CHARLES XI'S WAR

The Scanian War between Sweden and Denmark, 1675–1679

Michael Fredholm von Essen

'This is the Century of the Soldier', Fulvio Testi, Poet, 1641

Helion & Company

The series editor would like to thank Sergey Shamenkov
for his support and advice with this project

Helion & Company Limited
Unit 8 Amherst Business Centre
Budbrooke Road
Warwick
CV34 5WE
England
Tel. 01926 499 619
Fax 0121 711 4075
Email: info@helion.co.uk
Website: www.helion.co.uk
Twitter: @helionbooks
Visit our blog at http://blog.helion.co.uk/

Published by Helion & Company 2019
Designed and typeset by Serena Jones
Cover designed by Paul Hewitt, Battlefield Design (www.battlefield-design.co.uk)
Printed by Henry Ling Limited, Dorchester, Dorset

ISBN 978-1-911628-00-2

British Library Cataloguing-in-Publication Data.
A catalogue record for this book is available from the British Library.

Contents

Map 1. Scandinavia and Northern Germany

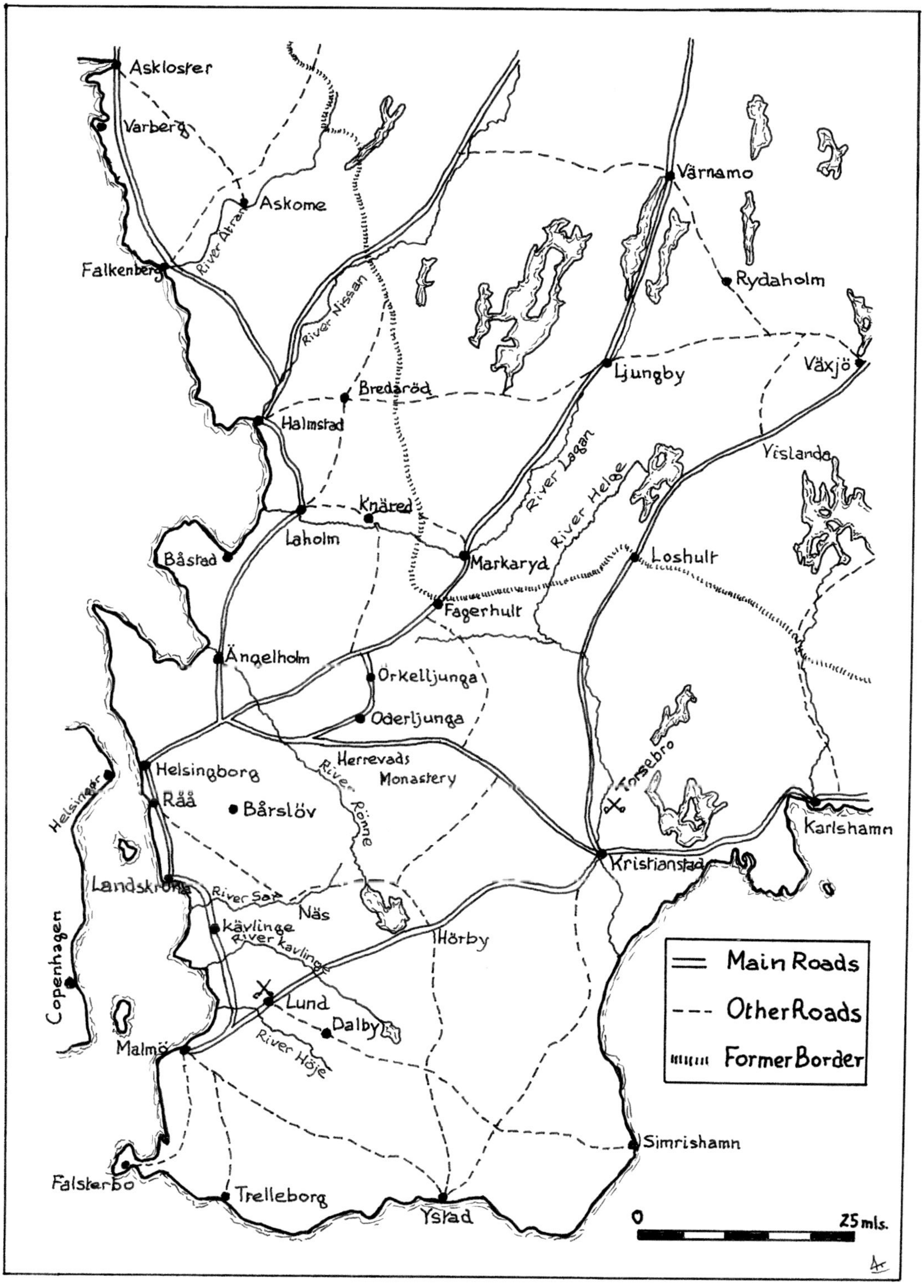

Map 2. Southern Sweden

Introduction

The Scanian War was fought from 1675 to 1679 between, on one side, a coalition of primarily Brandenburg and Denmark-Norway and, on the other, Sweden. The war was mainly fought in Scania (*Skåne*) and the surrounding provinces, which were former Danish lands, and in northern Germany. The conflict had complex origins and effectively constituted two separate wars, one from December 1674 to 1679 between Sweden and Brandenburg-Prussia, the Holy Roman Empire, and several German principalities, and a separate war from 1675 to 1679 between Sweden and Denmark and the Netherlands. The Danish objective, as desired by Denmark's King Christian V, was to retrieve the important provinces of Scania, Halland, and Blekinge, which a generation earlier had been captured by Sweden and in 1658 ceded by Denmark. Halland and Blekinge were border provinces that had adjusted well to Swedish rule. Scania, on the other hand, had been a key Danish province, its previously considerable wealth had derived from trade with Denmark which no longer was possible, and sympathies for the old country remained strong. Hence, the Danes invaded Scania, which also gave the war its name, the Scanian War.

However, the Danish invasion army was defeated by the young Swedish King Charles XI. Danish partisans carried out guerrilla operations in Scania, yet Swedish counterinsurgency operations were both harsh and efficient and the former Danish territories remained in Swedish hands. Although the Danish-Dutch combined fleet was victorious at sea, and an alliance headed by Brandenburg defeated the Swedes in Germany, the subsequent peace negotiations resulted in no major territorial changes. The Scanian War was vicious, even by contemporary standards, and from a military point of view, inconclusive. Yet, Sweden's experiences in the Scanian War laid the foundation for the first substantial reform of the Swedish army since the Thirty Years' War. Both the Danish and Swedish kings personally participated in the war. For young King Charles, who came from a warlike dynasty, the war was a pivotal experience. As a boy, he had eagerly anticipated going to war. As a king, he took an active part in all major battles. The Scanian War was very much Charles's war, and his role was, as we will see, equally that of a commander-in-chief and a junior company commander. Based on what he had learnt, King Charles restructured the Swedish army after the war and established a comprehensive and efficient military system that enabled Sweden repeatedly to mobilise trained armies during the even more devastating Great Northern War (1700–1721) which followed a generation later. But, based on the very same personal experiences, he henceforth laboured to keep Sweden out of further warfare. He had reaped the expected glory, but he had also seen the true cost of war.

The present book aims to combine and summarise the achievements gained during previous research on the Scanian War, as well as add some conclusions not drawn elsewhere. Nonetheless, there remain sources and data that have been underutilised in previous research, including the one that resulted in this book. In comparison to the preceding Thirty Years' War and the subsequent Great Northern War, the Scanian War is under-researched. In particular, much more could be gained from the genealogical field. Although the *names* of individual commanders and (through regimental records) even soldiers who took part in the war have been known ever since the events occurred, the *relationships* between these individuals have often not been examined. For instance, many of the commanders knew each other from previous wars, in some cases when they fought on the same side. Others were related by blood or marriage. Quite a few of the commanders of the Danish invasion force had close family members who lived in the towns they laid siege to, or had themselves lived in the same towns, or owned estates in Scania. How did these relationships affect their decisions? Some had considerable experience from previous wars, while others lacked military experience altogether. Such factors, too, must have impacted upon the decisions taken during the war. When such information was found, it was included in the present text. In addition, questions remain on the army organisation in the war below the regimental level. This also pertains to orders of battle, which is another under-researched field. Can we determine, through archival sources, the identity and real strength of the units that participated in the major battles? Moreover, battlefield archaeology has only recently been introduced in Scandinavia as an academic discipline. Here, too, much more remains to be done. Some data from recently carried out projects have been included in the text, and excavations at times give a more nuanced picture of the events that took place.

At the time of the war, some of the belligerent powers followed different calendars. The Gregorian calendar, named after the sixteenth-century Pope Gregory XIII who introduced it, had been developed as a correction to an observed error in the old Julian calendar. The visible result of the correction was that the date was advanced 10 days, that is, 4 October 1582 was followed by 15 October 1582. France and the Holy Roman Empire changed calendar on this date, as did most Catholic nations. However, many Protestant countries initially objected to adopting a Catholic innovation. The Duchy of Prussia was the first Protestant nation to adopt the Gregorian calendar. However, neither Brandenburg nor Denmark adopted the new calendar until 1700, while Sweden delayed yet longer. Most of the belligerents in the Scanian War accordingly used the Julian calendar, which for this reason differed from the one used in Catholic nations and at present. Old Style (O.S.) and New Style (N.S.) are terms commonly used with dates to indicate that the calendar convention used at the time described is different from that in use at present. Unless noted otherwise, the dates given here will be O.S., since this was the calendar style commonly used in archival documents relating to the war.

As for spelling, an attempt has been made to include, in addition to English-language translations, the original names of units in Danish,

Norwegian, Swedish, and German, where it seemed important to do so for reasons of clarity. However, since neither language had a codified system of spelling at the time, the forms used are not necessarily those used today. Still, anybody with a working knowledge of the language should be able to identify the word forms employed. The same goes for personal names, which were then spelled in a variety of ways. Moreover, names and titles were long and cumbersome, and we often do not know which of several given names an individual preferred.

Dramatis Personae

Denmark

Christian V (1646–1699, r. 1670–99), King of Denmark.
George (1653–1708), Prince of Denmark. Younger brother of the King.
Ulrika Eleonora (1656–1693), Princess of Denmark. Sister of the King and fiancée of King Charles XI of Sweden.
Gyldenløve, Ulrik Frederik (1638–1704), Count. Born as the illegitimate son of King Frederick III of Denmark, which made him the half-brother of King Christian V. A veteran of previous wars against Sweden, he served as the Danish governor in Norway and led the Norwegian front.
Johann Hans Adolf, Duke of Schleswig-Holstein-Sonderburg-Plön (1634–1704), Field Marshal. An experienced soldier who in various armies had fought both Ottoman Turks and the French.
Arensdorff, Carl von (1625–1676), General. A German officer from Mecklenburg who fought in Swedish service during the Thirty Years' War in Germany and Poland, then switched to Danish service a few years before the Scanian War began.
Arensdorff, Friedrich von (1626–1689), Lieutenant General. Brother of Carl von Arensdorff, he fought in first Danish, then Swedish service during the Thirty Years' War and also against Denmark in the previous war, beginning his military career as a common musketeer.
Baudissin, Gustav Adolph von (also known as Bauditz; 1629–1695), Lieutenant General. A proficient soldier, being the son of a Prussian field marshal in Swedish service during the Thirty Years' war.
Bibow, Siegwert von (1639–1677), Colonel. A Mecklenburg officer in Danish service who previously had fought the Ottoman Turks.
Cicignon, Johan Caspar von (*c.*1625–1696), Colonel. Born in Luxembourg, he first went into Venetian service and then moved to Norway, where he in time achieved high military rank and also served as a military and civilian engineer.
Croÿ, Charles Eugène de (1651–1702), Colonel. A duke of French-Belgian origin who in 1675 went into Danish service.
Degenfeldt, Hannibal von (1648–1691), Colonel. The son of a German general in Venetian service, he, too, went into foreign military service and eventually recruited a regiment for the Danish army.
Duncan, Jacob (d. 1685), Major General. A Scotsman formerly in Swedish service, who against his oath took service with the Danish Crown.

Goltz, Joachim Rüdiger von der (1620–1688), Field Marshal. A Prussian veteran of Imperial, French, and Brandenburg service who in 1675 entered Danish service while retaining his position in Brandenburg.

Juel, Jens (1631–1700), Ambassador. A supporter of royal absolutist rule and at times described as the most cynical diplomat of his day.

Juel, Niels (1629–1697), Admiral. Elder brother of Jens Juel; had a distinguished naval career, with the Dutch in the First Anglo-Dutch War as well as, later, against the Swedes.

Meerheim, Hans Wilhelm (1620–1688), Lieutenant General. An acknowledged expert of the small war, he was an Imperial veteran of the Thirty Years' War from Saxony, who went into Danish service during the siege of Wismar in 1675.

Rosencrantz, Maximilian (1630–1676), Colonel. After a long time in Dutch service, he returned to Denmark to lead a regiment of enlisted troops.

Rosencrantz, Niels (1627–1676), Lieutenant General. A veteran soldier who had been in Spanish service in Flanders and fought in the previous war against Sweden.

Rumohr, Detlef von (1634–1678), Major General. A Danish nobleman who had fought against the French and Swedes in foreign service.

Rysensteen, Henrik Rüse von (1624–1679), Lieutenant General. A Dutch fortification officer, previously in French and Venetian service, who wrote a well-known scientific work on fortification.

Sandberg, Anders (1620–1677), Major General. A veteran of the Thirty Years' war and previous wars with Sweden.

Schwanewede (Svanvedel), Herman Franz (1637–1697), Colonel. Fought for Sweden against Denmark in a previous war but was captured and went into Danish service; famous for his operations with irregular forces.

Tromp, Cornelis (1629–1691), Admiral. Having fought in the first three Anglo-Dutch Wars, he was appointed Admiral-General over the combined Dutch–Danish fleet.

Walter, Hans (1618–1677), Major General. A Thirty Years' War veteran from Schleswig, he was first in Swedish service, then in the army of Holstein-Gottorp, where he had stayed until King Christian's 1675 coup.

Sweden

Charles XI (1655–1697, r.1660–1697), King of Sweden.

Ascheberg, Rutger von (1621–1693), General, then Field Marshal. Rising from the ranks in Swedish service during the Thirty Years' War, which he had entered as a common cavalryman, Ascheberg in 1673 became King Charles's military mentor.

Baranoff, Klas Johan (1621–1686), Colonel. The son of a Russian nobleman who had entered Swedish service, he fought in Germany and then was commissioned to raise a cavalry regiment in Finland.

Bielke, Nils (1644–1716), Colonel. Commander of the Life Regiment of Horse and one of King Charles's few close friends.

Carlson, Gustav (1647–1708), Count. Half-brother of King Charles, he served as colonel in the army.

Creutz, Lorentz (1615–1676), Admiral of the Realm. A civilian official with neither naval nor military experience, he lacked the required skills and failed to fulfil King Charles' strategic objectives.

Dahlbergh, Erik Jönsson (1625–1703), Colonel. Military engineer and fortification officer with experience from European wars and the previous wars with Denmark; served as head of Fortification and Quartermaster General, among the duties of which was also military intelligence.

De la Gardie, Magnus Gabriel (1622–1686), Lord High Chancellor. Leader of the regency government during the minority of King Charles and chief among those responsible for Sweden's lack of fiscal and military preparedness.

De La Gardie, Pontus Fredrik (1630–1692), General. Younger brother of Magnus Gabriel De la Gardie.

Fersen, Fabian von (1626–1677), Field Marshal and Governor-General of Scania. Having participated in the previous war against Denmark, he defended Scania's chief town, Malmö.

Fersen, Wilhelm von (1623–1703), Lieutenant General. Fabian von Fersen's cousin, a veteran of the Thirty Years' War and the previous wars against Denmark and Poland.

Gyllenstierna, Christoffer (1639–1705), Colonel. One of King Charles's few close friends, he served as head of His Majesty's Life Guard on Foot.

Gyllenstierna, Johan (1635–1680), Counsellor to the King. A distant relative of Christoffer Gyllenstierna, he worked closely with the King, enjoyed his confidence, and was a firm supporter of the *reduktion* of former royal lands.

Helmfelt, Simon Grundel (1617–1677), Field Marshal. A veteran of the Thirty Years' War and the Muscovy war with particular expertise in fortifications and artillery technology, he from 1676 served as commander-in-chief of the Swedish army.

Hierta, Per (1613–1693), Colonel. An outspoken veteran of the Thirty Years' War.

Horn, Henrik Henriksson af Marienborg (1618–1693), Field Marshal. A veteran of the Thirty Years' War and the war in Poland.

Königsmarck, Otto Wilhelm von (1639–1688), Field Marshal. A veteran of European wars, he had particularly distinguished himself in French service.

Mörner af Morlanda, Hans Georg (1623–1685), Lieutenant General. A veteran of the Thirty Years' War and the war in Poland, who served as chief commandant in Gothenburg.

Mörner af Tuna, Lars Axel (1642–1676), Colonel. A veteran of the previous war with Denmark.

Mortaigne, Barthold de (d. 1690), Major General. An experienced Dutch soldier who had fought in Swedish service against Poland and Denmark.

Schönleben, Johan Benedikt von (1613–1706), Major General. A veteran of the Thirty Years' War and the previous wars against Denmark and Poland.

Schultz, Martin (1617–1682), Lieutenant General. The grandson of a Bohemian officer in Swedish service who had fallen at Kirkholm in 1605; he had a distinguished military career and his family later became known as von Ascheraden.

Siegroth, Hans Henrik von (1629–1676), Lieutenant Colonel. First commander of the Drabant Guard.

Siöblad, Erik (1647–1725), Admiral. The commander of the Gothenburg squadron, he early on spent several years in the English navy, where he reached the rank of captain, after which he returned home for service in the Swedish navy.

Sperlingh, Jöran (1630–1691), Major General. A veteran of the previous war with Denmark.

Stake, Harald (1598–1677), Lieutenant General. A veteran of Dutch service as well as the Thirty Years' War who once saved the life of King Gustavus Adolphus, he had also fought in the previous wars against Denmark and Norway.

Stenbock, Gustav Otto (1614–1685), Field Marshal and Admiral of the Realm. A veteran of the Thirty Years' War and all Sweden's subsequent wars, he nonetheless lacked experience of naval matters.

Uggla, Claes Johan (1614–1676), Admiral. One of few experienced Swedish senior naval officers, he was also a veteran of the Thirty Years' War, having participated in the 1648 siege of Prague.

Ulfeldt, Ebbe (1616–1682), Lieutenant General. A Scanian noble in Imperial and Spanish service during the Thirty Years' War, he willingly became a Swedish subject when the Danish Crown ceded Scania to Sweden.

Wachtmeister, Axel (1643–1699), Colonel. A younger son of a distinguished family, he was promoted to colonel in 1676.

Wachtmeister, Hans (1641–1714), Admiral-Lieutenant. The elder brother of Axel Wachtmeister, he was a veteran of service in the English navy and the Second Anglo-Dutch War.

Wittenberg, Leonard Johan (1646–1679), Major General. Joined the Swedish army in 1670, after distinguished academic studies in Tübingen and Heidelberg.

Wrangel, Carl Gustav (1613–1676), Field Marshal, Admiral of the Realm, and Grand Marshal of the Realm. A renowned veteran of the Thirty Years' War, but suffering from broken health.

Wrangel af Lindeberg, Wolmar (1641–1675), Lieutenant General. Half-brother of Carl Gustav Wrangel.

The German Coalition

Leopold I (1640–1705, r. 1658–1705), Emperor of the Holy Roman Empire.

Frederick William (1620–1688, r. 1640–1688), Elector of Brandenburg and Duke of Prussia.

Christoph Bernhard von Galen (1650–1678), Prince-Bishop of Münster.

Hedwig Sophie of Brandenburg (1623–1683), Landgravine of Hesse-Kassel. Mother-in-law of King Christian V of Denmark and regent of Hesse-Kassel.

1

The Two Kings

King Christian V of Denmark

King Christian V was born the first hereditary king of Denmark, growing up with the belief of the divine right of kings and absolute royal power. Although poorly educated, including in international affairs, and speaking only German and Danish, he had a reputation for honesty and was quite popular among the common people. Danish kings belonged to the House of Oldenburg, a noble family of northern German origin, so customarily distrusted the Danish nobility. King Christian was no exception. He favoured German officers, usually from Mecklenburg and the adjoining principalities, over Danish nobles. He also elevated commoners into senior positions and noble status, which might be one reason for his popularity among commoners.

King Christian was neither very gifted nor unwavering in his decisions. He was easily swayed by advisors and other rulers within the anti-Swedish coalition which he joined. As a result, he adopted military strategies that often produced less than ideal results. The King was no intellectual, and he was aware of the fact. In a well known letter from 1675, he requested that the advisors not confuse him with too complex arguments, nor too much eloquence, since this was "against his nature" and he did not understand how to handle overly intricate issues. Yet, he was quite aware of his status as an absolute ruler, and on the same occasion demanded that his advisors, in the presence of the King, not give any order that the King should have given.[1]

On 23 May 1676, King Christian appointed his secretary and Auditor-General, Herman Mejer, military councillor, which in effect made the secretary Minister of War. Mejer was conscientious and loyal, yet lacked strategic insights and the overview that a man in his position needed. But then, so did King Christian. From 1677, Mejer took charge of the royal correspondence concerning all military and naval issues which fundamentally put him in charge of most decisions except those that were solely of a tactical nature. By

1 K.V. Nielsen, "Dansk strategi och krigsföring", Göran Rystad (ed.), *Kampen om Skåne* (Lund: Historiska Media, 2005), pp.75–91, on p.76.

King Christian V of Denmark.

the end of the war, King Christian put so much trust in Mejer that he appointed him his personal representative in the army, in case he himself was absent. In comparison, the King's military commanders tended to have little influence. King Christian frequently replaced them, and in reality, the position of overall military commander was hardly more than an honorary title.

King Christian liked to lead meetings in his council of war. The King would sit silent during the meeting, while the advisors discussed the particular strategic or operational issue raised by Mejer. Finally, the King would decide, or at least Mejer, when he wrote the protocol of the meeting, would give the impression that King Christian had decided. Often King Christian would review the protocol, adding his comments where needed.

In many ways, King Christian's decision-making process resembled modern-day bureaucratic infighting. The Danish strategy was decided in committee meetings, in which the King carried the final decision. Yet individual members of the committee frequently disagreed, and there is no certainty that the King always made his opinion clear.[2] This led to a situation in which disputes and rivalry grew common among the senior military commanders, which in turn led to further divisions and errors of judgement in the conduct of the war. This corresponded poorly with the demands imposed by seventeenth-century battlefield conditions. As will be shown, King Christian's leadership style, procrastination, and inability to handle complex issues frequently resulted in indecision and delays that affected the army, and in extension the entire country, badly.

King Christian's need to emphasise his absolute rule also, as will be shown, had a less attractive side. When things went wrong, King Christian invariably would search for a scapegoat among his senior officers on whom to fix the blame, since the absolute political ideology of the Danish kings meant that mistakes under no circumstances could be attributed to the King. This was another reason why he frequently replaced his overall military commanders.

At the outbreak of war, King Christian was 29 years old. In the field, nobody could mistake King Christian for anything but a general. Contemporary illustrations show him dressed like a wealthy, noble officer, in a wide-brimmed hat, a luxurious French-style coat over his breastplate, and black, high riding boots.

King Christian died in 1699 from injuries sustained in a hunting accident, thus ending his life engaged in one of his favourite pastimes. He had eight

2 Ibid., pp.80–2.

children by his wife and another six by his official mistress. By all accounts, he was generally a pleasant fellow.

King Charles XI of Sweden

King Charles XI of Sweden

King Charles XI lost his father at an early age, so he grew up under a regency government. He assumed personal rule in December 1672, when, 17 years old, he came of age. By then he still trusted the regency government and believed, somewhat naively, that it acted in his best interests. When war broke out, he gradually realised the state of affairs under the regents and henceforth distrusted them.

King Charles was not a scholarly man. The extensive plans that had been drawn up for his education essentially failed. One reason was that he suffered from dyslexia. Beside his native Swedish, he had a good command of German, since many of his officers were Germans. However, he only had some limited understanding of French and never learnt Latin, nor Finnish. The problems in reading and writing continued to haunt him throughout his life.

However, the young king excelled early in military matters, which, together with hunting, was his real interest. The Florentine diplomat Lorenzo Magalotti, who visited Sweden in 1674 and wrote a comprehensive treatise of the country and its people, reported that King Charles showed great skill in commanding both infantry and cavalry. In fact, as a military commander, but only then, Charles acted with self-assurance and an authority that was remarkable for such a young man. Magalotti also concluded that the young king was not impulsive. In the past, he had occasionally relaxed by gambling. On those occasions, Magalotti reported, the King had never got carried away but instead "calculated and considered" before making a move. Besides, by the time of Magalotti's visit, King Charles had given up gambling altogether. King Charles was firm in his decisions, and unusually for a Swede, Magalotti argued, he did not reveal his inner thoughts and knew how to keep a secret. Yet, he was young, and he had a temper. It happened that he reacted with anger against subordinates, in particular on those few occasions that he got drunk, if he thought that they failed to show appropriate respect.[3]

3 Lorenzo Magalotti, *Sverige under år 1674* (Stockholm: Rediviva, 1986), pp.80–82.

When the war broke out, King Charles was only 19 years old. Yet, he rapidly learnt what was required of a Swedish king. Quite unlike his Danish equivalent, King Charles did not rule by committee. He would discuss strategy and tactics with his senior military commanders, but these meetings were brief, often took place on horseback, and were not documented in protocols since no clerical staff attended. While King Charles had a temper, and, like his Danish equivalent, might overrule his senior officers, he was not averse to taking responsibility for his decisions, and the continuing war eventually taught him the harsh lesson known to military commanders of all times, namely that wrong decisions lead to unnecessary deaths. He made mistakes, but he also learnt from them.

King Charles had strong opinions on the need to do one's duty. To fail in fulfilling the duty to one's King was to fail in one's duty to God. This viewpoint became evident during the war. Officers who showed cowardice in face of the enemy were court-martialled, and when the facts spoke against them, sentenced to death. The King had few close friends and, having discovered the mismanagement of the regency government, did not give his trust easily.

King Charles was frugal in his habits as well as choice of dress. In the field, he typically wore a dark wide-brimmed hat, a practical blue French-style coat over his breastplate, elk-skin buff gloves, and black, high riding boots. He regarded himself, and wanted to be regarded by others, as a soldier king.

King Charles died of cancer in 1697. He was succeeded by his son, Charles XII, who, like his father, almost at once found his country under attack by a coalition of enemies.

2

Organisation, Armament, Equipment, and Tactics

Tactical Doctrines

By the mid seventeenth century, the Dutch model of organisation and armament had been adopted throughout Western Europe, with the battalion as key tactical unit. On the field of battle, the battalions would form up in a linear formation, each with pikes in the centre and musketeers on each side of them. Several battalions would form a regiment. The army as a whole would form up in two to three lines. The Dutch model was designed to exploit firepower to the fullest extent, since it allowed all musketeers to fire by rotation of ranks. The model offered mobility, defined as rapidity of movement and ease of manoeuvre, although it was vulnerable to flank and rear attack. The Dutch model primarily used the rotation of ranks of musketeers defensively. Having fired, each rank retired to reload while the next rank took its place.

The Dutch model focused on mobility and firepower rather than shock. Moreover, it did not provide a significant role to artillery and cavalry. Artillery was typically dispersed along the front of the line of battle. Cavalry operated with the squadron as key tactical unit and normally employed caracole tactics. This meant that the cavalrymen would advance in deep formation, at less than a gallop. As each rank came into range, the men would discharge their pistols, then retire to the back of the formation to reload, and in due time repeat the manoeuvre. The whole unit might move slowly forward as each rank fired, or slowly retreat to keep its distance to an advancing enemy. The cavalrymen were armed and sometimes armoured for melee, and the intention seems usually to have been to follow the caracole with a charge, in effect using the caracole to soften up the enemy.

Both artillery and cavalry were accordingly relegated to what in effect was a support role, since the infantry was regarded as the chief means of winning a battle. Besides, warfare came to focus more on outmanoeuvring the enemy in an extended campaign than on defeating him in a major battle. Campaigns for this reason also tended to focus on fortified positions, since to deny the enemy an important stronghold was a means of wearing him down. Besides, during the siege there was finally an opportunity to fully utilise one's artillery.

During the Thirty Years' War, Swedish King Gustavus Adolphus had developed the Dutch model further. This gave rise to what can be called the Swedish model, which emphasised the offensive. Gustavus Adolphus typically formed up his army in two lines, with the infantry in the centre and the cavalry deployed in line on each wing. The musketeers would fire by rotation of ranks, but Gustavus Adolphus used rotation offensively, not defensively. Instead of retiring after firing, the musketeers would stop to reload while the ranks behind them moved forward. Moreover, the musketeers were trained to fire in volleys, several ranks at a time. A volley followed by an immediate pike charge might be devastatingly effective. In addition, Gustavus Adolphus deployed light regimental artillery which, unlike previous field artillery, would follow the infantry as it advanced and provide efficient supporting fire. The Swedish field artillery was both more numerous and lighter, that is, more manoeuvrable, than what was in use elsewhere on the Continent. In effect, Gustavus Adolphus aimed for a first shock derived from firepower followed by an almost immediate second shock, in the form of the charging pikemen. The combination of firepower and, above all, movement was decisive for gaining and holding the initiative, and since this reduced the men's exposure to enemy fire, the aggressive tactical behaviour actually worked for their protection. Additionally, the cavalry dispensed with caracole tactics and instead were ordered to charge the enemy, firing only at almost point-blank range. Although such cavalry tactics were practised by others as well, this fit in well with the Swedish model's emphasis on the offensive and on defeating the enemy's military forces during decisive actions on the battlefield instead of through lengthy sieges and campaigns of manoeuvre.

During the time of Gustavus Adolphus, Swedish cavalry advanced at a slow pace. The cavalry would only increase speed at a distance of 60 paces to the enemy, when it would move into a trot or gallop.[1] After the death of Gustavus Adolphus, Duke Bernard of Saxe-Weimar changed the tactical doctrine introduced by the Swedish king. He retained many aspects of the Swedish model but ordered his cavalry to charge at the gallop, independent of infantry support. Bernard later went into French service, where he recommended the adapted tactical doctrine to Henri de La Tour d'Auvergne, Viscount of Turenne, who then served under him. Turenne, who referred to this type of cavalry charge as in the Swedish manner (*à la suèdoise*) later recommended the doctrine to a young Swedish officer, Nils Bielke, who, as we will see, together with the Swedish General Rutger von Ascheberg in 1676 reintroduced it in the Swedish army, with considerable success (and, incidentally, calling it a charge in the French manner, *à la française*).[2]

1 Heribert Seitz, "Den karolinska värjans taktiska betydelse för kavalleriet", *Ny Militär Tidskrift* 8 (1944), pp.1–12, on p.2.

2 Ebbe Gyllenstierna, "Karl Gustav Wrangel och Henri Turenne: Svensk och fransk krigföring under trettioåriga krigets sista skede", *Meddelande 36* (Stockholm: Armémuseum, 1976), pp.39–51, on p.47.

Because over time, the offensive aspects of the Swedish model had gradually been forgotten. By the time of the Scanian War, the Danes essentially followed the Dutch model, although they, too, had learnt some practices from the Swedish experience in the Thirty Years' War, in particular with regard to organisation and cavalry tactics. The Danish infantry, when operating in an offensive role, would advance slowly, firing continuously, and not in volleys. The focus was on softening up the enemy through musket fire, not defeating him in hand-to-hand combat. Likewise, the Danish cavalry mostly relied on the Continental caracole model, discharging their pistols against the enemy rank by rank over a period of time, instead of aggressively charging home with rapiers.

The Swedes had not really changed their military system at the outbreak of war. Yet, a long period of peace had, paradoxically, made many of them, too, forget the offensive characteristics of the Swedish model. However, the Swedish army was still led by veterans of the Thirty Years' War, who remembered how war had been fought in their youth. As a result, the Swedish model regained its previous position. The caracole was explicitly forbidden, and the charge became the key means to gain victory. Moreover, it will be shown that the Swedish experiences during the Scanian War had a significant impact on the tactical doctrines of the Swedish army, consequences that became decisive a generation later, at the time of the Great Northern War.

Basic Organisation, Conditions of Battle, and Military Manoeuvres

By the time of the Scanian War, the basic organisation of most west European armies, including those of Sweden and Denmark, was fundamentally identical regardless of national origin. Most prestigious was the cavalry, which moved and fought on horseback. On the Continent, a few cavalry units remained heavily armoured. However, such troops were no longer used in Scandinavia. Besides, by the second half of the seventeenth century, another type of mounted troops became increasingly common, not least because they were cheaper to raise and arm. These were the dragoons, who moved mounted on horseback but fought on foot. They would also, on horseback, handle reconnaissance duties, patrolling, and so on. Then there was the infantry, even cheaper to raise and necessary, in particular, for siege work. On the Continent, infantry was also regarded as of key importance during set battles. Finally, there was the artillery, which again was primarily used during sieges. However, both Denmark and Sweden had field artillery as well.

The main tactical unit in the cavalry and dragoons was the squadron, which typically consisted of two companies. In the infantry, the main tactical unit was the battalion, which commonly consisted of four companies. In the Swedish army, the battalion was for historical reasons sometimes referred to as a brigade. The main administrative formation was the regiment, which often consisted of six companies in the cavalry and dragoons and eight companies in the infantry.

On the field of battle, armies were customarily formed up in three operational units in which the order of the tactical units often was fixed in advance, according to seniority or necessity. The three operational units were the two wings, which in Scandinavia chiefly or wholly consisted of cavalry and dragoons, and the centre, which consisted of infantry. The artillery was usually deployed between the infantry units. The operational units were commonly divided into a first and a second line. The second line was often weaker than the first and to some extent functioned as a reserve. In a large army, there might also be a third line, the real reserve.

The right wing was regarded as the prestigious one. In Scandinavia, it was typically led by the King himself, who would take an active part in the combat and risk his life to the same extent as the men among whom he fought. For this reason, and the fact that the best units often were deployed there, the right wing was often victorious. This commonly led to a situation in which the right wings of both opposing armies were victorious, while the left wings similarly were pushed back. We will see that this situation would repeat itself in several of the battles fought during the Scanian War. Both King Christian of Denmark and King Charles of Sweden led their troops in person, and there can be no doubt that both displayed personal bravery.

Because bravery was needed. Or, for most, strict discipline, used to suppress man's natural instinct, fear. The linear tactics exposed the men fighting in the line to exceptional danger as the lines closed with each other, and no man was permitted to take cover when under artillery or musket fire. It is likely that most men in the line entrusted their souls to God and merely hoped for the best, since it all too often seemed to be pure chance that decided who lived and died, exposed to artillery fire and enemy volleys fired at short range as they were. Seventeenth-century gunpowder weapons were lethal. Many soldiers loaded their weapons with excessively strong charges of gunpowder, which gave the musket ball a high velocity and produced grievous wounds. Moreover, it was common to load the musket with multiple and often irregular projectiles. Archaeological evidence from the Scanian War shows that many soldiers cut or otherwise distorted the musket ball so that the projectile would tumble and tear the flesh when it hit. But the projectiles were not the only things that resulted in grievous wounds and deaths. When projectiles hit gunstocks or pikes, the wooden parts would shatter and fragment, in effect producing shrapnel that burst through all men and horses in the vicinity. Perhaps yet more horrifyingly, the same result was produced by sharp bone fragments and, even more so, shattered pieces of teeth. In particular the tooth fragments resulted in vicious wounds, since they produced lethal infections even if the victim survived the immediate impact.

The effect of field artillery fire was even worse. Round iron shot could be seen while in motion, but due to weight and speed, they could not be stopped or evaded. It will be shown that even an admittedly brave man such as Frederick William, Elector of Brandenburg and Duke of Prussia, would hesitate to move on when round iron shot bounced under his horse and smashed into men in his immediate entourage. Yet worse was grape shot, that is, an artillery missile consisting of many musket balls, in effect functioning like a shotgun, and canister shot, artillery missiles consisting of metal fragments in canisters. With such munitions, the field artillery could mow down an entire unit of men. Soldiers knew this and would occasionally take their revenge on artillerymen, by sparing none if they surrendered.

Based on evidence from later, but similar, battles, we can expect that most men in the line would be in a state of psychological shock from seeing friends literally torn to shreds by enemy fire, probably to the extent that quite a few would be physically and psychologically unable to discharge their weapons or draw their side-arms. Which perhaps also indicated their strongest motivation to stay in the line, beside discipline. Almost all Swedish and Norwegian units, and many of the Danish ones, were raised from a particular geographical area. The soldiers accordingly stood in the line of battle together with family, friends, and neighbours. This provided a strong incentive not to let the others down, or to show oneself inadequate. It is probably fair to say that most men fought for their friends and comrades to a far higher extent than they fought for their country, which in the eyes of many was an abstract and artificial concept. Some might fight for their King, at least in those instances when the King provided an inspiring personal example. In the Scanian War, however, neither King Christian nor King Charles were able to provide the kind of truly inspired leadership that made men devoted to them. Both were able rulers in their respective manner, and we will see that in particular King Charles in some battles managed to rally his forces through personal example, but neither was truly charismatic.

Besides, we should not underestimate the difficulties in exercising command on a seventeenth century battlefield. First, communications were poor. Dispatch riders might or not reach their destination. Music and signals would not be heard over the gunfire. Geographical factors and indeed weather conditions might prevent visual observation of what was happening anywhere beyond the commander's immediate surroundings. Besides, the gunpowder used by firearms and artillery soon created a literal fog of war that was almost impenetrable. Moreover, on a dry day, sparks from the shot would set fire to any dry grass on the field, which produced smoke that reduced visibility even more. At the same time, the thousands of horses that took part in the battle raised dust clouds that mixed with the smoke. As a result, most successful commanders realised that they had to lead from the front, since this was the only way that they could control at least some of their troops. As for what happened elsewhere on the battlefield, there was usually no way of knowing.

Even before the coming of age of young King Charles of Sweden, his interest in military matters resulted in one important improvement in the army. In August 1672, when the King was still 16, what is generally regarded as the first military manoeuvres in Sweden took place. The manoeuvres took place on a royal hunting ground near Stockholm known as Gärdet ("The field"), which henceforth frequently was used for military manoeuvres (and still occasionally is). On this occasion, the manoeuvres lasted for three weeks and were carried out under realistic conditions, in fact so realistic that two soldiers were killed and several wounded in a mine accident when the army practised assault on fortified positions. In total, some 2,000 to 3,000 men from the Life Guard and several regiments in the vicinity of Stockholm took part, as well as the senior military leadership of the realm: Field Marshal, Admiral of the Realm, and Grand Marshal of the Realm (*riksmarsk*) Carl Gustav Wrangel, General Pontus Fredrik De La Gardie, Major Generals Axel Julius De La Gardie, Per Sparre, Wolmar Wrangel, Martin Schultz, and several others of high military rank. The young King Charles participated, too, in the role of a cavalry company commander.[3] Henceforth, similar manoeuvres, of a more or less serious nature, were carried out increasingly often wherever the King went to inspect troops, which he did on a regular basis.[4] During the war, too, King Charles insisted on regularly training his troops. Even when, for instance, a siege was underway, the King and his generals would train one or more units per day.[5]

In Denmark, similar training does not seem to have taken place. Troops would exercise during musters and on certain other occasions; however, military manoeuvres of the Swedish type seem not to have taken place.

Nonetheless, the military manoeuvres did not suffice to prepare for everything. This affected both the performance of the troops and the leadership of the commanders. During the war, there were frequent failures in leadership on both sides. This also brought other problems. One recurring failure that regularly affected both the Danish and Swedish armies was that lookouts and sentries maintained poor discipline. Lookouts were posted, but we will see that they frequently were unable to provide warning against attacks or indeed any movements among the enemy, even when the armies were close to each other.

Raising Troops

The Danish and Swedish Crowns had several ways of raising troops. On the Continent, it was most common to enlist soldiers. This was handled by an individual, usually a nobleman, who had received a patent or contract to raise a regiment. An enlisted regiment might consist of infantry or cavalry. Such men would typically be professional soldiers. Both Denmark and Sweden used enlisted (German: *geworbne*; Danish: *hvervede*; Swedish: *värvade*) troops. In Denmark, to enlist men was the most common means to raise troops, and Sweden used enlisted units in particular in its German possessions.

Sweden by tradition raised most of its regular cavalry units through an organisation known as *indelningsverket*, from a word perhaps best translated as the allotment authority. Established earlier in the century, it provided for the existence of cavalry units through the permanent allotment (*indelning*, "division") of sources of revenue for their needs. An individual who contracted to provide a cavalryman with equipment was awarded a farmstead the

3 Göran Rystad, *Karl XI: En biografi* (Lund: Historiska Media, 2003), p.36.

4 Ibid., pp.50, 52, 55.

5 Alf Åberg, *När Skåne blev svenskt: Två krig, två freder, snapphanar och försvenskning* (np: SMB, 2013), p.210. First published as Alf Åberg, "Rutger von Ascheberg och tillkomsten av den karolinska armén", *Karolinska förbundets årsbok* 1951, pp.170–92.

income of which together with tax exemptions would defray the costs. By the time of the Scanian War, Denmark, too, had copied the Swedish organisation.

Another common way to raise soldiers in northern Europe was conscription (Swedish: *utskrivning*), which was the arbitrary raising of men from a population, in most cases from peasants on Crown land. In Denmark, the absolute power of the King enabled him to decide about conscription as he pleased. In Sweden, conscription was granted through parliament. Either way, the result was much the same. The Swedish was the most comprehensive. The conscriptable male population (certain groups such as priests, nobles, their servants, miners, workers in the arms factories, and sons of widows were exempted) was divided into groups of 10, each of which had to provide one soldier. The conscripted soldiers then had to be armed, trained, and supplied by the Crown. They could then be used anywhere, overseas or at home, as well as indefinitely. Many peasants regarded conscription as a death sentence, which ultimately it often was, and many conscripts attempted to desert before they were shipped overseas. Yet, since conscripts from any given province usually would serve in the same unit, the system eventually tended to result in troops that due to family and community links performed well together. In Denmark, such units were known as national regiments, to distinguish them from the enlisted regiments which usually consisted of Germans. In Sweden, conscripts typically served in provincial regiments, each based on men from one particular province. Both kinds of regiments produced a certain esprit de corps.

However, neither enlistment nor conscription provided sufficient manpower in times of war. By tradition, the Crown in Scandinavia could also levy troops among the peasants. This was done through a quota that the farmers had to fill. Levied troops would not be trained, and they would have to pay for their own weapons and supplies. On the other hand, they were only required to serve at home. Levied troops were usually used to man defensive bastions along the external borders, in effect being a kind of border guard. The levied peasants would serve for a time, then be replaced by other levies from the same area. In Norway, it will be shown, conditions were somewhat different, and selected levied troops were extensively used during incursions into northern Sweden.

In times of need, the Crown also had the right to raise a general levy. A general levy consisted of all men able to bear arms and usually was called out to defend an external border. The levied troops would have to arm and supply themselves. Their use was accordingly restricted, for practical reasons, to certain geographical areas and short durations of time. Levies could also be called out in the form of burgher militias, which would have to take some responsibility for defending their towns when under siege. During the Scanian War, the Swedish Crown frequently called out general levies, and those from the province of Småland also had to serve with the field army. Results were mixed. At the Battle of Lund 1676, the levies failed to reach the field of battle in time but nobody seemed to notice. At the Battle of Landskrona 1677, they played a possibly crucial role, but as we will see, their role was a passive one and the result depended more on luck than fighting skill, since the general levy did not actually participate in the fighting.

In both Denmark and Sweden, certain geographical areas were exempt from conscription since they already were required to provide either cavalrymen or sailors. This was handled through organisational structures that had been used for centuries. For the raising of cavalry, a traditional means was to require the nobility to provide armed and equipped cavalrymen. This, originally a force of fully armoured cavalry called to arms in times of war, was recruited by members of the nobility from their retainers. Known as the retinue of nobles, it was financed by the nobility in exchange for their status as exempt from taxation. It was no longer required for a noble to serve in person, since he could hire a cavalryman to attend in his stead. However, all officers in these units tended to be men from the nobility. This traditional military duty was called by an old name that can be translated as military service but originally signified service on horseback (Danish: *rostjeneste* or *rusttjeneste*; Swedish: *rusttjänst*). Likewise, some towns and coastal regions in Sweden were still organised to provide sailors for the navy. This, too, was a longstanding organisational structure with roots in the distant past.

In times of war, the option remained to raise additional troops from those areas that otherwise were exempt from conscription. This was decided by the Crown on a case by case basis and, in Sweden, granted by parliament. In Sweden this was referred to as a take-out (*utskott*). The troops raised in this manner were armed, trained, and supplied by the Crown, yet only needed to serve in the nearest theatre of war within the country and only for as long as the present war lasted. They could accordingly not be sent overseas. They were, in effect, temporary troops intended to be disbanded when the war ended. Yet they frequently played an important role for the Swedish war effort. In the subsequent Great Northern War, temporary troops of this type (then known as *männing* units) were in great demand, as regular sources of military manpower dried up, but temporary troops were raised during the Scanian War, too.

In Sweden, the Crown in times of need also negotiated additional cavalry from any group in society that could afford to raise cavalrymen, such as the nobility, the civil service, the priesthood, and so on. Although the Crown then did not have to provide for men, horses, and weapons, such troops, similarly to the temporary troops of a take-out, only needed to serve within the country and only for as long as the present war lasted. Moreover, with the times being as desperate as they were during the Scanian War, the Crown soon realised that even when horsemen were provided, those who raised them might not be able to afford the full equipment of a cavalry unit. If so, they would instead raise dragoons, which were cheaper to arm and equip than the regular cavalry.

Since the Scanian War to a large extent was fought on Swedish territory, Sweden could and did make full use of all these means of raising additional troops. The anti-Swedish coalition, however, was more often limited to the use of enlisted troops, except Denmark which also fielded a number of conscripted units.

The Danish Military Establishment

In the years following 1660, Denmark's overall military commander, National Commanding General Hans Schack, had transformed the Danish army into a modern, disciplined, and properly trained and equipped military force.[6] The majority of the men were Germans, and the language of command was German, not Danish, but the army included a significant share of Danes. Although the retinue of nobles still provided some cavalry, many units, both horse and foot, including all guard units such as the King's Life Regiment Cavalry, which originally was raised in Mecklenburg, were enlisted in Germany.

In 1670, upon King Christian's ascension to the throne, Denmark had introduced what was known as national regiments. The reform was essentially a copy of the Swedish system. The national cavalry regiments were formed through a system in which the peasants with farmsteads were divided into groups, each of which was responsible for the provision of one cavalryman in exchange for a tax reduction.[7] In times of peace, the trooper had to support himself, his horse, and his equipment through farming or through payments from the group of farmsteads. In war, he was paid by the Crown, which also replaced equipment lost in combat. Because of the system used to raise these troops, most of the men in the national cavalry regiments were Danes. At first, the national cavalry regiments were five in number: one each from Zealand, Fyn, South Jutland, North Jutland, and Schleswig, respectively, with the last one at half-strength. As part of the reform, the old retinue of nobles was reformed into a single cavalry regiment with the same organisation as the national cavalry regiments.

At the same time, national infantry regiments were introduced. At first, they, too, were five in number: one each from Zealand, Fyn, South Jutland, North Jutland, and Schleswig-Holstein, respectively. The national infantry regiments were manned with conscripts.

In preparation for the planned war against Sweden, the Danish Crown in 1675 made additional changes to its military establishment. The number of fully-manned national cavalry regiments was doubled, from four to eight. Each original regiment was split into two, with only half the men as compared to before. The exception was the Schleswig regiment, which already was at half-strength and therefore was retained as one regiment. Henceforth, a cavalry regiment would consist of six companies, the life company of 94 men and the other five each of 83. The establishment strength of the regiment was accordingly 509 men. At the tactical level, two companies made a squadron. It follows that a regiment consisted of three squadrons, each of 166 to 177 men. The old retinue of nobles regiment, too, was split into two, with the same organisation: the Zealand Retinue of Nobles, which also included the island of Fyn in its intake, and the Jutland Retinue of Nobles.

---

6 The most easily accessible treatise on the Danish army is Olaf Hasselager and Torstein Snorrason, *Danish Uniforms, Colours and Standards 1675–1679* (published online, 2000; various web sites), which is the main source for this section. On organisation, see also Niels Peder Jensen, *Den skaanske krig 1675–1679* (Copenhagen: Det nordiske forlag, 1900), pp.42–6.

7 Nielsen, "Dansk strategi", p.90 n.22.

The Guard Cavalry and the King's Life Regiment Cavalry were reorganised like the others. Furthermore, three new enlisted cavalry regiments (under Gustav Adolph von Baudissin, Gottfried Rauch, and Jacob Gewecke) were raised in Germany and organised in the same way, as were three enlisted dragoon regiments (under Hans Walter, Detlef von Örtzen, and Detlef Rantzau). The dragoons, too, were organised (but not equipped) essentially like the cavalry regiments.

The number of infantry regiments was doubled, too. In addition to the Schleswig-Holstein Regiment, which was retained under the name Holstein Regiment, a new national infantry regiment was raised in Schleswig, named Plön after its commander, the Duke of Schleswig-Holstein-Sonderburg-Plön. Each of the two had a strength of eight companies.[8] The other infantry regiments were organised with 12 companies. Each infantry company consisted of 100 men. At the tactical level, four companies made a battalion, which accordingly had a strength of 400 men. In addition, six new infantry regiments were raised in Germany, each named after its colonel (Gustav Adolph von Baudissin, Detlef Lütken, Johan Otto Bremer, Hannibal von Degenfeldt, Henrik Harlov, and Gregor Alard Schönfeldt).

The artillery was traditionally divided among the forts and citadels in which the men served. In times of peace, the artillery had only skeleton crews. In 1675, a field artillery was for the first time organised as an independent service. It had a staff unit of 19 men and four companies, each of 111 artillerymen. The field park consisted of 58 guns (twelve-, ten-, and three-pounders). In addition, each infantry battalion was served by 2 three-pounders. Cannons were painted red with yellow iron fittings. Each cannon was handled by one artilleryman, assisted by a few soldiers taken from the infantry battalion, and with three horses to move the cannon.

As a result of the reform, King Christian found himself with a strong, modern, and well-organised Danish army (Appendix I). If the establishment strength can be taken at face value, the total number of troops would be 9,500 horse and 26,800 foot, in total 36,300 men including garrison and recruiting companies.

The unit organisation was not quite as straightforward as it might seem. First, battalions were often detached from their regiments. They were then frequently named after the battalion commander. Second, the new organisation did not long survive contact with reality. In January 1676, in preparation of the planned invasion of Scania, the infantry regiments of 12 companies were reduced to eight companies each of 107 men, who would take part in the invasion, and four garrison companies of 100 men each, who would not. An infantry regiment in the field therefore had an establishment strength of 856 men. The cavalry and dragoon regiments remained as established, each with 509 men (slightly fewer in case of dragoons).

However, it will be shown that the units suffered considerable attrition while on campaign, from disease (in particular dysentery), famine, and desertion far more than through enemy action. We can therefore assume

8 Jensen, *Den skaanske krig*, p.43.

that although the regiments may have been more or less up to establishment strength when they left Denmark, they would soon be severely understrength.

During the ensuing war, the system to raise both types of national regiments – cavalry as well as infantry – proved insufficient. The organisation could simply not cope with the demands. In December 1676, it was decided that the conscripted troops from the national regiments henceforth would be paid by the Crown in exchange for additional taxation of the peasants responsible for raising them. Moreover, over time an increasing number of conscripted troops were allocated to the enlisted regiments. Furthermore, a number of disrupted regiments were combined into new ones, regardless of whether they previously had been enlisted or national.[9]

On 24 January 1677, the Danish Crown ordered a reorganisation. The strength of a mounted company remained essentially as before. Each cavalry company would consist of 84 men, which resulted in a squadron establishment strength of 168 men. Each dragoon company would consist of 82 men, that is, with a squadron establishment strength of 164 men including officers. However, the establishment strength of an infantry battalion was significantly increased. Henceforth, each infantry company would consist of 148 men (including six grenadiers). Four companies constituted a battalion, which accordingly would have an establishment strength of 592 men, as compared to the previous battalion establishment strength of 400.[10]

However, there was not enough money to raise troops to man the new organisation. Besides, the units remained subject to attrition. It has been estimated that in the field during the war, a squadron on the average consisted of 125–135 men while a battalion on the average comprised 325–350 men.[11]

Then there was the navy. Although German officers dominated King Christian's army, his navy was mostly crewed and officered by Danes and Norwegians, with a significant share of Dutchmen. Unlike the army, which was divided into separate Danish and Norwegian establishments, the navy was a common undertaking. The Danish Crown had made great efforts to reinforce its navy, adding a significant number of major warships since the introduction of royal absolutism in 1661. In 1675, Denmark had a sailing fleet of warships consisting of 34 vessels, of which 10 were small. In addition, Norway maintained a fleet of six galleys for inshore operations.[12] The naval strength was deemed sufficient and had more or less reached the limit of what the country could afford.[13] Besides, the navy could also count on some 50 armed merchantmen. The owners were compensated for putting their

9 Henrik Didier Gautier, "Krigskostnaderna och den danska statens finanser", Göran Rystad (ed.), *Kampen om Skåne* (Lund: Historiska Media, 2005), pp.232–51, on p.242.

10 Otto Vaupell, *Den danske hærs historie til nutiden og den norske hærs historie indtil 1814*, Vol.1 (Copenhagen: Gyldendal, 1872), pp.165, 202; Jensen, *Den skaanske krig*, p.238. Both are valuable but contain some inaccuracies.

11 Arne Stade, "Slaget vid Lund", Göran Rystad (ed.), *Kampen om Skåne* (Lund: Historiska Media, 2005), pp.107–162, on pp.116–17.

12 Jan Glete, *Navies and Nations: Warships, Navies and State Building in Europe and America, 1500–1860* (Stockholm: Almqvist & Wiksell International, 1993), p.596.

13 Gautier, "Krigskostnaderna", p.246.

ships at the disposal of the Crown in times of war. About half of the armed merchantmen were Norwegian.[14]

The Danish navy was good, but possibly yet more important was that when war was declared, the Danes had already achieved the active support of the Dutch, a first-rate naval power.

The Norwegian Military Establishment

As noted, the Crowns of Denmark and Norway were united in a personal union under King Christian. Each kingdom maintained its own separate military establishment, although officers moved freely between them. As noted, Denmark and Norway also maintained a common fleet, although most of the sailors were Norwegians.

In Norway, unlike in Denmark, most troops belonged to national regiments, which first had been established in 1628. By the time of the Scanian War, there were six national infantry regiments, based respectively at Akershus in the capital of Christiania (modern-day Oslo), Bergenhus in Bergen, in Trondheim, and in the counties of Oppland, Smaalenene, and Vesterlen.

Following King Christian's 1670 ascension to the throne, Norway prepared for war. The Norwegian army was reorganised and additional fortifications were built at Akershus Fortress in Christiania and Frederikshald, where a Dutch fortifications officer and military engineer, Willem Coucheron, rebuilt Fredriksten Fortress. In addition, a new fort was built at Vinger (modern-day Kongsvinger). The fortification works were led by Henrik Rüse von Rysensteen, another Dutch military engineer, with work provided by conscripts from the national infantry regiments. Rysensteen had previously been in French and Venetian service and had written a well-known scientific work on fortification. Going into Danish service in 1661, he had immediately been appointed quartermaster general, chief inspector of fortifications, and colonel of an infantry regiment. Among other projects, he had led the reconstruction of the citadel in Copenhagen, and he was eminently qualified for the job.

Upon the outbreak of war in 1675, the Norwegian field army consisted of some 12,000 men (Appendix II). Of these, 6,000 were deployed north of the border to the Swedish province of Bohuslän.[15]

The enlisted companies were units that had been formed in Denmark, and then sent to Norway to serve as garrison units. At times, other Danish units, too, were deployed to Norway, although the majority of the troops in the Norwegian army were always Norwegians. All units in the field army were Norwegians, except Recke's Regiment, which had deployed from Denmark.

14 Christer Kuvaja, *Krigen kring Östersjön 4: Karolinska krigare 1660–1721* (Helsinki: Schildts, 2008), p.72.

15 Carl Eric Almgren, "Svensk strategi och krigsledning", Göran Rystad (ed.), *Kampen om Skåne* (Lund: Historiska Media, 2005), pp.33–74, on p.34. See also I. Gulowsen, *Gyldenløvefeiden 1675–1679* (Christiania: Videnskabs-Selskabet, 1906), for more details. Like the works of Vaupell and Jensen, Gulowsen's study contains some inaccuracies, but it also reprints many original documents.

King Christian ordered an increase of the Norwegian army in size. As a result, the Trondheim Regiment was divided into two, commanded by Colonel von Hoven and Colonel Coucheron, respectively. More men were enlisted or conscripted, too. To the infantry strength was added some thousand soldiers, while the cavalry strength (Recke's Regiment) was increased to 750, and that of the dragoons to a total of 654 men.[16]

The Norwegian army also made great use of levied peasants. It had previously been found that to call up all able-bodied men as a general levy was not always very efficient. On 16 August 1673, GovernorUlrik Frederik Gyldenløve accordingly issued instructions to form a selection (*utvalg*) of the best men of the general levy, which became known as the selected (*utvalgte*) levy. The selected levy was organised into companies and had orders to meet and exercise four times a year.

The Swedish Military Establishment

During the 1660s, when King Charles was a minor, the Swedish regency government had cut down on military spending, among other decisions reducing the army from a strength of 93,000 to some 46,000 men.[17] From a military point of view, Sweden remained a great power, and probably still had more troops than even the combined Danish and Norwegian armies. Yet, Sweden faced other adversaries as well, and was from any standpoint not quite as strong as in the past.

In 1673, the Swedish military command had formulated a defence strategy that was based on the capacity to act offensively, beyond the country's borders. Focus was accordingly placed on the mobile units. The troops in garrisons would be reduced from 24,000 to 14,000 men. The soldiers assigned to the navy's warships would be reduced from 6,000 to 3,000 men. Instead mobile units would be deployed with the field army in Germany, which would consist of at least 22,000 men, half of whom would be enlisted over there. A total of 12,000 men would be deployed to defend the border with Norway, which was regarded as the one under most serious military threat. In addition, there would be a *corps volant* ("flying body" a mobile corps intended for rapid movements) in Livonia consisting of 4,000 men that could be moved to whichever front needed it, whether the eastern front against Muscovy or Poland or the southern front in Germany which, in extension, formed the base for any offensive action against Denmark's southern borders. To fulfil this strategy, the military command foresaw a need for 13,000 cavalry, 4,500 dragoons, and 37,000 infantry, or 54,500 men in total. Most of these already existed (troops had recently been enlisted), so the Crown only needed to raise 668 cavalry, 1,720 dragoons, and 4,200 infantry to cover the demand.[18]

The strategy was based on previous experiences and permitted some flexibility depending on against which country Sweden went to war; however,

16 Jensen, *Den skaanske krig*, p.45.

17 Almgren, "Svensk strategi", p.66 n.15.

18 Ibid., p.36.

in the second half of 1675 Sweden faced threats on all these fronts at the same time. Moreover, the Swedish army was distributed throughout the Swedish possessions, which meant that although strong in numbers, it was not always possible to concentrate forces where they were most needed.

In 1675, the total number of Swedish troops in Germany, where hostilities began, were 8,575 horse and 16,210 foot.[19] However, these were dispersed throughout the Swedish German possessions and the total number was soon found to be inadequate.

Sweden, too, relied on a combination of enlisted and conscripted troops. As noted, the Swedish conscription system had served as the model for the Danish national regiments.

Since the Thirty Years' War, a Swedish cavalry regiment had an establishment strength of 1,000 men, divided into eight companies each of 125 men, plus officers. It follows that a squadron consisting of two companies then would have an establishment strength of 250 men. Indeed, when in early 1674, the Life Regiment was ordered to raise new companies, each would consist of 125 men.[20] During the Scanian War, however, attrition rapidly led to smaller units. In the summer of 1678, even the Life Regiment companies, which were favoured with regard to supplies, on the average consisted of only 95 men.[21] Based on the figures for the entire army just before the 1676 Battle of Lund, the average strength of a squadron was then a mere 107 men.[22] This is low but quite possible in light of the severe losses to disease and starvation just before the battle. Based on a similar calculation with the figures from just before the 1677 Battle of Landskrona, the average strength of a squadron was then 157 men.[23] This figure probably gives a fair indication of the real strength of a Swedish squadron under campaign conditions. If so, we can assume that a typical Swedish cavalry or dragoon regiment on campaign would consist of some 450 men divided into six companies each of which consisted of 75–80 men. Two companies, or 150–160 men, then constituted a squadron.

The situation was the same with the infantry. Since the Thirty Years' War, a Swedish infantry regiment had an establishment strength of 1,200 men, divided into eight companies each of 150 men. It follows that a battalion of four companies then would have a strength of 600 men, plus officers. Following this model, in December 1674 infantry companies in at least seven regiments were expected each to consist of 150 men and nine non-commissioned officers.[24]

However, this may have been an ideal not always achieved. It was not unheard of for an infantry regiment of eight companies each of 150 men

19 Tessin, *Die deutschen Regimenter der Krone Schweden 2*, p.23.

20 Sondén, p.10.

21 Ingvar Eriksson, *Nils Bielke (1644–1716): Firad i nådens dagar, fälld i onådens* (Stockholm: Atlantis, 2000), p.136.

22 Stade, "Slaget vid Lund", p.114.

23 Lars-Åke Götesson, *Skånska krigets verkningar i Landskronatrakten 1676–1679* (Visby: Nomen, 2014), p.129.

24 Lars-Eric Höglund, *Skånska kriget 1675–79: Fanor och uniformer* (Karlstad: Acedia Press, 1999), p.71; citing an archive document.

in the field to be reorganised into 12 companies of 100 men, plus officers.[25] Besides, by 1666 data on uniform cloth supplies to five provincial infantry regiments suggest that companies then had a lower strength than they should have, on the average about 100 men.[26] Company and accordingly battalion manpower strength was therefore reduced well below establishment strength, from attrition if nothing else. Based on the figures for the Swedish army just before the 1676 Battle of Lund, the average strength of a battalion was then only 175 men.[27] Again, this is low but possible due to disease and starvation just before the battle. Based on a similar calculation with the figures from just before the 1677 Battle of Landskrona, the average strength of a battalion was then 292 men.[28] Again, this probably indicates the real strength of a Swedish battalion under campaign conditions. If so, we can assume that a typical Swedish infantry regiment on campaign would consist of some 560–600 men divided into eight companies each of which consisted of 70–75 men. Four companies, or 280–300 men, then constituted a battalion.

For both horse and foot, it follows that most units on campaign had a real strength of less than half of their establishment strength. After the war, the Swedish army attempted to return to the former unit establishment strength. A battalion would then again have an establishment strength of 600 men. According to the 1694 regulations, which were the result of experiences from the Scanian War, the battalion would deploy for battle in four ranks, with the 200 pikemen grouped in the centre of the unit and with two equal wings of 200 musketeers on the flanks, the latter frequently flanked by grenadiers. But however much this organisation was influenced by practices during the Scanian War, it came later. During the Scanian War, it was not unheard of for infantry battalions to deploy in only three ranks, often because of a shortage of men. Cavalry units had been reduced to three ranks already during the Thirty Years' war, and probably then, too, because of manpower shortages.

Within the Swedish army, the most prominent unit was a very small cavalry unit known as His Majesty's Drabant Guard, a squadron also known, in French, as the Garde du Corps. Since 1657, it had formed part of His Majesty's Life Guard of Horse and Foot. From 1675, the Drabant Guard formed the only mounted unit of the Life Guard. It consisted of enlisted soldiers and had an establishment strength of 200 men and 12 officers. During the war, it was usually some 140–150 men strong, apparently organised in two companies like other squadrons.[29]

The foot contingent of His Majesty's Life Guard of Horse and Foot was in 1675 converted into a field regiment consisting of 12 companies of 150 men each, in total 1,800 men. The soldiers were enlisted. In many ways, the Life

25 Such a field reorganisation was ordered as late as in 1700, but then the plan was soon abandoned, with a return to the old company strength of 150 men. Folke Wernstedt, "Bidrag till kännedom om den karolinska arméns tillkomst", *Karolinska förbundets årsbok* 1954, pp.45–63, on p.60.

26 Erik Bellander, *Dräkt och uniform: Den svenska arméns beklädnad från 1500-talets början fram till våra dagar* (Stockholm: P.A. Norstedt & Söner, 1973), p.143.

27 Stade, "Slaget vid Lund", p.114.

28 Götesson, *Skånska krigets verkningar*, p.126.

29 Gustaf Petri, *Kungl. Första livgrenadjärregementets historia 2: Östgöta regemente till fot 1619–1679* (Stockholm: P.A. Norstedt & Söner, 1928), pp.67–8.

Guard functioned as a military school, from which officers would be sent to the provincial regiments.[30] King Charles held as a principle, perhaps with the example of his mentor Rutger von Ascheberg in mind, that an officer should begin training as a common soldier so that he would know the conditions of the men he was set to command. Ascheberg, in his mid fifties, was an experienced German officer in Swedish service who had risen from the ranks during the Thirty Years' War which he had entered as a common cavalryman.[31]

At the outbreak of war, the Swedish army was divided in a number of regiments that were distributed throughout its possessions (Appendix III). The origin and distribution of the regiments give evidence to the disjointed nature of the Swedish maritime empire, which was only held together by lines of sea communication. The unit organisation was not quite as straightforward as it might seem. Individual companies and squadrons or battalions were regularly sent overseas for garrison or other duty. Over there, they might be recombined as a new regiment. There were also independent squadrons and battalions, in particular among the enlisted troops in Germany. Likewise, old regiments were occasionally disbanded or combined, especially if they could no longer maintain their establishment strength. Moreover, as the war got underway, Sweden rapidly raised a large number of additional and temporary units.

Sweden had a substantial navy. In 1675, the Swedish navy had 41 warships, of which only seven were small.[32] The Crown could also make use of armed merchantmen. However, most of the navy's sailors were raised from the coastal population in the traditional manner. As a result, most were coastal fishermen rather than blue-water sailors, and their skills were no longer sufficient to man modern warships. Despite being obsolete, Sweden still relied on this tradition to man its navy. With the outbreak of war, its inadequacies would soon become evident.

The Brandenburg-Prussian Military Establishment

A few words need also be said about the military forces of Frederick William, Elector of Brandenburg and Duke of Prussia, although space does not permit a full study.

Frederick William, who had come to power during the Thirty Years' War, early on realised that his small domain only could compete with the major European powers surrounding him, or at least prevent them from marching through and devastating his lands, if he established a formidable army. He accordingly set out to create a standing army, the first ever in Brandenburg, exclusively out of enlisted troops. Like Denmark and Sweden, Brandenburg-Prussia depended on foreign subsidies for its military forces.

30 Lars-Åke Göthesson, *Ställningen vid Norrvidinge hösten 1678: Erik Dahlberghs bataljplan över Karl XI:s fältläger vid Norrvidinge och Dagstorp* (Kristianstad: Monitor Förlaget, 2005), p.85.

31 Alf Åberg, *När Skåne blev svenskt: Två krig, två freder, snapphanar och försvenskning* (np: SMB, 2013), p.203. Relevant section first published as Alf Åberg, "Rutger von Ascheberg och tillkomsten av den karolinska armén", *Karolinska förbundets årsbok* 1951, pp.170–92. See also Alf Åberg, *Rutger von Ascheberg: fältmarskalk och generalguvernör* (Malmö: Gleerups, 1950).

32 Glete, *Navies and Nations*, p.608.

Frederick William established the regiments and selected their colonels, who might derive from the traditional Brandenburger and Prussian nobility or be foreign officers in his service, who then recruited the other regimental officers and enlisted the men. An unusual feature of the Brandenburg-Prussian enlistment procedure was that the enlistment of peasants and artisans was forbidden, so all enlisted men were already soldiers. Moreover, all enlistment took place in the name of the Elector, not the Colonel who raised the regiment. Frederick William also introduced a system of military justice that was far more humane than what was common in his age, with the beating of the men by their officers and punishments such as running the gauntlet proscribed. Moreover, he established a cadet institution for the training of future officers. As a result, the Brandenburg army was a thoroughly professional force, although perhaps, despite Frederick William's intentions, somewhat less firmly linked to the state than the Scandinavian conscript armies. In fact, Frederick William did not quite trust the old Brandenburg-Prussian nobility, so employed an Imperial officer, Field Marshal Georg von Derfflinger, as his commanding general. Derfflinger was of non-noble origin, being the son of either a peasant or a tailor. Frederick William's army averaged some 7,000 men in times of peace, but this number was increased to 15,000 or even 30,000 when he went to war, according to what his funding and the availability of men allowed.[33]

Frederick William, Elector of Brandenburg. (Anselmus van Hulle, contemporary portrait although published only in 1717)

Brandenburg was no major naval power. In 1675, Frederick William had only four warships, all of them small and of little significance. Yet, this was the biggest fleet Brandenburg had ever had, and Frederick William was in the process of expanding his small navy, in the same way that he also worked to build an efficient army.[34]

Arms and Armour

With the basic organisation being the same in the armies engaged in the war, it is hardly surprising that armament, too, was essentially identical.

Officers brought their own arms and armour. Helmets and more extensive armour had grown obsolete already during the Thirty Years' War and at this time were little used, except when a senior officer posed for a portrait or participated in a parade. In battle, each would be armed with a

33 Hannsjoachim W. Koch, *A History of Prussia* (London: Routledge, 1978), pp.59–60.
34 Glete, *Navies and Nations*, p.686.

rapier and two wheellock pistols. Infantry officers usually added a half-pike (spontoon). An officer was expected to wear both breast- and backplate, and at sieges and most battles, officers would protect themselves. The armour was not always obvious, however, since many wore a coat above the cuirass. Still, not all officers bothered with the armour. In a letter written after the war, in 1683, King Charles asked his trusted mentor, Field Marshal Rutger von Ascheberg, if he wished to have a set of breast- and backplate. Charles knew that Ascheberg did not own any cuirass, but now he had received a new one for himself, which was quite comfortable, he wrote. So if Ascheberg wanted one, the King would order it for him from the same armourer. The combined breast- and backplate had a weight of 13.2 kg, but was 'comfortable to wear' and did not put additional pressure on any part of his body, Charles wrote, adding that it was tested as shot-proof for musket fire to the front and carbine fire from the rear.[35]

A non-commissioned officer, too, was armed with a rapier and perhaps pistols. Those serving in the infantry would carry halberds or half-pikes.

A cavalryman was armed with rapier, two wheellock pistols, and a carbine. At first, the individual or group of individuals who raised a cavalryman also had to arm him. However, firearms were soon provided by the Crown so as to achieve some uniformity in armament. Carbines were shorter than muskets, in Sweden typically 113 cm long. In comparison, muskets were about 150 cm long. Both types of weapon had a calibre of about 20 mm (the carbines were, at least in Sweden, technically 19 mm but used the same ammunition as the muskets since the ball in any case was smaller than the barrel).[36] In comparison, wheellock pistols had a calibre of about 16 mm in Sweden and 19 mm in Denmark. In Sweden, 20 mm muskets, 19 mm carbines, and 16 mm pistols subsequently became standard calibres.[37] By this time, Sweden had already established formal patterns for the manufacturers, although details are no longer known.[38] The carbine was hooked to a baldric, at this time possibly with the butt down,[39] while the pistols were carried in holsters fixed to the front of the saddle.

Swedish cavalrymen were supposed to wear heavy breastplates for protection, and it is likely that all cavalry regiments had, or acquired, them during the war. Swedish breastplates were heavy, with a weight of up to 7–8 kg. Tested for being shot-proof before distribution, they stopped most pistol and musket balls. Later the breastplates were commonly polished, but judging from contemporary paintings, blackened breastplates appear to have been more common at this time. Under the breastplate, but over the buff coat (see the section on uniforms, below), was worn a thick, padded vest, so as to provide additional padding under the breastplate. In Denmark, only

35 Josef Alm, *Blanka vapen och skyddsvapen från och med 1500-talet till våra dagar* (Stockholm: Rediviva, 1975), pp.266–7.

36 Josef Alm, *Eldhandvapen 1: Från deras tidigaste förekomst till slaglåsets allmänna införande.* (Stockholm: Rediviva, 1976), p.253.

37 Ibid., pp.252, 256

38 Ibid., p.232.

39 Ibid., p.262.

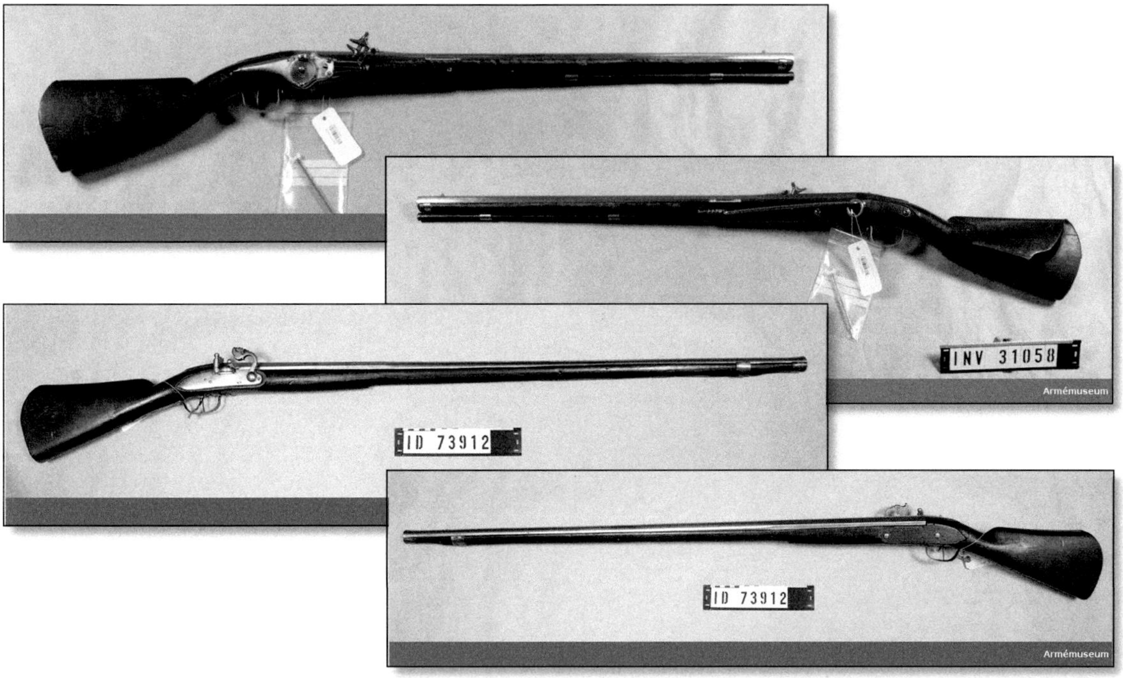

Top, left and right: Swedish Carbine, pattern 1680. The carbines used in Sweden during the Scanian War were essentially identical. (Army Museum, Stockholm, AM.031058)

Bottom, left and right: Swedish matchlock musket, late 17th century. (Army Museum, Stockholm, AM.102687)

the 1st Jutland Cavalry Regiment wore breastplates. Danish breastplates were apparently less heavy that the corresponding Swedish ones, each with a weight of about 5.8 kg, and were often blackened.[40]

Dragoons were armed with rapier or (possibly in Denmark late in the war) a sabre or curved hanger, a carbine or musket, and two wheellock pistols. They might also carry handy tools such as an axe or pickaxe. Swedish dragoons wore buff coats but probably not breastplates. This is an assumption based on the fact that they still were intended to fight on foot, and that unlike uniforms, which were the responsibility of those who equipped the troops, the Crown was expected to pay for armour, that is, buff coats and any breastplates. Since the Swedish Crown's finances always were poor, it seems unlikely that funding would have been available for dragoon breastplates, especially so since perhaps not even all cavalry regiments had been issued them. However, since dragoons increasingly often operated in a cavalry role, some units eventually may have been issued breastplates.

The chief infantry weapon was the musket, all of which at the outset of war were matchlocks. The musket was a sturdy weapon, when properly manufactured, and many soldiers loaded their weapons with excessively strong charges of gunpowder, which gave the musket ball a high velocity and

40 Alm, *Blanka vapen*, p.264.

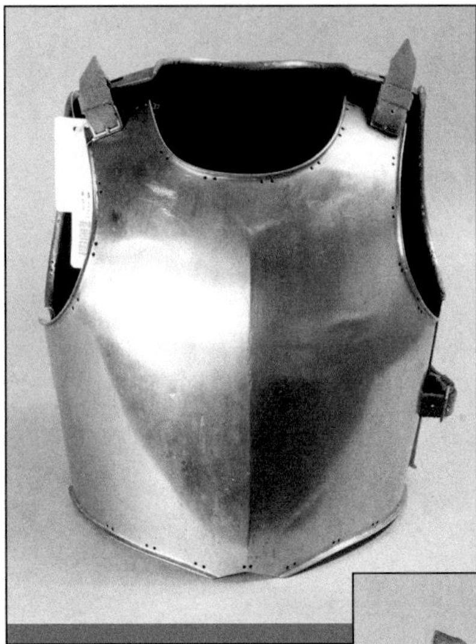

Clockwise from top left::

Swedish breastplate, 1680s. (Army Museum, Stockholm, AM.032357; Photo: author)

Swedish breastplate, late 17th century. Polished, but possibly at a later date. (Army Museum, Stockholm, AM.089709)

Swedish backplate, late 17th century. Polished, but possibly at a later date. (Army Museum, Stockholm, AM.089710)

Swedish breastplate, late 17th century. Painted black, like many cuirasses at the time. (Army Museum, Stockholm, AM.089711)

Swedish backplate, late 17th century. Painted black, like many cuirasses at the time. (Army Museum, Stockholm, AM.089712)

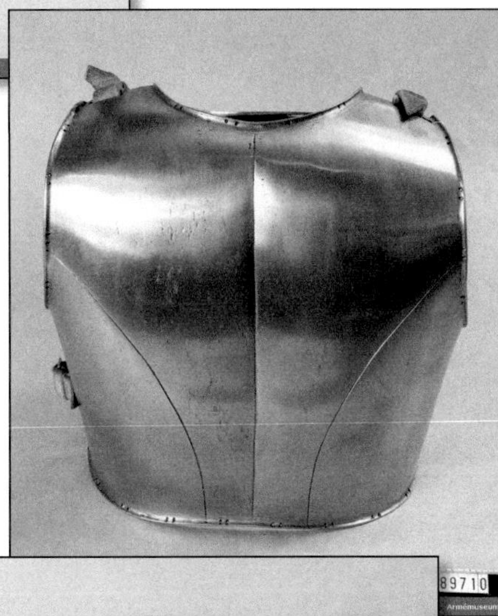

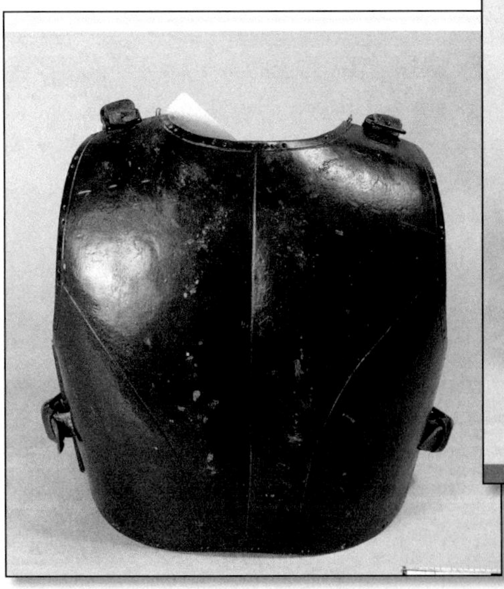

produced grievous wounds. Moreover, it was common to load the musket with multiple and often irregular projectiles, which might explain why during the war so many men and officers suffered from multiple wounds when they were shot. Wheellock pistols, too, might be loaded in this manner.[41]

In the past, muskets had been fired with the help of fork rests. This was no longer invariably the case, neither among Danish nor Swedish troops.[42] However, fork rests remained in use, and it will be shown that Swedish regulations issued during the war assumed that a third of the infantry (the second rank out of three) would carry fork rests. Regulations issued after the war referred to fork rests, too.[43] In a few regiments from Holstein or Germany, musketeers instead carried a swinefeather (elsewhere also known as a Swedish feather), which was a short pike with an attachment for resting the musket barrel that could be used as protection against cavalry. A unit of musketeers with swinefeathers firmly planted in the ground in front of them would give the appearance of a wall of spear points. Moreover, with the addition of logs to link them together, several swinefeathers could be arranged into a *cheval-de-frise*, an anti-cavalry obstacle that was positioned in front of the infantry ranks so as to provide protection against a cavalry charge.

From about 1677, the first flintlock muskets were distributed both in the Danish and Swedish armies (flintlocks had existed for some time but not seen general service). At first, only infantry guard units received the new weapons. In 1677, the first flintlock muskets were apparently distributed to the Swedish King's Life Guard.[44] Some Danish infantry units received flintlocks at more or less the same time. However, there is a terminology problem, since snaphance locks at the time were known as flintlocks, so one can only be reasonably certain that real flintlocks were meant when they were referred to as 'French flintlocks'.[45] Moreover, in the Netherlands snaphance muskets were used by marines, since matchlocks were regarded as less suitable at sea.[46] On 11 September 1678, the first supplies of what was then termed "the French armament" (*Franska Gewäret*) were distributed in the Swedish field army at Norrvidinge. It is likely that these were first flintlock muskets that went into general service in the Swedish army. The weapons may have been included in the shipment of weapons that arrived on 30 August 1678 with Colonel Robert Lichton.[47]

Musketeers armed with matchlocks would wear a leather bandolier slung over the left shoulder holding a powder horn and 12 or more wooden bottles for gunpowder (each with enough powder for a single shot). At about the same time as the flintlock was introduced, the bandolier was replaced by a cartridge box, which contained paper cartridges each containing a measured

41 Battlefield archaeology seems to confirm the use of such projectiles. Knarrström, *Slagfältet*, pp.60–61.
42 This is also obvious from Erik Dahlbergh's contemporary illustrations of the Battle of Lund 1676.
43 Alm, *Eldhandvapen 1*, p.242.
44 Göthesson, *Ställningen vid Norrvidinge*, p.85.
45 Alm, *Eldhandvapen 1*, p.230.
46 Ibid., p.234.
47 Göthesson, *Ställningen vid Norrvidinge*, 59; based on Alexander Magnus Hummerhielm's diary.

Top: Musket balls, excavated at Landskrona. The upper row balls retain sprues. (Photo: Bo Knarrström and Efron & Dotter, 2006)
Centre: Wheellock pistol balls with retained sprues, excavated at Landskrona. (Photo: Bo Knarrström and Efron & Dotter, 2006)
Bottom: Left: Musket ball with rust remnants indicating that it was cast around an iron wire. Right: Modern reconstruction. (Photo: Bo Knarrström and Efron & Dotter, 2006)

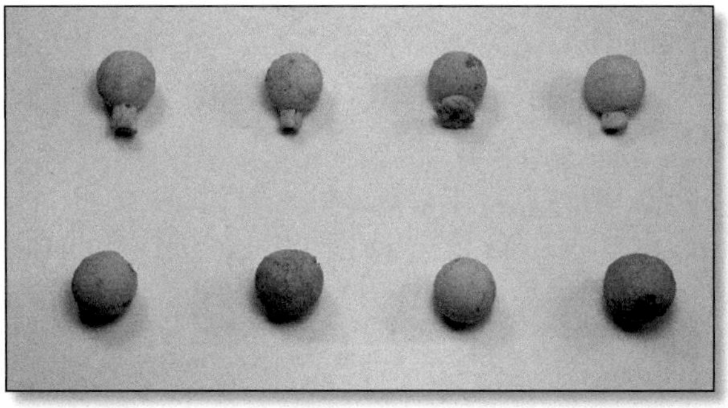

charge of gunpowder.[48] Archaeological evidence from the 1677 Battle of Landskrona indicates that paper cartridges then were already in relatively widespread use, and that many lead musket balls retained the sprue that resulted from the channel in which molten metal had been poured into the mould when cast. The sprue was probably retained since it could be tied to the paper cartridge, in effect anchoring the ball within the paper cartridge. A ball with sprue could also be expected to cause a more devastating wound. On the other hand, most musket balls found on the battlefield lacked a sprue. This would seem to suggest that the majority still loaded their muskets individually, without paper cartridges prepared in advance.[49] Or alternatively, cartridges were used, but the lead sprues were removed and melted down again so as to save lead. After all, the ball could be enclosed in a cartridge even without anchoring it on its sprue.

Archaeological evidence also indicates that the men employed other means to make sure that the musket balls became as devastating as could be. Some soldiers cast balls around an iron wire. Such a ball could be trusted to tear human flesh even more than a regular musket ball. Or perhaps the archaeological finds are the remains of a yet more devastating projectile, a group of perhaps four lead balls cast onto a metre-long iron wire, which when fired would whip through flesh, cut bones, and cause multiple wounds. Yet another method to make the musket balls deadlier was to cut a cross into the already cast ball. When hitting a target, such a ball would shatter on impact, producing horrible wounds in the manner of a modern expanding bullet, also known colloquially as a dumdum bullet. Or, if the ball was fully cut through, it would shatter already upon firing, thus producing a cluster of heavy projectiles.[50] The means to make a musket ball more devastating probably formed part of the soldiers' oral tradition, something that was learnt in camps and not necessarily taught by trained gunsmiths or condoned by officers.

Those infantrymen who did not carry muskets were armed with pikes. Pikes were up to 5.5 m in length and made of ash. The pike shafts may have been painted black, since this seems to have been a common practice in Germany and apparently also Sweden. Generally speaking, by the time of the Scanian War the share of

48 Alm, *Eldhandvapen 1*, p.244.
49 Knarrström, *Slagfältet*, pp.83–4.
50 Ibid., pp.85–8.

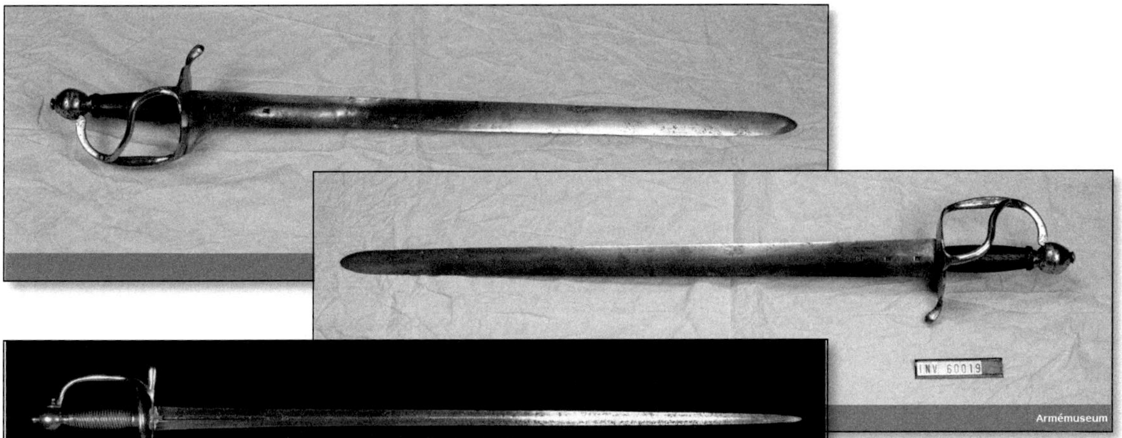

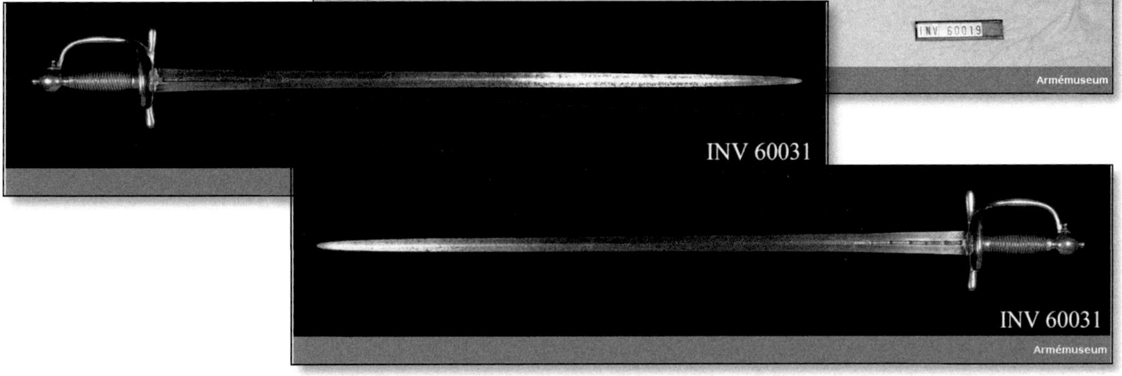

Swedish infantry rapier, 1660-1670. The hilt was originally of blackened iron with wire grip. (Army Museum, Stockholm, AM.060019)

Swedish rapier, 1670s, of the pattern that would become standard for Swedish rapiers. From Nils Bielke's armoury. (Army Museum, Stockholm, AM.060031)

pikemen in a unit was mostly less than a third, and probably closer to a quarter, of the total infantry. Most garrison regiments only carried muskets. In October 1678, King Christian ordered that pikes should be abandoned and replaced with muskets and swinefeathers. This had no effect on the outcome of the war, since re-armament took some time. The Swedish army took the opposite course and retained pikes for many more years to come, regarding it as an excellent offensive battlefield weapon. This fundamental difference in military thought between Danes and Swedes will show up again and again. The Danish military leaders thought in terms of defence, while their Swedish equivalents were far more interested in offensive capability.

In addition, each infantryman wore a rapier as a sidearm (socket bayonets had not yet been introduced, and although plug bayonets existed on the Continent, they were not yet in common use). Rapiers were used by both horse and foot, and those made for the infantry may have been somewhat shorter than those used by the cavalry. The rapier was worn hanging from a baldric slung over the right shoulder. Among officers and cavalrymen, waistbelts were coming into fashion but were not yet universal. Rapiers were double-edged and most were fairly crude. Sword hilts far more often consisted of blackened plain iron than brass. Although rapiers were similar in style and length, there were not yet any standard patterns. Blades had commonly grown longer since the mid seventeenth century. This was certainly the case in Sweden, where a cavalryman's rapier then typically had a blade length of 79–80 cm and a width of 3.7–4.5 cm. A blade that possibly was an infantry rapier of that time was only 73 cm long (although it may

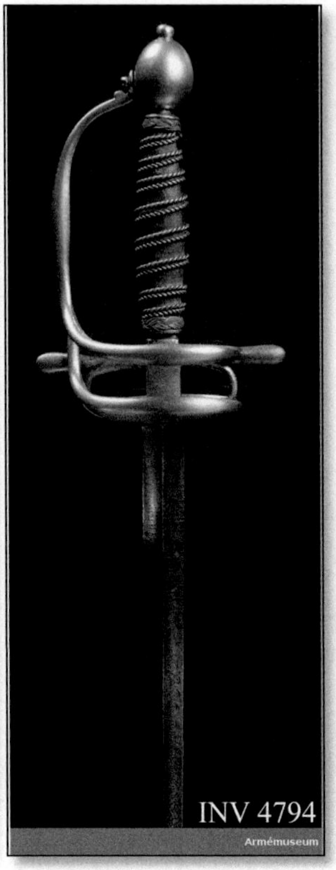

Above, left: Rapier for a Swedish officer, 1670s. The pattern became known as commander's rapier. (Army Museum, Stockholm, AM.004794; Photo: author)

Above, centre: Rapier for a Swedish officer, 1670s. The pattern became known as the commander's rapier. (Army Museum, Stockholm, AM.004794; photo: author)

Above: right: Rapier for a Swedish Drabant officer, *c.* 1670. The hilt pattern became known as the Drabant hilt. (Army Museum, Stockholm, AM.060057; photo: author)

have been shortened later) and a width of 4.5 cm.[51] At the time of the Scanian War, however, a Swedish rapier often had a blade length of 97 cm, with a total length including hilt of around 114–120 cm. King Charles carried a rapier with a blade length of 97.2 cm and a width of 2.5 cm. Immediately after the war, King Charles introduced the first known rapier pattern for the Swedish army. It was similar in style to his own but sturdier. Although detailed records of this pattern have not survived, the next pattern introduced, known as model 1685, had a blade length of about 93–97 cm and a width of more than 3 cm.[52]

Grenadiers carried muskets and several grenades each, carried in a dedicated container. Grenades intended to be thrown by hand were originally developed for siege work since grenades enabled the attackers to clear a breach of defenders before exploiting it. In Scandinavia, grenades were stored in Kalmar Castle, then held by Denmark, in 1611. Gustavus Adolphus was apparently the first ruler who formed dedicated units armed with grenades, that is, grenadiers. They were first used at the siege of Ratisbon (Regensburg) in 1632. However, these units were temporary and were not retained after the siege. At the 1658 siege of Copenhagen, Swedish musketeers reportedly fired grenades fastened to wooden sticks from their muskets.[53] From around this

51 Heribert Seitz, *Svärdet och värjan som armévapen* (Stockholm: Kungl. Armémuseum, 1955), pp. 143, 145, 147.

52 Alm, *Blanka vapen*, pp.55–61.

53 Alm, *Eldhandvapen 1*, p.250.

time, grenades were commonly used in set battles, too. France introduced grenadiers in 1667, and Count Raimondo Montecuccoli introduced grenadiers in Imperial infantry companies in 1670.[54] Denmark formed a dedicated but temporary grenadier unit at the siege of Wismar in 1675. In January 1676, in preparation of the invasion of Scania, King Christian ordered that all infantry companies should be organised into 60 musketeers, 24 pikemen, four grenadiers, and two carpenters (pioneers), in addition to drummers, fifer, clerk, and so on. A year later, the number of grenadiers was raised to 6, while in spring 1677 the carpenters were transferred to a special pioneer company. In 1677, the dragoon regiments, too, received grenadiers, in numbers about 10 per regiment.[55] Grenades were hollow balls filled with gunpowder 7–10 cm in diameter, manufactured from iron, lead, clay, and occasionally glass, with a fuse that was lit before throwing.[56] Fragments of such grenades have been found at the battlefield of Landskrona.[57]

Uniforms

By the 1660s, male civilian dress was strongly influenced by an entirely new fashion that originated in France. Its dominant garment was a long, tightly fitting coat with long cuffs and numerous buttons and pleats. Known as *justaucorps*, this long coat served as the model for the regimental uniforms that from this onwards became standard in west European armies. The coat, with lining and cuffs of a contrasting colour that enabled easier recognition of units at a distance, was worn with narrow breeches of a type that, despite being largely concealed under the coat, gradually replaced the old baggy ones. Long woollen stockings and square-toed, often buckled shoes completed the uniform, together with a brimmed hat or cap.

Regimental uniforms were not a new innovation. The Swedish army had for a considerable time aimed for uniform dress in at least some of its field units, including during the Thirty Years' War and even before. At the time of the Scanian War, the various regiments had all been issued proper uniforms, although there was no national uniform as such. Yet, because of the difficulties in supply, it can be assumed that many of the Swedish units in the field army soon

Justaucorps, supposedly brought to Sweden from France (or Prussia) as pattern for new uniforms. (Army Museum, Stockholm, AM.015470)

54 Generalstaben, *Karl XII på slagfältet 1* (Stockholm: P.A. Norstedt & Söner, 1918), p.181.
55 Hasselager and Snorrason, *Danish Uniforms, Colours and Standards*, pp.15–16.
56 Alm, *Eldhandvapen 1*, p.249.
57 Knarrström, *Slagfältet*, p.67.

Noblemen in French-style coats, with the royal castle Tre Kronor, Stockholm, in the background. (Lorenzo Magalotti, 1674)

displayed a rag-tag appearance, for the simple reason of wear and tear. In winter, in particular, there was probably much variation, according to what kind of winter clothing individual soldiers had been able to scrounge. Most would no doubt have acquired at least a grey homespun woollen cloak, cut in a circular shape. There was no formally issued winter uniform.

The Danish army had known the occasional uniformed guard unit during the Thirty Years' War but, generally speaking, the Danes only used uniforms after the 1661 introduction of absolute royal rule. The Danish army units in the Scanian War had all been issued uniforms. However, it can be questioned to what extent this applied to the enlisted German regiments. Even so, being closer to the Danish heartland and usually well-supplied, it can nonetheless be assumed that most Danish units presented a more uniform appearance than the Swedish ones.

Among Danish troops, the national cavalry regiments mostly wore light grey coats with lining in other colours. The coat might be decorated with shoulder ribbons or aiguillettes. Breeches were usually buff leather lined with linen, although later in the war, cloth breeches existed, too. Infantry wore stockings, typically in the regimental facing colour, white, or grey. The men also wore neckcloths. Most were white, black, or in the regimental facing colour.[58]

58 The main source for Danish uniforms is Hasselager and Snorrason, *Danish Uniforms, Colours and Standards*.

Infantrymen of unknown nationality, probably 1670s, with the hair tied up with a ribbon. (Johan Philip Lemke, based on observations before his arrival in Sweden but subsequently used as patterns for his paintings of events during the Scanian War)

Danish soldiers generally wore black or grey wide-brimmed felt hats. Alternatively, some wore caps which came in two varieties. The pointed cap (*spidshue*) was similar in shape to a nightcap with tassel. Another type of headgear was the *kahuds*, which was the equivalent of the Swedish *karpus*, a round woollen cap with flaps that could be turned down to protect the eyes, ears, and neck. Like the coat, the cap and its lining were typically in contrasting colours, so that the lining, in the regimental facing colour, would show when the flaps were turned up. Some cavalrymen may still have worn helmets.

Grenadiers were initially uniformed so as to distinguish them from the rank and file. At least initially, they commonly wore grey coats with red or blue lining.

As noted, only the 1st Jutland Cavalry Regiment wore breastplates. The Guard Cavalry wore buff leather jerkins.

Officers normally wore coats that conformed to the colour of the regimental uniform; however, there was great scope for variations since officers (and non-commissioned officers) provided their own clothing. As noted, many mounted officers wore cuirasses.

Danish dragoons were uniformed as infantry, except that they were dragoon boots, which were lighter and softer than the high riding boots used by the cavalry.

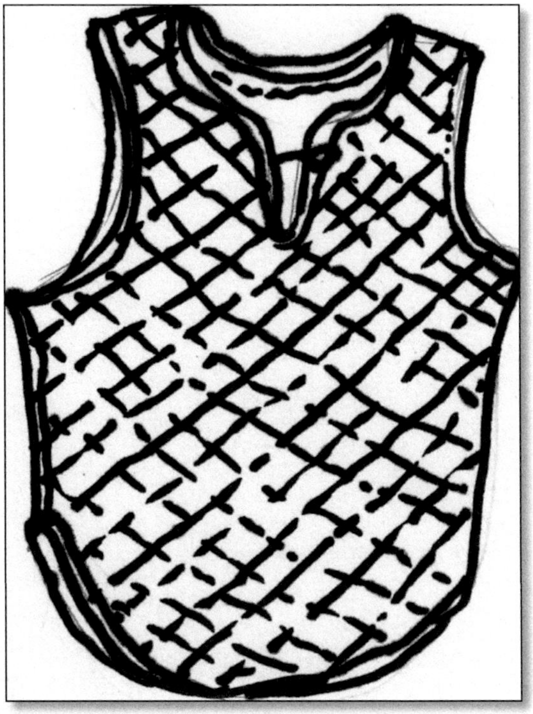

Left: Swedish buff coat, 1680s. (Army Museum, Stockholm; photo: author)

Above: Padded vest worn under the cuirass, made of leather and quilted linen. Buttoned on the left side, it was worn above the buff coat and under the breastplate. Drawing of a specimen in Swedish Royal Armoury.

Sweden had begun to introduce the new, French-style uniforms but not all units had received them. Officers provided their own uniforms, which usually but not invariably conformed to the colour of the regimental uniform.[59]

In the cavalry, the old-fashioned buff coat of leather made of elk skin remained in common use. It also provided a measure of protection against edged weapons. During the war, it was gradually replaced by the French-style coat, which the officers typically adopted before other ranks. It was by no means certain that all men would receive French-style coats at the same time. As a result, the cavalry might have men wearing buff coat and French coat in the same unit, without attempting to distinguish between the two.[60] As noted, cavalrymen were supposed to wear breastplates for protection, and it is likely that all cavalry regiments already had them, or acquired breastplates during the war, while dragoons wore buff coats but probably not breastplates. Most cavalrymen wore a wide-brimmed felt hat.

59 The best modern study of Swedish uniforms is Höglund, *Skånska kriget*.

60 Bellander, *Dräkt och uniform*, 172.

Young officers of unknown nationality, probably after 1670s. (Johan Philip Lemke, based on observations ***before*** his arrival in Sweden but subsequently used as patterns for his paintings of events during the Scanian War).

At the outbreak of war, most infantry regiments had received the new style uniform, although it was not yet in universal use. Some infantrymen, in particular the non-commissioned officers, instead wore old-fashioned buff coats. Non-commissioned officers might instead have worn grey coats, grey breeches, and grey stockings. Breeches were still baggy, knee-long, and made of wool. They had the same colour as the coat or were made of grey natural wool. Either way, they were worn with woollen stockings. A neckcloth and either a wide-brimmed felt hat or a *karpus* completed the uniform.

In the Swedish army, it was primarily the various guard units that first wore uniforms of the type that later would be recognised as a quintessential national uniform, or at least its prototype. The Drabant Guard, for instance, was uniformed as follows: in 1675, the men wore black hats with gold braids, blue coats with yellow lining and gilded buttons and gold braids, and grey cloaks. Corporals instead wore grey hats with gold-in-silver braids (in a bow or rosette), grey coats with gold-in-silver braids, buff coats, grey breeches and socks, and buff leather belts with braids.

By 1677, the men wore blue *karpus* with yellow lining, blue coats with yellow lining, golden braids, and gilded buttons, breastplates, buff coats, and leather breeches. The non-commissioned officers and corporals then wore blue *karpus* with yellow lining, blue coats with yellow cuffs and gold-in-silver threads in all seams, and blue cloaks with wide braided collars.

By 1678, the Drabants wore black hats with gold-in-silver braids. In combination with the previously issued blue coat with yellow lining, this became the archetypal Swedish Carolean uniform.

The Life Guard on Foot followed a similar path. In 1674, the musketeers wore pale blue coats with yellow lining, while the pikemen wore buff coats. All soldiers wore black hats, blue breeches, and blue stockings. In 1675, the pikemen had switched to blue coats with blue lining edged in yellow. Non-commissioned officers wore buff coats, grey breeches, grey stockings, and grey cloaks with gold and silver embroideries.[61]

The Geographical Setting and Logistical Requirement

Both King Christian of Denmark and King Charles of Sweden controlled significant territories (Map 1). The King of Denmark was the ruler of several quite different domains. He was King of Denmark, which comprised Jutland and the Danish islands of Zealand, Fyn, and Lolland. Denmark was commonly referred to as the Kingdom. He was also King of Norway. In addition, he was the suzerain of Schleswig-Holstein, which extended south of Jutland to the River Elbe in the vicinity of Hamburg. While the King of Denmark personally owned about half of Schleswig-Holstein, much of the rest belonged to the Duke of Holstein-Gottorp, with whom there was some rivalry. In addition, there were several other, formally independent counties and enclaves in the area, all of which depended on the King of Denmark. Schleswig-Holstein and the adjoining enclaves were commonly referred to as the Duchies. Finally, the King of Denmark had also obtained, by inheritance, sovereignty over Oldenburg and Delmenhorst, two German counties west of Bremen and the River Weser. These two possessions were commonly referred to as the Counties.

Since Gustavus Adolphus entered the Thirty Years' War two generations earlier and put Sweden on the path to great power status, Sweden had grown into what might perhaps best be described as a maritime empire, with diverse territories and responsibilities far beyond the country's old borders. Through the 1648 Peace of Westphalia, Sweden had emerged the ruler of several new territories in Germany, in addition to the lands on the east side of the Baltic that had been acquired earlier, namely, Finland, Ingria, Estonia, and Livonia. On the Continent, the Swedish maritime empire consisted of western Pomerania on the Baltic shore, which had limited agricultural resources but several important ports and towns such as Damgarten, Stralsund, Greifswald, Wolgast, Anklam, Demmin, and Stettin.

61 Ibid., p.160; Höglund, *Skånska kriget*, p.23.

Sweden controlled the exit of the River Oder into the Baltic Sea. Swedish Pomerania had land borders with Mecklenburg in the west (delimited by the River Recknitz) and Brandenburg in the south and east (in part delineated by the River Oder). Further to the west on the Baltic shore, with land borders with Mecklenburg, was Wismar, another important port under Swedish rule. The most western Swedish possession on the Continent was the Duchy of Bremen-Verden, formally the Duchy of Bremen and the Principality of Verden, two territories and immediate fiefs of the Holy Roman Empire. The Duchy was poor in resources, and the town of Bremen remained outside Swedish control. However, the Duchy's capital Stade was a substantial town of 14,000 inhabitants. Meanwhile, Carlsburg (modern-day Bremerhaven), at the exit of the River Weser, and the bastion Schwinge, built at the confluence of the Rivers Schwinge and Elbe, controlled the exits of the two rivers into the North Sea, which enabled the collection of significant toll revenues.

In Scandinavia, most operations took place in Scania and the surrounding provinces, although some raiding occurred on the mountains along the Swedish-Norwegian border further to the north as well. On the surface, Scania gave the impression of being a convenient territory for military operations, since the province predominantly consisted of fertile plains and accordingly was quite wealthy. However, the abundant farmland was crisscrossed with earth enclosures, fences, and dry-stone walls that impeded operations. Moreover, north-western Scania consisted of forestland, which offered good opportunities for defensive operations, including by local peasants who often were unfriendly to invading armies. And north of Scania was the province of Småland, which was heavily forested. The numerous rivers presented other difficulties. Although the rivers in southern Sweden were not comparable to the great continental rivers such as the Rhine and Danube, they were sufficiently large to present major obstacles for the armies. There were very few fords and only a few bridges, usually in built-up areas which impeded operations further. In addition, the river banks often merged into marshes, which made crossing yet more difficult away from the existing roads, which tended to follow the river valleys. The marshes also served as natural obstacles during siegeworks, since many towns were surrounded by wetlands.

For these reasons, it was far easier to move overland in winter than in summer. Although Denmark and Sweden had functioning road networks, to travel by sledge across the snow during winter was still considered more convenient than travel by cart in summer. Sledges could negotiate the frozen ground far easier than any cart. Besides, in Sweden frozen rivers were regarded as safe for sledge travel from late December to the end of March. In April, rivers tended to remain frozen, but then the ice was treacherous. In Denmark, sledge travel was common, too, but there the ice was always regarded as treacherous by seasoned travellers, since the country was located comparatively more to the south.[62]

It follows that logistics consistently presented difficulties during the Scanian War. During the summer, supplies may have been available in

62 Magalotti, *Sverige*, p.79.

Army camp. (Johan Philip Lemke)

the area of operations, but then it was difficult to move them. In winter, transportation was easier, but supplies were scant or non-existent. At the outbreak of war, neither side had made sufficient preparations for supplying their armies. Logistics remained difficult throughout the war.

Both the Danish and Swedish armies built field camps so as to help the soldiers survive the rigours of campaign.[63] This was particularly important in winter but also during autumn and spring, both of which might experience cold weather. The camps also served a strategic purpose. A camp could be used to maintain a position that prevented the enemy from manoeuvring into a more advantageous location.

Danish and Swedish camps were very similar. The camps were usually not fortified, although defensive bastions were occasionally erected in strong positions, and they were not very different from army camps elsewhere in western Europe. First, it was necessary to find a suitable location, with access to fresh water, supplies, and fodder. The camp was then laid out in order of battle, in two extended lines separated by a camp road which was used when calling up the army. It was thus easy to form up the entire army at once, since each wing and the centre camped in their proper position in the line of battle. For the same reason, the army could also form up in order of march very rapidly, as evidenced by the Battle of Lund when the Danish troops did so in no more than half an hour. However, this also meant that the camp was extended for a considerable distance, up to around 3.5 km in the case of the Danish army outside Lund in 1676. The troops lived in simple ridge tents, housing several men each. To give the men at least a modicum of shelter against the cold, King Charles would order his troops

63 See, e.g., Göthesson, *Ställningen vid Norrvidinge*, pp.39–46.

Supply cart. (Johan Philip Lemke)

to dig down, making dugout shelters which then employed the tent as a ridge roof.[64] Officers would bring larger tents for their own use. The supply train, with its numerous carts, horses, cattle, and other goods, was usually positioned in the rear of the two lines of tents. Cavalry horses, too, were tied up next to the supply train. An army with a large cavalry contingent, such as the Swedish, might easily bring up to 10,000 horses. If the King was present, he usually took quarters in a nearby castle, manor house, or the house of a parish priest. The army headquarters would commonly be set up in any convenient, existing building, but other houses and constructions in nearby villages would be demolished so as to provide construction materials for the camp. Any peasants there would be evicted, as their homes were torn down. Some of the materials would be used to provide workshops for the army's blacksmiths, bakers, and other craftsmen. The rest were used to build small cottages for officers.

Naturally, the camps also served as living quarters for other people than soldiers. The King would bring a limited court, which included cooks and servants but also civilian officials, foreign diplomats, and their respective households. The royal court, even when deliberately limited to essential personnel, was not only there for the King's personal pleasure but also constituted the national government as long as the King was on campaign. Sweden was governed from King Charles's camp for the entire duration of the Scanian War, not from the capital Stockholm. Likewise, Denmark was run from King Christian's camp, whenever he took to the field.

Then there were other civilians, ranging from merchants and traders to the dependents of officers and men, whether these be spouses, companions, or (but this was frowned on in the severely Lutheran Swedish army) prostitutes. An army camp typically had far more inhabitants than the nearby towns.

64 Sune Hildebrand (ed.), *Hakvin Spegels Dagbok* (Stockholm: Norstedt, 1923), p.41.

Supply trains. (Johan Philip Lemke)

Although the capitals, Stockholm and Copenhagen, at the time each had a population in excess of 40,000 inhabitants, most towns in Scania had a much smaller population. Scania's chief town, Malmö, had a total population of no more than 3,000 to 4,000 inhabitants. Others were smaller. For instance, Lund had a cathedral and a university but only some 1,700 inhabitants. In comparison, the Danish army camp in the field nearby at the time likely was the home of some 17,000 people.[65]

65 Wahlöö and Larsson, *Slaget vid Lund*, p.21.

3

Origins of the Scanian War

The Danish ambassador to Sweden, Jens Juel, on 30 March 1670 summarised his understanding of Sweden's foreign and domestic policy with the following words: 'As soon as unrest commences in Europe, the Swedes will get involved so as to receive financial subsidies... He who wishes ill to Sweden should wish the country 10 years of peace, because then its youth will take to luxury and affluence and its military will diminish, if not in numbers then in bravery and competent command.'[1]

In these two sentences, Ambassador Juel succinctly described Sweden's position in European politics. Sweden had a small population, was weak in resources, and the country's economy was poorly monetarised. Fundamentally, Sweden could not afford to go to war without having received subsidies from foreign allies, at the time primarily France. The subsidies were used to pay for Sweden's military needs, and war provided a means for many Swedes, not only nobles, to make a living and, indeed, to prosper. But this was individual prosperity, not state prosperity; the Crown did not necessarily prosper in any degree commensurate with the resources it had to spend on war, even though its army might subsist by operating in what essentially was a parasitic role abroad. Any war had to pay for itself, chiefly by being waged on the territory of foreign states which enabled Swedish armies to live off the land. However, if Sweden as a state could not afford war without subsidies, it could not afford peace either. In times of peace, the Crown tended to accumulate a burden of debt which it usually lacked the means to service. Yet worse, Sweden had ended its latest war with a government debt that surpassed two years' income.[2]

The peace between Sweden and Denmark in 1660 coincided with the death of Swedish King Charles X Gustav and the establishment of a regency government for young King Charles XI, led by the Lord High Chancellor Magnus Gabriel de la Gardie. The regency government, which was based around a narrow aristocratic group, was characterised by financial mismanagement and failed to safeguard the country's resources, at the same time that its members and their close associates had acquired a lifestyle in

1 Cited in Kurt Lundgren, *Regalskeppet Stora Cronan: Byggandet, slaget och undergången 1676* (np: SMB, 2014), p.23.

2 Rystad, *Karl XI*, p.27.

emulation of their European counterparts, which only could be sustained by largely tax-exempt, formerly royal lands donated by and alienated from the Crown. By the 1670s, some two-thirds of Swedish lands were owned by nobles. The Crown's share had fallen accordingly, in a process begun already during the Thirty Years' War. The royal domain could no longer support an army the size of the one of the 1630s.

Moreover, it was only a small share of the nobility which profited from the arrangement. Since senior military and administrative posts were generally reserved for nobles, the best way to find competent officers was to promote able men to noble rank. Accordingly, the nobility as a whole expanded considerably in numbers. By 1672, a full quarter of senior army officers, that is, of the rank of colonel and above, had been born as non-nobles.[3] Yet, this produced a large number of nobles who lacked access to wealth in the form of lands. In fact, most nobles depended on the salaries due for service as government officers. The Swedish nobility was accordingly growing in numbers but the result was something akin to a service nobility that depended on access to government posts – and thereby the ability of the government to pay their salaries.

It had already in the previous reign been decided to solve the state's poverty through a *reduktion*, a resumption of some royal lands. However, this was not in the interest of the regency government and the narrow group that constituted its immediate backers. Instead the government's then treasurer, Gustav Bonde, initiated radical cutbacks in government spending. While the cutbacks had little impact on the government debt, they compromised Sweden's military security by curtailing investment in fortifications and the navy, and by allowing the arrears of army pay to grow out of control.

Instead Sweden again sought for an alliance that would produce financial subsidies. After a few false starts, Sweden in April 1672, a month after the outbreak of the Dutch War (1672–1678) between France and the Netherlands, signed a treaty with the French King, Louis XIV. France guaranteed subsidies of 400,000 Riksdalers per year for Sweden to maintain 16,000 men in Germany, 6,000 horse and 10,000 foot. The subsidies would be raised to 600,000 Riksdalers in the event of Sweden entering the war. The French intention was that Sweden would guarantee to keep the German principalities out of any war between France and its then main rivals, the Netherlands and Spain. The French policy failed. In 1674, the Dutch War expanded to include the Holy Roman Empire, Denmark, and Brandenburg each of which in turn joined the war against France. The French, naturally, then put pressure on Sweden to enter the war. In April 1674, France offered to increase its subsidy to 900,000 Riksdalers in return for an increase in the size of the Swedish army in Germany to 22,000 men. However, no subsidies would be paid until the Swedish army moved against Brandenburg.

3 James Cavallie, *De höga officerarna: Studier i den svenska militära hierarkien under 1600-talets senare del* (Stockholm: Militärhögskolan, 1981), p.89.

The subsidies were important, which becomes readily apparent from a quick overview of the Swedish Crown's other revenues, presented according to geographical source of income in 1674 (Appendix IV).

The French offer accordingly corresponded to more than a fifth of total Crown revenues. Incidentally, the table also shows the relative importance of the German possessions with regard to revenue. Yet, the former Danish provinces were almost as important.

However, there were, from the Swedish perspective, several difficulties with the French subsidies. First, they were only paid twice a year, and then for the previous six months. The Swedish Crown accordingly had to raise money from other sources for immediate expenses. Second, the subsidies were paid in Paris, not Stockholm. The Crown accordingly had to work through a series of middlemen who would, in effect, lend the Crown money against surety of some kind. If the subsidies were not paid in the end (and they were not, it appears that only 1.5 million Riksdalers were actually paid), the Swedish Crown was in debt.

Denmark, meanwhile, had not forgotten that its former provinces across the Straits, chief of which was Scania, not that long ago had been captured by Sweden and subsequently ceded by the Danish Crown. Until then, Denmark had controlled both sides of the Straits, through which all maritime trade into and out of the Baltic had to pass. This trade had been a vital source of income in the form of customs duties, the Sound Tolls, which had to be paid by all who passed the Straits. Denmark still profited from the Sound Tolls, but less so than before. There was a feeling that a war of revenge on Sweden would be needed, to return the lost provinces and to regain vital income. Denmark, too, received financial subsidies from foreign powers, in particular the Netherlands and to some extent Spain, to maintain its military forces (by 1674, a total of 168,000 Rigsdalers in return for a Danish army of 16,000 men). Denmark used most subsidies for the enlistment of soldiers. The promised Dutch military subsidies eventually reached 1,037,000 Rigsdalers, of which 730,000 were supposed to be used for the army and 307,000 for the navy. The agreement with the Netherlands was concluded at the time of the Anglo-Dutch wars, when the Dutch wanted Denmark to maintain 40 warships with which to prevent the English navy from entering the Baltic Sea. Spain promised to pay the same amount as the Netherlands. Another subsidy of 67,025 was paid as a contribution to Danish diplomatic activities. The Dutch subsidies, as we will see, were withdrawn in 1677, and most of the Spanish subsidies were never paid. Eventually only 753,813 Rigsdalers were paid out (including 167,000 from Spain).[4] To put the figures in perspective, it has been estimated that Denmark's purely military (not naval) costs reached an average of three million Rigsdalers per year. In addition, naval costs reached an average of some 765,000 Rigsdalers per year, with increasing costs over time since the fleet was growing through the capture of Swedish ships and, with each ship captured, prize money to the equivalent of 10 percent of its

4 Gautier, "Krigskostnaderna", pp.233–4, 237.

value had to be paid to the admiral who won the victory.[5] Danish Admiral Niels Juel came out of the war a wealthy man. As a result, the subsidies were important, but in times of war they did not suffice to cover more than a limited share of the costs.

Moreover, in January 1661 Denmark's then King Frederick III had issued the Act Concerning Absolute and Hereditary Government which transformed Danish kingship from an elective monarchy to an absolute and hereditary monarchy that explicitly was freed from constraints. The nobility lost its tax-exempt status and its monopoly of many offices. Although the revolution from above, because a revolution it was, seemed more the culmination of a series of long-term developments that resulted from Denmark's experience in the previous wars, it undoubtedly offered King Frederick more choices and opened up for a new assertiveness in Danish foreign policy. This assertiveness was for the reasons already mentioned particularly aimed at Sweden, and it came close to fruition under King Frederick's son, King Christian V.

A particular case of Danish annoyance was the Duchy of Holstein-Gottorp, which occupied a strategic position south of the Danish heartlands. Duke Christian Albrecht of Holstein-Gottorp was Sweden's ally. Although the Duchy's small military was not a threat to Denmark on its own, its territory could conceivably function as a base for a Swedish attack from the south, emanating from the Swedish possessions in Germany. Assuming that the Swedish navy could maintain control over the Baltic shipping lanes, that is. The long-time rivalry between the Danish and Swedish kingdoms depended on two key naval vulnerabilities. First, the issue of the Sound Tolls, since whoever controlled the Straits, controlled the customs revenue. Second, both countries had territories that were separated by sea, including the important Danish possession of Norway and the Swedish possession of Finland, in addition to numerous islands and, for Sweden, overseas territories on the Continent. Both thus faced the very real need to maintain a naval power which could safeguard the supply lines between their different territories and possessions.

In late 1674, French pressure for Sweden to intervene in Germany grew too strong to resist. The French threatened to withhold their subsidy, while food supplies were growing scarce in Swedish Pomerania. As a result, a Swedish army of 13,000 men under Carl Gustav Wrangel moved into Brandenburg on 19 December 1674. Wrangel was a veteran of the Thirty Years' War who as a 19-year-old had fought in the Battle of Lützen, more than 40 years previously. The invasion was to a considerable extent carried out purely for logistical reasons; the Swedish army had to resupply itself, and it did this best by operating on enemy territory. Thus began the Swedish–Brandenburgian War. Meanwhile, the rest of the 25,000 Swedish troops in Germany were scattered in garrisons: 4,500 in Bremen-Verden, 1,400 in Wismar, and 6,000 in Swedish Pomerania. Facing a continued lack of supplies and poor weather, Wrangel's army did not move decisively against its opponents. On 18 June

5 Ibid., pp.245, 247–8.

1675, Frederick William, Elector of Brandenburg and Duke of Prussia, inflicted a defeat on the Swedes at Fehrbellin (see below).

The Swedish defeat spurred all those who had reason to dislike the Swedish presence on the Continent. Encouraged by Frederick William's victory, over the ensuing months Sweden's various adversaries entered the war. The Netherlands under William of Orange had declared war on Sweden already on 5 June, and the Holy Roman Emperor, Leopold I, followed suite on 8 July. With the Imperial declaration of war came an Imperial ban (*Reichsacht*) on the Swedish sovereign, in his role as an Imperial subject through his possession of lands within the Empire, which meant that the Swedish monarch's German subjects no longer were required, or even allowed, to serve him. Thus, Sweden suddenly found itself at war also with several Imperial subjects including the Prince-Bishopric of Münster, under the warlike Prince-Bishop Christoph Bernhard von Galen, and a number of principalities in the Lüneburg region, including those of George William, Duke of Brunswick-Lüneburg, at the town of Celle; Rudolph Augustus, Duke of Brunswick-Lüneburg, at Wolfenbüttel; and Ernest Augustus, Prince-Bishop of the Prince-Bishopric of Osnabrück. None formally declared war against Sweden, but they entered the war as Imperial subjects.

4

The Battle of Fehrbellin

Although Frederick William's victory at Fehrbellin on 18 June 1675 resulted in no real military gains, it was significant for its propaganda value, since it was the first major defeat of a Swedish army in Germany for a considerable time.[1] Militarily, the battle was a sideshow. We will see that Sweden eventually lost control over its German possessions not because of the defeat at Fehrbellin but because of its subsequent loss of supremacy at sea in the Baltic.

Nonetheless, the battle and the events leading up to it did show something of the malaise that had afflicted the Swedish military system during the years of peace under the regency government.

When Field Marshal Wrangel invaded Brandenburg in December 1674, it was because of pressure from France and the need to secure supplies, not because of any inherent Swedish military objectives there. There is no information to suggest that either the army or its commander was particularly enthusiastic about the task. Wrangel and Frederick William of Brandenburg knew each other personally, having fought side by side in the Battle of Warsaw in 1656. It had all boiled down to logistics. Wrangel had warned Stockholm that Pomerania was too poor to support the army. Brandenburg was only marginally wealthier. Both Pomerania and Brandenburg mostly consisted of sandy plains interspersed with marshes, rivers, and canals, which complicated military operations. Although few rivers were large, their riverbanks were marshy which made them obstacles to military operations, so existing bridges were strategically important. There was no initial animosity. Upon entering Brandenburg, Wrangel ordered his troops not to abuse the population and to pay for all supplies. However, the population fled before the Swedish army, so most provisions had to be taken without pay, regardless of Wrangel's intentions.[2] Besides, marauders had already passed through the area. Furthermore, on 20 May 1675 Frederick William of

1 The propaganda value of the victory was so great that the known events of the battle soon merged with myths. Recent studies of the battle include Uwe-Rolf Hinze, *Die Schlacht von Fehrbellin: Der Sieg Brandenburgs über Schweden 1675* (Karwe: Edition Rieger, 2010); Lars Ericson, Martin Hårdstedt, Per Iko, Ingvar Sjöblom, and Gunnar Åselius, *Svenska slagfält* (np: Wahlström & Widstrand, 2003), pp.215–22; Frank Bauer, *Fehrbellin 1675: Brandenburg-Preußens Aufbruch zur Großmacht* (Potsdam: Kurt Vowinckel-Verlag, 1998). Unfortunately, all contain inconsistencies and inaccuracies.

2 Ebbe Gyllenstierna, "Kriget i Tyskland", Göran Rystad (ed.), *Kampen om Skåne* (Lund: Historiska Media, 2005), pp.187–203, on p.187.

Brandenburg ordered the peasants to carry out guerrilla warfare against the Swedes, which for obvious reasons aggravated the situation.[3]

Moreover, Wrangel was old and soon incapacitated by illness, suffering from gout and other ailments, and was unable to take direct control of the army. His intended second-in-command was another, almost as old veteran of the Thirty Years' War, Field Marshal Simon Grundel Helmfelt, but he was unavailable; Helmfelt had gone south for reasons of poor health and had declined command. Command accordingly passed to Field Marshal Conrad Mardefelt, who was an able fortifications officer who previously served as quartermaster general, so was more used to logistics and intelligence than commanding armies in the field. Besides, he was even older than the others and frequently suffered from illness due to his age.

King Charles wanted most troops in Pomerania to be enlisted on the Continent, but many Swedish troops served there. Exact number of troops can only be estimated, although an invasion army of 13,000 men seems likely.[4] As noted, not only could the establishment strength of units vary, they also generally suffered from considerable attrition.

The war began in a leisurely fashion, since Wrangel for reasons of personal health and strategic concerns was reluctant to push on. Having acquired supplies, the army had dispersed throughout the country for further foraging, with most units returning to Pomerania. On 30 April 1675, Wrangel inspected his troops in the town of Damm in Pomerania. His field army then included squadrons from seven cavalry regiments, one dragoon regiment, and battalions from 10 infantry regiments. However, the troops had not been paid for four months, were not eager to fight, and through disease and desertions, he had lost some 1,000 men. Now the army only counted 12,000. The cavalry was mostly Swedish, while the infantry primarily consisted of enlisted Germans. Colonel Berndt Wangelin's dragoon regiment consisted of two Swedish, two Finnish, and two German companies. In addition, Wrangel had field artillery consisting of 38 light cannons.[5] Wrangel's army re-entered Brandenburg on 2 May, perhaps intending to cross the River Elbe at Magdeburg to join forces with John Frederick, Duke of Brunswick-Calenberg-Göttingen-Hanover, who at this time was a potential ally.

What nobody had taken into account was that Brandenburg-Prussia these days had acquired an efficient standing army. At the time of the Swedish invasion, Frederick William of Brandenburg was with his army at the Rhine, engaged in operations against the Marshal General of France, the Viscount of Turenne. The war against the French had not gone well. Now, learning that his own territory had been invaded, Frederick William had every excuse to return home. On 27 May, he set out to intercept the Swedish invasion force.

3 Georg Sello, "Fehrbellin", *Deutsche Zeitschrift für Geschichtswissenschaft* 7 (1892), pp.282–318.

4 Wrangel's army reportedly consisted of 48 companies of cavalry, 10 companies of dragoons, and 63 companies of infantry. Gyllenstierna, "Kriget i Tyskland", p.189.

5 Tessin, *Die deutschen Regimenter der Krone Schweden* 2, 24. There are conflicting accounts of the troops available, although most agree on the total of 12,000 men. See also Ericson et al., *Svenska slagfält*, p.216; which suggests that the army consisted of 30 cavalry squadrons and 11 infantry battalions.

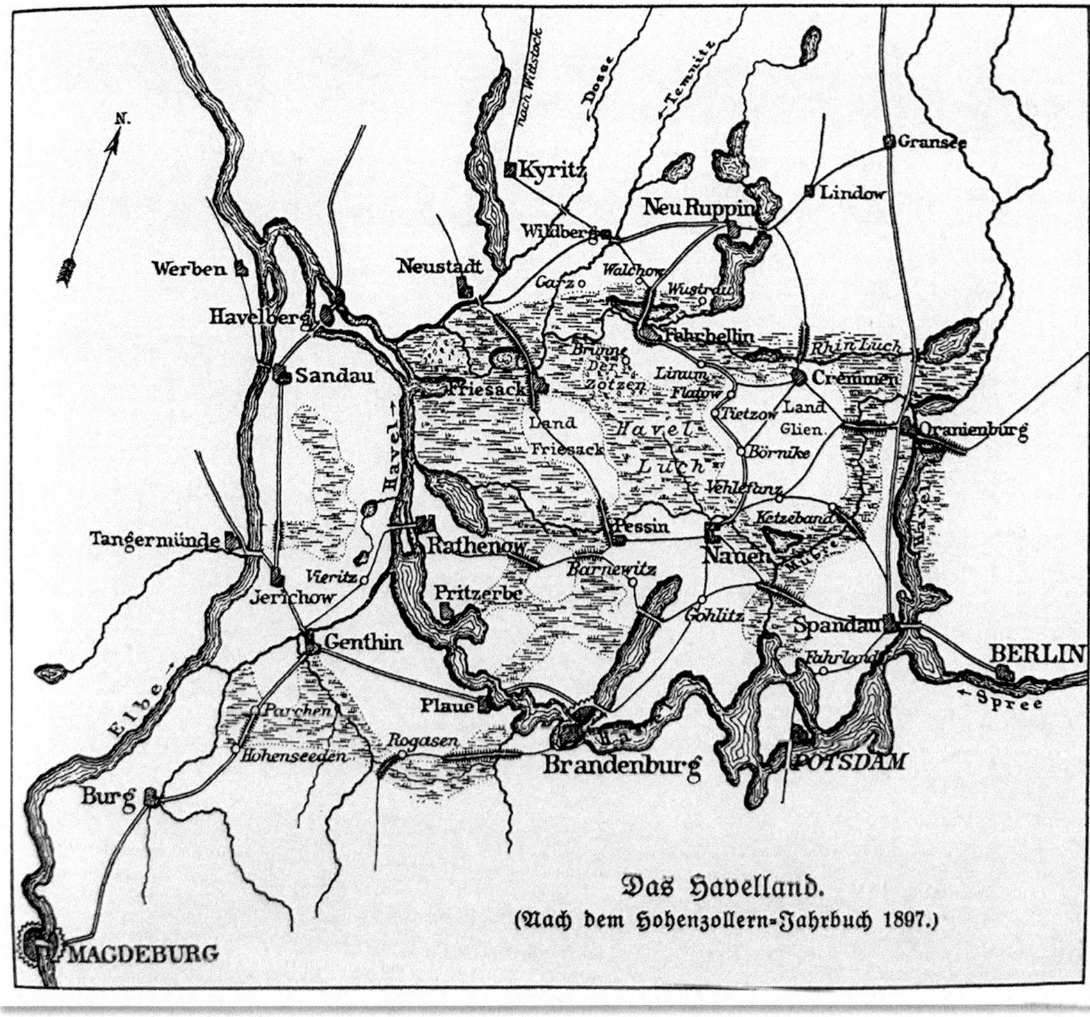

The Fehrbellin area, 1675. (*Hohenzollern-Jahrbuch*, 1897)

Through forced marches, he on 11 June reached Magdeburg. There he learnt that the Swedish army again had dispersed to forage for supplies. Wrangel was at Havelberg, on the River Havel. However, most of the army was at Alt-Brandenburg, west of Berlin, under Wrangel's half-brother, Lieutenant General Wolmar Wrangel. The road that connected the two Swedish formations passed through the town of Rathenow, the site of an important bridge over the River Havel. Rathenow was held by Colonel Wangelin and his six companies of dragoons.

Despite receiving intelligence that the Brandenburg army was on its way, the Swedes neglected reconnaissance. Standard Swedish practice since the Thirty Years' War was to follow up intelligence reports with further questions to the reporting officers and to send out cavalry patrols to gather intelligence in the area of operations. After the defeat, a Swedish commission of inquiry found that neither practice had been followed.[6] By pushing on with only his

6 Torsten Holm, *Översikt över Sveriges krig under 1600-talets senare hälft* (Stockholm: Militärlitteraturföreningen 148, 1927), p.14.

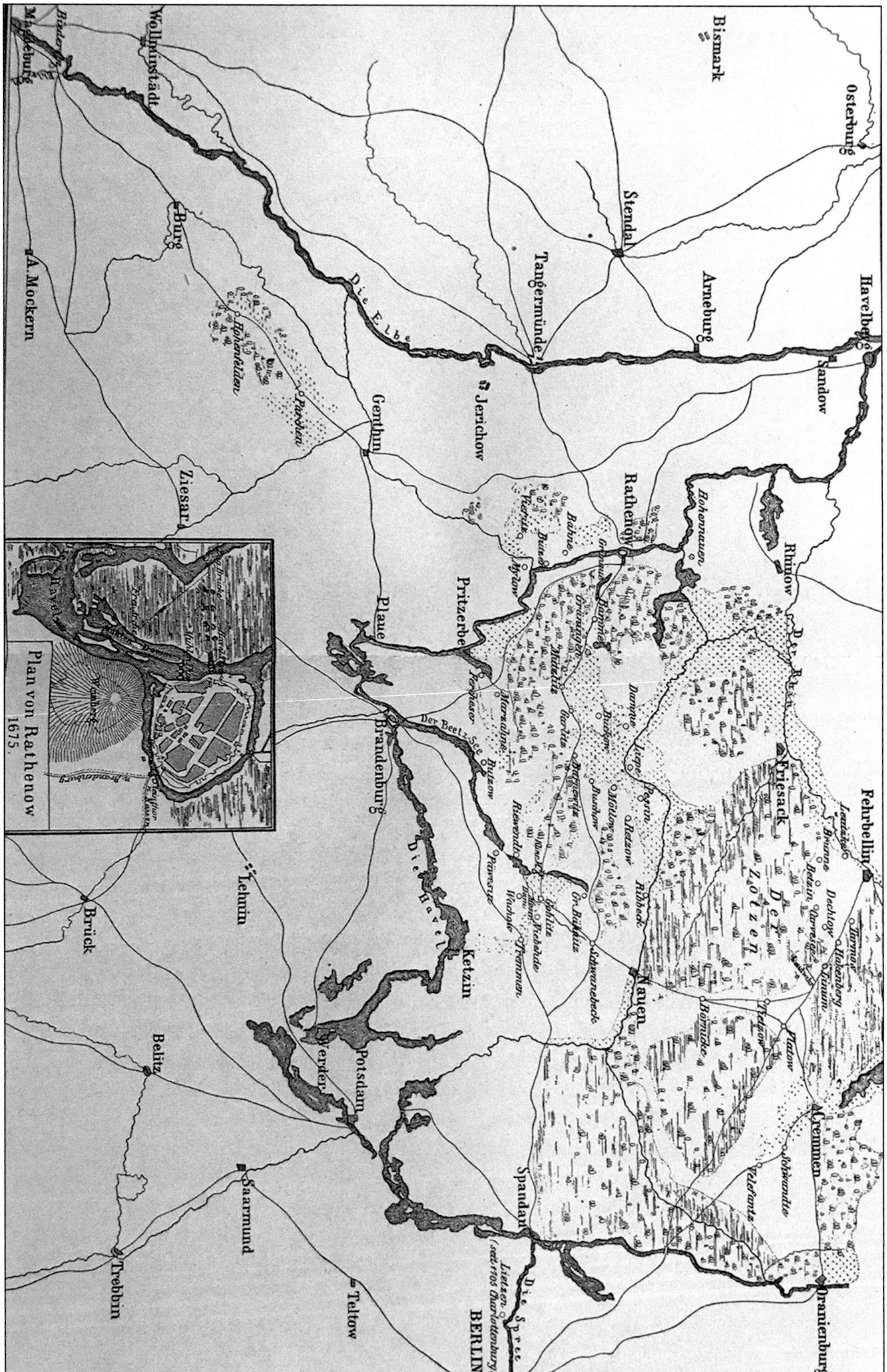

The Fehrbellin region.

cavalry and as much infantry as could load onto available wagons, Frederick William therefore managed to move a strike force of 5,000 to 6,000 cavalry, 800 dragoons, and 1,000 musketeers between the two Swedish positions without being detected.[7] He also managed to bring 13 to 15 light cannons. The Brandenburgers reached Rathenow very early in the morning of 15 June, led by Field Marshal Georg von Derfflinger, who, impersonating a Swedish officer, convinced the Swedish sentries to open the gates to himself and his dragoons. It was a dark and rainy night, and von Derfflinger had been in Swedish service during the Thirty Years' War so he knew how to be persuasive. He also knew some Swedish.[8]

Kettledrummer on horseback. (Johan Philip Lemke)

As the Brandenburgers entered Rathenow, they took Wangelin's men by surprise. As many as 390 of the Swedish troops were killed, and the rest, a total of 192, were captured, including Wangelin, his wife, and their maid. Derfflinger lost some 50 men. The aftermath of the conquest of Rathenow was customarily sordid. Wangelin's wife was apparently saved from being raped by Brandenburg dragoons, but not so the maid who was only recovered later when finally found "in the hands of a lieutenant", which probably sounds more romantic than it was.[9] The Brandenburgers also captured supplies, 500 to 600 horses, six dragoon standards, and a pair of kettledrums. Yet more importantly, they gained control of the important bridge over the River Havel.

Upon learning the news from Rathenow, Wolmar Wrangel realised that to re-unite his forces with those of his half-brother (a rendezvous had been planned in Wittstock further north), he had to make a detour by way of Nauen, and then cross the River Havel's tributary Rhin at the town of Fehrbellin, where there was another important bridge. Upon approaching Fehrbellin, Wolmar Wrangel received reports that some Brandenburg cavalry – 130 men led by Lieutenant Colonel Joachim Hennigs from Mörner's Cavalry Regiment – had reached the town before him and set fire to the bridge. Moreover, Frederick William's army was in close pursuit. On 18 June, Wolmar Wrangel ordered his artillery commander, Major General Jacob Staël von Holstein, to hasten to the bridge with 300 men to repair it. He then prepared for a delaying action against the pursuing Brandenburgers.

Frederick William had hoped that the destruction of the bridge would delay the Swedes until his main force arrived. Having then outmanoeuvred

7 Melle Klinkenborg, *Fehrbellin: Nach Berichten und Briefen der führenden Männer* (Leipzig: R. Voigtländer, 1913), p.45; citing Brandenburg's official report.

8 Ibid.,44–9; citing the official Brandenburg report..

9 Ibid., p.60; citing a contemporary witness.

Kettledrummer on horseback. (Johan Philip Lemke)

the Swedish army in the Continental fashion, he hoped that it would surrender. However, his General of Cavalry, Frederick, Prince of Hesse-Homburg, wanted to engage the Swedes and pushed on. While the main cavalry force thus attacked the Swedish rearguard, Frederick William led a couple of cavalry regiments, the musketeers, and the artillery on a flank march through the forest, hoping to catch the Swedes in a vulnerable position.[10]

By then, Wolmar Wrangel's infantry commander, Major General Henrik von Delwig, had deployed the expeditionary force in two strong lines of battle (Appendix V).

The Swedes were fewer than the Brandenburg army, but Delwig's force was clearly stronger than Prince Frederick's advance guard of some 1,500 men. As a result, the Brandenburgers were initially pushed back by the Swedes. However, in the meantime Frederick William's main force had arrived, deploying on a forested hill on the Swedish right flank with the Brandenburg artillery, which now opened fire with devastating effect. A battalion from Delwig's Regiment attempted to charge the hill, but was pushed back.

Wolmar Wrangel accordingly had the right wing reinforced with the battalion from Delwig's Regiment, with orders to cover the withdrawal of the rest of the army over the repaired bridge, before retreating itself. Unfortunately for the Swedes, the Östgöta Cavalry Regiment, under Colonel Adam Wachtmeister, for unknown reasons suddenly charged up the hill, then continued down on the other side, until they collided with no less than five Brandenburg squadrons under Colonel Berndt Joachim von Mörner. In the ensuing struggle, Wachtmeister possibly engaged and killed Mörner with his rapier (according to Field Marshal Wrangel's report; Prince Frederick of Hesse-Homburg, who was there, merely notes that Mörner was shot dead during the battle) but then fell himself. However, the Swedes were eventually pushed back. Badly disordered, the fleeing Östgöta cavalry then entered the remaining 10 Swedish squadrons, disordering them as well. This ended badly, since the Östgöta cavalry had been pursued by 10 Brandenburg squadrons personally led by Frederick William.

Meanwhile, Frederick William's right wing pushed back the Swedish left wing. As yet more Brandenburg reinforcements arrived, the Swedish cavalry pulled back. Delwig's infantry found themselves without support, and many were cut down. Wolmar Wrangel barely escaped capture. In the end, it was the Swedish deputy artillery chief, Lieutenant Colonel Paul Bethun, who had returned on his own initiative, who managed to restore some order among the Swedish troops.

10 Ibid., pp.49–52; which reprints Brandenburg's official battle report.

Frederick William, Elector of Brandenburg, at the Battle of Fehrbellin, 1675. (Reconstruction by Richard Knötel)

Joining Wolmar Wrangel and Colonel Wittenberg of Wittenberg's Cavalry Regiment, Bethun and his artillerymen got a defence line in order, then opened fire. Their artillery fire was dangerously well aimed, killing two men next to Frederick William himself, with the second round iron shot passing just under his horse, a terrifying experience for anybody. As a result, the Brandenburgers ceased pursuit. This gave the Swedes sufficient time to retreat over the repaired bridge. Swedish losses were between 500 and 600 dead and wounded, most of them from Delwig's infantry regiment, which also had lost its commanding officer, Lieutenant Colonel von Maltzahn, who died among his men. The Brandenburg losses were roughly equal in number. However, Frederick William

DE WONDERLYCKE SUCCESSEN
Van den
H.KEURVORST van BRANDENBURG
op de SWEDEN in Havellant;
En sijne generale Victorie van den 26 Juny tot den 2 July 1675.

Propaganda newsletter describing Frederick William of Brandenburg's glorious victory at Fehrbellin, published in Amsterdam, 1675.

retained the field, as the Swedes retreated, and the Brandenburgers then could capture six abandoned cannons and hundreds of supply carts, in addition to the 10 Swedish standards already taken.

The battle was a Brandenburg victory, but Swedish losses were small. Moreover, the determined Swedish rearguard action prevented the Brandenburgers from pressing home their advantage. Moreover, Frederick William did not pursue, since he assessed that his men needed rest. At first, Wrangel considered whether he should return and continue the campaign in Brandenburg. However, he was again overtaken by illness. Wrangel's army accordingly retreated into Swedish Pomerania, arriving on 27 June, to prepare defences against two anticipated invasions: the Brandenburgers and Imperial troops from the south and the Danes from the west.

After the battle, Sweden only controlled some 13,500 men in Pomerania.[11] Field Marshal Wrangel left the army because of his illness, although he retained command. Instead he assigned Field Marshal Lieutenant Otto Wilhelm von Königsmarck to defend the River Recknitz line against the Danes and Field Marshal Mardefelt to defend the River Trebel and the nearby River Peene against the Brandenburgers and Imperials. If successful, this would at least protect the important coastal towns. The rural south would have to be abandoned. Königsmarck was an educated man who knew Latin and classical Greek, and he had recently been in French service in the Netherlands, serving under the renowned commander Louis, Prince of Condé. Mardefelt was an experienced military engineer. Neither Königsmarck nor Mardefelt thought that the available Swedish forces were sufficient for the task, so they suggested that they instead should attempt to hold the port-towns themselves. Unfortunately, it was harvest-time, the army lacked supplies, and Wrangel argued that the farm areas could not be abandoned.[12] They had to attempt a defence based on the existing borders.

11 Almgren, "Svensk strategi", p.34.
12 Gyllenstierna, "Kriget i Tyskland", p.191.

5

The War on the Continent

Preparations for War

In Denmark, the immediate effect of Fehrbellin was that King Christian on 26 June had his brother-in-law, Duke Christian Albrecht of Holstein-Gottorp, thrown into prison. It was a coup d'état, pure and simple. Duke Christian Albrecht was the uncle of King Charles of Sweden and a Swedish ally, who from his domain to the south of the Danish heartland had formed a small but latent threat to King Christian's designs. King Christian also forced the Duke to hand over his troops to Denmark and deliver two fortresses into Danish hands. In effect, King Christian annexed Holstein-Gottorp, although this was not recognised by the other German principalities, or any other country. A few weeks later, on 13 August, King Christian joined the Danish army which had been deployed in Holstein. The Danish army there consisted of 5,500 horse, 1,200 dragoons, 9,600 foot, and 312 cannons. After some deliberation, King Christian agreed to join Frederick William of Brandenburg in a campaign to conquer Swedish Pomerania.[1] Denmark had already on 26 March 1675 secretly agreed with Brandenburg and the other allies to participate in an attack on the Swedish possessions in Germany.[2]

On 20 August, a joint Dutch-Danish fleet under the Danish Admiral-General, Cort Adeler, sailed into the Baltic Sea to prepare for a confrontation with the Swedish navy. A veteran of service with the Dutch navy, Adeler had returned to Denmark in 1663 and spent the period of peace together with Admirals Henrik Bielke and Niels Juel to reorganise the Danish navy (the Danish noble family Bielke had no relationship with the Swedish noble family of the same name).These preparations took place before war was declared. King Christian declared war against Sweden only on 2 September, and two days later he met Frederick William of Brandenburg in Gadebusch to discuss strategy. The Danes had planned an attack on the important port town of Wismar and the Swedish possession of Bremen-Verden; however, Frederick William persuaded King Christian to postpone these endeavours and instead co-operate in his planned

1 Ibid., p.190.

2 Nielsen, "Dansk strategi", p.86.

conquest of Swedish Pomerania.[3] King Christian dispatched some 19,000 men under General Field Marshal Lieutenant Adam von Weyher, a Brandenburger in Danish service, through the neutral Mecklenburg towards Pomerania, with orders to support Brandenburg and safeguard Danish interests. King Christian, too, joined the field army, in effect assuming command. Meanwhile, the army of Norway under Ulrik Frederik Gyldenløve, King Christian's half-brother, was ordered to safeguard the Norwegian border and also attack the Swedish provinces of Bohuslän and Västergötland.[4]

Actually, Swedish-Danish relations were then quite amicable. By the end of the previous year, a Swedish embassy had gone to Denmark to negotiate a treaty of neutrality in conjunction with the proposal to arrange a royal wedding between King Charles and Ulrika Eleonora, King Christian's sister. The Danish side had rejected the treaty but agreed to the wedding. The engagement between the young couple was announced soon before the Battle of Fehrbellin. The Swedish side proposed that the wedding should take place in August 1675. However, the Danish court postponed the wedding with the excuse that it would first be necessary to order a wedding dress from France for the royal princess, which would take time.

The delay meant that instead of announcing a date for the wedding, Denmark, as noted, declared war on Sweden on 2 September 1675, being the last of the anti-Swedish coalition to declare war.

The Danes knew that as long as Sweden retained territories in northern Germany, Denmark would, in case of war, be vulnerable to the threat of a war on two fronts. In the past, Sweden had shown that it could, through its German territories, strike at Denmark from the south. A primary element of the Danish strategy was, accordingly, to neutralise the threat from these territories, and this was best undertaken in co-operation with German allies. A second element of the Danish strategy was to search out and defeat the small Swedish naval squadron in the west, that is, the one based at Gothenburg. This would be undertaken in an alliance with the Dutch, whose sea power was second to none. Then a naval attack would be aimed at Gothenburg itself, in conjunction with a land invasion of Swedish territory from Norway. The next step would be, together with the Dutch, to move the naval war into the Baltic Sea, with the intention to neutralise the Swedish fleet from Stockholm. Then the island of Gotland would be occupied. Finally, the Danish army would be shipped across the Straits to reconquer Scania.

The Danish National Commanding General, Hans Schack, was ill (he died on 27 February 1676), so was unable to command the campaign in Germany. In his stead, Field Marshal Lieutenant von Weyher was designated nominal commander-in-chief, with General Carl von Arensdorff, an officer from Mecklenburg in Danish service, as commander of cavalry. Yet, as noted, King Christian took all decisions, supported by his secretary Herman Mejer. Besides, already before the death of Schack, King Christian appointed Johann Hans Adolf, Duke of Schleswig-Holstein-Sonderburg-Plön, his Chief Field Marshal.[5]

3 Ibid., 86; Gyllenstierna, "Kriget i Tyskland", pp.190–91.

4 Vaupell, *Den danske hærs historie*, p.98.

5 Nielsen, "Dansk strategi", p.78.

The Duke was an experienced soldier. He had first gone into Imperial service, among other duties fighting the Ottoman Turks in Hungary in 1664. Then he had been in Dutch service, and most recently, in 1674–1675, he had fought for Brunswick against the French, during which he also held his own against the famous Turenne. He had only gone into Danish service in early 1676. The Duke was popular with his soldiers, and he generously rewarded bravery.

Meanwhile, the combined Brandenburg and Imperial army that faced the Swedes consisted of some 20,000 men, and was growing towards 30,000.[6] To this was added the Danish army sent against Wismar and Pomerania which consisted of some 16,500 men.[7] The coalition deployed more than 7,000 men against Bremen-Verden alone.[8]

The Attack on Swedish Pomerania

The war in Germany, unlike the subsequent war in Scandinavia, came to be characterised by campaigns that were marked by manoeuvring and sieges. In effect, the Continental style of warfare remained prevalent.

In Pomerania, Field Marshal Mardefelt attempted to hold his long front, consisting of Rivers Trebel and Peene. Unfortunately, he in this way not only dispersed his forces but also neglected to carry out sufficient reconnaissance to determine where the enemy was approaching. When the Brandenburg and Imperial troops arrived, they easily broke through Mardefelt's defences. His troops had to retreat into Stralsund.

At the time, a Brandenburg expeditionary force under Major General von Schwerin also entered Swedish Pomerania from the east, across the River Oder. The Swedish commanders had not expected an attack there for geographical reasons. Schwerin accordingly managed to surprise and conquer the weakly defended island of Usedom and the town and island of Wollin, which fell on 3 October. When Königsmarck received the news about Mardefelt regrouping in Stralsund, he realised that he could not hold the Recknitz line without risking a rear attack. After a short battle against the Danes at Damgarten, he too retreated.

Having penetrated Mardefelt's defences, Frederick William on 21 October laid siege to the town of Wolgast. A lucky shot brought the gunpowder magazine to explode, after which (on 31 October) the commandant, Lieutenant Colonel Andreas Dubislaff von Blixen, surrendered. Since the Brandenburgers now controlled Wolgast and the islands of Wollin and Usedom, they also controlled the access to the Baltic Sea from the River Oder. It followed that the Swedish towns of Demmin, Anklam, and Stettin no longer could be supplied by sea. Frederick William wanted to take these towns, too; however, they were strongly defended and winter was approaching. He sent his troops into winter quarters.[9]

6 Almgren, "Svensk strategi", p.34.
7 Vaupell, *Den danske hærs historie*, p.99.
8 Almgren, "Svensk strategi", p.34.
9 Gyllenstierna, "Kriget i Tyskland", p.192.

King Christian V of Denmark at the conquest of Damgarten, 1675. (Detail from tapestry by Bernt van der Eichen, like the others of the series based on paintings by Claus Møinichen, Christian Morholt, and Peder Andersen from 1686–1688, Rosenborg Castle)

The Siege of Wismar

While the Brandenburgers and Imperials were busy in the east of Pomerania, King Christian ordered his Danish troops back into Mecklenburg to lay siege to Wismar, the most important Swedish port on the southern Baltic Sea shore. Wismar had natural defences consisting of wide marshlands. On the sea-side, the town was protected by logs pushed into the sea-bed. The town was also protected by a town wall and moat, and a citadel. Field Marshal Wrangel was governor of Wismar, while Count Gustav Carlson, the King's half-brother, served as its commandant. The garrison consisted of 1,400 men (200 horse and 1,200 foot), supported by some 60 cannons and about 1,000 levied burghers.[10]

King Christian, who led the Danish army of 18,454 men and 40 cannons in person and also received the support of two Imperial cavalry regiments under the Prince of Hesse-Homburg, appointed Lieutenant General Niels Rosencrantz to lead the siege. Rosencrantz was a veteran soldier who had been in Spanish service in Flanders and fought in the previous war against Sweden. By the end of October 1675, Danish Queen Charlotte Amalia came to visit. King Christian wanted to storm the town in her presence, as a birthday gift, but the siege work had not progressed sufficiently far, so his

10 Ibid., p.192; Vaupell, *Den danske hærs historie*, p.100.

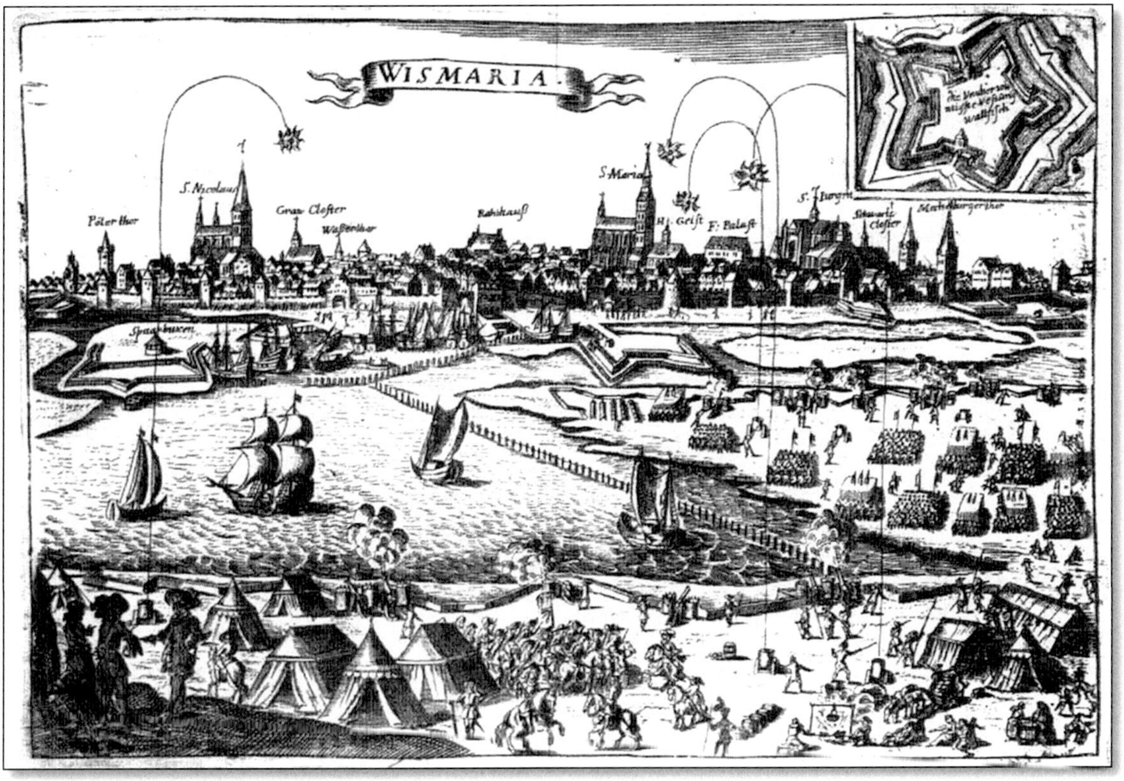

Danish Siege of Wismar, 1675.

generals advised against it. Actually, some argued that the army by then was in such poor shape with regard to disease, morale, and supply difficulties that a storm should not be attempted. King Christian hesitated, and then anyway decided to storm the town on 13 December. The Danes attacked in six columns, commanded respectively by Lieutenant General Rosencrantz and Colonels Hannibal von Degenfeldt, Maximilian Rosencrantz, Siegwert von Bibow, Johan Caspar von Cicignon, and Møller. Although three columns were repulsed with serious losses, Niels Rosencrantz, Bibow, and Cicignon fared better. In fact, after the first two assaults had failed, King Christian ordered them to retreat. However, the order reached Bibow and Rosencrantz too late, so they made a final, successful attempt to storm the citadel, after which the town surrendered. Although nobody yet knew it, this became typical for the war; King Christian would vacillate, his councillors argued, and meanwhile, daring generals such as Bibow and Rosencrantz would push on. On 14 December, the survivors of the Swedish garrison, some 650 men of whom many were wounded or ill, left the town, marching away with full honours of war. Many enlisted Germans instead went into Danish service.[11]

Following the conquest of Wismar, most of the Danish army returned home through Mecklenburg to prepare for the first step of King Christian's strategy: the invasion of Scania.

11 Vaupell, *Den danske hærs historie*, pp.100–102; Tessin, *Die deutschen Regimenter der Krone Schweden 2*, p.29; Nielsen, "Dansk strategi", p.86; Gyllenstierna, "Kriget i Tyskland", pp.192–3.

King Christian accepts the surrender of Wismar, 1675. Left: Danish Queen Charlotte Amalie of Hesse-Kassel. (Tapestry by Bernt van der Eichen, Rosenborg Castle; Photo: Medströms)

The Swedish Response Fails

When the Danish troops left Pomerania for the siege of Wismar, and the Brandenburg troops went into winter quarters, the Swedish commanders discussed how to respond. Königsmarck wanted to relieve Wismar, but Wrangel believed their available forces were insufficient. Instead, Wrangel ordered Mardefelt and Königsmarck to seek to retake Wolgast. The Swedes accordingly attempted to storm Wolgast. However, the commandant, Colonel Hallart, had the town walls reinforced with water which due to the cold immediately froze to ice, producing walls that were both structurally stronger and more difficult to climb. The assault failed.

The order to seize Wolgast was one of Wrangel's last. He died on 15 June 1676. Mardefelt, who should have assumed command since he was the next in rank, was recalled to Stockholm, since King Charles considered him too passive. Instead the King put Königsmarck in command of Swedish troops in Pomerania.[12] For the next three years, Königsmarck had the difficult task of carrying out a strategic delaying action in Sweden's German possessions while cut off from the Swedish heartland. Without reinforcements and supplies, there was no way that he could defeat the enemy coalition. The challenge was to avoid a total collapse of Swedish power in northern Germany, and while doing so, tie up as many enemy units and resources as possible, for as long as possible. And on this mission, he henceforth was on his own.

12 Gyllenstierna, "Kriget i Tyskland", p.193.

The Attack on Bremen-Verden

Otto Wilhelm von Königsmarck. (Jacob Gole)

When Frederick William of Brandenburg initially prepared for his invasion of Swedish Pomerania, he aimed to bring other rulers into the war by engaging them against the Swedes in Bremen-Verden, since Sweden then would be unable to unite its forces in Germany. However, the Dutch were occupied with a confrontation with France in the Flanders, while the Dukes of Lüneburg had deployed their troops at the Rhine. As for Denmark, it had then not yet declared war on Sweden. Nonetheless, Frederick William's strategy soon bore fruits.

In September 1675 the Prince-Bishop of Münster, Christoph von Galen, sent 3,000 troops into Bremen-Verden.[13] When King Christian received the news of the invasion, he was afraid to lose an opportunity, so he ordered Lieutenant General Gustav Adolph von Baudissin to advance into Bremen-Verden from the neighbouring Danish possession of Oldenburg, located to the southwest of Bremen-Verden, thus producing a strategic problem for the Swedes of the same type that the Danes had faced in Holstein-Gottorp. Baudissin brought 800 cavalry (Baudissin's Cavalry Regiment) and 2,000 infantry (Baudissin's, Lütken's, and – eventually – Bremer's Regiments). At about the same time, some 2,000 Brandenburg troops moved into the principality from the Brandenburg possession of Minden to the south. Somewhat later, in October 1675, 3,000 troops from Lüneburg invaded Bremen-Verden as well.[14]

The Swedish troops in Bremen-Verden, 4,500 men, were commanded by Field Marshal Henrik Horn, then in his mid-fifties. With less then half the force of the coalition at his disposal, Horn would have preferred to defend only Stade. However, he needed to control more of the territory in order to gain supplies for his troops.[15] Realising that such supplies were unlikely to last, Horn's young wife, Beata Wittenberg, went to Hamburg as their political agent (resident), to co-operate with other Swedish agents in northern Germany and to ensure that sufficient food supplies, funds, and intelligence reached Stade.[16]

Christoph Bernhard von Galen, Prince-Bishop of Münster, due to his rank assumed the post of commander-in-chief of the coalition forces in Bremen-Verden until October 1675, after which George William, Duke

13 Holm, *Översikt över Sveriges krig*, p.146.
14 Gyllenstierna, "Kriget i Tyskland", p.194.
15 Ibid., p.193.
16 Lars Rosander, *Sveriges fältmarskalkar: Svenska fältherrar från Vasa till Bernadotte* (Lund: Historiska Media, 2003), p.162.

Henrik Horn. (Photo: Medströms)

of Brunswick-Lüneburg, led the coalition there. The Prince-Bishop and the Duke also agreed, together with another Duke of Brunswick-Lüneburg, Rudolph Augustus, on how to divide up the territory of Bremen-Verden after the conquest.

By the end of 1675, the anti-Swedish coalition had taken all fortified positions in Bremen-Verden except Stade and the bastion at Schwinge. Postponing the siege of Stade until spring, they went into winter quarters.[17]

In early May 1676, some 10,000 to 12,000 coalition troops under Baudissin and Gustav Wilhelm von Wedel, a Prussian in Danish service, laid siege to Stade. Horn had a remaining garrison of 2,200 men (400 horse and 1,800 foot), of whom 200 horse and 600 foot were Swedish troops. Despite the numerical superiority, the coalition first aimed to starve Stade into submission, since its fortifications were among the strongest under Swedish control.[18]

Meanwhile, the small Swedish Gothenburg naval squadron in May 1676 left Gothenburg under Admiral-Lieutenant Erik Siöblad. Its objective was to relieve Stade, bringing supplies and fresh troops. When intelligence on this expedition reached the coalition commanders, they decided to storm Stade before the arrival of the Swedish warships. By concentrating artillery fire on the bastion at Schwinge, they forced its commander, Colonel Axel Wachtmeister, to surrender on 27 May. As a result, Siöblad found the River Elbe blocked, so had to return to Gothenburg without accomplishing his mission. During the return trip, Siöblad landed troops in Holstein, burned a town, but then had to embark the troops again and leave.[19]

The failed resupply attempt was the beginning of the end for Stade. By the end of July 1676, the town ran out of ammunition. On 2 August, Horn agreed to surrender Stade on the following day. Horn and his men had negotiated the right to march away with full honours of war. However, the survivors were not sent directly to Sweden but to remote Livonia, a location chosen by the Danes so that they could not immediately be redeployed where needed.[20]

17 Gyllenstierna, "Kriget i Tyskland", p.194.

18 Vaupell, *Den danske hærs historie*, p.159; Tessin, *Die deutschen Regimenter der Krone Schweden 2*, p.35; Gyllenstierna, "Kriget i Tyskland", p.195.

19 Vaupell, *Den danske hærs historie*, p.158.

20 Gyllenstierna, "Kriget i Tyskland", pp.195, 201.

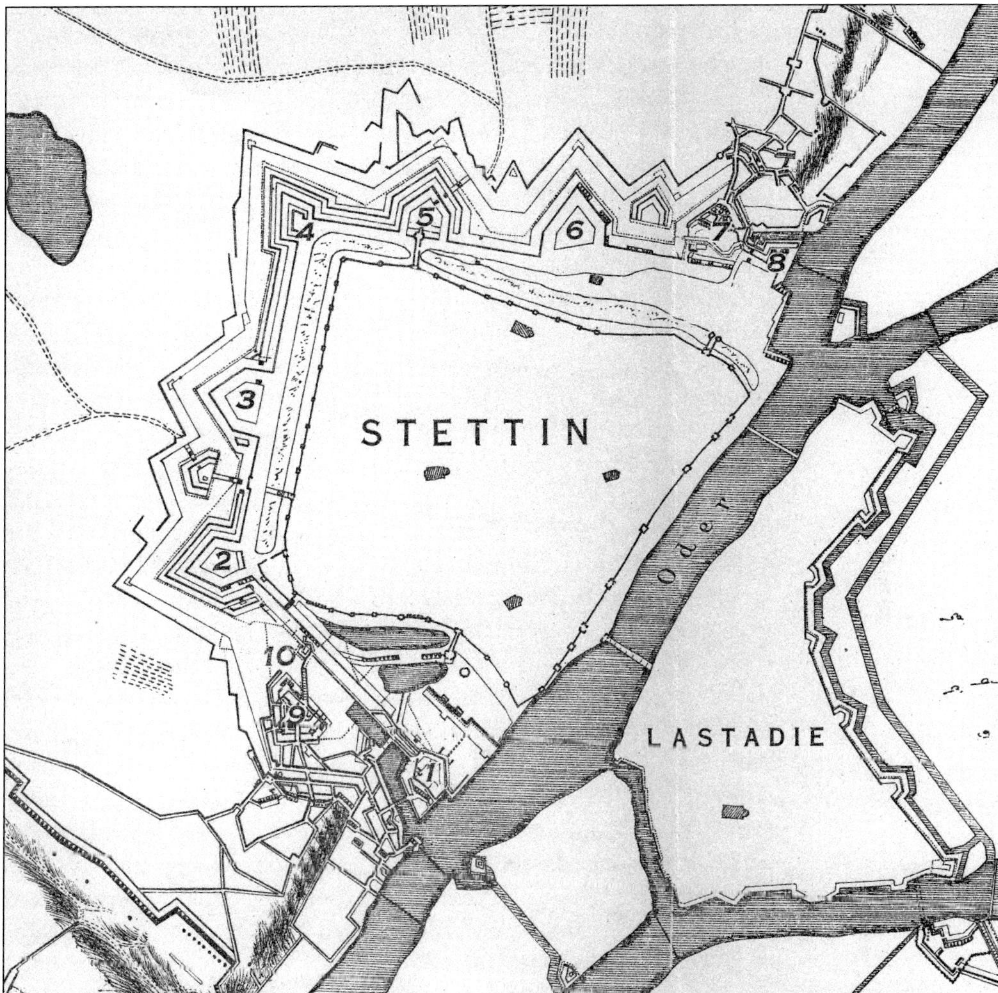

The Fortifications of Stettin, 1677.

The Siege of Stettin

Following the fall of the ports on the River Oder, Wismar, and Stade, only Stralsund and the island of Rügen remained available as transit points for Swedish reinforcements to the Continent.

In June 1676, Frederick William of Brandenburg continued the conquest of Swedish Pomerania, with an army of some 12,000 men, including three Danish and two Imperial cavalry regiments under the Prince of Hesse-Homburg. Following continental practices, he was careful not to bypass any fortified stronghold. On 17 August, he took Anklam, and on 30 September, Demmin. Only then did he turn towards Stettin, which was the more important town and the chief prize. He laid siege to Stettin for about a month, then abandoned the attempt and moved into winter quarters. By the end of the year, Sweden still held Stettin and Stralsund.[21]

In July 1677, Frederick William finally resumed the siege of Stettin. He then commanded a coalition army of 20,000 troops from Brandenburg, Denmark, and Lüneburg, and a large artillery park. Stettin was defended by Major General Jacob Johann von Wulffen, who commanded a garrison of no more than 2,300 men. Yet, it took until 10 December 1677 until the Brandenburgers had managed to get in position to attempt a direct assault. By then, the defenders were almost out of both ammunition and supplies. The town was essentially destroyed by the artillery bombardments, and no relief force could be expected, since, as we will see, the Danish and Dutch navies had acquired supremacy at sea. On 26 December, Wulffen found it necessary to surrender Stettin. The Swedish part of the garrison, by then some 700 men, was allowed free departure and a return to Sweden.[22] The energetic Frederick William had finally reached his goal, and he planned to make Stettin his new capital, instead of Berlin.[23] However, this was not to happen. Moreover, the victory had not been cheap, with as many as 4,000 Brandenburg troops lost during the siege. To give but one example, Lehnsdorff's Regiment of 1,600 men, which had been enlisted in Brandenburg on behalf of the Danish Crown but soon was transferred to Brandenburg, had only participated in the last three weeks of the siege, but still lost 195 dead and 316 wounded, that is, more than 30 percent of its strength in battlefield losses. And this figure did not include those who had died from disease, which by then was roughly another hundred men.[24]

Frederick William of Brandenburg had ordered his men to devastate Pomerania, but he made one exception. Field Marshal Wrangel's personal estate, where, increasingly ill, he also resided until his death, was spared for old times' sake. Wrangel reciprocated by sending Frederick William a case of the best wine he could find.[25]

21 Vaupell, *Den danske hærs historie*, 157; Tessin, *Die deutschen Regimenter der Krone Schweden 2*, p.34; Gyllenstierna, "Kriget i Tyskland", p.195.

22 Gyllenstierna, "Kriget i Tyskland", pp.195–6.

23 Ibid., p.202.

24 Vaupell, *Den danske hærs historie*, p.198.

25 Gyllenstierna, "Kriget i Tyskland", p.202.

6

Denmark Gains Supremacy at Sea

Based on history and experience, King Charles and his advisors aimed to follow the strategic plan from 1673, that is, to fight the war beyond Sweden's borders. This strategy would include an offensive from the south against the Danish heartland. This was a strategy that had worked well in previous wars with Denmark. Since no offensive could be carried out without the Swedish army in Germany, it was imperative to neutralise the Danish navy as soon as possible. This would safeguard the communication lines across the Baltic and simultaneously deny the Danes the opportunity to ship an army to Scania. It follows that the navy was the prerequisite for a successful implementation of the chosen strategy. In addition, King Charles envisaged an overland offensive into Norway, from the provinces of Bohuslän, Värmland, and Jämtland.[1] His strategic assessment was sound; however, King Charles did not yet know that it was out of touch with the current state of the Swedish military and naval establishment, following years of mismanagement by the regency government.

As noted, Denmark had greatly strengthened its navy since the introduction of royal absolutism in 1661. Denmark also had a geographical advantage. Denmark's chief naval base, Copenhagen, was located on a main shipping lane, enjoyed the use of an almost continuously ice-free harbour, and moreover was located in the southern Baltic, which was the main theatre of operations in any war between Denmark and Sweden. Besides, Copenhagen usually enjoyed a westerly wind, which made it easy for the Danish fleet to leave port.

For Sweden, the situation was quite different. The chief naval base, Stockholm, was well protected within an extensive archipelago, but with the prevailing winds, it was difficult to move the fleet out to sea. Moreover, Stockholm's harbour was blocked by ice until well into April each year. Finally, Stockholm was located far from the main theatre of operations,

1 Almgren, "Svensk strategi", p.37.

which caused communication and logistical problems, both with regard to supplies and when repairs were needed.

For these reasons, Danish naval crews were more experienced than Swedish ones. Their sailing season was longer, which meant that they had more time to get accustomed to their ships and tasks. Moreover, many of the Danish sailors, and an even larger share of the Norwegian ones, had previously served on Dutch merchant or warships. Besides, the Danish navy also employed many experienced foreign sailors, hired in Amsterdam and Hamburg. This, too, made their crews more skilled. In comparison, most Swedish sailors had, at best, a background as inshore fishermen, which did not necessarily make them experienced blue-water sailors.[2]

On the other hand, the fact that Danish naval crews were professionals also made it more difficult to retain them in service. When the Danish fleet returned to base in autumn, the crews were technically supposed to be paid off. If they were not paid, many would leave during the winter, securing employment elsewhere, which meant that in spring, too few trained sailors were available. At times, such as in 1675, the warships were not permitted to go into port until December, because funds for salaries had not yet been forthcoming. In 1676, the Admiralty suggested that no sailors would be allowed ashore until after the Dutch warships had left port, so that the men were not tempted to leave with them. Moreover, it was suggested to pay the sailors for an additional one or two months, and give them free lodgings, so that they would not think about leaving until they had run out of money.[3]

There were other differences as well, and again the Danish navy comes out ahead. When war broke out, the Swedish warships were, on average, both older and less well maintained than the Danish ones. Sweden had a larger fleet of warships; however, in terms of quality of both ships and crews, the Swedish navy was undeniably inferior to the Danish.[4]

Not only the sailors of the Swedish navy but its operational commanders, too, were non-professionals. The Swedish heads of the navy were Gustav Otto Stenbock in 1675, Lorenz Creutz in 1676, and Henrik Horn in 1677. Stenbock and Horn were army officers; Creutz a civilian administrator. We will see that none of them had the required skills to lead a fleet of warships at sea. It was only in 1678 and 1679 that an experienced naval officer, Hans Wachtmeister, was finally put in command of the navy.[5] Hans Wachtmeister was the elder brother of Axel Wachtmeister, who in 1676 had defended the bastion at Schwinge, and Adam Wachtmeister, who in 1675 had fallen at Fehrbellin.

In comparison, all the Danish operational commanders of the navy were experienced professionals: Cort Adeler, Niels Juel, and from 1676, the Dutch Admiral Cornelis Tromp.

In Denmark, naval planning for the coming war was already underway on 21 July 1675, when the war council met. This was before the declaration

2 Finn Askgaard, "Kampen till sjöss", Göran Rystad (ed.), *Kampen om Skåne* (Lund: Historiska Media, 2005), pp.171–86, on p.172.

3 Gautier, "Krigskostnaderna", pp.246–7.

4 Askgaard, "Kampen till sjöss", p.172.

5 Ibid., pp.172–3.

of war and while the wedding planning was still ongoing. Admiral-General Adeler proposed a bold operation: searching out and destroying the Swedish fleet at its anchorage at Dalarö, at the southern approaches to Stockholm, before it went to sea. This would be possible, since only a few Swedish vessels were out on patrol. The other Danish admirals were more cautious, proposing that the navy instead should patrol between Bornholm and Rügen, cutting off Swedish communications with Pomerania. If a Swedish fleet showed up, they might attack it, and if not, perhaps carry out an operation against Rügen. King Christian adopted the more cautious plan. Adeler received his orders on 28 July.[6]

On 4 August, the war council met again. This time they discussed what to do with the Swedish naval squadron in Gothenburg. Sweden maintained only a few warships there, its only mainland port facing the west. Gothenburg was important for trade, but it was also the port through which Sweden maintained communications with its possessions in Bremen-Verden. Cort Adeler, supported by Niels Juel and Henrik Bielke, suggested that the navy only should aim to blockade Gothenburg, instead concentrating on operations in the Baltic, while Marquor Rodsteen instead proposed to attack and destroy the Swedish warships while still in port. The blockade option was eventually chosen, and Rodsteen received orders to this extent on the same day. Having drawn up operational plans, the Danish navy left port on 13 August 1675.[7]

In Sweden, Field Marshal and Admiral of the Realm Gustav Otto Stenbock received his orders on 9 September, a week after the Danish declaration of war. Stenbock was a veteran of the Thirty Years' War and all Sweden's subsequent wars. There was no questioning his *military* experience; however, he lacked experience of naval matters. The Swedish navy was instructed to sail south, and then to patrol the waters between the islands of Öland, Bornholm, and Rügen so as to ensure communications between Sweden and Pomerania. If the Danish fleet approached Wismar, which due to its proximity to Denmark seemed a likely Danish objective, Stenbock was ordered to attack the Danes and relieve the town.[8]

There was also a previous, secret instruction for the navy, dated 31 August 1675. According to this instruction, Stenbock was in case of war to locate and destroy the Danish fleet, and cut it off from its base at Copenhagen. If this plan succeeded, Stenbock was to send home most of his warships, while the remaining ones should be used to take control of the Straits, with orders to take all Danish and Dutch merchant vessels there. The Dutch merchant ships in Danzig and Königsberg should be attacked and taken as well.[9] Brandenburg-Prussia and the Netherlands, it should be remembered, were already at war with Sweden. In addition, Admiral Stenbock had orders to transport troops to the Swedish possessions in Germany to reinforce the garrisons there.

6 Ibid., p.173.
7 Ibid., p.173.
8 Ibid., p.173.
9 Ibid., pp.173–4.

The Gothenburg squadron, under Major Mårten Kristersson Anckarhielm, was on 26 June 1675 ordered to take all Dutch ships that he could find. However, first there was a lack of supplies, so that he could not go to sea, and then Marquor Rodsteen's Danish squadron arrived. It had left Copenhagen on 6 September and effectively blockaded Gothenburg until the end of October 1675. Anckarhielm was unable to get out.[10]

On 9 October 1675, the Swedish main fleet at Dalarö finally left port, after a considerable delay caused by lack of supplies, poor organisation, and inexperience. Crews were untrained, and most senior officers, and not only Stenbock, lacked experience in naval operations. It was a large fleet: 33 warships, 11 armed merchantmen, and 22 other vessels, crewed by 7,640 sailors and 2,923 troops (excluding officers). By some accounts, the fleet's armament consisted of no less than 2,222 cannons (although establishment numbers did not always correspond to actual numbers).[11] In theory, it was a splendid fleet, even though it had set out very late in the season. Yet, ice conditions permitting, Scandinavian fleets often sailed throughout the winter, so this was not necessarily the wrong decision.

However, after only nine days at sea, most of the fleet returned to base. The fleet had encountered a storm, during which several warships had been damaged and two were lost. Others had been damaged due to the inexperience of the crews and officers. King Charles, furious, dismissed Stenbock from his post. Stenbock was also heavily fined for his negligence, which eventually ruined him.[12]

The Danish main fleet remained at sea until 2 November. Most of it, 23 Danish and Dutch warships, had patrolled the waters between Scania and Pomerania with orders to cut Swedish communications with Germany. Their presence prevented Sweden from moving additional troops to its German possessions, which had disastrous effects on the Swedish war effort there. By the end of the year, Swedish Pomerania had been reduced to a few towns, chiefly Stettin and Stralsund, and the island of Rügen. Meanwhile, Rodsteen's squadron had successfully blockaded Gothenburg. There had also been frequent Danish patrols in the Straits, so as to interdict Swedish activities there.[13]

During the winter, the Swedish fleet at Dalarö, blocked by ice, made yet another, somewhat desperate attempt to leave port. In early February 1676, weather improved slightly, so that only 20 km of ice separated the fleet from open sea. The naval command levied 900 workers for the dangerous task of sawing a channel through the ice. Work got underway, but then, with several ships already in the newly opened channel, a storm broke out. The ice began to move, crushing one of the ships. Moreover, the weather grew colder again, so the attempt had to be abandoned.[14]

10 Ibid., p.174.

11 Björn Axel Johansson (ed.), *Regalskeppet Kronan* (Höganäs: Bra Böcker, 1985), pp.104–5

12 Lundgren, *Regalskeppet Stora Cronan*, p.98.

13 Askgaard, "Kampen till sjöss", 174; Almgren, "Svensk strategi", p.34.

14 Lundgren, *Regalskeppet Stora Cronan*, pp.105–7.

There is no doubt that the Danish naval strategy succeeded in 1675. One might say that it succeeded by default, since the Swedish navy failed to carry out its tasks, yet the Danish strategy had been sound and the desired effects were achieved. However, Cort Adeler did not live to see the results. He died from natural causes on 5 November 1675, just a few days after the Danish main fleet had returned to Copenhagen.[15]

15 Askgaard, "Kampen till sjöss", p.175.

7

The Attack from Norway

Norway was a key Danish possession, with a long land border with Sweden. The western Swedish provinces of Bohuslän, Dal, and Värmland were traditionally most exposed to attacks from Norway, but previous wars had also engaged the northern Swedish provinces of Dalecarlia (*Dalarna*), Härjedalen, and Jämtland. Indeed, Härjedalen and Jämtland had belonged to Norway until 1645 and Bohuslän was one of the key territories lost to Denmark in the 1658 peace agreement that also deprived Denmark of Scania, Halland, and Blekinge.

In late October 1675, a Norwegian army moved into the formerly Norwegian province of Bohuslän. At the same time, further north a smaller Norwegian expeditionary force moved from Vinger (modern-day Kongsvinger) in Norway against the Swedish bastion at Eda.[1] These were the first military engagements of the war that took place in Scandinavia itself. The Norwegians were led by the energetic Danish governor in Norway, Count Ulrik Frederik Gyldenløve. Gyldenløve was born in Bremen as the illegitimate son of Prince Frederick, later King Frederick III of Denmark, who was at the time Prince-Archbishop of Bremen. When his father became King of Denmark in 1648, Ulrik Frederik assumed the name Gyldenløve which was customarily used by illegitimate sons of Danish kings.

Gyldenløve had orders to raise the population of Bohuslän for the Danish cause, then attack either Bohus Fortress or the port of Marstrand, if an opportunity arose. Otherwise he was merely to hold the border. However, unlike his half-brother the King, Gyldenløve was not shy about going on the offensive. He was popular among his men, since he was seen as sharing the dangers with them. Now Gyldenløve gathered 4,000 men under Lieutenant General Henrik Rüse von Rysensteen in Frederikstad (360 cavalry, 300 dragoons, and 2,550 infantry) and Frederikshald (60 cavalry and 800 infantry), and 2,000 men under Major General Hans Løwenhielm in Elverum, Vinger, and in the border passes of Smaalenene, near the Swedish border.

The fighting on the Norwegian-Swedish border may have begun with a minor Swedish incursion in the direction of Frederikstad. However, if so,

1 Almgren, "Svensk strategi", p.38.

Ulrik Frederik Gyldenløve

the Swedes soon retreated. Be that as it may, within days Gyldenløve moved into Bohuslän with 4,000 men, some by road, others by sea. Meanwhile, Løwenhielm made a first attempt, with 1,500 men, against Eda further to the north but was repulsed.[2] Gyldenløve's ultimate target was probably Gothenburg, Sweden's only mainland port to the west and a barrier between the Danish possessions in Norway and the former provinces in southern Sweden. However, the audacious Gyldenløve was checked by two Swedish officers who were no less capable than him. General Rutger von Ascheberg, the King's mentor in military affairs since 1673, had in 1675, when war seemed increasingly likely, been put in charge of the defences in Bohuslän. Then there was Colonel Erik Dahlbergh, who in 1674 had been appointed head of Fortification, and in 1675 was appointed quartermaster general. This meant that he, among other duties, also was responsible for military intelligence, which customarily was handled by fortification officers since they were responsible for military mapmaking. Dahlbergh, then in his early fifties and only a few years younger than Ascheberg, had experience from several previous wars including the ones with Denmark and had once learnt fortification skills from Conrad Mardefelt. Both came to play important roles during the war.

Now a Swedish force under Ascheberg intercepted and halted the Norwegians at Kvistrum (modern-day Kviström), the only crossing point over River Kviströmmen on the main north-south road through Bohuslän (Map 3).The invasion having failed, Gyldenløve in early November withdrew back into Norway.[3]

King Charles wanted to go on the offensive into Norway as soon as possible, with the forces already available in Bohuslän. This was again, in principle, a correct decision; however, such an offensive was then beyond the capability of the Swedish army. On 29 October, the King discussed the matter with Ascheberg and Dahlbergh. Despairing after all previous reverses, the young man yelled that he would rather die than not moving against Gyldenløve immediately, even if he had to go with only his Life Guard and the Life Regiment of Horse, and anybody who tried to prevent him would feel the point of his rapier. Dahlbergh, for whom this was a first personal meeting with King Charles, noted the King's outburst in his diary.[4] Nonetheless, Ascheberg's and Dahlbergh's cooler counsel prevailed. They advised the King that reinforcements and supplies had to be

2 Ibid., 38; Vaupell, *Den danske hærs historie*, pp.104.

3 Almgren, "Svensk strategi", p.39.

4 Herman Lundström (ed.), *Erik Dahlberghs dagbok (1625–1699)* (Uppsala: Almqvist & Wiksell, 1912), p.185.

Top: Rutger von Ascheberg. (Photo: Medströms)
Bottom: Erik Dahlbergh.

arranged, and besides, they had to await winter, so that rivers and roads became easier to cross.[5]

In January 1676, the Swedes were ready to move against Norway. Dahlberg went to Eda to supervise the extension of the fortifications there and collect intelligence. An expeditionary force under Lieutenant General Wilhelm von Fersen and Dahlbergh on 26 January moved towards Vinger in Norway from the Swedish province of Värmland, on a road that would enable the Swedes to threaten Norway's capital Christiania from the north. This attack was intended as a diversion, while the real invasion would take place further south, with a Swedish army setting out from Vänersborg. However, the expeditionary force was recalled, with orders merely to guard the border. Eventually only a few reconnaissance units penetrated into Norway, and only for short periods. It was not yet cold enough. The invasion was called off, too. More pressing problems had appeared elsewhere. Intelligence suggested that the Danes assembled troops in Zealand, preparing for a major naval landing in Scania. In April 1676, King Charles ordered his troops to gather there.

Sweden mobilised as best it could. On 5 May, King Charles inspected the Life Guard in Stockholm, which then marched south towards Scania. On 16 May, King Charles met the Life Guard and Life Regiment at Östra Karup in the province of Halland, from which they marched towards Ängelholm. While the regiments marched to Malmö, King Charles on 18 May arrived in Helsingborg, where the Governor-General of Scania, Fabian von Fersen, and the commandant in Helsingborg, Peter Hästesko, met him. On 22 May, King Charles arrived in Malmö. He continued to the town of Ystad, where he arrived on 26 May.[6]

5 Almgren, "Svensk strategi", p.39.
6 Wahlöö and Larsson, *Slaget vid Lund*, p.112.

8

The Conquest of Gotland

In January 1676, the Danes had set as their main objective for the year to carry out an invasion of Scania. Preparations for the invasion began on 26 January. Then plans for four separate contingency operations were drawn up:

1. A renewed attack on Bremen-Verden.
2. A renewed attack from Norway against the Swedish heartland.
3. An attack on Scania.
4. A simultaneous attack on all three regions.[1]

Four days later, the Danish war council recommended option 3, an attack on Scania. It was also noted that Norway would be able to support the invasion through an incursion with the troops already in position. The commanders also recommended to land troops on the island of Gotland in the Baltic Sea, with the purpose to make the island into a base for naval operations. No further decisions were taken; the subsequent operations were planned by the officers in the theatre of operations.[2]

On the same day as the strategic discussion had begun (26 January), the Danish Admiralty ordered the drawing up of a list of available ships and their total capacity. From 28 March onwards, the Danish navy was ordered to monitor shipping in the Straits closely and also to keep an eye out for any Swedish warships. There was a need for intelligence, since the Swedish main fleet at Dalarö remained strong and the Gothenburg squadron, too, had proven itself a force to be reckoned with.[3]

On 1 February, the Admiralty decided to occupy Gotland. This island had shifted hands a few times, but in 1645 Denmark had lost it to Sweden, together with the islands of Ösel and Dagö on the eastern side of the Baltic. The occupation of Gotland would greatly assist in acquiring supremacy at sea. The Danes could not expect the Swedish navy to be as passive in this year as it had been in the previous one, but fortunately, the Netherlands had promised

1 Nielsen, "Dansk strategi", p.87.
2 Ibid., p.87.
3 Poul T. Cohrt, "Landstigningen vid Råå", Göran Rystad (ed.), *Kampen om Skåne* (Lund: Historiska Media, 2005), pp.22–9, on p.23.

Niels Juel. (Photo: Medströms)

the use of a Dutch fleet. With the recent death of Cort Adeler, the position of Admiral-General was open. Although King Christian had an able Danish admiral at his disposal, Niels Juel who had served with the Dutch in the First Anglo-Dutch War and, later, against the Swedes as well, he for political reasons decided to give the vacant post to the experienced Dutch Admiral Cornelis Tromp, who would arrive in spring with the Dutch fleet.[4]

On 30 March, Admiral Juel and the Danish fleet left Copenhagen.[5] He had received his orders on 23 March, instructing him to interdict as much of Sweden's maritime trade as he was able. Only English ships would be exempted, as long as they did not carry troops or war materials. In addition, Juel was to destroy Swedish shipping, in particular to prevent troop transports to Pomerania. Otherwise he was to avoid battle with the numerically superior Swedish fleet. Finally, in a secret addendum, Juel was ordered to occupy the island of Gotland.[6]

Having reached Gotland on 28 April, Admiral Juel landed 1,500 soldiers under Morten Bærtelsen (in the official Danish report named Bartold), the commander of the 2nd Zealand Regiment, together with a few hundred commandeered sailors, at the port of Klintehamn. Colonel Michael Schultz, the Swedish commandant in Gotland's only town, Visby, had only 600 troops at his disposal. He attempted to prevent the landing, but had to retreat into Visby. Unfortunately for Schultz, on 30 April the townsmen decided to open the gates to the Danes. Schultz and his men took refuge in Visborg, the town's derelict fifteenth-century castle. Its broken walls were no match for shipboard artillery broadsides, so on 2 May, Schultz surrendered the castle in return for free departure with full honours of war. The townsmen then swore allegiance to King Christian. In June, some of Bærtelsen's men were amalgamated into a Gotland Battalion (*Gotlandske Bataillon*), intended as a garrison unit. Gotland remained in Danish hands until the end of the war. The Gotland Battalion was abandoned when the Danes withdrew from the island at the end of the war.[7]

---

4 Askgaard, "Kampen till sjöss", pp.174, 175.

5 Wahlöö and Larsson, *Slaget vid Lund*, p.111.

6 Askgaard, "Kampen till sjöss", p.175.

7 Vaupell, *Den danske hærs historie*, pp.108–9; Askgaard, "Kampen till sjöss", p.175. On the Gotland Battalion, see Hasselager and Snorrason, *Danish Uniforms, Colours and Standards*, p.27.

9

The Battle off Öland

In early 1676, the Swedish admiralty renewed its efforts to get a seaworthy fleet out to sea. King Charles, still inexperienced, appointed as new Admiral of the Realm the sixty-year-old Lorentz Creutz, a civilian administrator of some repute. Unfortunately, Creutz had never set foot on a ship, was not a soldier, and, in the words of a contemporary, had 'seen neither enemy nor death'. This did not prevent the choleric Creutz, who perhaps was sensitive about his lack of nautical knowledge, from quarrelling with his officers, on whom he laid the blame for the fleet's operational shortcomings.

Receiving his orders on 18 April 1676, Creutz was to sail to the Straits as soon as possible, there to attack and defeat the Danish fleet before the Dutch arrived. Having achieved victory, he was to transport some 2,000 soldiers as reinforcements to Pomerania.[1]

As usual, it took time to prepare the fleet, which left Dalarö on 19 May.[2] This was too late. Juel had already on 14 May joined his forces to a Dutch squadron of eight warships under Philips van Almonde. The joint Danish–Dutch fleet then consisted of 35 warships (25 ships of the line and 10 frigates) with 1,675 cannons.[3] The Swedish fleet on 19 May consisted of 32 warships, eight armed merchantmen, and 19 smaller vessels, with 2,172 cannons and 11,890 men: 8,770 sailors and 3,120 were soldiers.[4]

Admiral Juel was a skilled commander, and the Danish fleet had been at sea already for two months, which had given the Danish crews ample time to practice their skills. Even so, when the two fleets moved into contact on 25 May, they fought an inconclusive battle for two days west of the island of Bornholm. The battle of Bornholm, as it has become known, ended with a Danish withdrawal. If Creutz had been an experienced admiral, he would no doubt have been able to finish off his enemy, especially since the Swedish fleet was stronger, at least in numbers, and carried more cannons; however, Creutz confused his subordinates with faulty signalling, which resulted in the dispersal of the Swedish fleet. What seems to have happened was that Creutz

1 Askgaard, "Kampen till sjöss", p.175.
2 Lundgren, *Regalskeppet Stora Cronan*, p.131.
3 Askgaard, "Kampen till sjöss", p.175.
4 Johansson, *Regalskeppet Kronan*, p.112; Lundgren, *Regalskeppet Stora Cronan*, p.135.

Lorentz Creutz. (Photo: Medströms)

had seen one of his ships, the *Mercurius*, under threat from an enemy fireship. The captain on the *Mercurius* was Major Johan Creutz, the Admiral's son. Creutz had then ordered the crew of his flagship, *Kronan* ('The Crown'), to fall back, so that he could make sure that his son was safe. What Creutz had not realised, was that this command applied to the entire fleet. As a result, the Swedish pursuit ended, and the Danes could get away. What was particularly embarrassing was that King Charles had witnessed part of the battle from a church tower on the nearby shore, through a field-glass that he had borrowed from his intelligence chief Dahlbergh.

After the inconclusive battle, Creutz and his senior officers landed in Trelleborg, where they on 27 May met with King Charles. Creutz laid all blame for the failure on his officers, whom he accused of cowardice.

Embittered by this new failure, but not yet comprehending how utterly unable Creutz was as a naval commander, Charles believed Creutz and ordered him to attack the Danish fleet again. Based on the advice of Admiral Claes Uggla, one of few experienced Swedish senior naval officers, it was agreed to sail north to the shore beyond Öland, since from this position, the fleet had shorter communication lines to friendly ports. Since everybody agreed that Tromp surely would go on the offensive, it was better to meet him where the Swedish fleet might hold an advantage.[5]

Creutz then sailed north towards the island of Öland, but not before he had sent a letter to his family in which he, again, blamed his subordinates for everything that had gone wrong.

Meanwhile, Juel's fleet had on 28 May been reinforced by another nine warships and three smaller ships under Admiral Tromp, who had left Copenhagen two days previously, on 8 May having been appointed Admiral-General over the combined fleet.[6] Tromp and Juel were of the same age, being in their late forties. Juel was a very experienced naval officer, but Tromp was even more so; he had fought in the three Anglo-Dutch Wars and had the reputation of an aggressive commander.

Even the combined fleet was slightly smaller in number of vessels and cannons than the Swedish fleet. However, the two fleets were reasonably equal in number of warships, and the slight Swedish superiority in cannons was more than offset by the quality and experience of Tromp's crews. Besides,

5 Johansson, *Regalskeppet Kronan*, p.134.

6 Askgaard, "Kampen till sjöss", p.175.

the recorded number of cannons may be irrelevant. At least the artillery of the Swedish flagship *Kronan* was not up to establishment strength, and we do not know if the records concerning the other ships, on both sides, are any more correct.

Cornelis Tromp (Peter Lely, *c.* 1675; Photo: Medströms)

On 30 May, the two fleets got in sight at the southern promontory of Öland. On 1 June, they engaged each other in what became known as the battle off Öland. By noon, Creutz emerged from his lunch. Misunderstanding the tactical situation, he ordered his men to signal the entire fleet to turn. Then, and against the advice of his officers, Creutz ordered his own ship to carry out a sharp turn under too much sail, a very dangerous manoeuvre. His sailing officers should have made allowance for the admiral's lack of nautical experience and taken measures to reduce the risk; however, the acrimonious relationship between Creutz and his officers made cooperation impossible. The manoeuvre failed, *Kronan* capsized, her gunpowder magazine ignited, and the entire ship exploded, taking about 750 men with her into the deep, including Creutz. Only 41 men managed to save themselves, coming ashore on Öland. Among those lost were major elements of the Västerbotten Regiment, which had been assigned as reinforcements for Pomerania.[7]

Admiral Uggla then tried to assume command. However, the Swedish fleet was now dispersed, and his ship, *Svärdet* ("The Sword"), was badly damaged. Tromp asked Uggla to surrender. According to Tromp, Uggla accepted. However, the popular story went that Uggla refused, replying 'When did you ever see an owl (Swedish: *uggla*) being caught in the middle of the day!' There is probably some truth in both stories. It is likely that Uggla surrendered in order to save his men, because he had looked out for them in the past. However, when against Tromp's orders, a Dutch fireship, *t'Hoen* under Captain Willem Willemsen, suddenly closed with and set *Svärdet* aflame, Uggla and his crew did not extinguish the fire. Perhaps preferring to see their ship burned than taken as a prize, Uggla instead attempted to evacuate his crew, remaining aboard until the last. However, the gunpowder magazine exploded, and Uggla was thrown into the sea where he perished, along with most of his men. Only some 50 survivors out of 650 were saved and brought to Copenhagen as prisoners of war. Angry over the loss of Uggla and his ship, which Tromp had hoped to take as a prize, Tromp later had Willemsen arrested. The latter died within days because of harsh treatment.[8]

7 Johansson, *Regalskeppet Kronan*, pp.112, 143.

8 Ibid., pp.140, 145.

Above: The Swedish flagship ***Kronan*** before her explosion, battle off Öland, 1676. (Tapestry by Bernt van der Eichen, Rosenborg Castle; Photo: Medströms)

Below: The Swedish flagship ***Kronan*** explodes, battle off Öland, 1676. To the right: Admiral Uggla's ship Svärdet. (Claus Møinichen; Photo: Medströms)

The combined fleet had destroyed five Swedish ships including the flagship and dispersed the rest. Yet, the battle had not been without losses also for Tromp's men. Tromp's flagship *Christianus Quintus* had taken serious damage. After the battle, Tromp wrote that his first captain, Adrian Akersloot, had been killed, his second captain, Isaak van Enten, had lost his right arm, the commander of his infantrymen had lost an eye, and more than a hundred of his crew were dead or wounded.[9]

Besides, although the Swedish fleet had suffered major losses, it had not been annihilated. In the final account, Admiral Uggla's advice to King Charles to have the fleet fight in a position closer to the Swedish heartland saved the survivors of the badly mauled fleet.

On 4 June, King Charles attended mass in a church in Malmö. During the sermon, he could hear, from across the Straits, the Danish cannons firing a salute in celebration of the recent naval victory.[10] King Charles received the news about the defeat off Öland on 7 June.[11]

Claes Uggla.

In western Sweden, Admiral-Lieutenant Siöblad's Gothenburg squadron remained undefeated. At the same time as Creutz's fleet went out, the Gothenburg squadron left port, too. As noted, Siöblad's objective was to relieve Stade. Arriving too late, Siöblad had to return to Gothenburg without accomplishing his mission. But then the fortune of war changed. The Danish Admiral Marquor Rodsteen had again sailed to Gothenburg to blockade the town, according to orders dated 6 July. On 16 July, Siöblad's Gothenburg squadron went out to engage the Danish warships. In the battle, the Danish frigate *Kiöbenhaffn* (Copenhagen) ran aground and was burned by the Swedes. Although Rodsteen's action tied up the Gothenburg squadron and prevented it from operating elsewhere, Rodsteenn either defeated the Gothenburg squadron, nor managed to provide naval support for Count Gyldenløve's offensive in Bohuslän. By the end of July, Rodsteen returned to Copenhagen. This allowed the Swedes first to bring in six newly equipped warships from England, then for Siöblad to leave port and ravage the Danish communication lines by taking several prizes among Danish merchant ships. Rodsteen was removed from his command, and a new Danish squadron under Lieutenant Colonel Johan Vibe sailed towards Gothenburg. Vibe was a Norwegian army officer, the son out of wedlock of a Danish noble and a French woman. Although known for his bravery and ability, Vibe had no more success than Rodsteen in maintaining the blockade.[12]

9 Vaupell, *Den danske hærs historie*, p.112.

10 Wahlöö and Larsson, *Slaget vid Lund*, p.113.

11 Almgren, "Svensk strategi", p.41.

12 Vaupell, *Den danske hærs historie*, pp.128–9; Askgaard, "Kampen till sjöss", p.176.

10

The Danish Invasion of Scania

With the combined fleet victorious at sea, it was time to move an invasion army across the Straits. On19 June, Tromp was informed about the imminent invasion and ordered to carry out a diversion at the Scanian town of Ystad.[1]

Having achieved naval supremacy, the combined Dutch-Danish fleet under Tromp on 25 May cast anchor off Ystad, at a musket shot's distance from the shore. On the following day, Tromp sent a trumpeter ashore to demand the surrender of the town. Lieutenant General Wilhelm von Fersen refused, and in response Tromp opened fire on the town from eight frigates and two bomb vessels. The latter were vessels the primary armament of which was not cannons (long guns) but mortars mounted forward near the bow and elevated to a high angle, projecting their fire in a ballistic arc. Explosive shells (known as bombs or carcasses) were employed rather than solid shot. With almost unopposed broadsides from the warships, the garrison had little hope of success. The citadel walls were soon destroyed by the cannon fire.

On 27 June, more than 2,000 Danish troops (battalions from the 1st Zealand Regiment and 2nd Fyn Regiment, together with a corps of sailors) were sent ashore in hundreds of small boats, which had been towed, empty, from Copenhagen. They breached the town defences in two locations. The Swedish garrison consisted of eight squadrons of the Life Regiment and a few companies of infantry and dragoons, in total some 1,500 men.[2] The Swedes were forced out and retreated towards Kristianstad, leaving 120 dead and wounded. Tromp garrisoned Ystad with a battalion of the 2nd Fyn Regiment.[3]

Despite the serious firepower and large number of troops, the attack on Ystad was a feint. The plan was instead to land an invasion force much further to the west. The main invasion took place at Råå two days later, on 29 June 1676. Some 14,000 or more Danish troops landed on the beach at Råå, disembarking from some 500 vessels of various sizes and wading ashore. They were unopposed; there was no Swedish military force of similar size in Scania.

As noted, preparations for the invasion had begun already in January 1676. The army began its planning somewhat later. The cavalry regiments tasked

1 Cohrt, "Landstigningen vid Råå", p.26.

2 Almgren, "Svensk strategi", p.43.

3 Vaupell, *Den danske hærs historie*, p.114.

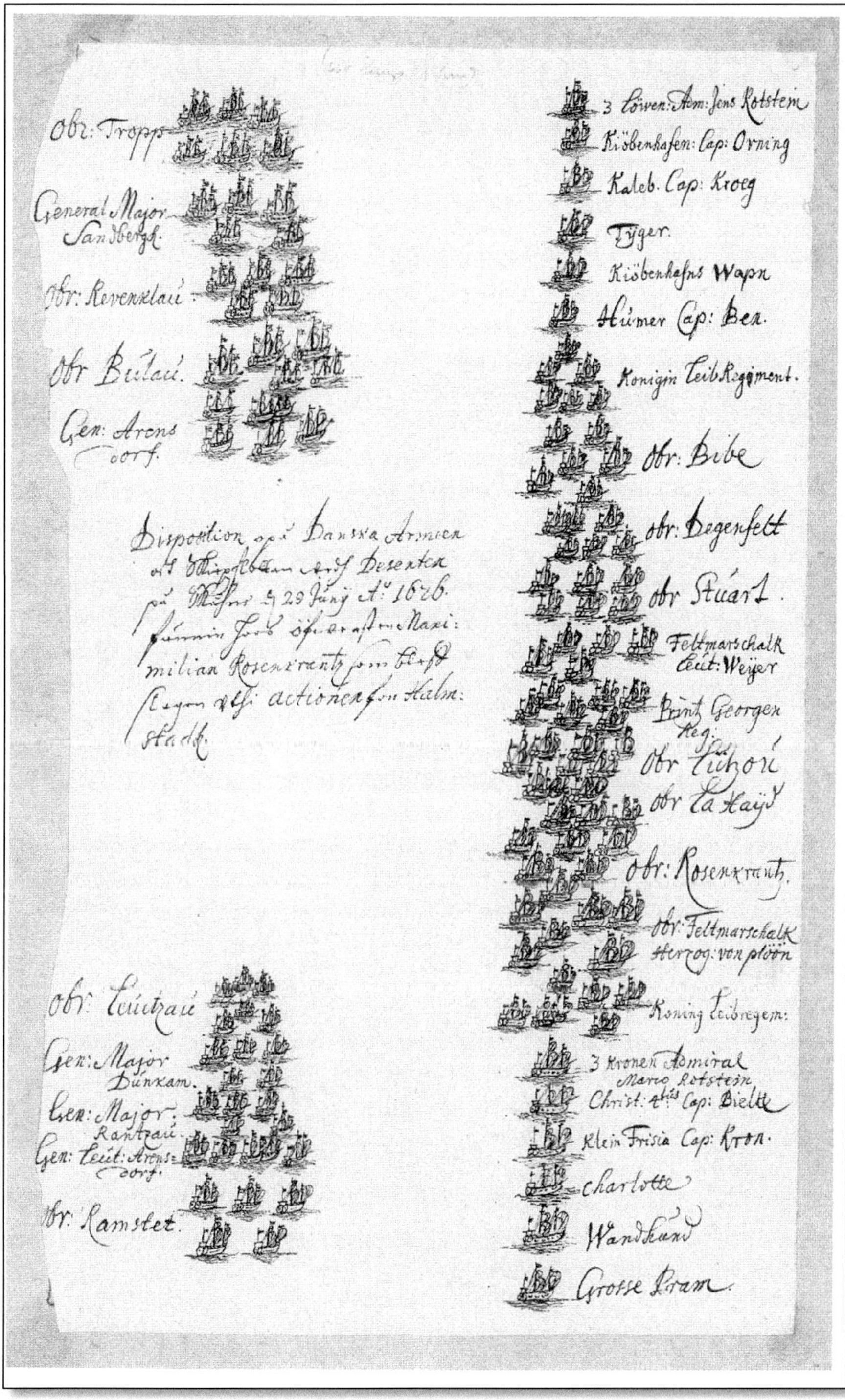

Disposition of the Danish invasion fleet, 1676. Document found among Colonel Maximilian Rosencrantz's papers, captured after the Battle of Halmstad later in the year. (Swedish Military Archives, Kungsboken, 12:4)

to join the invasion force received their marching orders on 11 April.[4] The infantry regiments had suffered major losses in the war on the Continent, in particular during the siege of Wismar, so additional troops were conscripted and enlisted in April and May, until all units had reached their establishment strength. Ammunition and other military equipment were purchased from merchants in Lübeck and Hamburg, which had the necessary production facilities, in exchange for surety in the form of the promised military subsidies.[5] On 5 June, the invasion army began to gather in a camp at Lyngby immediately north of Copenhagen, where King Christian inspected it on 14 June. By then the army was some 14,000 men strong, according to Frederik Giese, a Danish official involved in the activities.[6]

The crossing is described in an order issued on 22 June. Warships would sail on both sides of the vessels that transported the infantry. The latter vessels were drawn up and sailed by regiment, with the regimental colour flying from the main mast of the vessel with the colonel so as to guide the others. Each regiment would use 18 vessels, of which the first four also would carry a light cannon each. In addition, each regiment would have three barges for ammunition and other supplies. At sea, the colonel and other regimental officers would be subordinated the naval officers.

The artillery would be shipped on six barges and 38 vessels. The heavy artillery would follow the senior command staff and the King.

The cavalry would follow behind the infantry, with the right wing on the right side of the fleet, and the left wing on the left side. The same applied to the dragoons, who would be embarked in order of rank.

Upon landing, the warships would be ready to support the landing through shipboard artillery fire, on either flank of the invasion army.[7] The flotilla of four ships of the line and six frigates that was dispatched to provide cover for the invasion was led by Admirals Marquard Rodsteen and Jens Rodsteen, two brothers.[8]

In total, the Danish invasion force that was actually landed consisted of eight cavalry regiments and two dragoon regiments, each with a strength of 509 men, and 11 infantry regiments, each of 856 men (divided into eight companies of 107 men each). All in all, the establishment strength of the invasion force was 14,506 men (Appendix VI).[9] In addition, there would be a number of artillerymen to man the cannons. Although those who were ill or unfit for duty were left in Denmark, the invasion army counted at least 14,000 men, which corresponds to the number mustered at Lyngby. The infantry was landed first. Most of the cavalry was reportedly landed only on the second day of the invasion.

First the invasion fleet sailed to Landskrona, but since conditions there were unfavourable, it then moved on to the north and landed at Råå, a fishing

4 Cohrt, "Landstigningen vid Råå", pp.23–4.
5 Gautier, "Krigskostnaderna", pp.240–1, 243.
6 Cohrt, "Landstigningen vid Råå", p.24.
7 Ibid., p.25.
8 Vaupell, *Den danske hærs historie*, p.115.
9 Cohrt, "Landstigningen vid Råå", pp.23, 28 n.23; Vaupell, *Den danske hærs historie*, p.115.

The Danish invasion fleet at the landing at Råå, 29 June 1676. (Claus Møinichen, 1686-1688; Photo: Medströms)

village. The invasion force was formally led by King Christian but, in reality, by his overall military commander, Johann Hans Adolf, Duke of Schleswig-Holstein-Sonderburg-Plön.

The Swedes were aware of the Danish invasion force, but they lacked information on where it would land. There were several possible alternatives: Landskrona, Råå, Barsebäck, and Limhamn. On the other hand, the landing spot hardly mattered, since the Swedes lacked troops to oppose the landing. It remains unclear how many troops Sweden had in Scania at the time. Sthen Jacobsen, a contemporary observer who wrote a chronicle after the war, mentions a field army of 5,568 men, which probably is reasonably correct.[10] In addition, there were garrison troops of some 5,200 men distributed across the territory, in Malmö, Landskrona, Kristianstad, and Helsingborg (Map 2).

Of these troops, some 2,300[11] men were garrisoned in Scania's chief town, Malmö, under the efficient Governor-General, Fabian von Fersen, who had fought in all Sweden's war since the Thirty Years' War. Another garrison of 1,800[12] men was in Landskrona, north-west of Malmö, under the faint-hearted Colonel Hieronymus Lindeberg and his able second-in-command, Lieutenant Colonel von Metzstacken. In Helsingborg, yet further to the northwest, Lieutenant Colonel Peter Hästesko commanded a garrison of 300 men.[13] In Kristianstad, in the inland to the east, Colonel Henrik Ulfvenklou led a garrison of 800 men.[14] Kristianstad, a town founded by King Christian IV of Denmark and named after him (as Christianstad), was the key to eastern Scania.

After the Danish feint at Ystad, King Charles had moved, with a handful of men, to Landskrona personally to reconnoitre the situation. From Landskrona, he sent a man in a boat to the Danish side of the Straits. The scout returned, explaining that the Danish army had embarked upon a large invasion fleet and would raise anchor at any moment. The scout was right; soon King Charles could see the Danish invasion fleet approach with his own eyes. There was little he could do, however, without soldiers to oppose the

10 Sthen Jacobsen, *Den Nordiske Kriigs Krøniche* (Lund: Gleerups, 1897), p.35.
11 Göthesson, *Ställningen vid Norrvidinge*, p.18.
12 Vaupell, *Den danske hærs historie*, p.116.
13 Almgren, "Svensk strategi", p.65 n.9.
14 Vaupell, *Den danske hærs historie*, p.116.

Landing the cavalry horses at Råå, 1676. (Photo: Medströms)

landing. King Charles had less than half the number of men in the field army as compared to the Danish invasion force. Moreover, the Danish supremacy at sea meant that the Danes also would receive naval artillery support in any engagement near the coast. King Charles accordingly rode to Malmö with his men. The Swedish army then retreated north by way of Lund and Hörby to Kristianstad, arriving on 2 July.[15]

Marches were forced, and the general feeling within the Swedish army was one of despair, as if it had already been defeated. The French Ambassador, Isaac de Pas, Marquis de Feuquières, described in a letter home that the retreat was confused and in haste, and that both soldiers and officers complained, asking to be taken into battle or at least to be brought into view of the Danes, so that they could see their enemy. The men began to lose confidence in their young king, who was as yet untested. And as for Charles, he finally realised the magnitude of which the regency government had neglected matters of defence. Neither supplies nor equipment were prepared, to an extent unanticipated not only by the King but by most of his men as well.[16] Sweden had been utterly unprepared for war.

The Fall of Helsingborg

On 30 June, the town of Helsingborg fell to a Danish force under the capable Lieutenant General Niels Rosencrantz, who previously had taken Wismar. He was also said to have been the first Danish officer of the invasion force to land in Scania. The townsmen were very positive to the idea of returning

15 Wahlöö and Larsson, *Slaget vid Lund*, pp.113–14.

16 Claes-Göran Isacson, *Skånska kriget 1675–1679* (Lund: Historiska Media, 2000), p.17; citing Feuquières.

to Denmark, and in fact, the town notables handed over the key to the town and swore loyalty to King Christian as soon as he arrived.[17]

Nonetheless, Helsingborg Citadel remained under the control of Swedish troops under Lieutenant Colonel Peter Hästesko. However, the garrison turned out to be unwilling to fight. When a lucky Danish shot exploded a group of 14 barrels of gunpowder, the soldiers surrendered, despite a strong position and plenty of supplies. On 3 July, Hästesko surrendered without further ado,[18] on the following day bringing his remaining 250 men into Danish captivity.[19] The Danes had only lost some 20 men during the short siege. However, one of them was the able Rosencrantz, who was hit by a shot to the head when he exposed himself to enemy fire and soon died from his wound. Rosencrantz was succeeded by Colonel Siegwert von Bibow, an experienced officer from Mecklenburg who, together with Rosencrantz, had led the final assault on Wismar. Since 1675, Bibow had been the commander of the newly raised 2nd Fyn Regiment but now he was appointed head of the King's Life Regiment, replacing Rosencrantz in this position. As for Hästesko, he was subsequently exchanged and returned to Sweden, where he was court-martialled and sentenced to death for cowardice.

Meanwhile, detachments of the Danish field army were sent north, including Walter's Dragoon Regiment, which on 2 July took the little town of Ängelholm to secure the strategically important bridge over the River Rönneå.[20]

The Fall of Landskrona

Other detachments, under Major General Joachim von Schack, were sent south, to Landskrona. Although ably defended by the garrison's second-in-command, Lieutenant Colonel von Metzstacken, the Swedish garrison there was too small to hold the entire town when the Danes broke through the bastions. As the battle turned into street fighting, Metzstacken withdrew into the citadel, having lost possibly 400 men dead, wounded, or captured. The Danes suffered serious losses, too, including Jean de la Haye, the commander of the 1st Zealand Regiment, who fell in combat. Nonetheless, on 11 July, the Danes had taken the town, although Metzstacken still controlled the citadel, with a remaining garrison of perhaps 1,400 men and a hundred cannons. When King Christian, who had joined Schack's men, asked Metzstacken to surrender, he replied: 'Unless the devil brings me alive up into the air, I will not surrender the citadel!' Soon afterwards Metzstacken was fatally wounded leading a sally at night, while on the Danish side, Colonel Stuart was wounded.[21]

With his second-in-command Metzstacken lost, Colonel Hieronymus Lindeberg reluctantly had to take charge of the defences. He was not up

17 Wahlöö and Larsson, *Slaget vid Lund*, p.113.
18 Nielsen, "Dansk strategi", p.87.
19 Wahlöö and Larsson, *Slaget vid Lund*, p.114.
20 Vaupell, *Den danske hærs historie*, p.119.
21 Ibid., p.118.

Above: King Christian of Denmark (left) and Johann Hans Adolf, Duke of Schleswig-Holstein-Sonderburg-Plön (right), at the conquest of Landskrona, 1676. Behind King Christian stands his brother, Prince George, while Friedrich von Arensdorff is visible just behind the Duke. (Tapestry by Bernt van der Eichen, Rosenborg Castle)

Right: King Christian accepts the surrender of Landskrona, 1676, with King Christian (right) and Johann Hans Adolf, Duke of Schleswig-Holstein-Sonderburg-Plön (left). Behind King Christian stands his brother, Prince George, while Friedrich von Arensdorff is visible just behind the Duke. (Peder Andersen; Photo: Medströms)

Overleaf: Landskrona, 1676. The map shows the town at the time of the Swedish surrender and departure. (Johan Husman, 1683)

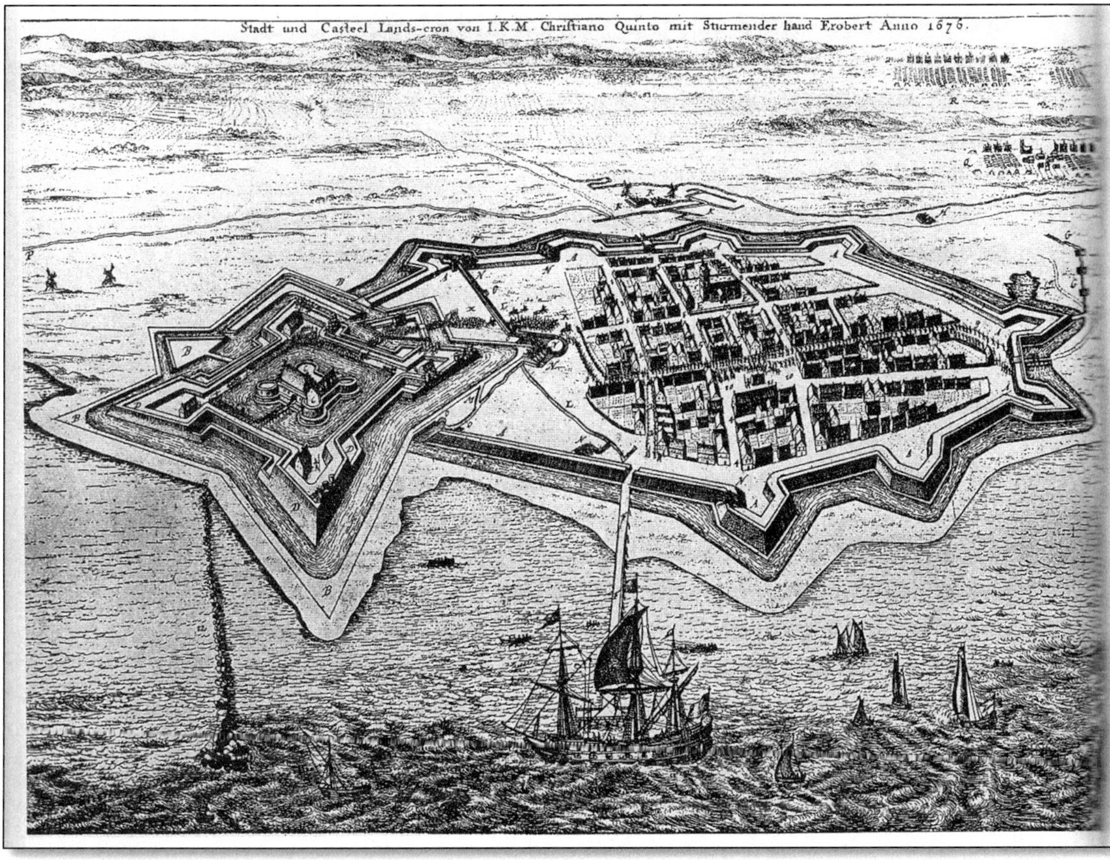

to the challenge. Moreover, his wife argued that he should surrender and not risk their lives. The citadel was well-supplied and defences were strong. However, the Danes brought up yet more artillery, and the bombardment caused constant losses. On 2 August, Lindeberg, to the consternation of his officers, sent a trumpeter to Schack to initiate negotiations. Schack coolly informed Lindeberg that unless he surrendered the citadel at once, Schack on the following day would send a hundred Danish swimmers across the moat to build bridges, after which he would storm the citadel, then offering quarters to nobody. This was too much for Lindeberg, who on the following day surrendered. His men, who had been reduced from 1,800 to 1,300, were moved to Denmark, despite the agreement that they would be shipped to Riga. (Lindeberg was later exchanged and returned to Sweden, where he was court-martialled for cowardice and executed on 31 December.)

Upon gaining the citadel, the Danes marvelled that Lindeberg had surrendered. Although outnumbered in men, the citadel was the most important one in Scania and also one of the most modern. It had plentiful supplies of water and food, as well as a large number of muskets and, amazingly, 120 cannons and plenty of gunpowder. The Danes had captured it for the loss of no more than 100 dead and 190 wounded. King Christian

Landskrona today. (Photo: Medströms)

awarded the plunder to his Field Marshal, Duke Johann Hans Adolf, who distributed it as cash gifts to the troops.[22]

For the rest of the war, Landskrona became the key Danish outpost in Scania. The port town was used to bring in supplies by sea, and when the Danish army subsequently was defeated in battle, it could still retreat into the town, where it remained well protected under the citadel's cannons.

King Charles's First Victory

Simon Grundel Helmfelt.

Faced with the invasion, the numerically inferior Swedish field army under King Charles retreated to Kristianstad, the key to eastern Scania. Fortunately for Charles, Field Marshal Simon Grundel Helmfelt, a veteran from the Thirty Years' War, was with him. Helmfelt, who as noted had been in southern Germany to cure his poor health at the outbreak of war, had after many difficulties managed to return. From Hamburg, where he almost was captured by Danish agents, Helmfelt had travelled to England, where he found a ship to Sweden. He had arrived in Stockholm on 1 April, whence he continued south with King Charles.[23]

Conditions were difficult, and it was most likely the experienced Helmfelt who really negotiated the perils that threatened the retreating army, with the victorious Danes advancing behind them. This was not an easy task; both the King and the army felt as if they already were defeated. Besides, the Danish field army outnumbered the available Swedish troops.

On 6 August, King Christian and Johann Hans Adolf, Duke of Schleswig-Holstein-Sonderburg-Plön, moved the Danish main army against Kristianstad. By then, King Charles and Helmfelt had retreated towards Karlshamn (where he arrived on 26 July), presumably wishing to retain the field army's mobility. Instead he left a garrison in Kristianstad, Colonel Henrik Ulfvenklou with 800 men.

The young King was still clearly unsure of himself, and after a few days, he changed his mind and returned to Kristianstad. However, the situation had changed. Ulfvenklou had destroyed the main bridge, Långebro, so as to prevent the Danes from crossing River Helgeå and entering the town. Now this also prevented access to the Swedish army. There was another bridge across the River Helgeå at Torsebro, north of the town. However, upon reaching Torsebro on 1 August,[24] King Charles found that a squadron of

22 Vaupell, *Den danske hærs historie*, p.121.

23 Wahlöö and Larsson, *Slaget vid Lund*, p.111.

24 Ibid., p.115.

Danish dragoons had reached the position first. The Danes had taken cover in a redoubt on the other side of the river, and the bridge itself was destroyed. However, there were boats nearby. King Charles decided to attack.

The King joined some of his men in the boats, then crossed the river under fire from the Danish dragoons and attacked. The Swedish cavalry, too, crossed the river, on horseback, half wading, half swimming, then joined the King and his men. In the ensuing battle, a number of Danes fell, and many were captured. Swedish losses were slight, despite the river crossing. More importantly, King Charles passed his baptism of fire with courage and success, both in his own eyes and in the eyes of his men. The Swedish retreat was not yet over, but the skirmish had shown that the Swedish army still could charge and win.

Despite this, the engagement also showed King Charles the futility of regaining Kristianstad. Even if he could get inside, he could then not easily get out again. He would have to trust Ulfvenklou to defend the town. King Charles accordingly decided to return across the River Helgeå, and then retreat further until he could join the reinforcements from the Swedish heartland that were on their way to the town of Växjö under Lieutenant General Martin Schultz. As we will see, Schultz was a very able officer, even though courtiers, including Magalotti, described him as of dissolute habits and with a weakness for beautiful women and good food.[25]

Skirmishes around Malmö

Malmö was Scania's chief town and had the largest Swedish garrison, 2,300 troops under Field Marshal Fabian von Fersen, the Governor-General of Scania and a veteran soldier. At first, the Danes were content in keeping Malmö under cavalry surveillance. Some of these missions were reconnaissance in force, such as when on 6–7 July 1676 Major Herman Franz von Schwanewede led 700 troops through Lund to Malmö. Schwanewede had fought for Sweden against Denmark in a previous war but, when captured, had gone into Danish service. During the Scanian War, he primarily served with irregular forces and was so successful that he eventually was promoted to Major General.

In August, the Danes deployed a containment force of 600 men so as to restrict Swedish movement in and out of the town. In September, a number of sallies and skirmishes took place outside Malmö, but the Danes did not attempt a proper siege and most withdrew on 27 September, burning their camp.[26] They may have aimed to go into winter quarters, but as will be shown, other events interfered.

---

25 Magalotti, *Sverige*, p.85.

26 Wahlöö and Larsson, *Slaget vid Lund*, pp.15, 114, 117.

The Fall of Kristianstad

The Danes controlled western Scania through Helsingborg and Landskrona, but to regain eastern Scania, they had to take Kristianstad.

With King Charles retreating to Växjö, King Christian led an army of 3,000 men across Scania to positions outside Kristianstad, deploying there on 10 August. Nonetheless, Colonel Ulfvenklou and his 800 men refused to surrender.

Kristianstad was protected by marshlands, moats, walls, and bastions. However, following the summer drought, the town's moat was almost empty, and the marshlands had dried out, too. It was easy to wade across the moat.

The Danes prepared an assault force of 2,000 foot divided into columns of 500 men each, with troops from the 1st Fyn Regiment, 4th Jutland Regiment, Schönfeldt's Regiment, and Ramstedt's Dragoon Regiment, led respectively by Colonels Johan Caspar von Cicignon, Ægedius Kristof Lützow, Gregor Alard Schönfeldt, and Nicolaus Helmich Ramstedt. Cicignon and Lützow attacked from the northwest, while Schönfeldt and Ramstedt attacked from the southwest. In addition, a fourth column of 500 men from the Queen's Life Regiment under Lieutenant Colonel Wilhelm Erhorn carried out a feint attack on the east side of the town. A turncoat from Kristianstad named Per Persson volunteered to guide them.

At 2:00 a.m. on 12 August, the Danes began to break through the outer palisades. The Danish infantry advanced into the moat, which they crossed, carrying their muskets above the head. They then climbed the walls. The Swedes had not maintained proper lookouts, so they only noticed the Danes when the first climbed into the bastions. Still, the fight was hard, but after several hours, the Danes were victorious.

Losses had been high, however. The Queen's Life Regiment alone had suffered casualties of 20 officers and 165 men. In total, the Danes lost 24 officers and 124 men dead, and 392 wounded. The Swedes lost some 500 dead and an unknown number of wounded. The Danes captured some 300 Swedes, including Ulfvenklou, as well as 78 cannons and a number of colours and standards. King Christian allowed his men three hours of free plunder in the town, and large numbers of valuables were shipped back to Denmark. Much of the plunder was awarded to the Field Marshal, Johann Hans Adolf, Duke of Schleswig-Holstein-Sonderburg-Plön, who characteristically distributed it as cash gifts to the men. King Christian deployed a garrison of 2,300 men in Kristianstad, under Colonel Lützow.[27]

Ulfvenklou was not court-martialled upon his return to Sweden, since he had fought to the end. However, he was taunted for the defeat by a colleague, Colonel Gustav Tungel, who recently had surrendered Wismar. The argument between the two colonels, who both had lost their towns, in 1677 resulted in a duel between the two near Kalmar in which Ulfvenklou was killed. As for the turncoat, Per Persson, he was later executed by the Swedes for treason.

27 Vaupell, *Den danske hærs historie*, pp.122–3.

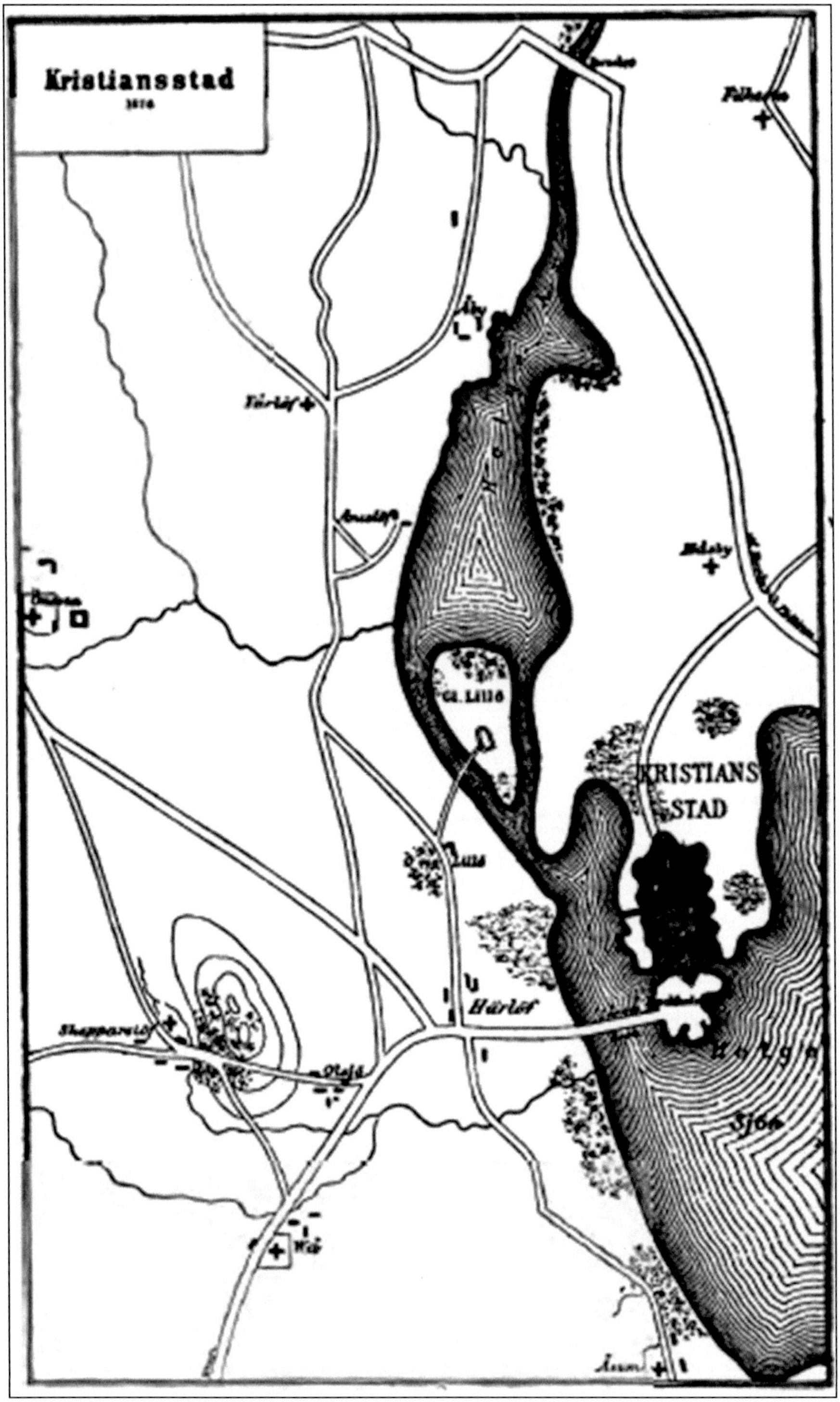

Kristianstad. (Gustaf Björlin, 1885)

Fall of Kristianstad, August 1676. (Romeyn de Hooghe, Rosenborg Castle)

The Fall of Öland

In July, the Danish fleet ravaged and burned the island of Öland. When Swedish troops finally arrived, they forced the Danes to depart on 17 August. However, by then almost all settlements on the island had been looted and burned.

By autumn 1676, the Danish supremacy at sea prevented the Swedes from reinforcing the faltering Swedish garrisons in Germany. However, not all went the coalition's way. On 2 August, Admiral Tromp's combined fleet attempted to support an invasion of Rügen. A coalition force consisting of, from Denmark, the Life Regiment Cavalry, Gewecke's Cavalry Regiment, and a battalion of the 2nd Fyn Regiment, and from Brandenburg, three infantry regiments, attempted a landing on the east shore of Rügen. However, the Swedish commander Königsmarck was prepared for such an eventuality, and easily repulsed the invasion force. The combined fleet was then ordered to return the cavalry to Ystad, then to proceed into the Gulf of Bothnia to prevent the Swedish troops in Finland from crossing to the Swedish heartland. However, they were too late; the reinforcements from Finland had already arrived.

Tromp then returned south, disembarking the Fyn battalion in the province of Blekinge, where they took control of Kristianopel, which surrendered on 25 September 1676.[28] This was hardly surprising; the town had been built, and named, by Danish King Christian IV as a border fortress, and since there no longer was a border there, the Swedish government had in 1675 already began to demolish the town's fortifications.

In September, the Dutch fleet returned home, while most Danish ships returned to Copenhagen.

28 Vaupell, *Den danske hærs historie*, pp.130–1.

The Fall of Karlshamn

Denmark retained two naval squadrons in the Baltic Sea. One, under Rear Admiral Christian Bielke, kept guard at Gotland. The other, under Admiral Jens Rodsteen, operated off the Blekinge coast. There, the Danes decided to take the little port of Karlshamn. Although Karlshamn had a citadel, its construction had only begun in 1675, under Lieutenant Erik Palmquist. However, the work was not yet completed.[29]

Palmquist was a Swedish fortification and intelligence officer who in 1673–1674 had participated in an embassy to Moscow, with the task to prepare a military intelligence report on the Muscovite army and military geography. In this endeavour he had been successful.[30] Palmquist was less fortunate in his present mission. Involved with the fortifications of Kalmar, Kristianstad, Kristianopel, and Karlshamn, he was captured in August 1676 by Danish troops while attempting to get out of Karlshamn on his way to Kalmar. Palmquist apparently died in Danish captivity soon afterwards. He was likely executed as a spy.[31]

Because on 7 August, Karlshamn had been surrounded by a levy of Blekinge peasants who had mobilised in support of Denmark, their old country. The peasant levy remained outside Karlshamn until 4 October, when Jens Rodsteen landed a battalion from Colonel Lützow's 4th Jutland Regiment commanded by Major Herbst at the port. They built several redoubts, brought in artillery, and opened fire against the town. Meanwhile, another Danish force under Colonel Sten Brahe, composed of pro-Danish guerrillas, invested the town from the inland.

There were food supplies in Karlshamn, but as the port began to suffer shortages of fresh water, on 7 October the Swedish commandant, Lieutenant Colonel Carl Olof Hård, surrendered. Again, the Danes were amazed. The Swedish garrison of 400 men had occupied a fort with 242 cannons (not all in operational order), a large quantity of firearms, and two newly built ships. The Danes installed a garrison in Karlshamn, consisting both of regular troops and peasant levies, under Captain Krumsee. (Hård eventually returned to Sweden, where he was court-martialled for cowardice and executed in 1677.)[32]

---

29 "Karlshamns Castell – Frisholmen", *Karlshamns historia*, Karlshamn municipality, n.d. (<www.karlshamn.se/Global/Karlshamn/Forvaltning/Kommunledning/Arkiv/Karlshamns%20historia/Kastellet.pdf>).

30 See, e.g., Michael Fredholm von Essen, *Muscovy's Soldiers: The Emergence of the Russian Army 1462–1689* (Warwick: Helion, 2018), parts of which to a significant degree are based on Palmquist's report.

31 "Palmquist (Palmqvist), släkt", *Svenskt biografiskt lexikon* 28 (Stockholm, 1992), p.659.

32 Vaupell, *Den danske hærs historie*, 131–2; Jens Lindström, *Skeppsvarvet och vraken i Vindhamn vid Boön: Arkeologisk förundersökning av varv, RAÄ Karlshamn 36, samt utbredning av fartygslämningar, RAÄ Karlshamn 47* (Vejbystrand: Nordic Maritime Group Rapport 2017:8, 2018), p.12; citing Edward Lindahl, *Om staden Carlshamn: några historiska och statistiska anteckningar* (Dissertation, Lund University, 1868), p.4.

11

The Small War, Insurgents, and Paramilitary Forces

A persistent problem for the Swedes, both civilians and soldiers, during the war was the continued operations of pro-Danish guerrillas in major parts of Scania and, although far less so, in other former Danish or Norwegian provinces. The Swedish authorities referred to the guerrillas as *snapphanar* (sing. *snapphane*), a term of unclear origin that most likely was an old expression for brigand or robber. It was certainly a pejorative term, and it is unlikely that anybody would have called himself a *snapphane*, unless it was to scare one's victims.

However, during the war *snapphanar* came in two main varieties: genuine *snapphanar*, who were outlaws in the true sense of the word, and 'freeshooters'(in Danish German: *Freyschützen*), paramilitary soldiers who regarded themselves as in Danish military service.

The *snapphanar* were outlaws who made a living from crime. Often hardened brigands who lived in makeshift camps in the forest, they were violent, had no formal organisation, and did not co-operate with Danish troops except when they found it convenient. As the war continued, their gangs were swelled by the influx of destitute farmers and army deserters. A typical example of *snapphanar* was the notorious gang known as the "Owl Lords" (Swedish: *Uggleherrarna*). The core of the gang was seven brothers named Trued, Per, Sven, Nils, Erik, Olof, and Karl, and the gang's name derived from their farm, which was known as Uggletorpet ("Owl Cottage"). Per was conscripted in 1674. However, he deserted and joined his brothers, who were led by Trued, the eldest of them. Although mainly engaged in brigandage and cattle-rustling, the Owl Lords gathered a number of other desperate men to their gang, at times more than 50, and they occasionally took part in open fighting on the Danish side. However, they did not hesitate to rob locals as well. Trued was killed already in 1676, whereupon the ex-soldier Per assumed command of the gang. Their farm was burned by Swedish troops in 1677, almost certainly in retaliation for their activities. In 1678, Per received a pardon, but he almost immediately returned to brigandage. Nor did he and his brothers end their violent activities when Denmark and Sweden concluded a peace agreement. Sven and Nils were

Danish irregular. (Johan Philip Lemke)

captured and sentenced to death in Kristianstad in 1680. However, they managed to escape and rejoined their brother Per. The three men carried on criminal activities as outlaws until autumn 1683, when they were captured, convicted, and executed.[1]

The 'freeshooters', on the other hand, were recruited for Danish military service. In 1643–1644, during a previous war between Denmark and Sweden, the Danish Crown had attempted to exchange the old levy system of local defence in Scania with a more up-to-date military organisation, consisting of men who had received some military training. The Danish noble Ebbe Ulfeldt accordingly organised units of voluntary freeshooters, recruited from the locals, who would operate as guerrillas against the Swedish communication lines, including on operations that reached into Swedish territory.[2] During the Scanian War, the Danish Crown repeated the experiment. Immediately after the invasion force had landed at Råå in late June 1676, the Danish Crown called for volunteers from the population in Scania, Halland, Blekinge, Bohuslän, and Jämtland who were willing to join the Danish cause in exchange for a payment of five Rigsdalers upon enlistment and monthly payments thereafter. During the autumn, when King Christian still felt secure in his new conquests, a number of patents to raise companies were given to experienced soldiers. These were apparently intended as regular companies, not freeshooters of the old type. However, it turned out to be difficult to enlist more than a handful of local men. Besides, a few months later, following the Danish defeat at the Battle of Lund, the policy changed. On 20 March 1677, King Christian issued an order to recruit voluntary freeshooters from the population in Scania, Halland, and Blekinge. They would be organised into units and paid as dragoons by the Danish Crown. They would also be entitled to supplies like other troops. In addition, after the war the freeshooters would be free of taxation, as a further benefit.[3]

While units of freeshooters were raised, little is known about how they were recruited. It was previously generally believed that each company was recruited from a particular area. However, it seems more likely that they were recruited in major towns such as Landskrona and Kristianstad, among individuals who had heard about the freeshooter companies and travelled there to enlist. Few were freeholders. About a tenth of those who have been identified were former artisans, often shoemakers or tailors. Others were peasants who lacked land, being either sons of a freeholder or his former hired hands. Some were deserters from the regular army.[4]

1 Göran Rystad, "Snapphanarna och 'det lilla kriget'", Göran Rystad (ed.), *Kampen om Skåne* (Lund: Historiska Media, 2005), pp.283–98, on pp.296–7.

2 Knarrström and Larsson. *Hans Majestäts friskyttar*, pp.70–74.

3 Ibid., pp.94–5.

4 Ibid., p.96.

Top: Danish irregulars ambushing a Swedish convoy. (Johan Philip Lemke)
Bottom: Danish irregulars carrying out an ambush. (Erik Dahlbergh)

The freeshooter companies varied in size, also over time, but they were commonly from around 20 to 150 strong. Total numbers remain unknown. Personnel rolls for 17 freeshooter companies have been preserved, with the names of a total of 949 men. In addition, the names of another eight companies are known, which might have consisted of another 400 men or so. Among preserved documents one can find the names of several freeshooter captains who cannot be connected to any known company. All in all, a total of perhaps some 1,200–1,500 freeshooters seems likely for the duration of the war.[5] Others have suggested a slightly higher number, suggesting approximately 2,000 in total.[6] However, that many would never have been in service at the same time.

The freeshooters fulfilled several important tasks for the Danish field army. Perhaps most importantly, they carried out reconnaissance tasks and provided intelligence on the Swedish army and its activities. Furthermore, they carried out raids against the Swedish supply and communication lines. Raiding also provided a means of supplying the Danish army, since the freeshooters' raids often brought in stolen cattle and other supplies. Furthermore, they intercepted a large number of Swedish couriers, thus disrupting the Swedish communication line between King Charles's headquarters and Stockholm, and between the various Swedish armies and garrisons. The Danish national archives contain a large number of intercepted Swedish letters and documents, which were taken by the freeshooters at the time of the Scanian War. But freeshooters also functioned in a general support role, providing couriers, escorts, and patrols to the regular army.[7]

Sometimes the freeshooters operated in conjunction with regular units. The indefatigable Major General Hans Wilhelm Meerheim personally led raids combining regular and irregular troops on numerous occasions. Meerheim was an Imperial veteran of the Thirty Years' War whose forte was the small war. His military career began when, eight years old, he ran away from home to join a cavalry regiment. Meerheim had entered Danish service during the siege of Wismar in 1675. In Scania, he frequently led cavalry on raiding and reconnaissance missions and became a link between the Danish army and pro-Danish guerrillas. So did Colonel Schwanewede, who as noted had fought for Sweden against Denmark in a previous war but then gone into Danish service. From 1677, Schwanewede commanded a regular cavalry regiment in Landskrona, but from spring this year led several raids against the Swedes, capturing men and cattle.[8] In fact, large numbers of cattle had to be procured for the army's use, and the easiest was to have freeshooters move into the Swedish province of Småland to take them.[9]

The freeshooters primarily operated from the Danish bases in Landskrona, Kristianstad, Karlshamn, and Kristianopel.[10] There they received food supplies, gunpowder, and ammunition. They depended on the Danish

5 Rystad, "Snapphanarna och 'det lilla kriget'", p.288.
6 Knarrström and Larsson. *Hans Majestäts friskyttar*, p.95.
7 Ibid., p.102.
8 Vaupell, *Den danske hærs historie*, p.165.
9 Ibid., p.193.
10 Knarrström and Larsson. *Hans Majestäts friskyttar*, 103.

Crown for these commodities, unless they managed to capture supplies from the Swedes. It is unknown whether the freeshooters also received grenades, but this is certainly conceivable, since the Danes regarded the freeshooters as Danish soldiers.

The armament of the freeshooters and *snapphanar* varied, between the two categories of men as well as between different individuals. Some no doubt carried regular army muskets. New freeshooter recruits were given weapons by their captains. Others would have received, or captured, carbines. Some would have carried pistols, and many would have carried rapiers as sidearms, or long, single-edged fighting knives which seem to have been fairly common. Many freeshooters and *snapphanar* used civilian hunting guns, which fired smaller balls than the regular army muskets. Scania had many skilled gunsmiths, and it was common to use rifled weapons for, in particular, bird hunting. Northern Scania was indeed known for the prevalence of poaching. As a result, some of the guerrillas were likely skilled marksmen armed with long-range rifled guns. Some probably also operated on the battlefield as snipers in support of the regular troops. Archaeological evidence suggesting the use of small-calibre rifled guns on the field of battle has been found at Landskrona.[11]

The Danish Crown soon after the invasion made public announcements that effectively legitimised the looting of the private property of Swedes who happened to live in Scania, as well as those locals who still remained loyal to Sweden. On numerous occasions, the families of Swedish soldiers based in Scania suffered harassment and plunder by their neighbours.[12]

There was also popular peasant opposition to the Crown (both the Swedish and the Danish, one can assume). These two sentiments came together when on 20 July 1676, a treasury convoy from the Swedish heartland arrived in Loshult, where it because of the general confusion following the invasion remained for several days just south of Loshult Church. The convoy held heavy copper coins the equivalent of what most reports claimed was some 30,000 or 50,000 Riksdalers in silver. This treasure, packed in barrels and stored on 250 carts, was guarded by seven regulars under Captain Gustav Lilliesträm of the Scanian Cavalry Regiment and a number of Småland peasant levies.

Whether it was the proclamations of King Christian, or mere human greed, that set the events in motion remains unknown. In any case, the existence of the treasury convoy proved too tempting for the locals. Peasants from Loshult, Osby, Hästveda, and Broby soon got together with some local cavalrymen from Glimåkra, Emisslöv, and Knislinge, and 10–15 Danish cavalrymen from the Danish camp at Landskrona, whom the peasant leaders had persuaded to go on unauthorised leave to join the endeavour.[13] On 24 July, this diverse group looted the convoy. The Småland levies who were supposed to guard the convoy had been enticed into joining the other locals, which meant that only Captain Lilliesträm and his seven men were available to defend the treasury convoy. This was clearly inadequate, and they were soon

11 Ibid., pp.107–9, 129–31.

12 Ibid., pp.155–6.

13 Göthesson, *Ställningen vid Norrvidinge*, p.11.

Johan Gyllenstierna.

overwhelmed. The carts were then brought to Älmhult in Småland, by the Småland levies, where the coins were distributed among the participants.

The amazing thing about the raid was not that the peasants saw an opportunity to enrich themselves, but that they still relied on age-old military practices to do so. Those among them who took the initiative to the raid distributed messages among the neighbouring settlements with instructions to mobilise, just as they would have done in face of an outside threat centuries earlier. They then assembled their forces at a pre-selected location, from which they marched to Loshult, formed up in warbands according to village of origin. Some brought their women and children, perhaps as a safety measure.[14] It was a general levy, but one raised by the peasants themselves, not the Crown. And although there were some repercussions, the endeavour was a success. Most of the stolen coins were never recovered.

Attacks on Swedes and locals who remained loyal to Sweden grew in scope over time. They also grew increasingly vicious. Both freeshooters and *snapphanar* would, for instance, seek to capture Swedish officers, since the Danes paid a good prize for them. However, captured common soldiers were usually killed on the spot. The same treatment was handed out to civilians and non-combatants. After the Battle of Landskrona (see below), freeshooters raided the Swedish camp while the field army was away. They later reported that they had killed all ill and wounded Swedes they could lay their hands on.[15]

The Swedes attempted to deal with paramilitaries and other insurgents through such means that they had found efficient under similar circumstances in the past, in Scania during the previous war and also in Poland. First, they sought to separate the unruly elements who had taken refuge in the forests from the peasants who remained with their farms. The latter were presented with thinly veiled threats that they all had to swear, individually and in writing, loyalty to the Crown, and then surrender all insurgents, or face very severe penalties. Johan Gyllenstierna, a councillor to the King, personally led a large number of public meetings in which all participating peasants had to swear loyalty and individually sign legal documents to this effect. Since meetings were held at the parish church, and the church's birth records were consulted, it was impossible for any parishioner to avoid swearing

14 Åberg, *När Skåne blev svenskt*, pp.105–9.

15 Knarrström and Larsson. *Hans Majestäts friskyttar*, p.141.

loyalty. Moreover, the parishioners were held collectively responsible for the behaviour of those who lived among them.

When the peasant communities had been thus pacified, the Swedish army turned its attention to the active insurgents. For them there was no mercy. Special detachments of, usually, irregular troops were sent out to deal with them. Operating as paramilitary militias, they could strike back with the same tactics as the freeshooters and *snapphanar* used, including ambushes and surprise attacks. Some Swedish officers were experienced in this kind of warfare, among them Rutger von Ascheberg but even more so Georg Henrik Lübecker, a veteran of the Thirty Years' War and previous wars against Denmark who already in 1659 had set up the first cavalry regiment to be based in Scania, comprising men enlisted in the Swedish heartland whose primary role became to fight brigands and *snapphanar*. Moreover, the Swedes introduced a system of reintegration which included amnesty for past crimes for those guerrillas who accepted the offer. As a result, former guerrillas, if they repented, were employed as scouts tasked to find the hideouts of the remaining ones.[16] The Swedes in particular relied on levies from Småland to carry out counter-guerrilla operations in Scania. They were also used for convoy duty, so as to secure the communication lines.[17]

Since most of the guerrillas were Swedish subjects, the Swedish authorities regarded them as traitors and outlaws. They accordingly did whatever it took to suppress them. Punishments were ruthless. When captured, most would be executed, and many would be put to death in particularly gruesome fashion, for instance by being broken on the wheel or by impalement. They also did not distinguish between freeshooters and *snapphanar*; the freeshooters were not regarded as soldiers and both categories of men were treated as traitors if captured.

At the end of the war, the Danish Crown attempted to integrate their freeshooters into the regular forces. This turned out to be difficult, since the freeshooters did not accept military discipline. First, they spent considerably more time looting their fellow Scanians than fighting the Swedes. Second, the freeshooters refused to accept regular Danish officers within their companies, since they claimed only to accept the authority of their own leaders. In the end, some 400 surviving freeshooters were shipped across the Straits to Denmark. Of these, only 46 accepted service as dragoons in the Danish army. The rest preferred to demobilise. This produced its own set of problems. In the end, the Danish Crown found itself having to handle the reintegration of its freeshooters into civilian society. Most had never lived in Denmark, so it was often difficult to find them employment and accommodation. Most ended up in poverty, as second-class citizens.[18]

16 Ibid., pp.135–7, 159–60.

17 Ibid., p.88.

18 Ibid., pp.141, 142, 178.

12

The Siege of Bohus Fortress

On 8 June 1676, already before the invasion in Scania, Count Gyldenløve led a new offensive into western Sweden from Norway, with the support of his political advisor, Jens Juel, and his two generals, Rysensteen and Løwenhielm. His Norwegian army consisted of 400 cavalry, 3,600 infantry divided into nine battalions, and 12 cannons, in total some 4,000 men.[1]

There was no organised Swedish defence there, merely a few small and frequently isolated regular units, reinforced with several thousand peasant levies. The latter could provide a modicum of security against irregular Danish forces and banditry, which grew increasingly common during the war. This relieved the few regular units of at least this responsibility, even though the Swedish communication lines remained vulnerable.

Gyldenløve defeated a Swedish force of 1,600 men under Lieutenant General Hans Georg Mörner af Morlanda on 16 June at Kvistrum. Mörner was a veteran of the Thirty Years' War and the war in Poland who served as chief commandant in Gothenburg. He did not lack experience, but he lacked trained troops. Gyldenløve then pursued the retreating Swedes to Uddevalla, which he took on 17 June.[2] Then he moved against Vänersborg, which Mörner defended with some 3,000 men, most of whom were untrained levied peasants. Mörner had Vänersborg evacuated, burned the supplies stored there, and then he abandoned the town, which Gyldenløve took on 26 June 1676. Then Gyldenløve sent out detachments, some by boat on Lake Vänern, that ravaged the provinces of Bohuslän, Dal, and Västergötland.[3] Meanwhile, Gyldenløvein July led his 3,800 remaining men further south to Gothenburg, which he hoped to blockade both from land and sea. However, Admiral-Lieutenant Siöblad's squadron was still in the area, and, as noted, forced the Danish fleet under Marquor Rodsteen to withdraw. Without a fleet, and without the opportunity to move heavy siege artillery by sea, Gyldenløve concluded that he could not take Gothenburg. Instead he in mid-August attempted to lay siege to Bohus, a key fortress in western Sweden with a garrison of 1,400 men. Gyldenløve did bring some siege artillery overland. A

1 Vaupell, *Den danske hærs historie*, pp.112–14.

2 Ibid., p.112.

3 Wahlöö and Larsson, *Slaget vid Lund*, pp.113, 117.

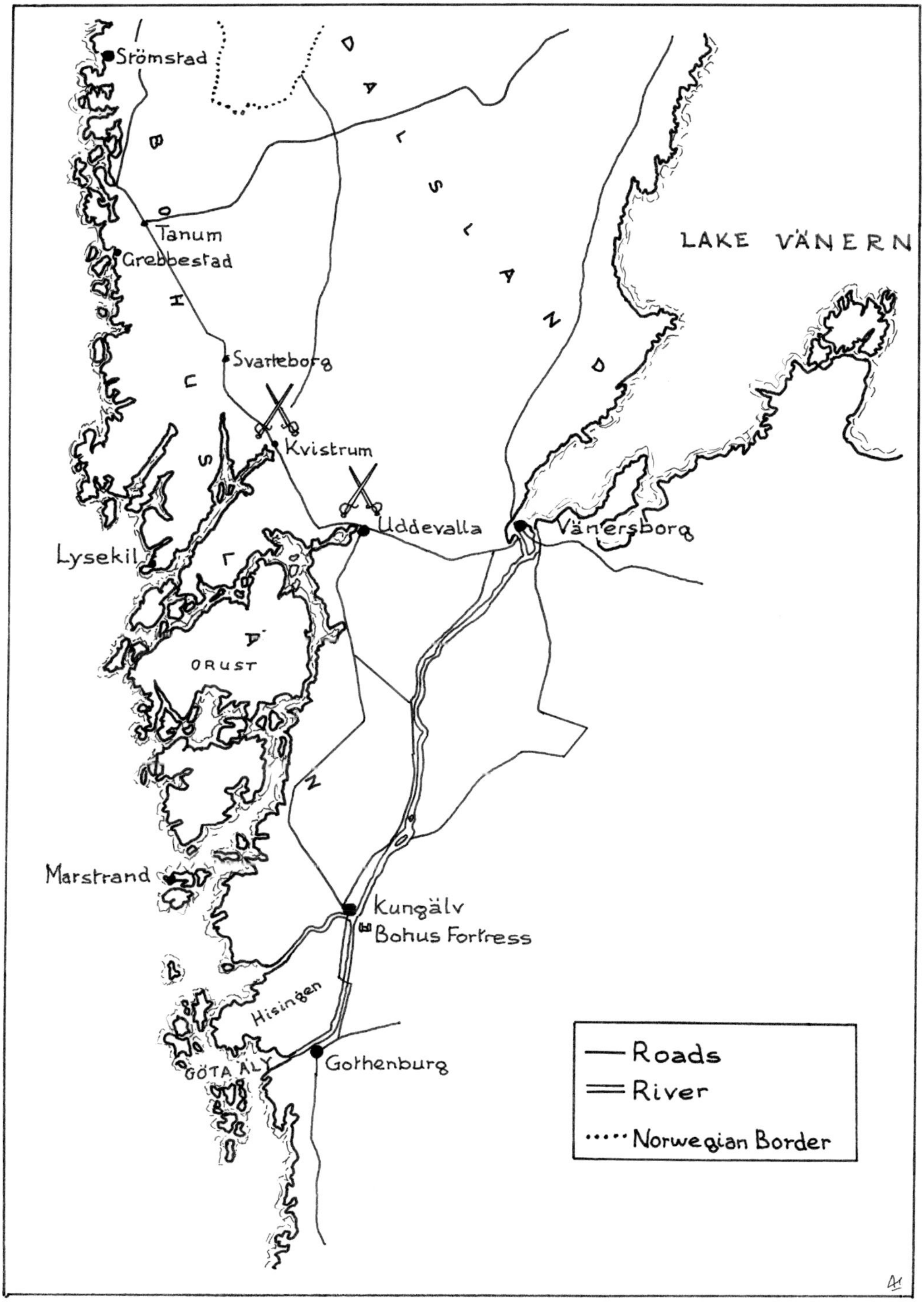

Map 3. The Gothenburg Region

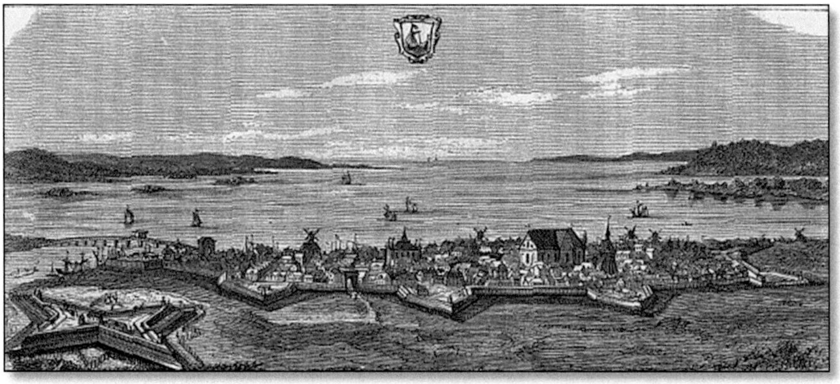

Vänersborg, late seventeenth century.

Swedish force of 3,000 men from Värmland under Colonel Jonas Hansson Gyllenspetz, head of the Närke-Värmland Regiment, attempted to oppose the Norwegians. However, he had only a few companies of regulars, the rest of his force being levied peasants, so he failed and had to return to Värmland.[4]

Bohus Fortress was defended by Lieutenant General Harald Stake, the governor of Bohuslän. Stake was a veteran of many wars, both in Dutch service and the Thirty Years' War. He had, in 1631, once saved King Gustavus Adolphus from being captured by Imperial troops. Since then he had fought in the wars against Denmark and Norway. By now 78 years old, Stake could only mount his horse with assistance, but this had not reduced his belligerence one bit.

Stake first attempted to prevent the Norwegians from reaching Bohus. Successful for a while, he was too short of men to prevent a Norwegian detachment from bypassing him. As the Norwegians then threatened his flank, Stake retreated, meanwhile burning bridges and making the road impassable. On 12 August, he also burned the town of Kungälv, under his fortress walls. The little that remained of the town after he had withdrawn into the fortress, he had burned with heated shot from the fortress's artillery, that is, round iron shot that had been heated before firing from cannon so that they would set fire to flammable objects.

Gyldenløve then laid siege to Bohus. Having succeeded in positioning an artillery battery in a captured bastion within range of the fortress, he sent a letter to Stake, asking for his surrender. Stake's reply, renowned in his own time for its insolence, in graphic terms described how he had used Gyldenløve's letter for wiping his behind.

Moreover, Gyldenløve had received intelligence that a large Swedish army under Lord High Chancellor Magnus De la Gardie was approaching, according to an incorrect report with a strength of 20,000 men. The Lord High Chancellor had led the regency government during the minority of King Charles and was chief among those responsible for Sweden's lack of fiscal and military preparedness. He had now been given the task to organise the defences of western Sweden.

4 Vaupell, *Den danske hærs historie*, pp.128–30.

Gyldenløve then lacked supplies of all sorts, not least since Stake had burned whatever had existed locally before withdrawing into his fortress. On 16 September, Gyldenløve abandoned the siege and retreated.[5]

The Danish plan seems to have been for Gyldenløve to advance to Gothenburg with his men to join forces with a 4,000-strong Danish expeditionary force under Major General Jacob Duncan, who from Scania had orders to take Halmstad, the key town in the province of Halland, and then march north to unite his forces with those of Gyldenløve. Certainly Gyldenløve was on his way to Gothenburg in July, and it would make sense that Duncan, who was sent north in early August, aimed to meet up with him. (There is no contemporary document that explains the Danish intention with Duncan's expedition. Yet, his men were too few to have a strategic impact on their own.)

Duncan, too, was an experienced officer. A Scotsman, he had entered into Swedish service in 1657 and achieved the rank of Lieutenant Colonel. He had sworn never to go to war against Sweden, but as we will see, this oath had been sworn lightly and Duncan did not even pay it lip-service. In 1671 Duncan took service with the Danes, with whom he advanced in rank to Major General.

In western Sweden, only a small Swedish force under Lieutenant General Mörner and Major General Jöran Sperlingh, the chief commandant and commandant in Gothenburg, respectively, opposed the Norwegians. The Swedish troops were unable to match the Norwegian invasion force. Yet it was imperative for the Swedes to prevent Duncan from joining forces with Gyldenløve.

The only Swedish formation that might be able to accomplish this was King Charles' field army, then in Växjö.

On 12 August 1676, Duncan had laid siege to the town of Halmstad. Halmstad was defended by Lieutenant General Johan Hård, of the af Segerstad family, who commanded 300 men. The fortifications were in poor condition. Moreover, Hård could not count on the townsmen, many of whom sympathised with the Danes.

5 Ibid., p.130.

13

The Battle for Halmstad

Having on 10 August received intelligence that Duncan was moving towards Halmstad, King Charles ordered his men to march the following day. The Swedish army covered 130 km in forced marches, with the men taking turns marching for one hour at a time, then riding on supply carts for the next hour. On 16 August, the Swedish army had reached Knäred, where supplies for once were plentiful. Knäred was about 15 km from the main road between Halmstad and Laholm.

The Danes had learnt that the Swedes were advancing, and King Christian did not want Duncan to be separated from Scania and the communication line to the Danish main army, so he ordered Duncan to retreat to the town of Laholm. Duncan accordingly abandoned the siege, burned his camp, and moved south across River Nissan. He could have stayed, preparing a defensive position north of the river. However, King Christian's orders said otherwise. So when the Swedish army reached Knäred, Duncan was preparing to slip away into Laholm.

Following six days of forced marches, most of the Swedish senior leadership advised King Charles that the army needed a night of rest before battle. However, General Ascheberg saw the danger in delay. He advised the King to continue moving, so as to prevent Duncan from escaping. King Charles agreed, and in the evening of 16 August, the Swedish army moved on, continuing the forced march towards the road between Laholm and Halmstad for another four to five hours under conditions of heavy rain.

During the night, King Charles and Ascheberg sent an advance party of 60 men from the Queen-Dowager's Life Regiment of Horse under Captain Roos with orders to seize and destroy the bridge over River Lagan at Laholm so as to prevent the Danes from retreating further south. A few hours later, Duncan sent a lieutenant and a few men to inspect the condition of the bridge. However, by then Roos and his party had already got there, and the Danish lieutenant had to return to Duncan, reporting that the bridge was destroyed. This, incidentally, also prevented the Danes from sending scouts to determine the position of the Swedish army.

Duncan's men had spent the night at rest, because of the rains. Early in the morning, they broke camp and continued the march towards Fyllebro, where a bridge across the River Fylleå once had enabled communications with Laholm. However, Duncan had previously had the bridge demolished. The river could be forded, but unwilling to abandon his supply train and artillery, Duncan delayed crossing while his men repaired the bridge.

At dawn on 17 August 1676, the Swedish army had seized the road between Halmstad and Laholm, thus cutting Duncan's communication line to the south. Despite the six days and one night of forced marches, the Swedish troops were ready to give battle, having had only three hours of sleep. Known as the Battle of Halmstad, the action really took place at Fyllebro (Appendix VII).[1]

General Ascheberg accompanied a cavalry unit of 300 men (three squadrons) under Lieutenant Colonel Ernst Johan Lode of the Scania-Bohuslän Dragoon Regiment that set out to scout for the Danish army. They reached the hill above River Fylleå just as the Danes had completed repairs of the bridge and begun to cross. Duncan, who did not know that Ascheberg was on the hill, ignored the Swedes, believing that they only were a small scouting party. However, he realised that time was of the essence, so while he crossed with his cavalry and infantry, he this time ordered the supply train to be burned, since it would only delay his retreat into Laholm further.

However, Lode and Ascheberg deployed their men in two lines, between two areas of marshland, and at a distance of only a musket shot from the Danes. Meanwhile, they sent a message to the King, demanding immediate reinforcements. It was by then between 8:00 and 9:00 a.m., and there had already been daylight for several hours, allowing the Swedish forces some rest after the forced marches.

Field Marshal Helmfelt immediately dispatched three additional cavalry squadrons. Then King Charles, tired of all reverses and retreats and eager to fight, rapidly followed with his Life Regiment of Horse and Drabant Guard, which together counted at least 8 squadrons. The infantry was left behind.

The rapid Swedish advance was risky, since a built-up area with fenced gardens and some marshland blocked access and forced the Swedish cavalry to advance in column, despite the proximity to the enemy. In fact, the terrain was so broken and difficult that many horses stumbled and broke their legs during the last stage's rush to get into position. Duncan could have ordered a general advance against the Swedes, but he failed to do so, since he did not realise that the entire Swedish army was moving up. He still believed that he dealt only with small scouting parties, since all were cavalry. In fact, Duncan had not been idle during the rainy night. In addition to the small force sent to River Lagan, Duncan had also dispatched cavalry scouts to determine if any Swedish troops were approaching. The Danish scouts had encountered a Swedish cavalry unit, and under cover of darkness and rain joined the rear ranks of the Swedish cavalry, trusting that they would not be recognised. Nor were they, and having ascertained that no Swedish infantry was to be seen, they had broken off and returned to Duncan to report. Since no

1 The best modern study of the battle is Arne Stade, "Slaget vid Halmstad (Fyllebro)", Göran Rystad (ed.), *Kampen om Skåne* (Lund: Historiska Media, 2005), pp.95–106, which also lists the primary sources.

Nils Bielke, 1679. (François de Troy)

Swedish infantry was near, Duncan had drawn the conclusion that the Swedish field army still was far away.

Duncan and his 3,500 men had now crossed the river. At this point, Ascheberg ordered his six squadrons, some 600 men, forward against the Danes. Although this was too small a force actually to defeat the Danish army, Duncan realised that he could no longer move on towards Laholm. He also could not retreat, since the bridge across River Fylleån could not accommodate all his men. Furthermore, the river valley was too narrow for him to deploy all his units in a line of battle. It was not only the Swedes who suffered from the broken terrain.

On the Swedish side, Field Marshal Helmfelt deployed his cavalry in two wings, with a considerable gap in-between so as to give the infantry and artillery sufficient space to form up in a centre when they finally arrived. The artillery, which was drawn on horse carriages, arrived first, deployed, and opened fire. It took an additional hour before the infantry approached. However, by then the Danes, who had been unable either to move forward or to retreat, were outnumbered. The Swedish army consisted of almost 7,000 men as compared to the 3,500 men in Duncan's army. On the other hand, the Danes were rested, while the Swedes had spent days and the greater part of two nights on forced marches with a minimum of food.

The Swedish army deployed in its customary manner, in two lines. Duncan, too, deployed his units in the traditional manner, with two wings and a centre, although due to his weakness in cavalry, he seems to have deployed them in only one line. In addition, he ordered a number of infantry units to deploy with the cavalry in the wings, so as to reinforce the cavalry.

Duncan sent his infantry and dragoons forward, under artillery cover, against the Swedish infantry just as the latter was arriving. Trop's Dragoon Regiment, led by Major Hein, charged the battalion from the Skaraborg Regiment, led by Colonel Friedrich von Börstell, a veteran of the wars with Denmark and Poland who spent his life at war and never married. Despite not quite having deployed in the line, the Swedish infantry managed to repulse the Danish dragoons, who fought by caracole. Still, Major Hein and some dragoons managed to break through the Skaraborg infantry. However, behind the Skaraborg troops advanced a squadron (of no more than company strength) of the Scanian Cavalry Regiment under Lieutenant Colonel Georg Johan Maydell. Hemmed in, Hein surrendered to Maydell.

Meanwhile, more Swedish infantry arrived, including eventually three infantry battalions of His Majesty's Life Guard on Foot under Colonel Christoffer Gyllenstierna, a close friend of King Charles's. The first battalion of the Life Guard faced the two Danish battalions from Rosencrantz's Regiment, which were protected by swinefeathers and mobile *chevaux-de-frise*. The Danes had improved the concept by making the *cheval-de-frise* mobile by adding wheels, like a cart.

Still, and despite heavy losses including Gyllenstierna who was hit by a shot to the shoulder, the Life Guard managed to push through the defences and break the Danish battalions. Major Jacob Johan Hastfehr, the commander of the Life Guard's third battalion, pushed on towards the river. On the Danish side, Colonel Maximilian Rosencrantz attempted to cover Duncan's retreat across the bridge with his own infantry regiment and the support of Lieutenant Colonel Joachim Frederik Lützow, who commanded a squadron of Trop's Dragoon Regiment. It did not work. Three Danish battalion commanders were lost; Colonel Rosencrantz fell from a shot to the forehead. Lieutenant Colonel Frederik Wilhelm von Warnstedt, of Rosencrantz's Regiment, received no less than 10 wounds, and was captured (he survived and was subsequently exchanged). Lieutenant Colonel Lützow fought until the end, killing no less than 17 Swedes before he fell, 'wounded, but fighting' as the Swedes wrote on a subsequent memorial at the site. The survivors of their battalions fled across the River Fylleån.[2]

On the Swedish right wing, King Charles, Ascheberg, and Dahlbergh led the charge. Ascheberg was shot, receiving two serious wounds in his left upper arm, by a Danish cavalry captain who then himself fell. Colonel Nils Bielke charged with the Life Regiment in what he described as *à la Françoise*, "in the French manner", which meant that the cavalrymen fired their pistols, then immediately charged home with rapiers.[3] Bielke was hit by a shot that was deflected by his rapier hilt, then he was wounded by a Danish officer with a partisan.

Having defeated the Danish cavalry, Bielke and the Life Regiment waded across the river and prepared to fall on Colonel Burchard Heinrich Münchhausen's cavalry and the retreating Danish centre from the rear. For Duncan and the Danes, the retreat ended in chaos. Duncan had no other option but to send a trumpeter, offering his surrender.

The battle had been over quickly. According to the Danes, combat lasted only for an hour. Swedish sources said that the action had been over in 15 minutes. Since not all units had arrived at the same time, the time probably depended on the observer's position in the line. So much is clear, however, that the action was short but fierce.

The Danes lost almost 3,000 men, of whom more than 2,000 were captured. According to the official report, 1,567 were captured, including both Major General Duncan and Colonel Trop. In addition, 469 men accepted enrolment in the Swedish army. These were distributed among various Swedish units.[4] No more than 500 to 600 Danish troops managed to withdraw from the battle to re-join the Danish main force in Scania.

2 Vaupell, *Den danske hærs historie*, pp.126–7.

3 Per Sondén, *Nils Bielke och det svenska kavalleriet 1674–1679* (Dissertation, Uppsala University, 1883), p.28.

4 Stade, "Slaget vid Halmstad", p.106 n.33.

Swedish losses were small. According to the official report, total losses were 185 men, of whom 3 officers and 38 common soldiers were dead. Six officers were wounded including Ascheberg, Gyllenstierna, and Maydell.

King Charles rewarded his men after the victory. Among those who were particularly honoured was Major Peter Weinholtz of the Scania-Bohuslän Dragoon Regiment who had captured a Danish standard.[5] The Swedes captured 13 cannons, 2 mortars, and 45 standards which were sent to Stockholm.[6] Colonel Gyllenstierna was promoted to Major General after the battle.

The Swedish victory at Halmstad may have saved Gothenburg, since it prevented Gyldenløve and Duncan from joining forces. However, from a Danish perspective, the battle was not regarded as a serious reverse. The Danes expected that Gyldenløve would be able to take Gothenburg on his own. However, Gyldenløve returned with his army to Norway in September, having received news from King Christian that the Danish army was moving into winter quarters.[7]

For the Swedes, the victory reinforced morale. Perhaps they could still turn the tide.

However, immediately after the victory at Halmstad, King Charles received the news that Kristianstad had fallen a few days previously.

After the victory, the Swedish army marched to Halmstad to destroy the siegeworks begun by Duncan. Following a day engaged in this venture, the army continued northwards. The Swedish army remained too weak to confront the Danish main army.

5 Gustaf Björlin, *Kriget mot Danmark 1675–1679* (Stockholm: P.A. Norstedt & Söner, 1885), p.90. Like the works of Vaupell, Jensen, and Gulowsen, Björlin's popular history is useful but contains some inaccuracies.

6 Wahlöö and Larsson, *Slaget vid Lund*, p.116.

7 Almgren, "Svensk strategi", p.48.

14

The Danes Go into Winter Quarters, the Swedes Take the Offensive

King Charles's situation was not enviable, despite the victory. The Swedish army at this time consisted of only 3,500 cavalry and 1,800 infantry. The eagerly awaited reinforcements from the Swedish heartland, the north, and Finland had not yet arrived. The navy, on which the King had pinned his hopes for an offensive strategy, had been defeated and would not be able to set out again this year. Siöblad's Gothenburg squadron had arrived too late to save the Swedish territories in Bremen-Verden. Gyldenløve remained undefeated in Bohuslän, with some 3,800 men, all of which he controlled except Gothenburg and a few forts. His men had ravaged the provinces of Västergötland and Dal. Gyldenløve also threatened Gothenburg, which had a garrison of only 1,500 men. Moreover, Gothenburg was also under threat from the sea, where Johan Vibe commanded a Danish squadron. However, at least Siöblad's decisive patrolling prevented Gyldenløve from bringing any heavy siege artillery across the sea.[1] The ravaged provinces suffered from famine and disease. And immediately after the victory, King Charles had learnt that Kristianstad had fallen, as well.

Meanwhile, considerable Danish reinforcements had been shipped across the Straits. Entire new regiments had arrived. Having just taken Kristianstad, King Christian ordered another attempt to lay siege to Halmstad, since the Swedish army had left. He then led his field army across Scania, from Kristianstad to Halmstad, adding the reinforcements to his own army while underway. Three cavalry regiments from the campaign in Pomerania now joined the field army (the Life Regiment Cavalry under Major General Hans Wilhelm Meerheim, the Schleswig Cavalry Regiment under Colonel Henrik Sehested, and Rauch's Cavalry Regiment under Colonel Gottfried Rauch, together with two infantry battalions (Schönberg and Bremer) from Mecklenburg. The King also ordered four of the battalions in Holstein (one each from the Holstein

1 Vaupell, *Den danske hærs historie*, pp.128–9

Regiment, 1st Fyn Regiment, Baudissin's Regiment, and Lütken's Regiment)to be sent to Scania.[2] However, it was autumn, and despite the massive number of Danes outside Halmstad, the commandant, Lieutenant General Hård, refused to surrender, so King Christian abandoned the siege.

The Danes followed Continental habits and accordingly prepared to send the army into camp for the duration of the winter. On 25 September, the Danish army left the region around Halmstad and returned south. They prepared winter quarters along the River Rönneå in northern Scania. On 5 October, King Christian, Prince George, and Field Marshal Johann Hans Adolf, Duke of Schleswig-Holstein-Sonderburg-Plön, returned to Copenhagen, where living conditions were better. The active campaign season was over, or so they thought. The King's return was celebrated with luxurious fireworks.[3] King Christian then dismissed the Duke as commander of the Danish army, since the latter did not always agree with him.[4]

However, King Christian had neglected that northern armies more often than not continued operations also in winter. King Charles had no reason to wait for spring. Rather, he had more to lose than gain by delaying, since conditions in the field were appalling, he lacked supplies, and men were dying from disease and starvation. The communication lines suffered from repeated attacks by guerrillas and bandits. On the other hand, the Danes had comfortable quarters, were well supplied, and could bring fresh reinforcements across the Straits from the Danish heartland, which was within easy reach. Charles had only some 5,000 men, but having waited in Åskloster for almost a month, he led the army south, in the direction of Malmö, which remained in Swedish hands.

On 1 October, a new Danish containment force had been sent to Malmö, consisting of the recently arrived Life Regiment Cavalry, under Meerheim, and Rauch's Cavalry Regiment, under Rauch. King Charles attempted to reach Malmö without being detected by the Danes. This failed, however. The Danish army left its winter quarters, again prepared for battle, and King Christian and Prince George returned from Copenhagen, by way of Helsingborg, reaching the army on 17 October. On 16 October, Major General Anders Sandberg had set out on a reconnaissance ride with 200 cavalry of his 3rd Jutland Cavalry Regiment to the border against the province of Småland. On 20 October, he returned, able to report that all was calm; King Charles was not moving.[5] His information was correct, but unknown to the Danes, the timing of his patrol was wrong.

King Charles had finally received some of the reinforcements from the Swedish heartlands. On 19 October, Lieutenant General Johan Galle arrived with reinforcements from the north and Finland, where he lived. On 20 October, a general review of the army counted some 12,000 fighting men, formed in 50 squadrons and 9 battalions, with 30 cannons. It was supposed

2 Ibid., pp.127–8.
3 Wahlöö and Larsson, *Slaget vid Lund*, p.118.
4 Nielsen, "Dansk strategi", p.78.
5 Wahlöö and Larsson, *Slaget vid Lund*, pp.17, 117, 118.

to be 18,000, but all reinforcements had not arrived and diseases had taken their toll.[6] On 21 October, King Charles again led the field army to Scania.

There was a basic divergence between the Danish and Swedish understanding of the principles of war. The Danes, following continental practices, paid more heed to outmanoeuvring their enemy than searching out and destroying his military units. It follows that there was also a focus on fortified strongpoints and siege warfare. Accordingly, the Danes thought that King Charles was trying to get to Malmö, the only remaining fortified position in Scania in Swedish hands.[7] However, the Swedes, looking back to the winning strategies employed during the Thirty Years' War and the previous wars against Denmark, argued that the only objective that counted was to engage and decisively defeat the enemy's military forces on the battlefield.[8]

The Danes thought that King Charles would take the newly built road from Älmhult over Loshult to Kristianstad, so they tried to block this approach. However, King Charles instead followed the old road over Markaryd, where the army arrived on 23 October. Yet, he found that this road had been temporarily blocked, too – not by Danish troops but by pro-Danish peasants in Fagerhult just south of the traditional border who had built timber obstacles, that is, abatis, or barricades of felled trees. This was a traditional feature of northern warfare. The Swedish advance guard had to spend the night between 23 and 24 October clearing the road.[9] The peasants were led by Colonel Detlef von Örtzen and two companies of his dragoon regiment. Örtzen's objective does not seem to have been to resist the Swedish army, only to gather intelligence on it. Having ascertained the Swedish strength, Örtzen abandoned the timber obstacles and returned to the Danish headquarters.

At the same time, two small Swedish expeditionary forces, one under General Pontus Fredrik De la Gardie and the other under Ebbe Ulfeldt, moved into Blekinge. The regular units were reinforced by peasant levies from Jönköping, Kronoberg, and Kalmar counties. Ulfeldt, it will be remembered, was the former Danish noble who had set up the original Danish freeshooter companies in the 1643–1645 war with Sweden. A Scanian noble in Imperial and Spanish service during the Thirty Years' War, Ulfeldt had returned to Denmark in 1641, married a daughter of King Christian IV, and become county governor in Kristianstad. However, a dispute with the Danish Crown made him move to Sweden in 1652. Since he was a Scanian, he willingly became a Swedish subject when the Danish Crown in 1658 ceded Scania to Sweden. With the outbreak of the Scanian War, Ulfeldt again raised local irregulars, but this time on behalf of the Swedish Crown. His formal rank was Lieutenant General, although he never served as such.

On 29 October, a Swedish unit encountered a Danish column with 270 mostly wounded and ill Danish soldiers at Hyllinge. According to a

6 Almgren, "Svensk strategi", pp.49, 69 n.49.

7 Jensen, *Den skaanske krig*, p.164.

8 Generalstaben, *Karl XII på slagfältet 1*, p.167.

9 Wahlöö and Larsson, *Slaget vid Lund*, pp.18, 119.

contemporary rumour, the Danish column had been commanded by a German captain, known as Michel Smeihler, who refused to continue the journey until he had finished drinking at the local inn. By ill luck, the delay meant that the Swedish unit caught up with them. The Danes were taken away in captivity, but those who were ill, that is, most of them, were killed on the spot.[10]

On 30 October, the Swedes attacked Helsingborg, which was defended by Colonel Møller with three infantry and one mounted company.[11] The town fell, although the citadel remained in Danish hands. The Swedes looted Helsingborg, then on 31 October withdrew to Bårslöv, southeast of Helsingborg. A force of 1,000 Swedish troops were left to contain the town and citadel.[12]

The Swedish army remained at Bårslöv for nine days. The camp became known as the 'dirt camp' (*lortlägret*),[13] since it had the worst sanitary conditions by far that the soldiers had ever experienced, in an age when camps all too often were unsanitary. It was November, with heavy rains, cold, and frost. Everything was soaked. There was some bread and salt, but no lodgings, dry firewood, fresh water, food, or fodder. The men died from diseases, and in particular dysentery. The 12,000 Swedes were soon reduced to 10,000.

As for King Charles, he had taken lodgings in the house of the parish priest at Bårslöv. Although certainly far better than the dirt camp, this soon posed another problem. The Danes learnt about his location and on 4 November aimed to destroy the house and kill King Charles through a sudden artillery bombardment. No less than nine cannon shot hit the house, destroying the roof. Some shot penetrated the bedroom used by the King Charles. King Charles survived, but a passing peasant was killed.[14]

The Danish field army took up positions at Kvisttofta opposite the Swedes. However, in between the two armies was a gorge, River Råå, which prevented the adversaries from attacking each other, since doing so would have resulted in certain ruin. This did not prevent skirmishes, several of which took place.

Although well-supplied, the Danish field army suffered from disease, like the Swedish one, but it did receive reinforcements.[15] Major General Meerheim abandoned his containment of Malmö on 30 October, bringing his two regiments to join the field army. Malmö would remain uncontained by Danish troops until 11 November.[16]

Finally, King Christian retreated south towards Glumslöv. He hoped that the Swedes would follow, so that he could defeat them at a suitable location north of Landskrona. However, King Charles on the evening of 9 November left the dirt camp at Bårslöv and crossed at Tågarp.[17] He then moved on towards Kävlinge, so as to separate the Danes from easy access to Malmö and

---

10 Jacobsen, *Den Nordiske Kriigs Krøniche*, p.63.

11 Vaupell, *Den danske hærs historie*, p.137.

12 Wahlöö and Larsson, *Slaget vid Lund*, pp.119–20.

13 Martin Weibull (ed.), "Johan Adolph Clodts anteckningar", *Historisk Tidskrift* 3 (1883), pp.203–24 and pp.279–322, on p.295.

14 Wahlöö and Larsson, *Slaget vid Lund*, p.120; Isacson, *Skånska kriget*, pp.39–40.

15 Vaupell, *Den danske hærs historie*, pp.139–40.

16 Wahlöö and Larsson, *Slaget vid Lund*, p.119.

17 Ibid., p.120.

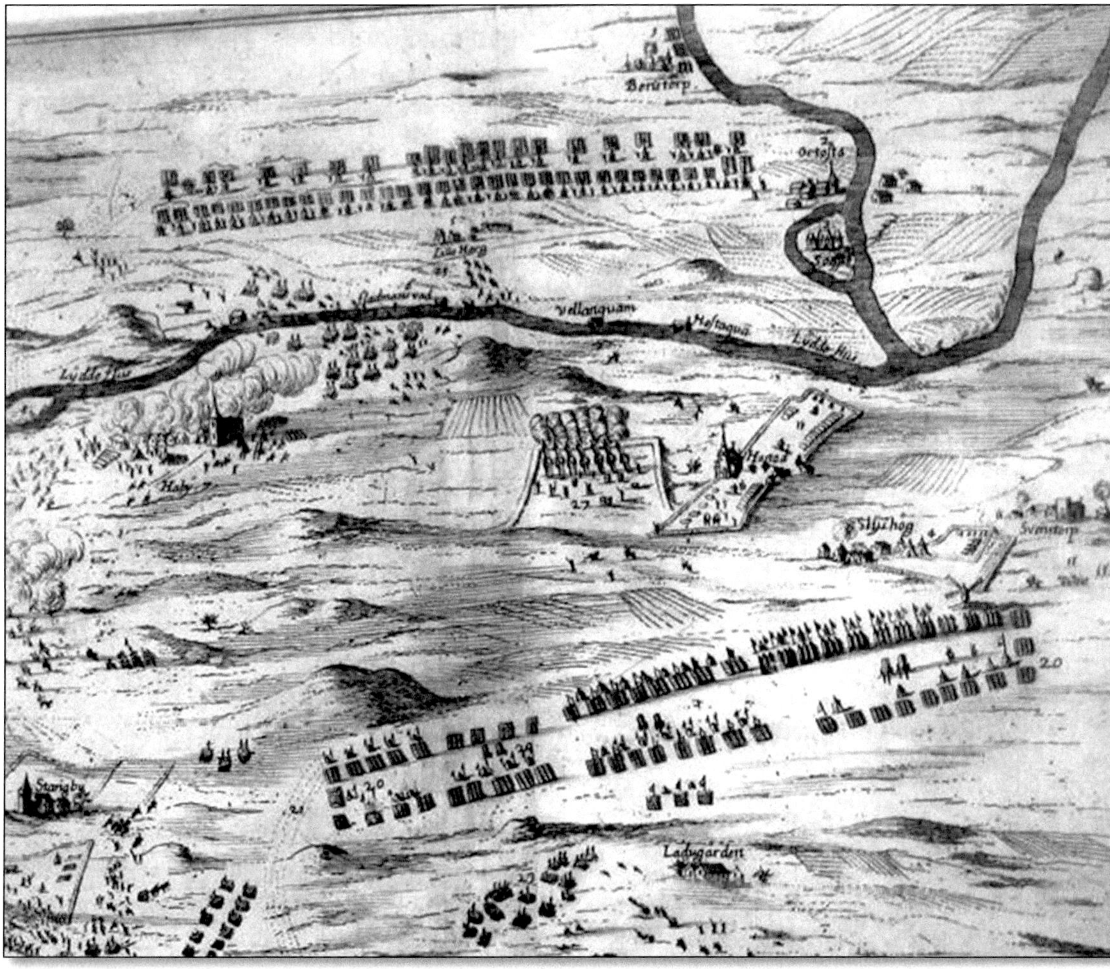

The two camps, on each side of River Kävlinge, at the Battle of Lund, 1676. (Erik Dahlbergh)

Kristianstad. Danish scouts discovered the Swedish army, and the Danish army began to move southeast, following the Swedish army (which was on its left flank) at a distance of less than 10 km.

The Danes reached River Kävlinge (*Kävlinge Å*) and on 10 November moved into camp south of the river, on a ridge south of Svenstorp Castle (which provided quarters for King Christian) at the village Skälshög, where the headquarters was established. The location blocked one of the main roads to Lund, and thereby Malmö as well, and was located close enough to the other two so that they could be blocked as well.[18] The Swedes, arriving at the river but finding the road to Malmö blocked, on 11 November established a camp at Lilla Harrie, with King Charles and his headquarters in the village Benstorp. This location was even worse than the hated dirt camp. There was hardly any food, fresh water, or beer, and no fodder for the horses. Disease continued to take its toll among the Swedish troops. Several hundred men were incapacitated by illness or died each day. The corpses were laid up in piles in cemeteries or next

18 Ibid., pp.21–22.

to churches, or were simply stacked along the roads. With the ground frozen, it was impossible to bury them as fast as men died.

King Christian may not have realised how eager King Charles was for battle. So far, the war had been little different from the kind of warfare common on the Continent, with a focus on outmanoeuvring the enemy and laying siege to his strongholds. As a result, King Christian did not expect a set battle. With the cold becoming worse, and the rivers freezing, he should have realised that River Kävlinge could not protect his camp for much longer. He could have moved the camp to the heights just north of Lund, where he could have blocked the road to Malmö just as easily. Instead he made preparations seemingly unrelated to what was to come. On 10 November, the dismissed overall commander Johann Hans Adolf, Duke of Schleswig-Holstein-Sonderburg-Plön, returned to the Danish camp, but only formally to relinquish command. It would have been natural to appoint Field Marshal Lieutenant Adam von Weyher in his stead; however, Weyher had died in October.[19] The Duke was accordingly replaced by Carl von Arensdorff, an officer born in Mecklenburg, who had served with the Swedish, Danish, and Dutch armies in several wars. And on 11 November, King Christian sent a cavalry force of 1,000 men to Malmö, which had been left uncontained since Meerheim's departure.[20]

On 12 November, the Danes brought up artillery on the other side of the river across Lilla Harrie, then fired at the Swedish camp for several hours. Apparently, no major damage was inflicted. In response, the Swedes moved artillery to the river and during the evening fired at the village of Västra Hoby with heated shot. The village burned down, but again no particular damage was caused to the Danish army.

On 14 November, Count Gyldenløve visited the Danish camp at Skälshög, coming from Norway to co-ordinate strategy with King Christian. Admiral Tromp had arrived as well, and Gyldenløve and Tromp left together, on 29 November. Gyldenløve then returned to Norway by ship. As soon as Tromp had departed, Admiral Juel went to see King Christian in his headquarters.[21] Their journey was not free of risks, since then both sides launched frequent scouting and reconnaissance missions, and this often led to minor engagements between the cavalry units involved. On 17 November, King Charles, too, participated in one such mission, as did on different occasions other senior officers. On the night between 20 and 21 November, Major General Meerheim and Colonel Conrad Reventlow led a Danish cavalry force across the River Kävlinge. This kind of small war was Meerheim's speciality; he and his men regularly raided the villages on the Swedish side of the river, burning food and fodder, so as to deny the Swedes supplies.[22]

19 Nielsen, "Dansk strategi", pp.78–9.

20 Wahlöö and Larsson, *Slaget vid Lund*, p.120.

21 Th. Bjerre, *Fra Flådens arkiver: Dannebrog fra kongebanner til orlogsflag og fane; Niels Juel og bådsfolkets skæbne i slaget ved Lund, 4. december 1676* (Copenhagen: Våbenhistorisk Selskab, 1958), pp.54, 60.

22 Wahlöö and Larsson, *Slaget vid Lund*, pp.21–27, 121.

15

The Battle of Lund

Since the Battle of Halmstad, it had been a war of manoeuvre, in the Continental fashion. King Charles and his senior commanders understood that this could not continue. They had no choice; if they returned north with the starving army, the Danes would no doubt retain their grip on Scania indefinitely. If he attacked the Danes, it was far from certain – in fact, quite unlikely – that his ill-fed men would win. The Swedish army consisted of about 7,500 men (with non-combatants and those unfit for duty included, probably some 9,000 men), as compared to at least some 11,000 to 11,500 Danes. In addition, the Danish army was reinforced by some 1,000 to 1,500 sailors, although they were of dubious ability in a land battle. A third option was to push forward, attempting to cross the River Kävlinge despite the nearby Danish camp and then move into Malmö, where there still were supplies.

Moreover, yet more reinforcements had arrived from the Swedish heartland, the north, and Finland, including but not limited to two infantry companies from the Hälsinge Regiment, commanded by Ascheberg's son, the 25-year-old Lieutenant Colonel Georg Friedrich von Ascheberg, who arrived on 24 November, and Colonel Klas Johan Baranoff's Finnish cavalry, the Åbo-Viborg Cavalry Regiment, a newly raised, enlisted unit which arrived on 27 November (Appendix VIII).[1] Baranoff was the son of a Russian nobleman who had gone into Swedish service; now in his mid fifties, Baranoff had previously fought in Germany after which he was commissioned to raise a cavalry regiment in Finland, which he now led.

On the evening of 30 November, the first strong winter cold came, together with snow, so that the nearby rivers began to freeze. Since this would facilitate the army's ability to move across the country, King Charles decided to attack. Yet, was the fresh ice strong enough to carry the whole army? Each night, Dahlbergh and Ascheberg, at times probably accompanied by King Charles as well, went to measure the thickness of the ice. On 2 December, King Charles decided to attack. On this date, he signed and dispatched a letter, in code, to Fabian von Fersen, the Governor-General of Scania and commandant in Malmö, informing him of his decision. Dahlbergh and

1 Ibid., p.121.

Ascheberg again inspected the thickness of the ice in River Kävlinge during the night. Dahlbergh determined that the ice was 10 cm thick, which, he concluded, was sufficient. On the evening of the following day, King Charles wrote a letter to his mother, informing her that he would 'be victorious or die'. The letter, which in effect was his last will, also specified where he wanted to be buried, if he fell in the battle.[2]

On the same evening, everybody prepared for the ensuing battle, which would be fought on 4 December 1676. The Swedish troops wrapped a wreath of straw around their left arms and put a whisk of straw in the band around their wide-brimmed felt hats, so as to distinguish themselves from the Danes who used white arm bands and put white paper sheets into their hatbands as markers.

The Reintroduction of Proven Tactics

King Charles and Rutger von Ascheberg had already before the battle ordered the troops to utilise more aggressive tactics, and on the eve, they reminded them again. The essence of the new tactics was not merely to engage with muskets or carbines but actually to charge home into the enemy formation. The new instructions applied to both infantry and cavalry.

King Charles had ordered Field Marshal Helmfelt to deploy the infantry units in three ranks. When the infantry had reached a distance of 80 paces from the enemy, they would fire by rank, that is, the first rank would stop to fire a first volley. This would immediately be followed by a volley from the second rank, which marched through the first rank, then halted to fire. The third rank would then continue through the second, and discharge a third volley. Having reloaded as rapidly as possible, the troops would continue the advance until reaching a distance of 10–12 paces, when the enemy's white of the eye was visible, Then, all three ranks would fire, simultaneously, a final volley. The first rank would kneel and fire, the second rank would fire from the fork rest, and the third rank standing ("with raised head"). After the final volley, the infantry would charge, 'with the rapier in hand and the musket reversed', as King Charles said, that is, with hand-to-hand weapons and musket butts. Helmfelt had, at first, been doubtful about this, telling the King that although he had participated in 10 campaigns including during the Thirty Years' War, he had never experienced infantry charging into other infantry under such conditions. The weaker infantry force would likely retreat, thus evading the charge, he suggested. Yet King Charles was convinced of the value of the new tactics, and henceforth, the Swedish infantry would employ them. On the eve of the battle, King Charles repeated these instructions to the Life Guard and other units.[3]

The cavalry would employ more aggressive tactics, too. During the Thirty Years' War, Gustavus Adolphus had ordered his cavalry to charge home with

2 Wahlöö and Larsson, *Slaget vid Lund*, pp.30–31, 32, 122.

3 Weibull, "Johan Adolph Clodts anteckningar", pp.299–300. The words between King Charles and Helmfelt, as related by the junior officer Clodt, suggest a prearranged, motivational performance.

Plate A

The Swedish Army, Battle of Lund, 1676

1. Mounted Drabant, His Majesty's Life Guard of Horse; 2. Trooper, Life Regiment of Horse; 3. Trooper, Baranoff's Åbo-Viborg Cavalry Regiment

(Illustrations by Sergey Shamenkov, © Helion & Company) See Colour Plate Commentaries for further information.

Plate B

The Swedish Army, Battle of Lund, 1676

1. Musketeer, Dalecarlia Regiment; 2. Artilleryman, Artillery Regiment; 3. Pikeman, Västgöta-Dal Regiment

(Illustrations by Sergey Shamenkov, © Helion & Company) See Colour Plate Commentaries for further information.

Plate C

The Danish Army, Battle of Lund, 1676

1. Trooper, Life Regiment Cavalry; 2. Officer, Prince George's Regiment; 3. Musketeer, the Queen's Life Regiment

(Illustrations by Sergey Shamenkov, © Helion & Company) See Colour Plate Commentaries for further information.

Plate D

The Danish Army, Battle of Lund, 1676

1. Musketeer, Sailors' Battalion; 2. Danish Irregular; 3. Pikeman, 1st Fyn National Regiment

(Illustrations by Sergey Shamenkov, © Helion & Company) See Colour Plate Commentaries for further information.

Plate E

Swedes, Danes, and Norwegians

1. Officer, Swedish Naval Regiment, 1676; 2. Musketeer, Norwegian Akershus Regiment; 3. Swedish Sailor

(Illustrations by Sergey Shamenkov, © Helion & Company) See Colour Plate Commentaries for further information.

Plate F

Swedish Standards

1. Cavalry Regimental Standard, Baranoff's Åbo-Viborg Cavalry Regt., 1676;
2. Cavalry Standard, Vadsbo Company, Life Regiment of Horse, 1679;
3. Infantry Company Flag, Dalecarlia Regiment, 1676;
4. Infantry Company Flag, Västgöta-Dal Regiment

(Illustrations by Sergey Shamenkov, © Helion & Company) See Colour Plate Commentaries for further information.

Plate G

Danish Standards, Battle of Lund, 1676

1. Infantry Regimental Colour; 2. Infantry Flag, Sailors' Company;
3. Infantry Company Flag, 3rd Jutland Regiment

(Illustrations by Sergey Shamenkov, © Helion & Company) See Colour Plate Commentaries for further information.

Plate H

1

3

2

4

Swedish, Danish, and Norwegian Standards

1. Swedish Infantry Colour, Naval Regiment, 1676;
2. Danish Cavalry Standard, 1676;
3. Danish Infantry Colour, Sailors' Battalion;
4. Infantry Flag, Norwegian Sailors' Company

(Illustrations by Sergey Shamenkov, © Helion & Company) See Colour Plate Commentaries for further information.

the sword, with only the first or, at most, the first two ranks discharging their pistols and then only when they saw the whites of the enemy's eyes. Carbines were not used at all during a charge (commonly employed during the caracole, after the 1632 Battle of Lützen Imperial supreme commander Albrecht von Wallenstein, too, forbid their use[4]). Although this practice had since fallen into disuse, Charles and Ascheberg now wanted to revive it. At King Charles's request, Ascheberg had on 23 November issued new orders for the cavalry. The new regulations decreed that a cavalryman was not allowed to discharge his pistol until he saw the whites of his enemy's eyes, and then he was to press home the attack 'with force' (*medh gewalt*), that is, charging home with rapier alone without wasting time discharging his second pistol, so as to penetrate into the enemy formation.[5] There would be no caracole. When during the ensuing battle, a Swedish squadron still tried to caracole, Helmfelt ordered them not to. The same went for other senior Swedish officers, such as Lieutenant General von Fersen, who actively discouraged the use of carbines, since their use, because it took place at a greater distance than pistols, dissuaded the men from getting close enough to the enemy to see the whites of his eyes. In addition, Ascheberg ordered the cavalrymen to stay in close order even when the enemy was fleeing. No dispersing or looting was permitted.[6] Ascheberg's instructions included the command that when a squadron had broken through an enemy formation, it must be prepared to meet the enemy reserve behind it. Then, and only then, should all officers and men be ready to fire their second pistol.[7] In other words, speed, shock, and the discipline to maintain close order formed the essence of the tactics to be employed, and the objective was to penetrate and break through the enemy formation so as to scatter it.

Henceforth, carbines were primarily used when dragoons fought on foot, on picket duty, or when foraging. Moreover, Ascheberg's instructions eventually formed the foundation for the 1685 regulations which specified that cavalry, in a line formation consisting of three ranks, would trot until it reached a distance of 200–300 paces from the enemy formation, then charge rapidly. The first rank, only, discharged pistols at a distance of 50–75 paces. Then the entire unit would charge home.[8] By the last quarter of the seventeenth century, this was also, incidentally, the approach used by the French cavalry.

---

4 Richard Brzezinski, *Lützen 1632: Climax of the Thirty Years' War* (Oxford: Osprey Campaign 68, 2001), p.90 with note.

5 Alf Åberg (ed.), *Fältmarskalken Rutger von Aschebergs journal och korrespondens till år 1680* (Stockholm, Historiska Handlingar 34:1, 1951), pp.1–267, on pp.188–90 (Paragraph 4). Based on this paragraph alone, some historians eventually drew the erroneous conclusion that Ascheberg's tactics were new and did not allow the cavalryman to discharge even one of his pistols, since he forbid the men to fire before the enemy (to prevent them from the temptation of opening fire while still too far away). Not so. The tactic was a revival of the practice introduced during the Thirty Years' War.

6 Ibid., (Paragraph 7).

7 Ibid., (Paragraph 5), which also shows that the first pistol then already was discharged.

8 Generalstaben, *Karl XII på slagfältet 1*, p.227.

Preliminary Skirmishes

With the exception of a few patrols, the Swedish army began to move at 1:30 a.m. (Map 5).[9] The ice had been reinforced with wooden planks in two locations to provide temporary bridges for the artillery and supply carts. It is likely that the ice had been reinforced elsewhere as well, in the traditional manner of adding straw and slush which gradually reinforced the ice as the slush refroze, but the sources are silent on this point. Moonlight was strong, and the men risked being spotted against the snowy fields. So as not to be seen, the army awaited the setting of the moon, which took place at 2:25 a.m. The army formed up in five columns, each facing the river. Furthest to the west was the infantry and artillery of the centre. To the east of them stood the right wing, divided into two columns. Furthermost to the east was the left wing, again divided into two columns. Despite the darkness, it was easy to march across the snow-covered ground, since the white snow provided a measure of illumination and also enabled the columns to maintain the proper direction and the appropriate distance between columns, since tracks were easily visible.

The army soon crossed River Kävlinge, beginning about 4:00 a.m. The right wing crossed first, each man leading his horse. At 5:30 a.m., the entire army had crossed. Last followed parts of the supply train, after the artillery. The advance guard moved south first, followed by the right wing, the centre, and finally the left wing. It remained dark, since the moon had set long ago and it still was a long time until dawn. Yet, the Danish lookouts, only some 3 km away, must have maintained poor discipline, since they failed to notice the crossing of the entire Swedish army. At one point of leaving camp, even a fire broke out, which destroyed some 20 hovels. There was noise as well, in particular from the horses and the supply train. Dahlbergh later claimed that the sound must have been heard as much as 10 km away, an exaggeration but probably not a great one. That this went unnoticed says something about how noisy and ramshackle army camps usually were. In other words, the Danish sentries must have noticed the commotion, but the Danes failed to heed it. Probably their officers concluded that the Swedish army was retreating. Alternatively, they may have thought that a single Swedish unit was attempting to bypass the Danish camp and move to reinforce the garrison in Malmö. At least such rumours later flourished among the Danish senior officers, then overheard by a Swedish prisoner of war, Wilhelm von Fersen. Or possibly, they thought the commotion was just a regular, everyday disturbance. For the failure to pay attention to the commotion when the Swedish army moved out, King Christian eventually needed a scapegoat, so he blamed Major General Anders Sandberg,

9 It is impossible to reconcile all sources to the battle, or for that matter most secondary works, because of numerous inconsistencies. The best modern study is Arne Stade, "Slaget vid Lund", Göran Rystad (ed.), *Kampen om Skåne* (Lund: Historiska Media, 2005), pp.107–162, which also describes the primary sources. The description here fundamentally follows Stade, although some additional details have been added. The second-best is Wahlöö and Larsson, *Slaget vid Lund*, who fundamentally follow Stade's interpretation.

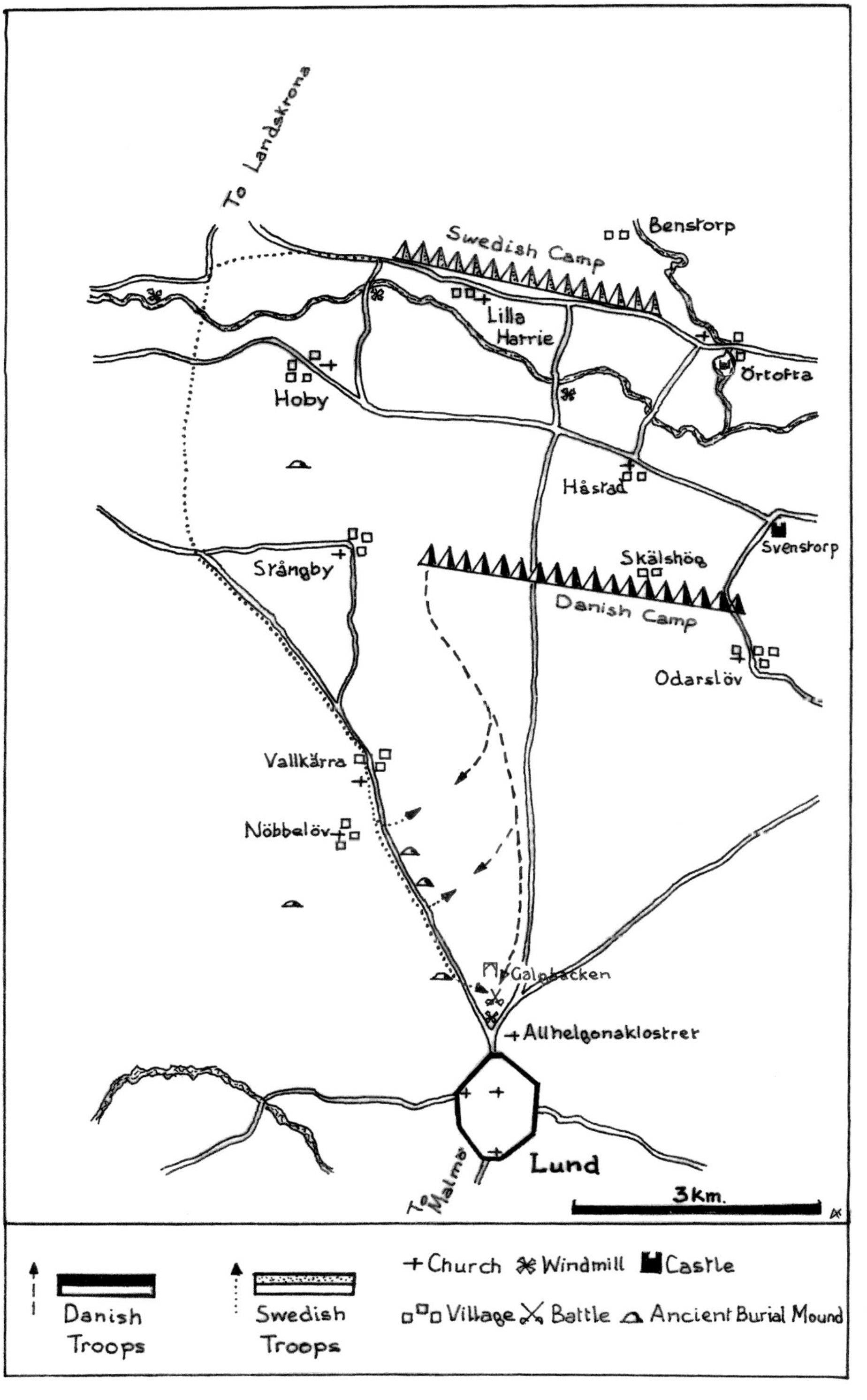

Map 4. Battle of Lund Preliminary Skirmishes

the commander of the left wing. However, Sandberg was only informed about the crossing later, just before 7:30 a.m.[10]

By pure chance, the Danes might have noticed the preparations for the crossing already by 10:00 p.m. the night before. No doubt because of the commotion in the Swedish camp, the indefatigable Major General Meerheim brought a company or two (50 or 100 men) of cavalry across the frozen river to monitor the Swedes. Some later claimed that he set out to sober up after having enjoyed a hearty dinner with King Christian. It sounds far more plausible that he wanted to ascertain whether the Swedes were retreating, as most Danes believed, or advancing. Be that as it may, Meerheim and his men stumbled on a Swedish outpost. The alarm being raised, Lieutenant General von Ascheberg personally gathered some cavalry and engaged Meerheim's men. Shots were fired. Following a confused skirmish that left one Swedish ensign and several men on both sides dead, the Danes were pushed back across the river. They never realised that the entire Swedish army was preparing to march.[11] Indeed, they probably believed that the continuing commotion was a reaction to the recently concluded skirmish.

There are no written records of the Swedish battle plan from the council of war, which took place in the field, but by all accounts, King Charles planned a sudden surprise flank attack on the Danish camp. We know little of contingency plans, but we know that the Swedish commanders on the previous evening had discussed other options, since achieving surprise was no certainty. For instance, Wilhelm von Fersen had suggested the possibility of marching towards Lund, if the surprise attack failed.

Having moved to the village of Stångby, west of the Danish camp, King Charles sent out Colonel Rolshausen to scout the possibility for a cavalry charge; however, Rolshausen returned to report that there were so many fences and stone walls between the two armies that the plan was not feasible. Although still dark, it was then around 7:00 a.m. The opportunity to make a surprise attack on the Danish camp had passed. The King then ordered the army to move past the Danes in the direction of Lund. Outside the town, they could take up positions on the high ground just north of Lund with the rear shielded by the town. In addition, this would cover an escape route to Malmö, if needs be. King Charles ordered von Fersen to take command of the advance guard (two squadrons, or some 300 men[12]). He himself took command of the right wing. Fersen decided, on his own initiative he later said, to march towards Lund.[13] In any case, Rolshausen led the advance guard towards Lund, followed by the right wing, the centre, and the left wing, in this order.

However, with the break of dawn a Danish outpost had finally discovered the Swedish army. The Danes formed up in order of battle rapidly, in only half an hour, and then left camp, marching south towards Lund in two columns, with the left wing leading the way. Already when he received the first report, at about 7:30 a.m., Sandberg ordered the cavalry of the left wing

10 Wahlöö and Larsson, *Slaget vid Lund*, pp.33–5.

11 Ibid., p.122.

12 Stade, "Slaget vid Lund", p.109.

13 Björlin, *Kriget mot Danmark*, p.125; citing Fersen.

to mount. The left wing was also the first to move. Nonetheless, the other Danish units formed up quickly, too. The Danish orders were to shadow the Swedish army, move when enemy moved, and halt when the enemy halted, according to Cavalry Captain Heinrich Otto Artmar, from the left wing, who served under Lieutenant Colonel Adam Hans Basse in the advance guard.[14] The Danish left wing was formally led by Sandberg, but he had been joined by several higher-ranking personages – the overall commander of the army, Carl von Arensdorff, but also King Christian and his brother Prince George – who effectively took command over his head. The two armies then marched on roughly parallel, although slightly converging, courses. Both sides attempted to reach Lund before the other. Both armies almost certainly navigated towards the same landmark, Lund's towering cathedral.

The terrain remained difficult, with both armies suffering from fences, ditches, and dry-stone walls. The cavalry often had to dismount to tear down the dry-stone walls so that the army, and its artillery, could pass in reasonable order.[15]

The Swedish army marched in two columns, with the right wing under King Charles, Helmfelt, and Ascheberg leading. The left wing was commanded by Lieutenant General Johan Galle and Major General Johan Benedikt von Schönleben.

The Swedish advance guard, under Fersen, reached the windmill hill (Möllevångshöjden) north of the town of Lund, just before the Danes. The Danish advance guard, under Lieutenant Colonel Basse, took up positions just north of Lund, south of the gallows hill (Galgbacken) and immediately north of the windmill hill. They were soon accompanied by King Christian, Prince George, Carl von Arensdorff, and the increasingly neglected Sandberg. King Christian was accompanied by a company or perhaps a squadron of his Guard Cavalry.[16] However, they were far ahead of the Danish main army.

The First Phase

The Swedish Right Wing Versus the Danish Left Wing

The sun rose at 8:30 a.m., and as soon as there was sufficient light to see their whereabouts, the small Swedish advance guard chosen from the squadrons under Lieutenant General von Fersen attacked the Danish advance guard. Fersen by then only had a squadron (some 150 men, regiment unknown) under Colonel Rolshausen, since the other squadron (150 men) under his command, dragoons under Lieutenant Colonel Lode of the Scania-Bohuslän Dragoon Regiment, had been dispatched by Ascheberg to hold the village of Vallkärra and only joined the battle later. A squadron was insufficient, but he soon received reinforcements in the form of the Drabant Guard under Lieutenant Colonel von Siegroth which pushed on to assist the advance

14 Stade, "Slaget vid Lund", p.111.
15 Wahlöö and Larsson, *Slaget vid Lund*, p.36.
16 Arne Stade, "Christian V i slaget vid Lund: En huvudvärk för den danska krigspropagandan", *Historisk Tidsskrift*, New Series 15 (Copenhagen, 1983–1985), pp.23–54, on p.29.

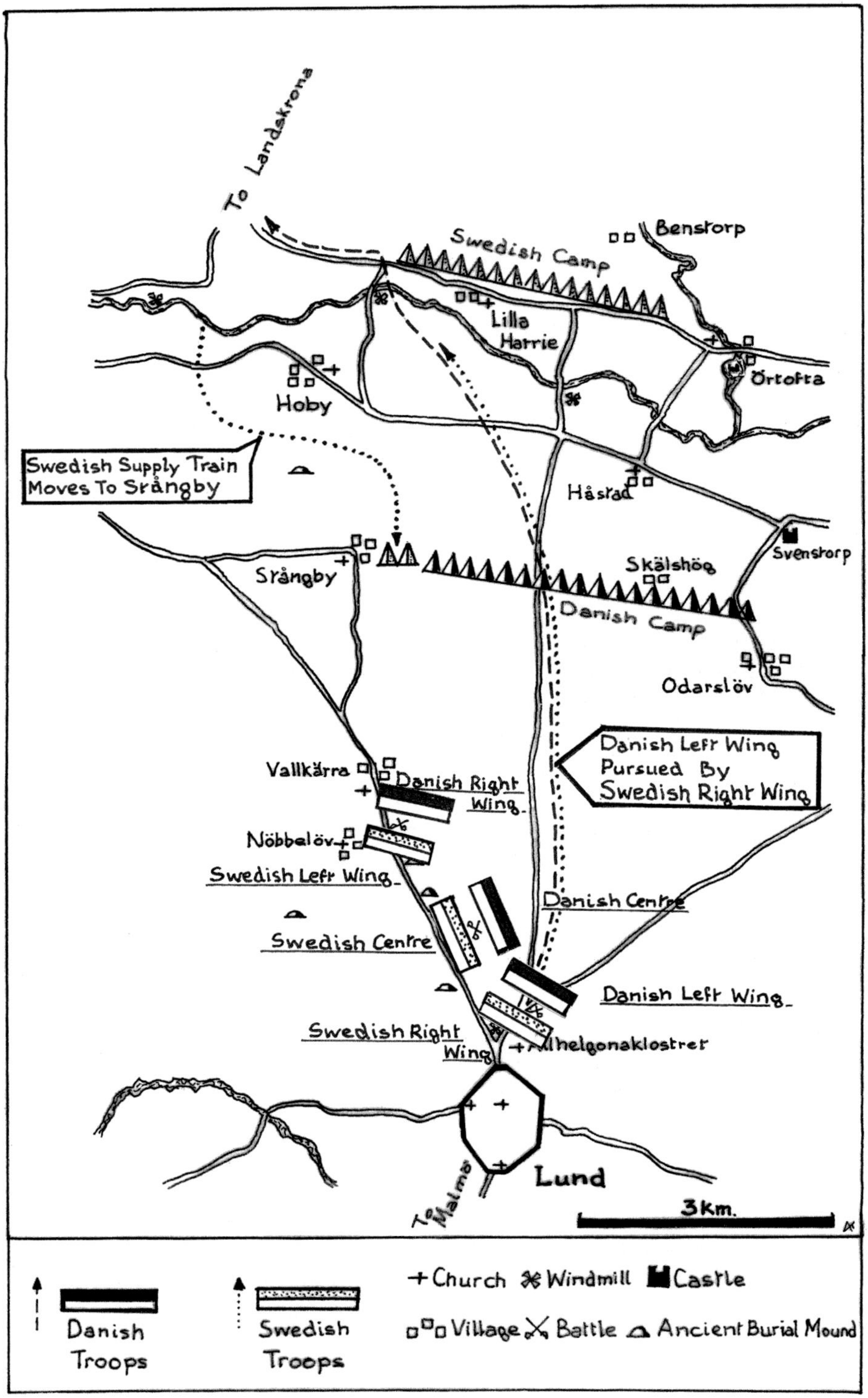

Map 5. Battle of Lund 1st Phase

Carl von Arensdorff on horseback at the Battle of Lund, 1676.

guard. The reinforced Swedes pushed back the Danish advance guard. However, the Danish left wing soon caught up with the advance guard, which reformed, reinforced by Colonel Jørgen Brockenhus's dragoons, and counterattacked under the personal command of Danish overall commander Carl von Arensdorff (Map 6). As for King Christian and Prince George, they apparently remained behind the Danish line, since neither appears to have taken part in the struggle at this point. The Swedish line was reinforced, too, by the arrival of Colonel von Budberg's Viborg Dragoon Regiment. They were no match for Brockenhus's Dragoons. Budberg himself was wounded in the first Danish volley and then taken prisoner.

Moreover, Colonel Rolshausen fell, too, mortally wounded.[17] But the Danish commanders suffered losses, too. General von Arensdorff was wounded by a shot to his right arm and was carried from the battle. Arensdorff never returned; he died from gangrene within a week despite being shipped to Copenhagen for medical treatment, where his arm was amputated. Because of the loss of General von Arensdorff, King Christian gave overall command to the man's brother, Lieutenant General Friedrich von Arensdorff.

The two sides then separated, neither being able to best the other. The remaining Swedes took hold of the position around the windmill, at the same time as both sides received additional reinforcements, as units arrived in order of march. On the Danish side, these included Colonel Henrik

17 Wahlöö and Larsson, *Slaget vid Lund*, p.102.

Friedrich von Arensdorff.

Sehested's Schleswig Cavalry Regiment and the wounded Arensdorff's own regiment, the 4th Jutland Cavalry Regiment.

It is likely that it was the loss of Arensdorff that secured the Swedish early victory at the windmill. Another reason may have been the more aggressive Swedish cavalry tactics, which probably helped to push the Danes back. It was about 9:00 a.m., and the sun had now risen.[18]

But the battle had only begun. By this time, the main forces of the two armies had arrived and formed up in regular lines of battle. The Swedish right wing had formed up opposite the Danish left wing, furthest to the east, just north of the windmill. The distance between the two armies was some 200 metres.

The Swedish right wing now charged the Danish left wing. The battle was hard fought. The Swedish Drabant Guard, consisting of 150 men in a single squadron under Siegroth, fought hard but had already suffered losses. Colonel Baranoff's Åbo-Viborg Cavalry Regiment was pushed back, with Baranoff himself wounded, too (command was then assumed by the King's half-brother, Colonel Gustav Carlson, the former commandant at Wismar). Budberg's Viborg Dragoon Regiment, having already been rudely handled by Brockenhus's Dragoons, were not in a shape to push forwards. Then only the Life Regiment of Horse, in five squadrons, under Colonel Nils Bielke, remained fighting, together with the surviving members of the Drabant Guard and, indeed, King Charles.

The Swedish second line, under Major General Wittenberg (promoted since the Battle of Fehrbellin),was slow to reach the field of battle, being delayed by the dry-stone walls and ditches along the Kävlinge road, which led north from Lund to Vallkärra and later Kävlinge. Fersen, upon noticing that Wittenberg's line was no longer behind him, where he expected it to be, reportedly exclaimed, 'Jesus save us, what is General Wittenberg doing who is not following me?'[19] If this statement is correctly attributed, it shows something of the chaotic character of the battle at this point.

Yet, the Life Regiment under Bielke stubbornly refused to give in. Surrounded by superior numbers of Danes, they still repulsed the Danish attack and pushed back the first Danish line in a furious counter-charge, which also drove the second Danish line backwards. The Danes regrouped and counterattacked, yet failed to make an impact on the Life Regiment. The battle had then raged for about an hour. The Life Regiment had suffered heavy losses, including most officers.

18 Ibid., pp.41–2.
19 Ibid., p.47.

King Charles, accompanied by Erik Dahlbergh, orders a Danish squadron to charge, having mistaken it for a Swedish one at the Battle of Lund, 1676. (Johan Philip Lemke; Photo: Medströms)

Then finally the Swedish right wing's second line reached the battle. Seven squadrons under Major General Wittenberg joined the fray. The battle continued. Many Swedish officers fell, including Siegroth of the Drabant Guard, and both Major General Wittenberg and Colonel Christoffer von Güntersberg, who commanded the Reinforcement of Nobles in Götaland, were wounded. Wittenberg, shot in the shoulder which produced a nasty wound, was carried out of the battle. Güntersberg suffered a lighter wound and continued to lead his unit.

It is difficult to reconstruct the details of this part of the battle, since it was extremely hard-fought by both sides, with charges and counter-charges taking place repeatedly. The participants, too, later found it hard to describe the exact events. Bielke noted that there had been "such a struggle on both sides that it was impossible to describe precisely how it occurred." He simply did not know 'how many times we charged each other' but "we all were, it seems to me, for more than an hour almost continuously *à la charge*, with pistols and even more with rapiers."[20]

King Charles took an active part in the combat. During the fighting, he accidentally ended up in a Danish squadron. Fortunately for him, the lack of national uniforms and his own relatively simple officer's dress meant that the Danes failed to notice his mistake. As soon as Charles had realised his position, he managed to withdraw, and so saved himself. But before this, one of the more remarkable incidents during the battle took place. Bielke later described what happened:

20 Ingvar Eriksson, *Nils Bielke (1644–1716): Firad i nådens dagar, fälld i onådens* (Stockholm: Atlantis, 2000), p.110; citing Bielke.

> Both units had merged to the extent that they stood mixed among each other. Nobody could recognise the other because of the gun smoke, with the result that His Majesty ordered a Danish squadron to advance and the kettledrums to play, believing, since it stood between two Swedish squadrons, that it was Ramsvärd's Old Smålanders, who carried red standards, which however upon closer inspection turned out to have white crosses, since they belonged to the King of Denmark's Life Regiment Cavalry.[21]

In fact, Bielke was wrong on one account. The Danish squadron did not belong to the Danish Life Regiment Cavalry, which was on the Danish right wing, but can almost certainly be identified as one of the three squadrons of Colonel Sehested's Schleswig Cavalry Regiment, which carried red standards of the type described and was in the right location. Moreover, Sehested had fallen in the battle, which no doubt contributed to the confusion of the men of his regiment.

Soon after 10:00 a.m., the Danish left wing broke. Men began to retreat in disorder, which soon turned into headlong flight. On the Swedish side, King Charles by then had personally taken command of his right wing. He sent some squadrons to assist the centre, but to pursue the fleeing Danes he then led what remained of 10 squadrons: the Drabant Guard, the five squadrons of the Life Regiment, the two squadrons of the Retinue of Nobles under Colonel Johan Drake, one squadron of the Reinforcements of Nobles in Götaland, and the squadron of Old Smålanders, who were cavalrymen who had served in the previous war, after which they had been disbanded, only to be recalled to duty with the outbreak of the present war. They were then raised as the Blekinge Cavalry Regiment but three quarters of the men were former cavalrymen from Småland.[22] He also brought with him Helmfelt and Ascheberg. On the Danish side, Major General Sandberg made desperate attempts to reform and hold the fleeing Danish left wing, going so far as using his rapier to 'animate and punish' the fleeing men. The pursuit was, indeed, not free of risks. King Charles's horse, a black stallion named Thotten, took a shot to the head. The shot ricocheted into the King's hat, and the horse, although still standing, began to behave erratically, forcing King Charles to mount his spare horse, the white stallion Brillant which he had received as a gift from French King Louis XIV.[23] For the rest of the day, King Charles rode Brillant.

King Christian, who apparently had observed the struggle from behind his left wing, was caught up in the flight, too. Moreover, he ordered Brockenhus and his dragoons to follow him, instead of going in support of the right wing which apparently was the original plan.[24] One may suspect that King Christian felt that he needed them to guard his royal person. This was not necessarily a reflection on his bravery, since Christian undoubtedly was brave and fought hand-to-hand in battle on other occasions, but had he

21 Isacson, *Skånska kriget*, p.47; citing Bielke.

22 Stade, "Slaget vid Lund", p.131.

23 Wahlöö and Larsson, *Slaget vid Lund*, p.47.

24 Stade, "Christian V i slaget vid Lund", pp.29–30.

Left:
King Charles XI of Sweden, mounted on Brillant, at the Battle of Lund, 1676. (David Klöcker Ehrenstrahl, 1682)

Overleaf:
Top: Soldiers looting the Danish camp, the Battle of Lund, 1676. (Erik Dahlbergh)

Bottom: Soldiers looting King Christian's supply train, the Battle of Lund, 1676. The carts are marked with the royal cypher of King Christian. (Erik Dahlbergh)

been lost, this would have cost the Danish Crown the entire war. The same fate, of course, would have affected Sweden, had King Charles been lost, but by all accounts, Charles considered the Swedish situation so desperate that he willingly took the risk.

The Danes abandoned three artillery batteries, which were captured by the Swedes. Many Danes sought refuge in their camp; however, when the Swedes approached, the Danes fled in panic. As a result, the pursuing Swedes killed a number of Danes there, including, no doubt, many of those who were too ill to have participated in the battle. Dahlbergh wrote that the ill and the wounded were "massacred". Later the wording was changed into 'taken prisoner'. Probably the original word choice was the correct one. The Swedes also looted the camp, probably without any level of control and accompanied by further violence. Massacres of the ill and wounded were, as we have seen, common occurrences on both sides during the war. King Charles then pursued the Danes all the way to the River Kävlinge, where many Danes drowned as the ice broke when they crossed. Either the Danes were careless in their flight, or, more likely, the morning sunshine had weakened parts of the ice, which then no longer was safe to cross. King Christian, his brother, and separately, and later, Sandberg managed to cross the ice. Somebody

told Lieutenant General von Fersen that King Christian had fallen into the river, as the ice was breaking up, so he hurriedly rode down to the river to investigate and secure the capture of the Danish King. Instead he was shot at, suffering two wounds, one in the face and one in the right shoulder.[25] Fersen had to be carried from the field to seek medical attention (and he was then taken prisoner by the Danes who by chance captured his cart on the road to Malmö). Besides, the rumour of King Christian having fallen into the river was wrong; he had by then already left the field.

It was then about 11:30 a.m.

The Struggle between the Two Centres

King Charles, Ascheberg, and Helmfelt stayed near River Kävlinge for several hours. At first, it was no doubt prudent to allow the horses some rest and see to that the Danes did not rally and return to the battle. It is, however, unclear why they delayed further. The long pursuit engaged in by King Charles when the Danish left wing fled was a serious mistake that might have cost him the battle. The pursuit, which diverted both himself and the overall commander, Field Marshal Helmfelt, can probably be explained by his youth and lack of experience. A wiser choice would have been to send a smaller cavalry force in pursuit, then return with the bulk of his cavalry to engage the Danish centre from the rear. But instead King Charles disappeared for several hours.

Meanwhile, both the Swedish centre and left wing were losing ground to the Danish army. The Swedish centre and left wing entered the battle later than the cavalry of the right wing under King Charles. By around 10:00 a.m., the Swedish infantry had turned left, forming up in two lines on the east side of the Kävlinge road, to meet a Danish attack. Between the two lines, separated by a few hundred metres, was a shallow valley bisected by a frozen stream, Vallkärrabäcken. The Danes, under Major General Joachim von Schack, enjoyed higher ground, standing about five metres above the Swedes, and had more artillery. The second Swedish line included some dragoons and cavalry, while the Danish lines were all infantry.

The battle began with an exchange of artillery fire. The Swedes had at least eight cannons, while it remains unclear how many of the 56 Danish cannons had been brought forward. To avoid excessive losses from the artillery fire, the two armies advanced down into the valley against each other. The Swedes were inferior in numbers, by some accounts only half as many as the Danes, and were pushed back uphill, whence they had come. The Danes followed, capturing the Swedish cannons, despite the efforts of Colonel Lars Axel Mörner and his battalion of the Västgöta-Dal Regiment to protect them. Mörner, a veteran of the previous war with Denmark, fell in the battle. Colonel George Ashton, an experienced English officer who commanded the Swedish artillery, fell, too, killed by a shot to the head. Ashton was newly re-enlisted; he had returned from England to Gothenburg only on 8 November, so survived less than a month's service in Sweden.[26]

25 Wahlöö and Larsson, *Slaget vid Lund*, pp.48–50.
26 Ibid., p.120.

However, the Danish success was incomplete. The Swedish Life Guard, three battalions under Colonel Christoffer Gyllenstierna, not only resisted but then successfully broke through the Danish centre's first line (Prince Frederick's Regiment and the Queen's Life Regiment). Gyllenstierna's men then continued into the Danish second line, where they were opposed by a battalion of the Plön Regiment. The Life Guard lost several officers, including Gyllenstierna who suffered nine wounds to the head and some 10 more elsewhere. At that point, the third battalion of the Life Guard wavered, seeming to share the fate of the rest of the Swedish infantry, even though two other Life Guard battalions were advancing. Moreover, Budberg's Viborg Dragoon Regiment were supposed to support the Life Guard, but they remained reluctant to enter the battle, having lost their colonel and been thoroughly beaten already in the previous engagement.

The Life Guard's charge might have stopped there, had not, as we have seen, King Charles's half-brother Gustav Carlson assumed command of the remnants of Baranoff's Åbo-Viborg Cavalry Regiment. With the Swedish right wing victorious, Carlson now returned to support the centre, finding a place in the second line. There were already deployed Colonel Otto Vellingk's and Lieutenant Colonel von der Pahlen's respective squadrons of the Old Östgötian cavalry, a regiment of recently re-enlisted veterans. Now the second line's cavalry pushed through the gaps in the Swedish first line and charged the Danes.

Then, finally, two other cavalry squadrons from the Swedish right wing, under Colonel Christoffer von Güntersberg (commander of the Reinforcement of Nobles in Götaland and himself already wounded) and Lieutenant Colonel Axel Rehnskiöld (commander of the Civil Service's Temporary Regiment), respectively, also came to the aid of the centre, charging into the flank of the Danish infantry.

Those Danish officers who survived the battle and later described it, among them the experienced Colonel Cicignon who commanded the Danish second line and Captain Hans Schack of the Queen's Life Regiment, explained that the Swedish cavalry had surrounded the Danish infantry which then fled from the field. Some of the Danes, including Cicignon, managed to reach the distant River Kävlinge, which had already been crossed by those Danes who fled from the left wing. The fleeing Danes suffered severe losses as their lines broke.

However, the Swedes, too, had lost many men. In fact, it was uncertain whether any of the Swedish battalions still could be described as fit for service. Lieutenant General Martin Schultz, commander of the Swedish centre, accordingly withdrew his survivors into cover of several ditches and fences to regroup, despite having won the struggle. He was also well aware that he had lost his artillery. It was now about 12 noon.

Meanwhile, the commanding officer of the Swedish Life Guard, Gyllenstierna, was left on the field, seriously wounded. Found by enemy looters, he was again shot, but the ball ricocheted off his cuirass, wounding but not killing him. Nonetheless, the marauders undressed him, stealing whatever he had carried, and left him naked to freeze to death. But Gyllenstierna was lucky. A young captain-lieutenant (the rank between

Soldiers, possibly snipers with civilian rifled guns, firing muskets without using fork rests, the Battle of Lund, 1676. (Erik Dahlbergh)

lieutenant and captain)named Fabian Gustav Wrangel from Baranoff's regiment passed by. Wrangel recognised Gyllenstierna, dismounted, and gave Gyllenstierna his own horse. Despite his wounds, Gyllenstierna then managed to return to his regiment, although at first, due to his dishevelled state, nobody recognised him. He was identified only from his voice. Against all odds, Gyllenstierna had survived the battle and eventually recovered fully from his wounds.

Young Wrangel, however, was taken prisoner by Count Reus, a Danish Guard Cavalry captain. Contrary to good form, Reus also stole his money and personal belongings. A few hours later, the Guard Cavalry unit to which Reus belonged found itself defeated and at risk of being overrun. To save his own skin, Reus then surrendered to Wrangel. Nonetheless, the battle continued, and within another few hours, Wrangel was killed in combat.[27] Reus survived, and was later exchanged.

The Danish Right Wing versus the Swedish Left Wing

Around 10:00 a.m., the Swedish left wing, the first line of which was commanded by Lieutenant General Galle, marching in two columns, had reached the vicinity of Vallkärra. There the Swedes were charged by the Danish right wing under Lieutenant General Friedrich von Arensdorff, who

27 Isacson, *Skånska kriget*, pp.48–9.

aimed to turn the Swedish flank. The Swedes may have had to wheel to the left to form a line of battle, taking casualties while doing so. Among those lost was Galle, who, exposed in front of his men, fell in the first Danish volley. Major General Schönleben, the commander of the second line, had to assume command of the entire Swedish left wing. There are few reports or other records from this section of the battle, and little is known for sure except that fighting was extremely hard and confused.

Furthermore, the Danish cavalry managed to break through the Swedish line and separate the two squadrons of the Savolax Dragoon Regiment, under Colonel Herman von Burghausen, and the Västgöta Cavalry Regiment, four squadrons under the 63-year-old Colonel Per Hierta, from the other Swedish units. Fighting dismounted as dragoons, Burghausen's Finns were first attacked by the Danish Life Regiment Cavalry. Many Finns fell, including Burghausen. Colonel Hierta's Västgöta Cavalry Regiment suffered casualties, too, and Hierta (together with Schönleben probably the oldest man on the battlefield) was wounded, which did not prevent him from staying with his men.

The other Swedish units suffered casualties, too. The commander of the Viborg and Nyslott (Karelian) Cavalry Regiment, Colonel Bernhard Mellin, suffered a wound in the throat, but remained in the battle. But several of his officers were killed, including Lieutenant General Galle's son, the last of the family, who served as captain in Mellin's regiment. The New Retinue of Nobles, under Colonel Robert Lichton, also suffered serious losses. Born in Finland as the son of an English soldier in Swedish service, Lichton had begun service as a common musketeer during the Thirty Years' War. He was known as an incredibly strong man and was quick to anger, which resulted in several cases of manslaughter and duels. Now Lichton was wounded by several shots (one to the arm and six to the torso, most of which could never be removed) but, due to his remarkable strength, stayed in the battle and eventually recovered. His Lieutenant Colonel, Georg Johan Lode (the brother of the aforementioned Lieutenant Colonel Lode of the Scania-Bohuslän Dragoons), was killed. The same fate struck several other officers in the regiment.

By then only five of the originally 19 squadrons of the left wing remained as coherent units. Major General Schönleben temporarily deployed his surviving troops behind a dry-stone wall at Nöbbelöv Church in order to re-form the units. Soon after noon, Schönleben got the left wing in order, and then he moved, in two columns, in the direction of Lund, where he by 1:00 p.m. joined his wing to the centre, under Schultz.

Perhaps the Danes could have prevented this, had they pushed on with their cavalry. Instead they lined up in a formal line of battle. Arensdorff was close to a complete victory, but possibly he did not know this, since the battle was such a confused affair. The wind was not very strong, and smoke must have covered major parts of the battlefield.[28] Yet, both the Swedish and the Danish left wing had seen itself defeated. The Swedish centre had suffered significant losses and, although somewhat victorious, been forced to

28 Wahlöö and Larsson, *Slaget vid Lund*, pp.58–62.

Previous page:
Top: Cavalry with pistols, the Battle of Lund, 1676. (Erik Dahlbergh)
Bottom: Cavalry with rapiers, the Battle of Lund, 1676. (Erik Dahlbergh)

retreat. Nobody knew where King Charles and the Swedish right wing was. Arensdorff may have felt obliged to prepare for the return of the victorious Swedish right wing. The two armies then regrouped. This took about an hour, which offered the surviving men some much-needed rest.

Meanwhile, the remnants of the Swedish centre and left wing united and regrouped. The Swedish centre then marched towards Lund to use the town to safeguard its rear.

The new line of battle was significantly different from the original one. The Swedes had lost a considerable number of men and only about half of the units were still able to function. They had also lost all artillery. For this reason, the order in which the units deployed was not the same as before. Under the overall command of Schultz, a new right wing was formed, consisting of nine cavalry squadrons. The centre under Schultz with Major General Barthold de Mortaigne in command of the second line was built of five or six (now combined) infantry battalions, and the left wing consisted of nine cavalry squadrons. The right wing was commanded by Schönleben and the wounded Güntersberg, while Admiral Lieutenant Hans Wachtmeister, a naval officer who had commanded a squadron of the Västgöta Cavalry Regiment and also had played an active role in reorganising the line of battle, took command of the left wing, with Colonel Vellingk as the commander of the second line. Hans Wachtmeister, as noted, was the elder brother of Axel Wachtmeister, who had fought in Bremen-Verden, and Adam Wachtmeister, who had fallen at Fehrbellin.

However, the Danes, although somewhat shaken, remained superior in numbers. Of their 18 infantry battalions, five regular battalions remained in condition to fight, but the Danish line now also included the three sailors battalions that finally had reached the line, too. A total of 21 cavalry squadrons remained, as well as almost all artillery and the captured Swedish artillery.[29]

The three sailors battalions deserve some additional comment. Having been raised from some 1,500 sailors from the navy, which had been laid up for the winter, each battalion was subdivided into companies of the same type as the army's infantry. There were apparently 12 companies, although there is some confusion on whether the total manpower of these battalions was 1,500 or only 1,000 men. In any case, there is little doubt that each battalion consisted of four companies. The sailors were commandeered to serve as infantrymen, something for which they were untrained. Most were Danes and Norwegians, but quite a few Dutchmen also served. In addition to snaphance muskets (used by the Dutch navy as shipboard weapons), they received 308 pikes. In addition, many were armed with half-pikes, crude

29 Stade, "Slaget vid Lund", pp.127–8; Wahlöö and Larsson, *Slaget vid Lund*, p.63.

morning stars, pistols, and cutlasses.[30] The morning star was a spiked club which, in similarity to the Flemish *goedendag*, had a sharp metal spike inserted in and extending out of the head, like a short pike. As for uniforms, most sailors had received red coats to look like soldiers, which they wore possibly with white stockings.[31] Their standards were captured and most remain in the Swedish Trophy Collection. However, as we will see, their lack of appropriate training made them inadequate for a modern battle, regardless of their coats and standards.

Having regrouped, the two armies, deployed for battle, moved to the southeast, marching side by side on each side of the Kävlinge road, only separated by some hundred metres and the dry-stone walls alongside the road.

The Danish commander Arensdorff may have been concerned about the whereabouts of Swedish King Charles and the victorious original Swedish right wing, but if so, he was not the only one. On the Swedish side, it was paramount to locate King Charles, or at least to find out whether he was dead or captured. For this reason, the Quartermaster General, Erik Dahlbergh, who as noted also led military intelligence, set out to the north together with the Hofmarschall (*hovmarskalk*), Bengt Rosenhane, the Supervisor of the Royal Household, to locate the King.

The Second Phase

Just north of Lund, the two armies prepared for renewed battle (Map 7). By 1:15 p.m., they again faced each other, the Swedes to the south, just north of the windmill, and the Danes to the north.

Before the battle re-commenced, suddenly a Danish captain left the line, approaching the Swedish Life Guard, which by then was commanded by Major Jacob Johan Hastfehr. The commander of the third battalion, Major Hastfehr had assumed command when Life Guard commander Colonel Gyllenstierna was seriously wounded. He had also merged his much depleted third battalion with the second battalion. The Dane now challenged Hastfehr to single combat. However, Hastfehr was the only remaining senior officer and was then sorely needed, so a Life Guard officer in his mid-twenties, Captain Bernhard von Liewen, volunteered to fight on behalf of Hastfehr. The single combat then took place between the Swedish and Danish lines. It ended with Liewen killing the Dane, bringing back the latter's rapier as a sign of victory.[32]

The Danish artillery then initiated the general action by opening fire, having first fired a Danish salute (three cannon shots in rapid succession). The Danish artillery fire was unopposed, since the Swedes had lost their artillery. The Danes then charged. The Danish left wing pushed back the new Swedish right wing, which had to take cover behind the infantry in the centre.

30 Bjerre, *Fra Flådens arkiver*, pp.26, 51–2.

31 Hasselager and Snorrason, *Danish Uniforms, Colours and Standards*, pp.28–9.

32 Wahlöö and Larsson, *Slaget vid Lund*, p.54.

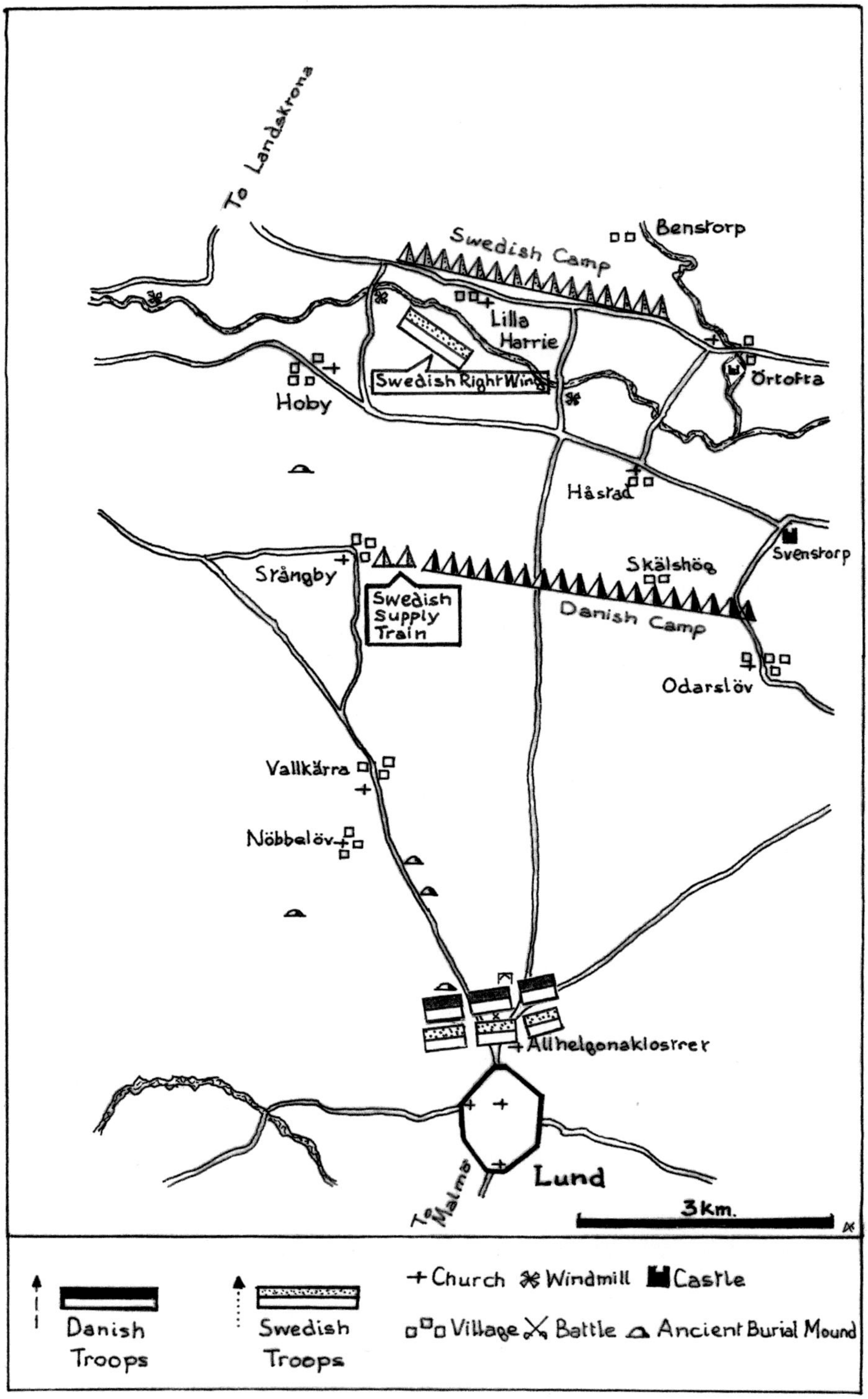

Map 6. Battle of Lund 2nd Phase

On the other hand, the Swedish left wing succeeded in pushing back the Danish right wing. Meanwhile, the battle in the centre was inconclusive. Although the Danes were superior in numbers with regard to infantry, the numerical superiority consisted chiefly of the three sailors battalions. Besides, the infantry on both sides eventually ran out of ammunition. Having to fight with rapiers and musket butts, both sides grew exhausted and by around 2:15 p.m., the inconclusive battle was temporarily over as both sides stepped back.[33] Admiral-Lieutenant Wachtmeister, who commanded the Swedish left wing, had three horses shot below him, but yet managed to find a fourth horse and, more importantly, remained unharmed himself.

However, the Swedish right wing was losing the battle, being gradually forced back. So as not to be divided, the entire Swedish army then had to follow suit, slowly withdrawing until they stood with their backs against Lund itself.

The Third Phase

The Swedes had again regrouped, this time with the left wing pushed back further south all the way to Lund's medieval town wall. The Swedish line now faced the north-west.

Meanwhile, Arensdorff had regrouped the Danish troops, too, and prepared for yet another charge, this time with good hope of wiping out the Swedes, many of whom literally were fighting with their backs against the town wall. It was around 3:00 p.m., and the sun was already close to setting.

At this point, something unexpected happened. Arensdorff suddenly turned the Danish lines around, then had his army moved towards the northwest (Map 8). For the reportedly third and last time, Arensdorff fired a Danish salute, this time in the faint hope of recalling King Christian and the dispersed Danish left wing. What had happened? The Danes had discovered a Swedish cavalry unit approaching into their rear from the direction of Vallkärra. The cavalry unit was small, but the Danish command believed that it probably was the advance guard of a larger force. They decided to defeat the approaching cavalry first, then return their attention to the embattled Swedish main army.[34]

Then it became clear that it was King Charles who returned from his extended pursuit. Finally, Erik Dahlbergh and Bengt Rosenhane had located the King, bringing news from the battle and strongly suggesting that the King had to return. It had then been 1:45 p.m., at the latest.[35]

When the pursuit began, King Charles had set out with 10 squadrons. These were the Drabant Guard of which only some 50 men remained, the five squadrons of the Life Regiment of Horse, the two squadrons of the Retinue of Nobles under Drake, one squadron of the Reinforcements of Nobles in Götaland, and the squadron of Old Smålanders under Colonel Ramsvärd. When recalled by Dahlbergh and Rosenhane, the King left Ramsvärd

33 Ibid., pp.64–6.

34 Ibid., pp.67–9.

35 Ibid., pp.50–51.

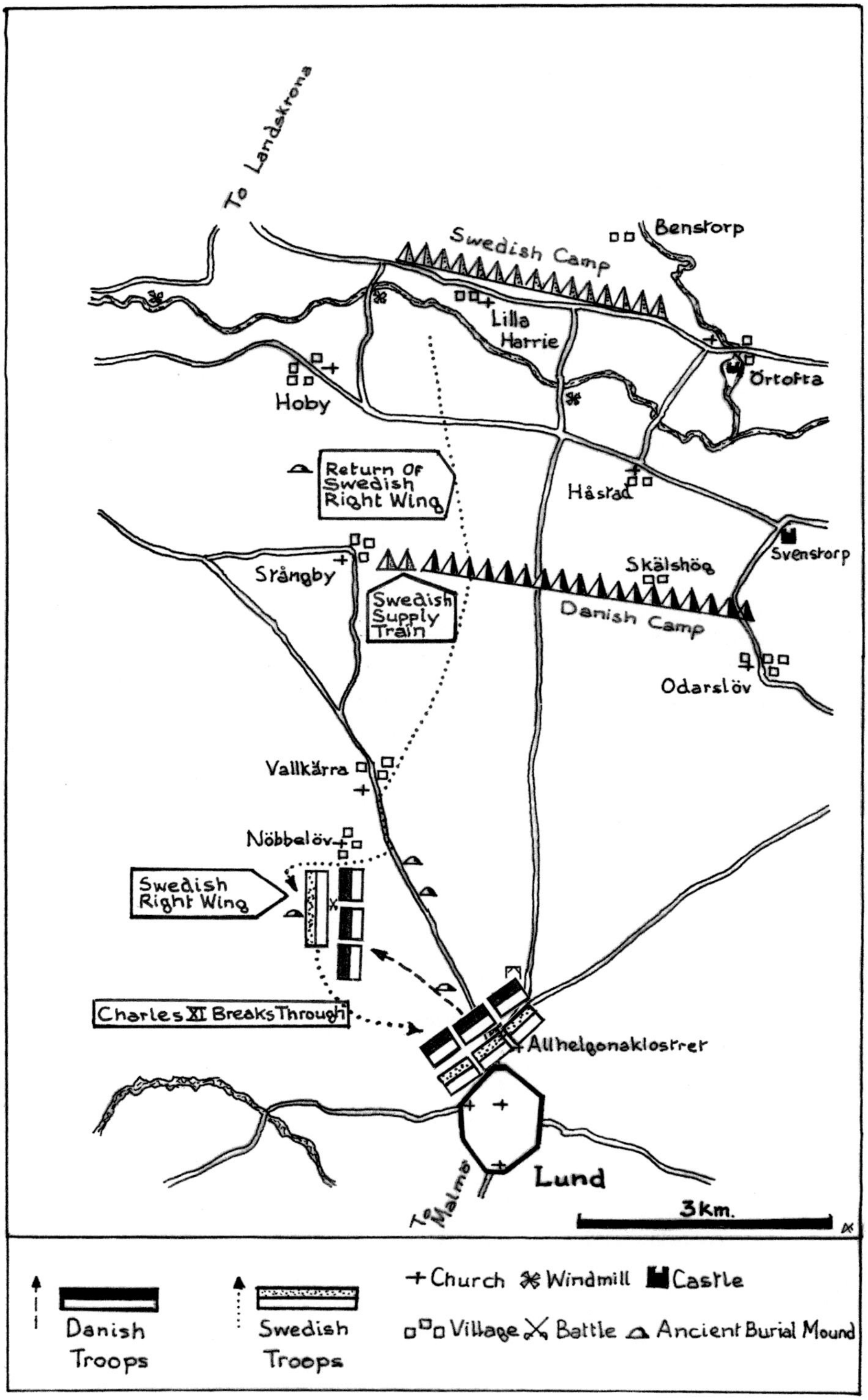

Map 7. Battle of Lund 3rd Phase

and his Old Smålanders, the Reinforcements of Nobles in Götaland, and one squadron of the Retinue of Nobles to defend the crossings over River Kävlinge. The King then returned with seven squadrons (the Drabant Guard, the five squadrons of the Life Regiment of Horse, and one squadron of Drake's Retinue of Nobles). However, on the way back King Charles had also picked up what remained of two of Budberg's dispersed dragoon squadrons. As a result, he returned with nine depleted squadrons.[36] This renewed hope among the Swedes, but caused dismay among the Danes, whether outside Lund or more far away. King Christian, already safe and way beyond the River Kävlinge, was overheard saying that the day had been unlucky and it was best to withdraw slowly to Landskrona. Soon rumours spread that King Christian had left the battle.[37] At around 2:00 p.m., King Christian rode off to Landskrona, where he spent the night after the battle. During the night, he also dispatched a patrol to Svenstorp Castle, to retrieve some personal belongings he had forgotten there.[38]

King Charles first led his nine remaining squadrons to the west, in an attempt to bypass the Danish army. However, the Danes formed up to the north, facing King Charles and his cavalry with more than 20 squadrons and five battalions. It suddenly looked to the Swedes, including Colonel Bielke, that there was no longer any hope for victory. As the Danes advanced, King Charles noticed that the Danish right wing, under Meerheim, during the march had become separated from the Danish centre and left wing. King Charles accordingly charged the Danish left wing. Against all odds, the Swedish cavalry pushed back the Danes, so that the Danish cavalry and infantry collided in disorder. However, the Swedes were not sufficiently strong to maintain their momentum, in particular against the Danish pikemen, and the Swedish cavalry soon recoiled. Some of the Swedish squadrons were dispersed, and Budberg's two dragoon squadrons again seem to have fled from the field.[39] Yet, already during the successful first charge King Charles actually managed to push through the Danish lines together with Ascheberg, Dahlbergh, and an unidentified Drabant who had become separated from his unit and accordingly decided to follow the King. Although repeatedly shot at (Dahlbergh's coat and saddle were ruined by stray bullets), amazingly the four men reached the Swedish lines without suffering a single wound, and King Charles resumed command over whatever remained of the Swedish army.[40]

The Fourth Phase

The return of their King reinvigorated the Swedes. By 3:15 p.m. or soon thereafter, they formed up in three columns (Map 9). The northernmost column, formed from the (new) right, including two squadrons of Baranoff's Åbo-Viborg Cavalry Regiment, and led by King Charles, moved north, aiming

36 Stade, "Slaget vid Lund", p.131.
37 Stade, "Christian V i slaget vid Lund", pp.33–4.
38 Wahlöö and Larsson, *Slaget vid Lund*, pp.85, 122.
39 Stade, "Slaget vid Lund", pp.135, 157 n.76.
40 Ibid., pp.135–6; Wahlöö and Larsson, *Slaget vid Lund*, pp.70–71.

for a pincer movement, until they could attack the Danish right wing in the rear. Schultz led the Swedish infantry centre along the Kävlinge road until they could attack the Danish centre in the rear. Ascheberg, taking command of the Swedish left wing, led it in an attack on the rear of the Danish left wing. At the same time, Helmfelt and Bielke attacked with their cavalry from the west. The Danish army was suddenly attacked from all sides.

The attack also eased the pressure on Helmfelt and Bielke, the senior officers left in the original right wing. After the King's dash for Lund, the cavalry of the right wing had been pushed back and had to regroup. This was no easy matter in their current condition; of Bielke's originally five squadrons, by then there was only enough men left to form up in one, combined squadron. Bielke's hat had been shot through, and his cuirass was dented by glancing shots. Bielke's horse, Plaisant, had been wounded by a shot to the head, but both rider and horse stayed in the battle. He and his men were exhausted. Most of his officers were dead or wounded.

By then, the Danes were still probably numerically stronger, perhaps an estimated 4,500 Danish troops as compared to 4,000 Swedes. However, their position was now hopeless, and like the Swedish troops, the Danes, too, were exhausted. The final battle lasted only around 15 minutes. The Danes, thoroughly defeated, suffered great losses and many fled in to the direction of Vallkärra, where some Danes made a stand under the steadfast Colonel von Bibow, who took charge despite his wound. The Swedish centre under Schultz, being infantry and accordingly slower than the cavalry, seems not to have reached the battle before the Danish lines already had collapsed.[41]

About a thousand sailors surrendered; however, the survivors from Baranoff's Åbo-Viborg Cavalry Regiment and the Life Regiment of Horse were not inclined to show mercy. The Finns and Swedes reportedly argued that 'Sailors are paid to fight at sea but not on land. Therefore you do not deserve any mercy!' Be that as it may, certainly no quarter was given and many sailors were killed, before Field Marshal Helmfelt regained control of his men.[42] According to one report, only 60 of them were taken captive, while another contemporary witness described how 500 sailors were taken captive and subsequently repatriated to the Netherlands without ransom by way of Gothenburg.[43] Another 500 had already departed for Landskrona and did not take part in the battle (they were returned to Copenhagen on 6 December with Admiral Juel, who had stayed in King Christian's camp until the morning of the battle and possibly participated in it).[44] The battle was over by 5:00 p.m., when it was already dark. The darkness prevented further pursuit. The Swedish army held a short religious service to give thanks for the victory, then fired a Swedish salute (two cannon shots in rapid succession).[45]

The surviving Danes, 10–12 squadrons and the remnants of 3–4 battalions (perhaps some 1,500 cavalry and 500 infantry) commanded by Bibow, withdrew

41 Wahlöö and Larsson, *Slaget vid Lund*, pp.74–5.
42 Ibid., pp.76–77; Isacson, *Skånska kriget*, p.55.
43 Stade, "Slaget vid Lund", p.158 n.83.
44 Bjerre, *Fra Flådens arkiver*, p.60.
45 Wahlöö and Larsson, *Slaget vid Lund*, p.77.

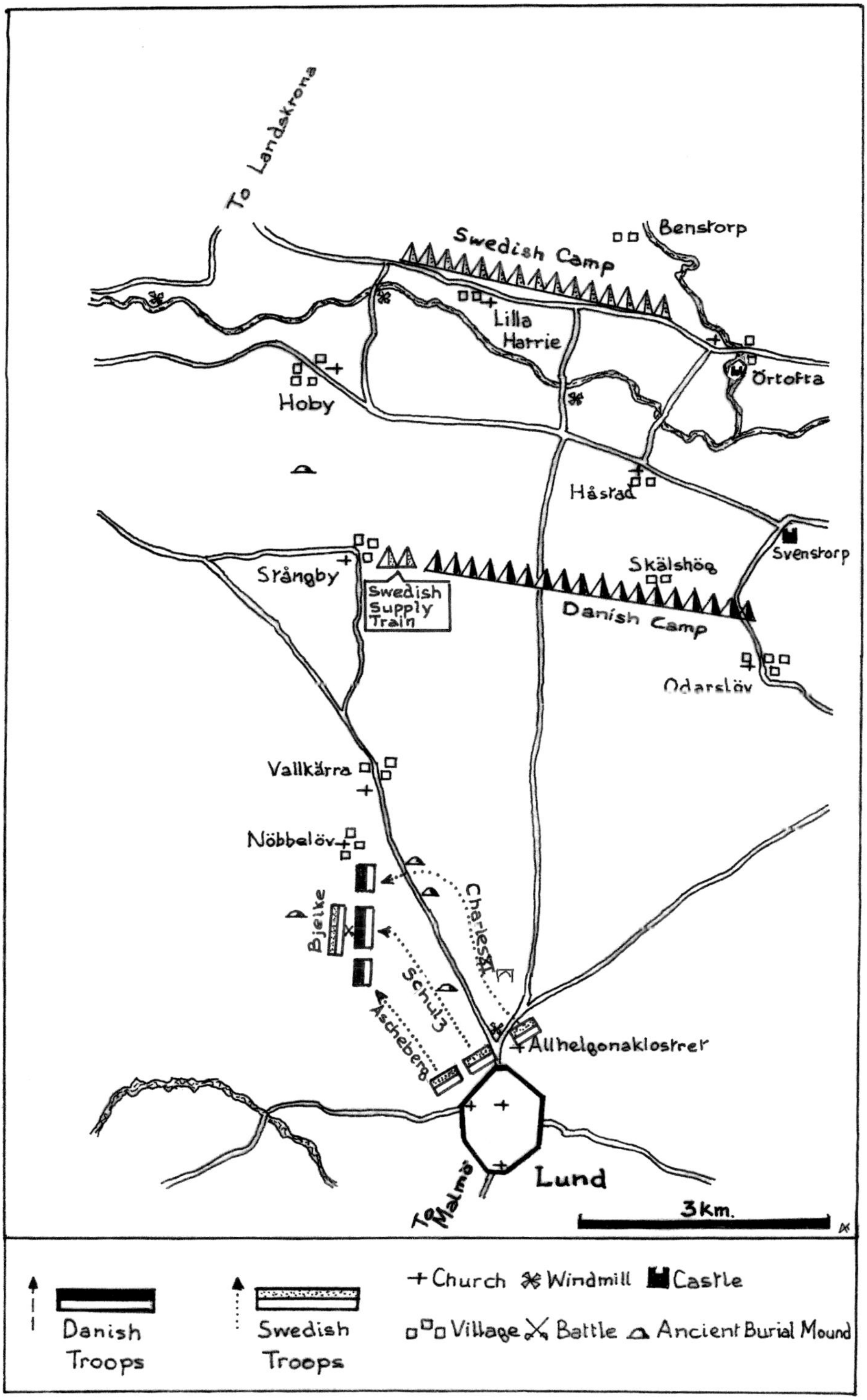

Map 8. Battle of Lund 4th Phase

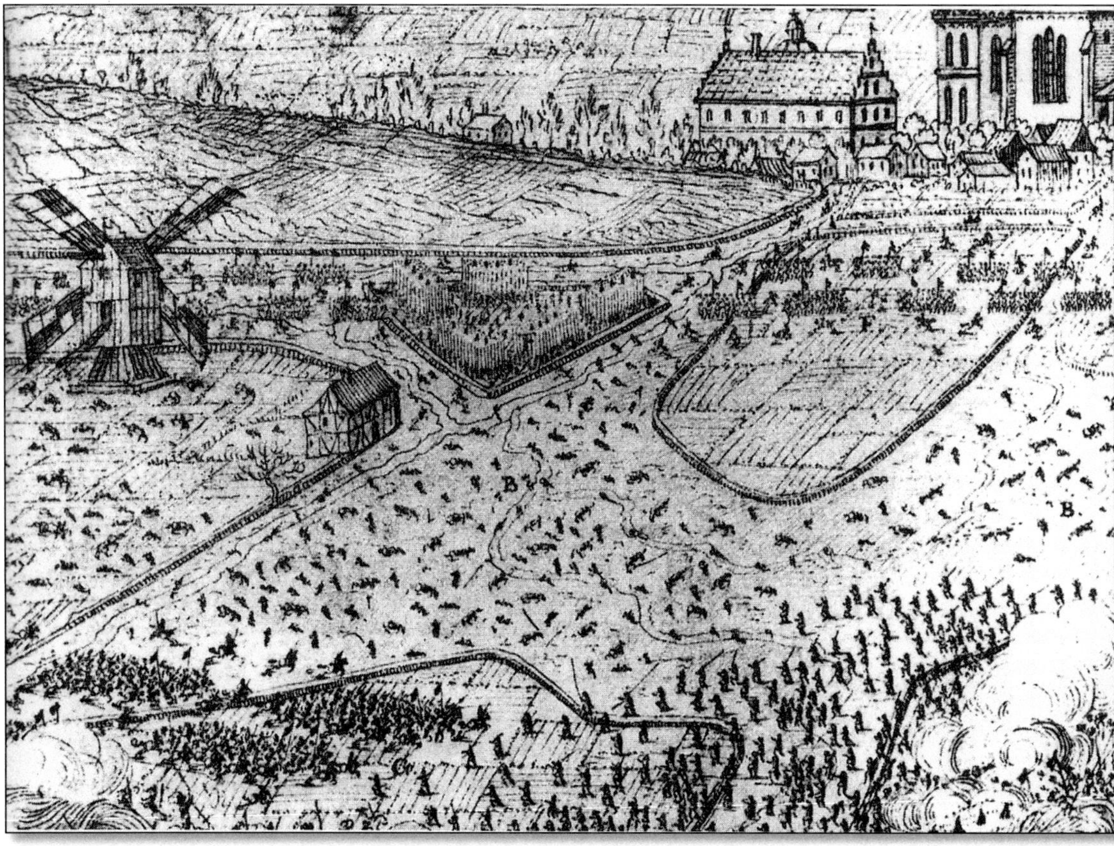

Third phase of the Battle of Lund, 1676, showing the Swedish battalions with their backs to the town, with the Cathedral in the upper left. (Erik Dahlbergh)

in the direction of Landskrona.[46] Bibow's improvised rearguard defence saved whatever remained of the Danish army. Nonetheless, the Swedes were unable to pursue, since the Swedish units were essentially used up. The Swedish army spent the night on the field of battle and in the abandoned Danish camp, where the Swedish soldiers stayed for eight days. By 11:00 p.m., King Charles took night quarters with Bishop Peder Winstrup in Lund, which already had prepared a banquet for whichever king would win the battle.[47]

The Aftermath

On the following morning, in Landskrona, King Christian reviewed his remaining troops, who only counted some 4,000 men.[48] He thanked the troops of the right wing for having fought courageously but ignored those of the left wing, which had fled. In time, he also convened a court-martial to determine who was responsible for the failure to detect the Swedes as they advanced across the River Kävlinge. Major General Sandberg was held responsible, probably unfairly, but at least he was not condemned to

46 Stade, "Slaget vid Lund", p.138.

47 Wahlöö and Larsson, *Slaget vid Lund*, p.79.

48 Stade, "Slaget vid Lund", p.140.

The Battle of Lund as seen from the north, immediately after the return of King Charles, with Lund and its cathedral at the top. (Johan Philip Lemke; Photo: Medströms)

death. As for Bibow, he was promoted to Major General. The fact that King Christian had fled with the left wing was later smoothed over in the official account of the battle which was prepared by the King's close advisor Mejer.[49]

As for King Charles, he after the battle repeatedly expressed his thanks to Bielke and the Life Regiment. To the French ambassador Isaac de Pas, Marquis de Feuquières, King Charles explained that for this victory, next to God he had to give thanks to Bielke and his Life Regiment. He later said: 'On that day, my crown hang on Bielke's rapier point.'[50]

The Battle of Lund was an exceptionally bloody contest. Almost half the participants remained dead on the field, and yet more died within days. Casualties were also exceptionally high among the senior commanders, which in the later stages of the battle meant that it was difficult even to try to exercise any semblance of unified command. The total number of dead was counted but nobody tried to separate them by nationality. Ascheberg mentioned 8,893 dead, while Erik Dahlbergh first wrote 8,892 dead, then in his official report gave the number as 8,357.[51] The different figures can no doubt be explained by the fact that local peasants had to count and then bury the dead in mass graves. It would be surprising if mistakes were not made, especially so since many corpses remained on the field of battle for months before graves could be dug in the frozen soil. Most estimates suggest

49 Stade, "Christian V i slaget vid Lund", pp.52–3.

50 Wahlöö and Larsson, *Slaget vid Lund*, p.77.

51 Ibid., p.82, citing the official Swedish newsletter *Swenska Mercurius*, 11 April 1677.

King Charles, Rutger von Ascheberg, and Erik Dahlbergh, followed by an unnamed Drabant, break through the Danish lines, Battle of Lund, 1676. (Johan Philip Lemke)

that some 2,500–3,000 Swedes died, together with 6,000–6,500 Danes.[52] In addition, some 1,500–2,000 Danes were captured or wounded.[53]

Danish casualties included one general, 11 colonels, and at least four lieutenant colonels. Among the senior Danish officers killed in the battle or from wounds sustained in it were General von Arensdorff, Colonels Sehested, Holck, and Örtzen, and Lieutenant Colonels Holstein, Blücher, and Kremberg. In addition, Colonels Bibow, Lewetzow, Kaas, Styrke, Haxthausen, and Schilden were wounded, as was Colonel Schulenburg, who was wounded and then also captured.[54] Many Danish units were effectively wiped out. In the Zealand Retinue of Nobles, 13 out of 18 officers were dead. The Jutland Retinue of Nobles had lost more than three quarters of its men. The 4th Jutland Regiment had participated in the battle with one full battalion fresh from Denmark, and after the battle it only had about 50 men left.[55]

Swedish casualties included three generals, 14 colonels, and at least two lieutenant colonels. The fact that more senior Swedish than Danish officers were lost, despite being fewer to begin with, is an indication of the aggressive tactics employed by the Swedes. Even very senior officers led their men from the front. Among the senior Swedish officers killed in the battle were Lieutenant General Galle, Colonels Ashton, Burghausen, Mörner, and Rolshausen, and Lieutenant Colonels Siegroth and Lode. In addition, Major

52 Stade, "Slaget vid Lund", p.141; Wahlöö and Larsson, *Slaget vid Lund*, p.83.

53 Wahlöö and Larsson, *Slaget vid Lund*, p.78.

54 Vaupell, *Den danske hærs historie*, p.152.

55 Stade, "Slaget vid Lund", p.159 on n.98.

Above: King Charles at the Battle of Lund, 1676. (Johan Philip Lemke)

Left: Nils Bielke's hat at the Battle of Lund, with alleged bullet hole. (Photo: Medströms)

General Wittenberg, Colonels Gyllenstierna, Hierta, Güntersberg, Kruuse, Lichton, Börstell, Mellin, Baranoff, and Örneklou were wounded, as were Lieutenant General von Fersen and Colonel Budberg, who were wounded and then also captured by the Danes.[56] The Danes had taken 50–70 prisoners, who were brought to Landskrona.[57]

For King Charles and the Swedes, the victory at Lund served two main purposes. First, it gave the Swedish army operational freedom in Scania, with access to the province's rich agricultural supplies, and reopened communications with Malmö. Second, the victory reinforced morale, which

56 Vaupell, *Den danske hærs historie*, p.152.

57 Wahlöö and Larsson, *Slaget vid Lund*, p.78.

Soldiers looting the dead, the Battle of Lund, 1676. (Erik Dahlbergh)

was much needed, in the general population perhaps more so than in the field army. Moreover, Scania remained, at least in some manner, in Swedish hands, so there was no longer any risk that the next campaign season would have to begin outside the southern provinces.

The Battle of Lund was fought not as one set battle but as several, separate actions. There were key differences between the two armies. First, the Swedish army included a significantly higher share of mounted troops than the Danish one. The Swedish ratio was almost 3:1, while the Danish corresponding ratio was close to 1:1, in actual numbers with more foot than horse.[58] Second, the Danish army included more foreign enlisted troops, who might not have been eager to give up their lives merely to win another province for King Christian. Third, and possibly more significant, the Swedes had been out of supplies for most of the campaign and no doubt realised that their only chance to avoid starvation during the winter was to win, and get hold of the plentiful supplies that supposedly existed in Lund and in the Danish camp. In the final account, the Swedes might simply have been the

58 According to Dahlbergh, the Swedish army included 4,700 mounted versus 1,750 foot, officers excluded, which gives a ratio of almost 3:1. In the Danish army, cavalry and dragoons constituted at least some 4,700 to 5,000 men, while infantry strength was some 5,800 men, which gives a ratio close to 1:1. Stade, "Slaget vid Lund", p.114.

more desperate of the two opponents, with far more to lose and consequently a higher motivation to fight on against all odds.

Yet there were also tactical differences. The Danish cavalry mostly relied on the Continental model of discharging their pistols against the enemy rank by rank, instead of aggressively charging home with rapiers. This tactic was often futile against aggressive cavalry, and at Lund, it usually failed to make an impact on the Swedish infantry as well. The battle demonstrated the superiority of the aggressive Swedish style of fighting. It was the Swedish cavalry and the return to aggressive tactics prescribed by Ascheberg which decided the battle. It was perhaps the use of such tactics that best explained the panic engendered particularly in the Danish left wing, a panic that carried everybody including the King and his senior command from the field. The Swedish tactics made an impact on the Danes, and by the end of the war, the Danish cavalry, too, had been ordered to abandon the Continental model. Yet, they still failed to emulate the aggressive tactics of their Swedish counterparts.

There were shortcomings in command on both sides. King Charles, his senior command, and entire right wing were swept up in an ill-advised extended pursuit of the cavalry of the Danish left. After the battle, the 63-year-old Colonel Hierta rebuked the King: 'You do not understand the service of the Crown, you who rode away from the squadron.' King Charles apparently understood the validity of this critical remark, since he soon after promoted the fuming Hierta to Major General.[59] And as for King Christian, his choice to withdraw from the battle before it had truly ended demonstrated that overall command was less than excellent on the Danish side as well.

59 Isacson, *Skånska kriget*, pp.56–7.

16

The Swedes Retake Helsingborg

Having somewhat recovered, the Swedish army on 14 December proceeded to and on the following day laid siege to Helsingborg. Swedish troops again entered the town, and Schultz laid siege to the citadel. Under Schultz served Colonel Bernhard von Sahnitz, who earlier in the year ably but futilely had led the defence of Anklam in Pomerania, an endeavour that had ended in the free return home of the Swedish contingent of the garrison (six companies of the Södermanland Regiment, of which Sahnitz was the commanding officer). Helsingborg was largely abandoned, since many townsmen had fled across the Straits to nearby Helsingør (immortalised by Shakespeare as Elsinore). However, the citadel held out under Colonel Schönfeldt until 30 December, when he surrendered.[1] The huge, 7 x 17-metre swallow-tailed Danish flag (*Dannebrog*) which had been displayed on the citadel since the invasion, was captured. It still remains in the Swedish Trophy Collection in Stockholm.[2]

Danish flag (Dannebrog), captured at the surrender of Helsingborg, 30 December 1676. (Army Museum, Stockholm, AM.084406)

1 Almgren, "Svensk strategi", p.51.

2 Arne Danielsson, "1676 års Dannebrog på Kärnan i Hälsingborg", *Meddelande* 29 (Stockholm: Armémuseum, 1968), pp.25–46. Large sections of the flag have gone missing over the years, so exact length can only be conjectured.

King Christian had specially ordered the huge flag on 5 July, the day after the surrender of Helsingborg's citadel, with specifications to be identical to the great flag over Kronborg Castle in Helsingør, and it was ready only three days after the order.[3]

Schönfeldt and his survivors were sent to Norway. Two thirds of the men were lost during the march. Upon his return to Copenhagen, Schönfeldt was dismissed from the army.[4]

3 Wahlöö and Larsson, *Slaget vid Lund*, p.114.

4 Vaupell, *Den danske hærs historie*, p.155.

17

Another Norwegian Incursion

Winter was coming, and on 17 December 1676, Count Gyldenløve returned from Norway, with an army of 500 horse, 1,200 foot, and 6 cannons. He moved through the province of Bohuslän into that of Västergötland. In Toftedal in Dal province, his cavalry commander Hans Løwenhielm defeated three Swedish squadrons from the Retinue of Nobles and the Old Östgötian Regiment. Løwenhielm personally cut down a Swedish ensign, taking his standard. However, on 20 December, Gyldenløve received news of the defeat at Lund and was ordered not to proceed too deeply into Sweden. Moreover, and apparently more significant, was that the weather suddenly grew unexpectedly mild. The thaw and melting snow resulted in difficult road conditions. As a result, Gyldenløve decided to withdraw to Frederikshald. However, he left a garrison of 140 men and 4 cannons in a blockhouse near Strömstad under Captain Conrad Henneberg, in an attempt to block the port town. Unfortunately for the Norwegians, two days after Gyldenløve's departure, a Swedish force of 1,200 men from Uddevalla under Colonel Claes Breitholtz showed up outside the blockhouse. Most of the Norwegians promptly ran away, hiding in the nearby forests. Those who remained, Captain Henneberg, four officers, and some 15 men, attempted to defend their position, but soon had to surrender. Those who had run away were later court-martialled, with most subsequently executed or forced to run the gauntlet, which in effect often was a death sentence. Henneberg was upon his return dismissed from the army since he had been unable to maintain command.[1] As for the blockhouse, Breitholtz had it burned, after which he returned to Uddevalla.

1 Ibid., pp.155–6.

18

Denmark Again Mobilises

On 7 December 1676, King Christian had ordered Major General Meerheim to Kristianstad with three cavalry regiments and one dragoon regiment (the Life Regiment Cavalry, 2nd Jutland Cavalry Regiment, Rauch's Cavalry Regiment, and Örtzen's Dragoon Regiment), a total of 1,000 cavalry and dragoons. He had to fight his way through the Swedish containment force to enter Kristianstad. He then defended the town for half a year.

Having ordered Meerheim to Kristianstad, King Christian returned to Copenhagen on the same day.[1] A major part of the remaining army was shipped to Denmark later in December, for reorganisation and to be brought up to establishment strength with new troops. Since several infantry regiments had been ruined in the Battle of Lund, some were combined. So was, for instance, the King's Life Regiment reinforced with the remnants of Croÿ's Regiment, Prince George's Regiment was reinforced with the survivors of Stuart's Regiment, the Queen's Life Regiment was reinforced with the remnants of Lütken's Regiment, and Prince Frederick's Regiment was reinforced with the survivors of Schönfeldt's Regiment. Bremer's Regiment was joined with Maximilian Rosencrantz's Regiment and renamed Prince Christian's Regiment.[2]

By the end of 1676, Landskrona remained in Danish hands, and Danish ships could resupply the town indefinitely by sea. Kristianstad, too, remained in Danish hands, under the command of Meerheim. The town and its garrison dominated eastern Scania and accordingly threatened the rear of the Swedish army. However, following the defeat at Lund, it became increasingly difficult for the Danes to raise taxes in Scania, which had been one major reason for the invasion. Likewise, supplies in most cases had to be brought in from Denmark. By then, Denmark also faced a two-front war. On 28 August 1676, France had declared war on Denmark. Although no French military operations against Denmark took place, King Christian had to take the threat of a possible French attack into account. He accordingly negotiated agreements with first Christoph Bernhard von Galen, Prince-Bishop of

1 Vaupell, *Den danske hærs historie*, p.152; Wahlöö and Larsson, *Slaget vid Lund*, pp.109, 123.
2 Ibid., pp.152, 166.

Münster, then with his mother-in-law, Hedwig Sophie of Brandenburg, in her role as Regent for the Landgrave of Hesse-Kassel. The Landgrave, Charles I, was Hedwig Sophie's son and therefore, of course, King Christian's brother-in-law. However, the 22-year-old Landgrave had not yet been able to wrench political power from his mother's grip.

Both the Prince-Bishop and Hedwig Sophie agreed to send reinforcements to Christian's army in Scania in exchange for subsidies. Münster eventually, in 1677, sent 3,500 infantry (Grandvilliers's, Netzow's, Tecklenburg's, and Braun's Regiments), 500 cavalry (Grandvilliers's Cavalry Regiment), 200 dragoons (Schumacher's Dragoon Regiment), and 60 artillerymen, for which Christian promised to pay 52,000 Rigsdalers for a campaign season that lasted until October 1677. The troops were handed over in Holstein in April 1677. Hesse-Kassel first sent a regiment of 10 infantry companies under Colonel Johann auf dem Keller and a dragoon regiment of 270 dragoons in two squadrons under Lieutenant Colonel Wilhelm von Hornum, assisted by Lieutenant Colonel Kristof Lorenz Reitzenstein. Both these regiments, as will be shown, first were deployed for battle on Rügen. Later Hesse-Kassel sent another two cavalry squadrons as well. The troops arrived in Scania in July 1677.[3] King Christian also received the permission of Frederick William of Brandenburg to have an infantry regiment of 1,600 or 1,800 men, the aforementioned Lehnsdorff's Regiment, enlisted on his territory. Elsewhere in Germany, King Christian's emissaries enlisted a dragoon regiment and two other infantry regiments.[4]

Meanwhile, the Norwegian army had been increased to 16,500 men. Three regiments of 1,800 horse were raised or moved to Norway (Jacob von Bülow's Dragoon Regiment, Life Dragoon Regiment, and Brockenhus's Dragoon Regiment, several squadrons of which were transferred to Norway). So were nine regiments of 14,000 infantry, three of which were newly raised: Coucheron's Regiment, under Colonel Willem Coucheron; the 2nd Trondheim Regiment under Colonel Hieronymus Friderich van Iddekinge, another Dutchman; and the Garrison Regiment consisting of enlisted troop under Marthin Jørgen Rochlinge, a Curonian. In addition, a ski company with wheellock muskets was raised under Captain Frantz Wilhelm von Folckersahm. Some of the troops were sent to Denmark to support the Danish field army.[5]

King Christian again attempted to send the army into winter quarters, this time between Helsingborg and Ängelholm. However, the Swedish army remained active throughout the winter, harassing the Danes whenever possible, and hunting down the irregulars whenever an opportunity arose.

On 9 January 1677, King Charles led his army towards Kristianstad. On the whole, the winter of 1676/1677 was unusually cold. The Swedish army again suffered supply problems and famine. The Swedish command found it difficult to maintain control, as troops had to search for food wherever they could. On 12 January 1677, the Swedish army reached Vä. Although

3 Ibid., p.166.

4 Isacson, *Skånska kriget*, p.79.

5 Vaupell, *Den danske hærs historie*, pp.166–7; Gulowsen, *Gyldenløvefeiden*, pp.32–3.

an attack on Kristianstad would have been technically feasible, since the ice meant that the army could cross the wetlands around the town, the King learnt that the Danish garrison had been reinforced to a strength of more than 3,000 men. To storm the town seemed unlikely to succeed. As a result, King Charles let the army move into winter quarters at Vä.

King Charles again wanted to go on the offensive, to take the war to the lands of his enemies according to traditional Swedish doctrine. On the eastern front, Tsar Aleksey Mikhailovich of Muscovy had died in 1676. Perhaps this would give King Charles sufficient respite to march the Swedish army in Livonia south along the Baltic shore to Prussia and Pomerania, to attack his adversaries from the rear? Poland might support such a venture. In addition, King Charles again put his hope in the navy's ability to regroup and reopen his supply lines.

Again, the King's plans made strategic sense, but the recurrent lack of resources made them impossible to carry out. A Livonian expeditionary force was indeed prepared and equipped; however, all supplies were lost in a fire in Riga in 1677, which prevented it from setting out.[6] Moreover, the appointed expedition commander, Field Marshal Bengt Horn (a distant relative of Henrik Horn), failed to leave on time, instead wasting time in Stockholm until he was caught in the ice late in the year.[7] The expedition had to be postponed.

It should not be assumed that King Charles and his senior commanders were delusional and made grandiose plans without any link to reality. Although many archive documents remain from the war, hardly any remain from the strategic discussions of King Charles and his commanders in their field headquarters. They may well have had access to more information than has survived into modern times, information which suggested that there was a real chance, after all, to take the war to their enemies. Besides, it will be shown that they eventually were proven to be right.

6 Gyllenstierna, "Kriget i Tyskland", p.199.

7 Rosander, *Sveriges fältmarskalkar*, pp.202–3.

19

The Reconquest of Karlshamn and Kristianopel

Soon after the Danish invasion, King Charles had dispatched his trusted counsellor, Johan Gyllenstierna, together with Ebbe Ulfeldt and General Pontus Fredrik De la Gardie to raise the Småland peasants for the Swedish cause. The plan was to initiate operations in Blekinge in October 1676. In particular, their task was to fight guerrillas and to retake those small towns previously lost. However, there had been delays, and the attempt to retake Kristianopel by the end of the year had failed.

Now King Charles provided Gyllenstierna with the help of Colonel Axel Wachtmeister and his brother Admiral-Lieutenant Hans Wachtmeister. The Wachtmeister brothers were tasked to assist Gyllenstierna in retaking Blekinge.

In addition, the Swedes established a number of supply depots along the marching routes north of the area of operations. Several were located in Småland. The Danes could not reach the depots, so they had to rely on their freeshooters to attack the convoys bringing supplies to the Swedish field army instead. As a result, Danish operations in Scania increasingly came to focus on a scorched-earth policy. The intention was to deny the Swedes the supplies they needed. However, since most supplies came from the depots in the Swedish heartland, the Danish policy mainly harmed the Scanian population, who increasingly became the target of looting and raiding by both Danish regulars and guerrillas. In many ways, the Danish policy was counterproductive, since it harmed those pro-Danish sentiments that otherwise might have lingered among the population.[1]

In the middle of the winter, Axel Wachtmeister led 1,700 peasant levies to the Blekinge port of Karlshamn, which since its capture by the Danes had been held by Captain Krumsee. Karlshamn's garrison consisted of 400 infantrymen from three companies of respectively the 1st Zealand, 3rd Jutland, and 4th Jutland Regiments. Krumsee also had two warships, but both were locked in by the ice.

On 8 February 1677, Axel Wachtmeister attempted to storm the citadel by advancing across the frozen sea. However, they were repulsed. Krumsee then

1 Knarrström and Larsson. *Hans Majestäts friskyttar*, pp.92–3.

Left: Swedish siege of Karlshamn, 1677. (Preliminary sketch by Erik Dahlbergh)

Below: Swedish siege of Karlshamn, 1677. (Erik Dahlbergh)

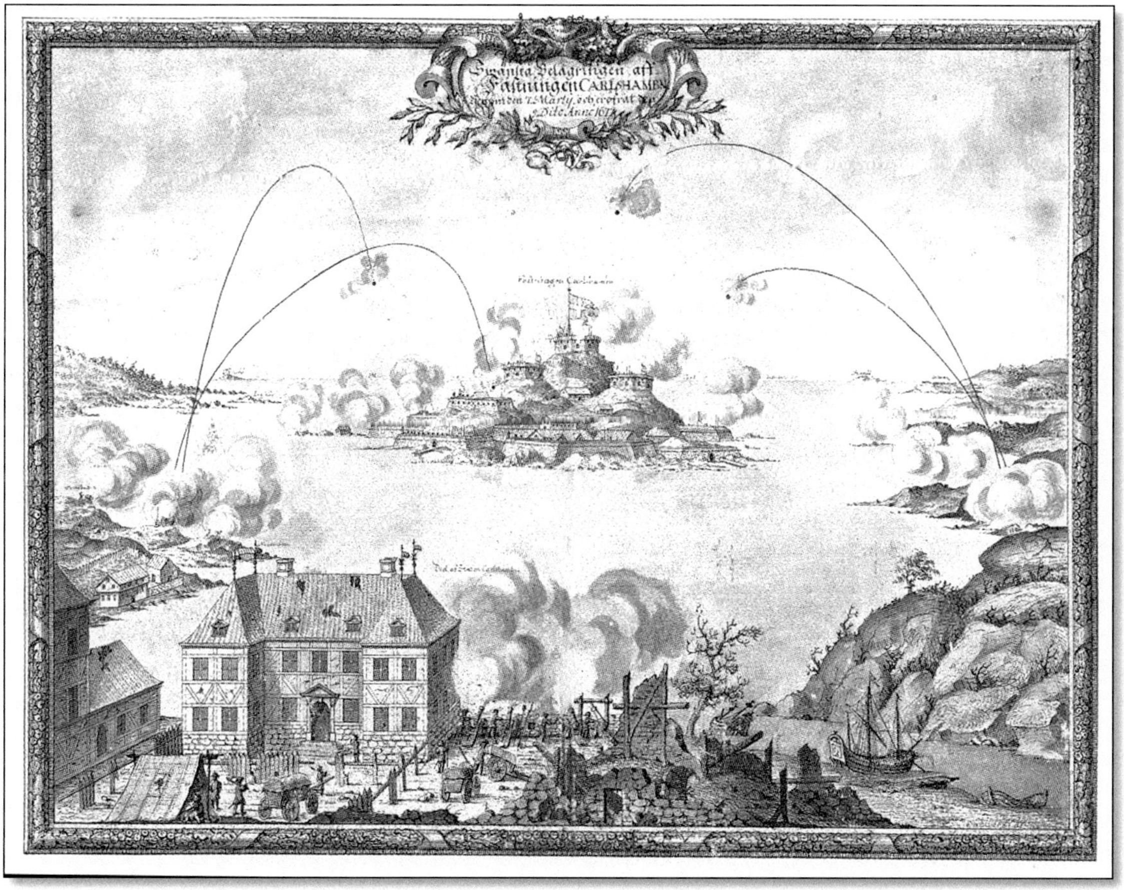

had a large part of the ice in front of the citadel and ships sawn up so as to prevent a second attempt. Yet Wachtmeister made the attempt. Nonetheless, the Swedes again failed, suffering many casualties from the citadel and shipboard artillery fire. The Swedes then withdrew, rejoining other Swedish troops outside Kristianopel.

King Charles then ordered Gyllenstierna and Wachtmeister to make another attempt to take Karlshamn. On 1 March, they again stood outside the citadel, this time with a larger force and several cannons. The Swedish bombardment of Karlshamn continued until Krumsee on 8 March was compelled to surrender. Karlshamn was again in Swedish hands. Krumsee negotiated a free departure, but he and his men had to march to Norway. Back in Denmark, Krumsee was court-martialled for the surrender, but he was freed of all blame.

However, the Swedes did not know that Danish reinforcements under Colonel Otto Heinrich von Aderkas, a German of Livonian origin who had gone into Danish service, were on their way from Kristianstad. Including irregulars, the Danish detachment consisted of some 700 to 1,000 men, of whom 400 were mounted. During the night after Krumsee's surrender, Aderkas and his men carried out a night attack against the Swedish besiegers. The Swedish lookouts had maintained poor discipline, so were taken by surprise. However, Wachtmeister took charge of the situation, rallied the troops, and pushed back the Danes. The captured irregulars were executed.[2]

Johan Gyllenstierna and Ebbe Ulfeldt were also tasked to deal with the little Blekinge town of Kristianopel. On 11 February, Gyllenstierna and Ulfeldt led an army of a few regular soldiers and several thousand peasant levies to lay siege to Kristianopel. They surrounded the town, and on 14 February, the Swedish artillery opened fire. Kristianopel was then defended by Lieutenant Colonel Bernhard Valentin von Lützow, the commandant since early October. His garrison consisted of a battalion from Prince Christian's Regiment and four companies from the 1st Zealand and 2nd Fyn Regiments (in total, 750 soldiers), 150 burgher militiamen, and 60–70 irregulars. On 25 February, the Swedish artillery had breached the walls, so that it would be possible to storm the town. Lützow surrendered, under terms that he and his men would be allowed to depart with full honours of war. This honour was not bestowed on the irregulars, who all were executed by being broken on the wheel, a gruesome method of execution.

As for Lützow and his men, they had been promised to embark upon the Danish ships waiting at sea nearby, to be shipped to Zealand. However, the ships departed as soon as the town fell, before Lützow's men had time to embark. With no other transport available, they were sent on a long march to Norway, during which the majority died from famine and illness. Lützow later returned to Copenhagen, where in November 1677 he was court-martialled for having surrendered the town. First sentenced to death for cowardice, he was subsequently pardoned by King Christian.[3]

2 Vaupell, *Den danske hærs historie*, pp.163–4.

3 Ibid., p.163.

20

King Christian Wavers

By March, the Danes began to engage in operations from their base at Landskrona. On 22 March 1677, they attempted to retake Helsingborg with 300 cavalry and 1,400 infantry. They took the town but failed to take the citadel, which was ably defended by Colonel Carl Hård. King Christian ordered his men to abandon the siege and leave Helsingborg.[1]

Meanwhile, the Swedish army left its winter quarters. Spring was coming, and King Charles was eager to search out the Danes and defeat them in the field. He left Lieutenant General Schultz with 2,300 men, a significant share of the field army at the time, to keep the Danes contained in Kristianstad. Nonetheless, the Swedish army remained at Nääs until 17 May, awaiting reinforcements from the Swedish mainland. The Swedes hoped to gather some 12,000 men, assuming that the contingents from distant Finland and the Baltic provinces arrived.[2]

The Danes had already received reinforcements. On 16 May, the Danish field army in Landskrona consisted of 4,200 cavalry, 800 dragoons, and 7,800 infantry, in total 12,800 men.[3] In addition to these troops, Landskrona had a garrison of some 1,800.[4] In addition, some 4,000 German and Imperial troops were on their way, together with two cavalry regiments newly raised as a retinue of nobles, which remained under training in Denmark.[5] In addition, a Colonel Dubsky had raised a reinforced company of Croats in the Empire for Danish service. The Croats were armed with lances and carbines, some with matchlocks and some with flintlocks. (Placed under the Guard Cavalry or Life Regiment Cavalry, the Croats turned out to be uncontrollable, mutinied in 1678, and were finally sent home in May 1679.)[6] The Danish infantry regiments had in most cases received replacement troops to reach

1 Isacson, *Skånska kriget*, p.65.
2 Almgren, "Svensk strategi", p.71 n.62.
3 Jensen, *Den skaanske krig*, pp.245–7.
4 Almgren, "Svensk strategi", p.71 n.62.
5 Isacson, *Skånska kriget*, p.66.
6 Hasselager and Snorrason, *Danish Uniforms, Colours and Standards*, pp.48–9.

their establishment strength. However, the cavalry on the average seems to have been at only about 80 percent of establishment strength.[7]

On 17 May, the Swedish army marched to Rönneberga, only 7 km north-east of Landskrona. King Charles wanted to restrict the mobility of the Danes, until the Swedish navy again could set out. However, this was an overly bold move. The Swedish army was too small to confront the Danes, consisting of only some 5,000 men and 20 cannons, compared to the more than 12,000 men and 50 cannons that King Christian had at Landskrona.[8] King Charles's generals advised him to withdraw. King Charles refused. Despite the disadvantage, he would not retreat.

King Christian, learning about the Swedish position, drew the conclusion that this time, he might end the war by defeating the smaller Swedish army and killing King Charles. During the night between 26 and 27 May, the Danes left Landskrona and marched to Rönneberga.

When King Charles in the morning saw the Danish army, which had greeted the morning, and the Swedes, through the firing of a Danish salute, he deployed his army in line of battle and responded with a Swedish salute.

The two armies lined up facing each other, separated only by some 400 m of marshland. Then the Danes noticed the approach of a Swedish cavalry unit at some distance. In reality, this was only a scouting party returning to the main army, but King Christian grew worried and called one of his war councils. The Swedish audacity, bordering on lunacy, had apparently given him second thoughts. Had King Charles perhaps planned a trap of some kind? Did Charles have more troops than he had shown? King Christian's advisors, too, wavered. Clearly, more intelligence collection was needed before committing their forces to battle. As usual in such situations, it was easier to find arguments against a proposed course of action than in support of it. After about an hour, King Christian decided to withdraw, hoping for a better opportunity to attack on the following day.

The Swedes withdrew, too, in good order. Meanwhile, the Swedish commanders, thanking their good fortune, again attempted to persuade King Charles to save the army from what they considered certain defeat in light of the superior Danish numbers.

Finally, King Charles agreed. During the night, the Swedish army withdrew under the cover of darkness. They left a few men who lit camp fires and made the occasional noise so as to make the Danes believe that the army remained in camp.[9] As so often during the Scanian War, lookouts maintained poor discipline, and the Danes failed to notice the Swedish withdrawal. King Christian's hesitation had wasted the probably best opportunity he had to defeat his opponent decisively.

The Swedes returned to Kristianstad in forced marches, destroying the bridges after crossing so as to delay the Danes, who followed behind them.

7 Gautier, "Krigskostnaderna", p.242.

8 Almgren, "Svensk strategi", p.53.

9 Göran Rystad, "Slaget vid Landskrona", Göran Rystad (ed.), *Kampen om Skåne* (Lund: Historiska Media, 2005), pp.163–8, on pp.163–4.

On 30 May, the Swedish army rejoined the containment force under Lieutenant General Schultz outside Kristianstad. Some skirmishes followed, including when the Kristianstad commandant, Meerheim, true to form, led a major raid out of Kristianstad. The Danes captured some standards and cannons, but the cost was high since the experienced Colonel Rauch fell in the fighting.[10]

King Christian on 1 June moved his field army to the walls of Kristianstad. The Swedes were, again, too few so withdrew. King Christian replaced Meerheim with first Colonel Christoph Hans Schack, then Major General Carl Henrik von der Osten. Meerheim was promoted to Lieutenant General. King Charles then led the Swedish field army to Mölleröd and Herrevadskloster, leaving a small containment force under Lieutenant General Schultz outside Kristianstad as before.[11]

10 Vaupell, *Den danske hærs historie*, p.170.

11 Isacson, *Skånska kriget*, pp.67–8.

21

The Siege of Malmö

Denmark was wealthy, but the war was costly, and after two years of warfare, Denmark was showing signs of financial bankruptcy. Taxes had already been raised to the extent that little more could be collected, and foreign subsidies failed to materialise from 1677 onwards.[1] Hoping to force an end to the war, King Christian aimed to take Malmö, Scania's chief town which still was in Swedish hands. Malmö was not easy to lay siege to. From the sea, the water was too shallow to allow efficient artillery fire from large warships, while approaches overland had to negotiate a series of marshes. However, if the summer was warm, it happened that the marshland dried out.

On 3 June 1677, the Danish field army left Kristianstad and moved towards Malmö. On the way, the reinforcements from Münster joined the Danes on 6 June. The Münster contingent included both horse (Grandvilliers's Cavalry Regiment and Schumacher's Dragoon Regiment) and foot (Grandvilliers's Regiment, Netzow's Regiment, Tecklenburg's Regiment, and a battalion of Braun's Regiment), as well as artillery (8 three-pounders). Arriving at Malmö on 8 June, the Danish army had reached a strength of 14,000 men.[2]

Realising early on that the Danes eventually would besiege Malmö, the Swedish Field Marshal Fabian von Fersen had taken all possible precautions. In the town and citadel, he had 2,277 soldiers, but of them, sadly only 1,463 were fit for duty.[3] The garrison included six companies from the Mountain County Regiment, an old formation that originally had been set up in Bergslagen, a large mining district in the north-western parts of the Swedish heartland. Regarded as loyal to the Crown and raised from a region traditionally hostile to Denmark for historical reasons that went far back in time, the unit had been moved to Malmö in the early 1670s as a garrison regiment.

In addition to the regular soldiers, Fersen had organised somewhat more than 500 men from the town's total population of 4,000 (including women and children) into a burgher militia consisting of four companies. These were armed with halberds, pikes, and morning stars, the latter an improvised weapon with a long history of use by city militias. However, they had, after some hesitation

1 Nielsen, "Dansk strategi", pp.81, 84.

2 Vaupell, *Den danske hærs historie*, pp.173–4.

3 Göthesson, *Ställningen vid Norrvidinge*, p.18.

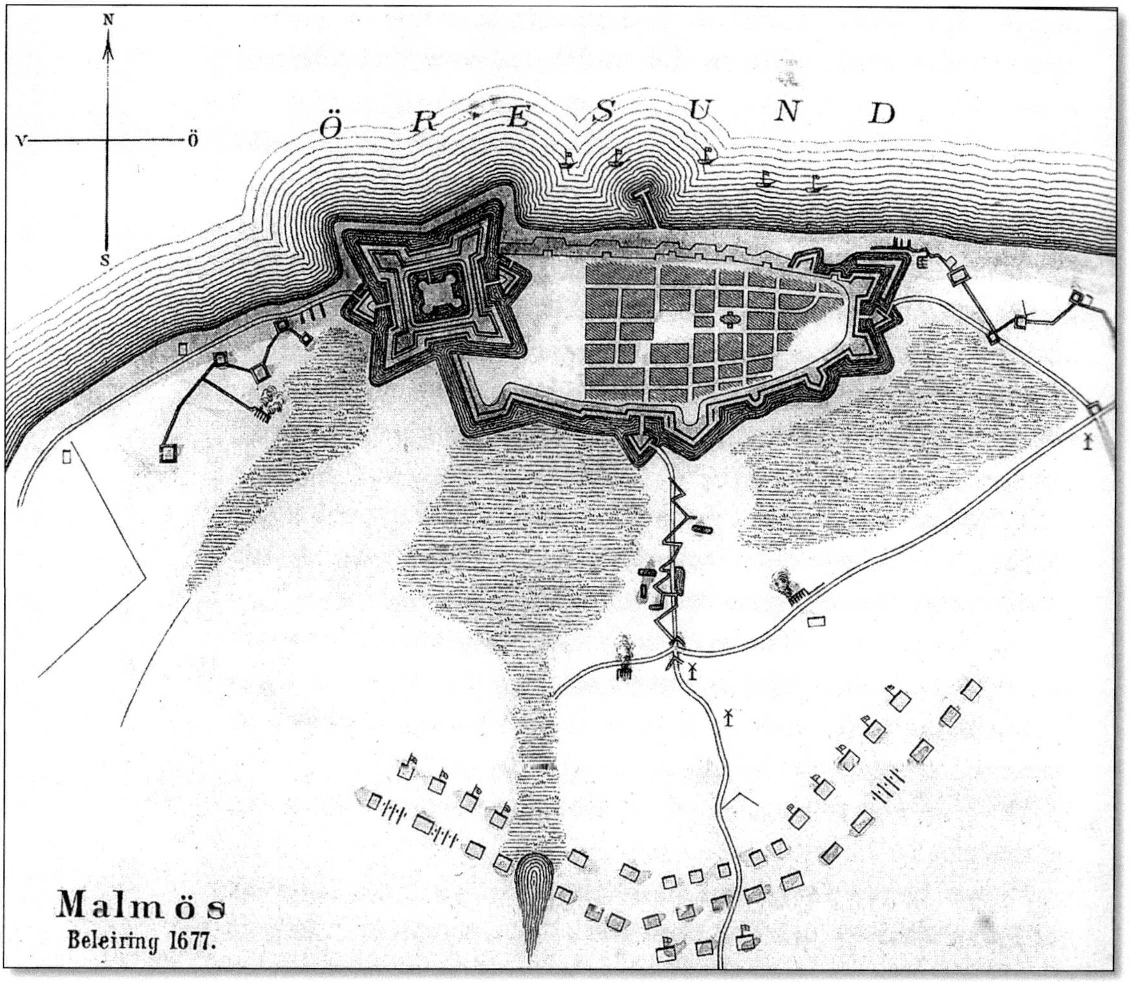

Siege of Malmö, 1677

(since their loyalty was not yet tested), also received a number of army-issue muskets. Other townsmen had been detailed as temporary firemen, since a large number of fires could be expected during a bombardment or assault.

Under Fersen's command, the townsmen had repaired and improved the town's fortifications, in the process also tearing down a number of outlying buildings which might facilitate an attack. Each officer had to sign a warrant that they would not surrender under any circumstances. The chain of command was clarified, too. In short, von Fersen made thorough preparations.

On 10 June 1677, the Danes fired a triple Danish salute into Malmö, that is, nine shot. The Swedes responded with a double Swedish salute: four shot. The two sides having issued their formal challenges, the siege could begin. Real operations began as night fell. The Danes dug trenches and built bastions so that they could get closer to the town. However, for reasons of personal rivalry, they did not involve, in the planning process, their most experienced siege engineer, Rysensteen, who had arrived from Norway. The work continued for several days and nights. On 13 June, the heavy siege artillery from Copenhagen finally arrived with a warship that would provide shipboard artillery support from the sea. It soon became obvious to Fersen that he

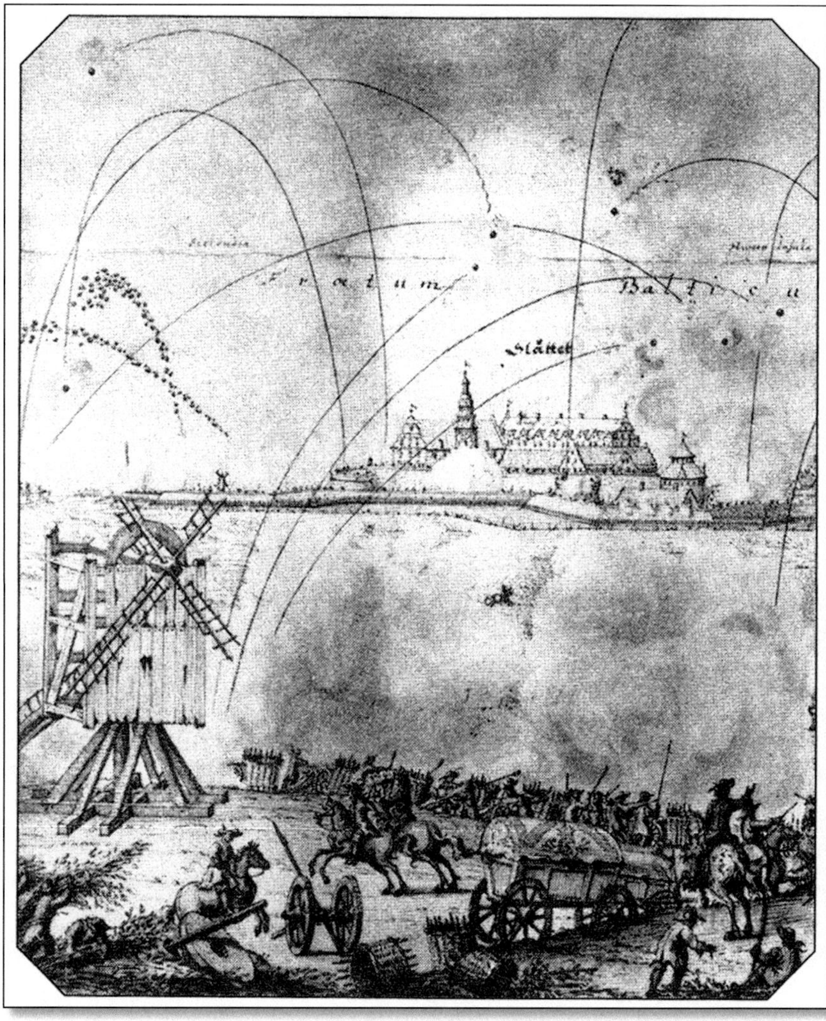

Siege of Malmö, 1677. (Erik Dahlbergh)

had to disrupt the siegeworks. On 15 June, Fersen dispatched a squadron of cavalry, who harassed the Danes engaged in the siegeworks, killing many of them. On the night of 18 June, another force was dispatched, 60 men under regimental quartermaster Willensen. Armed with half-pikes and pistols, they cleared the nearest trenches, also capturing a couple of Danish officers and men. And hours later, at 5:00 a.m., Fersen dispatched Lieutenant Colonel Fritz Wachtmeister with 250 cavalry and 150 musketeers to raid one of the Danish bastions. They reportedly killed about a hundred Danes including four officers and brought back a prisoner, losing only a captain-lieutenant named Kratsch, a cavalryman, and a musketeer during the sally.

Meanwhile, both sides employed artillery fire to strike the other. On the night between 21 and 22 June, the Danes attempted to storm three of the town's bastions. However, they were repulsed, reportedly suffering 300 casualties.

On the night between 25 and 26 June, the Danes attempted a full-scale attack, accompanied by a strong artillery barrage. They attacked in eight different points, led by Major General Bibow and Lieutenant Colonel Plessen, with two battalions (1,000 men) from the King's Life Regiment, and Colonels von Warnstedt (previously wounded and captured at Halmstad) and Busch, with battalions from Prince Christian's and Prince George's Regiments; Croÿ, with the 2nd Zealand Regiment (2 battalions, or1,000 men); Brockenhus, with 400 dragoons; Rumohr, with 1,000 men; and General Grandvilliers, with the Münster troops. By 1:00a.m., they had taken parts of two bastions as well as certain segments of the town wall. Others still attempted to cross the moat by building pontoon bridges, or climb the walls with siege ladders. Finally, the east gate was breached. Bibow immediately led an assault force through the gate, taking another bastion. Additional Danish units joined Bibow. However, the pontoon bridge on which they crossed was soon destroyed by Swedish artillery fire. Bibow and his men, trapped inside the town, could not withstand the counter-attack, being cut down to the last man, including Bibow. The Danes still outside, losing hope, retreated. The battle was over. The Danish army had lost close to 4,000 men. Entire battalions had to be reconstituted. The Danes also suffered significant losses among officers: Major General Bibow, Colonels Busch and Warnstedt, and Lieutenant Colonels Plessen and Ellebrecht had fallen, while Grandvilliers, Croÿ, Fuchs, the Scotsman Meldrum, Ramstedt, and Otto von Vietinghoff, a Livonian in Danish service, were wounded. So was Brockenhus, who eventually died from his wounds.[4] In comparison, Swedish losses were slight, being described as 'very few in number' in the official report.[5] Swedish losses were some 1,000 of whom most were civilians.[6]

It is possible that the Danish assault was premature, because King Christian worried that the Swedish navy might appear with a relief force. After all, King Christian knew that the contest between the Swedish main fleet under Horn and the Danes under Juel (see below) had not yet been resolved. Swedish warships had reportedly been sighted, and it was perhaps to be expected that they would aim to reinforce Malmö. Indeed, on 1 July three badly damaged Swedish warships, the *Kalmar Slott*, *Mercurius*, and *S:t Hieronymus*, cast anchor off Malmö. However, they were survivors of the Danish victory at Køge Bay on the same day, and already on the following day, five Dutch warships arrived to attack the Swedish ships. In the ensuing struggle, all three Swedish ships were lost, primarily from poor seamanship, with the captain on *Kalmar Slott* deliberately setting his ship on fire after having evacuated the crew, so as to deny it to the Dutch.

Nonetheless, after the failed assault, King Christian had lost the will to continue the siege. On 5 July, the Danes abandoned camp and departed. Malmö had not fallen, but the siege had been costly. Less than a month later, on 30 July, the 51-year-old Fabian von Fersen died, from a head wound sustained during the siege.[7]

4 Vaupell, *Den danske hærs historie*, pp.176–8.
5 Isacson, *Skånska kriget*, pp.70–73.
6 Göthesson, *Ställningen vid Norrvidinge*, p.19.
7 Rosander, *Sveriges fältmarskalkar*, p.193.

22

The Battle of Køge Bay

The Swedish navy had again left port, with the same tasks as in the previous years. However, again it failed to fulfil them. A new admiral was appointed, Field Marshal Henrik Horn, who was an experienced soldier and until recently had attempted the task, against all odds, to defend Stade, but he knew that he lacked nautical experience and argued against his appointment. Nonetheless, he had to accept.

Both the main fleet in Stockholm and the squadron in Gothenburg were supposed to leave port around 20 May, in the hope that they could defeat the Danish fleet before the Dutch fleet returned. However, only the Gothenburg squadron left on time. Admiral Siöblad, by then promoted, on 15 February received orders immediately to dispatch a couple of warships to sever the communication line between Denmark and Norway. When his entire squadron was ready, he was to sail to Helsingborg for further orders, before the Danish fleet left port. He then should join the Swedish main fleet in the Baltic. It is unclear if the Swedish command, including King Charles, understood exactly what they asked Siöblad to do. He would have to run the gauntlet between the Dutch and Danish fleets through the narrow sea lanes in the Danish heartland. Nonetheless, Siöblad sailed on 20 May with his squadron consisting of three warships and five smaller ships with a total of 386 cannons.[1]

The Swedish main fleet, too, was ordered to leave port. Horn on 3 April received orders to bring reinforcements to Stettin. King Charles in a letter dated 21 April repeated the urgency for speed, so that the fleet could defeat the Danish fleet before the expected Dutch fleet arrived. Horn was ordered to join forces with Siöblad's squadron, and then attack the Danes. King Charles, now knowing that the Dutch crews were better artillerymen than their Swedish counterparts, advised Horn not to engage in artillery duels but to close with the enemy and board his ships. In effect, King Charles asked Horn to follow the aggressive tactics that had proven so useful on land. The Swedish main fleet, a total of 34 ships with 1,745 cannons, finally left Dalarö only on 9 June.[2]

1 Askgaard, "Kampen till sjöss", pp.176–7.

2 Ibid., p.177.

The Danes, too, understood that it was advantageous to have their fleet set out well before the Swedes. In fact, Niels Juel was ready to sail on 23 May, when intelligence arrived that Siöblad had left Gothenburg. On 24 May, King Christian ordered both Tromp and Juel to intercept the Swedish Gothenburg squadron. Since Tromp already on 8 February had returned to the Netherlands to push for an earlier departure of the expected Dutch fleet, Juel took command of the available 11 warships with 584 cannons. This was fortunate for the Danes, since Tromp only returned with the Dutch fleet on 2 July, which meant that the Dutch fleet did not participate in the battles this year.[3]

Siöblad almost carried it off, but only almost. He charted an audacious course through the Great Belt, through the very core of the Danish lands, and harried coastal towns so as to give an impression of strength, since he could not avoid being seen. On 28 May, the inevitable happened, as somebody observed the squadron passing through the Great Belt and sent intelligence to Copenhagen. On 1 June, Juel managed to intercept Siöblad's squadron as it negotiated a way through the Danish sea lanes. Both Siöblad and Juel were experienced sailors, but Juel had more ships and men. In a desperate battle with the numerically stronger Danish fleet off Rostock, later known as the Battle of Møn, Siöblad had to surrender, together with most of his surviving men. Of Siöblad's squadron, only two ships managed to break through and reach the Swedish main fleet.[4]

Amarant, one of the Swedish warships taken by Danes at the Battle of Møn, 1677. (Model in Maritime Museum, Stockholm; Photo: Medströms)

By then, the Swedish main fleet had not yet left port. When it did, on 9 June, the fleet commanded by Field Marshal Horn consisted of 21 ships of the line, three frigates, between six and eight armed merchantmen, six fireships, and 11 smaller vessels. It was armed with some 1,600 cannons, carried a crew of 8,600 men, and also carried 600 soldiers intended as reinforcements for Pomerania.[5]

Admiral Juel had no intention to approach the Swedish fleet immediately. First, he was still waiting for the arrival of Tromp's Dutch fleet. Second, the failure of King Christian's army at Malmö meant that if the Danish fleet was lost due to recklessness and Horn gained supremacy in the Straits, then King Christian would be cut off from the Danish heartland. Besides, the Danish fleet was still slightly inferior in numbers. It consisted of 19 ships of the line, five frigates, one armed merchantman, two fireships, and seven smaller vessels. Armed with some 1,400 cannons, it had a crew of 6,700 men.[6]

3 Ibid., p.177.
4 Vaupell, *Den danske hærs historie*, pp.171–3; Askgaard, "Kampen till sjöss", p.178.
5 Ericson et al., *Svenska slagfält*, p.241.
6 Ibid., p.241.

Top: Battle of Køge Bay, 1677, as depicted in an incorrect but near-contemporary painting. (Claus Møinichen; Photo: Medströms)
Bottom: Battle of Køge Bay, 1677, as depicted by a later artist. (Anton Melbye, 1858; Photo: Medströms)

Horn searched out Juel's fleet in the hope of engaging in battle. On 1 July, the two fleets entered into contact in Køge Bay, east of Zealand. The battle was hard-fought and lasted for 10 hours, but eventually, the superior Danish skills in seamanship turned decisive. When Horn disengaged, he had lost five ships of the line. In the aftermath of the battle, he lost another three (the *Kalmar Slott*, *Mercurius*, and *S:t Hieronymus*, which, as noted, were taken at Malmö). As for personnel losses, Swedish casualties totalled some 3,000 dead, wounded, and captured. Juel lost 100 dead and 275 wounded.[7]

7 A recent study of the Battle of Køge Bay is Ericson et al., *Svenska slagfält*, pp.238–46.

Hans Wachtmeister. (Photo: Medströms)

After the battle, Horn was removed from the position of Admiral of the Realm. Instead he was sent to take charge of the army in Livonia, which King Charles still hoped would be able to go on the offensive against Brandenburg-Prussia. As new head of the navy, King Charles chose Hans Wachtmeister, who had commanded a squadron of the Västgöta Cavalry Regiment at the Battle of Lund and later led irregular troops in Scania together with his brother. But more to the point, Wachmeister *was* an experienced naval officer, had commanded a squadron at Køge Bay, and indeed was the first mariner to be appointed head of the navy during the war.

Admiral Wachtmeister withdrew the Swedish fleet to Kalmar, from which he continued to threaten the Danes. When Tromp arrived with the Dutch fleet immediately after the battle, Wachtmeister realised he was unable to challenge the combined Danish-Dutch fleet directly, yet his continued presence in Kalmar meant that the Danes could not act with impunity in the southern Baltic, as they had done until then.

Despite the Danish success at sea, King Christian remained in an exposed position in Scania. Having failed to conquer Malmö, King Christian was desperate for the navy to ease the pressure on his army. King Christian on 9 July accordingly ordered Tromp to sail all the way to distant Stockholm, and on the way attack the Swedish mainland towns of Norrköping and Västervik as well as the island of Öland. King Christian described the purpose of the operation: 'through such diversions force the enemy to detach its army in Scania; and for this reason, burn and defile, take ransom, plunder, kill or abduct the population, so that the enemy will think that we are serious when visiting them.'[8] In addition, King Christian on 15 July ordered Juel to locate and destroy the Swedish fleet at Kalmar. In August, Juel considered an attack on Kalmar. However, this being unfeasible, he instead ravaged and burned almost all settlements on the nearby island of Öland. He also captured 2,000 heads of cattle. In addition, Juel raided Småland and Västervik. As for Tromp, King Christian by then entertained plans to send 6,000 to 7,000 men on an expedition to Stockholm, to land them there so as to put additional pressure on the Swedes. However, this plan was abandoned on 11 August. Instead, the focus henceforth lay on coastal raiding.[9]

Yet, neither the victories at sea nor the ravaging of Öland and other coastal areas succeeded in alleviating the strategic situation on land.

8 Cited in Askgaard, "Kampen till sjöss", 179;Ericson et al., *Svenska slagfält*, p.246.

9 Askgaard, "Kampen till sjöss", p.179 with n.27.

23

The Battle of Landskrona

Despite the losses at Malmö, King Christian was not too shaken. Landskrona was the strongest fortress in Scania and a port town, he retained supremacy at sea, his communication lines to the Danish heartland were short, and he received yet more German reinforcements from Hesse and Münster. His army numbered some 11,000 to 12,000 men, not quite as much as before the debacle at Malmö but close.[1] The Danish army regrouped at Billeberga outside Landskrona.

On 12 July 1677, King Charles led the Swedish army towards Rönneberga, only 7 km northeast of Landskrona. It consisted of about 9,000 to 10,000 troops, in addition to some 4,000 Småland levies led by their county governors, Augustin Leijonsköld and Gustav Lilliecrona.[2] The respective share of horse and foot was about 1:1. The levies were normally used to combat guerrillas. Armed with spears, scythes, hay forks, morning stars, and other improvised polearms, with a sprinkling of pikes, muskets, and reportedly even crossbows, they could handle brigands and irregulars but were not sufficiently trained to face regular troops. When it came to regular troops, the Danes still held the advantage.

Nils Bielke, after the Battle of Lund promoted to Major General, on the evening of 12 July set out on a reconnaissance mission. On the morning of 13 July, he found that the Danes had taken up a strong, fortified position on the hills of Rönneberga, in fact, the same position that the Swedes held in May. Upon his return, Bielke and the senior leadership attempted to dissuade King Charles from attacking under such unfavourable conditions. To no avail; King Charles lost his temper, replying that he would attack under any circumstances.

The Swedish army rested on 13 July, since this was a religious holiday. King Charles was genuinely pious, and he did not wish to profane the holy day. This was a calculated risk, since the Danes knew the Swedish position and could take additional precautions, which, as we will see, they did.

At midnight, after the day of rest and prayer, the army began preparations to march. By 2:00 a.m., the men had formed up in their units, and by

1 Almgren, "Svensk strategi", p.56; Rystad, "Slaget vid Landskrona", p.163.

2 Almgren, "Svensk strategi", p.56; Rystad, "Slaget vid Landskrona", p.164.

3:00 a.m., the march towards Tirup began. The summer night was short and never really dark, it was warm, and the following day would be sunny, with high temperatures. Not yet quite dawn, but there was enough light to march.

When approaching Rönneberga, the Swedes realised that the Danish army had left its positions. Were they walking into an ambush? King Charles sent out Ascheberg to locate the Danes. Ascheberg brought only a couple of men. At the Tirup church, the small party suddenly encountered Major General Walter, who, like Ascheberg, rode with only a few companions. Ascheberg and Walter knew each other. Back in 1642, during the Thirty Years' War, Walter had saved Ascheberg's life in the Second Battle of Breitenfeld (also known as the First Battle of Leipzig). This was 35 years ago. Ascheberg, then a mere cavalryman in his early twenties, had been seriously wounded, fallen to the ground, and his belongings had been taken. Walter, then a cavalry captain in Swedish service, had found and carried him back to safety. Walter, who came from Schleswig, later joined the army of Holstein-Gottorp, where he stayed until, following King Christian's 1675 coup, he received a written order from the Duke to surrender and go into Danish service. So now he and Ascheberg were on opposing sides. The two parties exchanged shots with their pistols. Both had been looking for the enemy army, and when the parties ran into each other, both realised that the opponent would not be far away.

Having returned to the Swedish army, Ascheberg reported the situation. The army halted, and a Swedish salute was fired, as a challenge to the Danes. For some reason, the Danish army did not respond, but in the distance, the Danes at Landskrona responded with a Danish salute.

Ascheberg then set out again. From the hill at Billeberga church, he finally saw the Danish army. The Danes had regrouped on a plain called Ylleshed, behind a line of recently prepared earthworks. Ascheberg returned to the King to report. It was around 6:00 a.m. on 14 July 1677.[3]

King Christian had expected King Charles not to be so foolhardy as to attack his fortified position at Rönneberga. Yet, he, too, wanted a battle, since there was no other way to win the war. He had accordingly moved his army out of the prepared positions and into the new position at Ylleshed so as to tempt King Charles to attack. And Charles was only too willing to bite.

Lieutenant General Friedrich von Arensdorff had temporarily assumed his brother's post as commander-in-chief at the latter's death in the Battle of Lund and he stayed in this post until February 1677. However, from March 1677 King Christian had replaced him with Lieutenant General Gustav Adolph von Baudissin, the conqueror of Bremen-Verden, as interim overall commander until May 1677. When King Christian on 15 May returned to Landskrona for a new campaign season, he brought a Prussian officer, Field Marshal Joachim Rüdiger von der Goltz, as his new overall commander.[4] Goltz had fought at Fehrbellin in the service of Brandenburg. Now he ordered a few infantry battalions to be moved to the wings, in order to support the cavalry, despite

3 Modern studies of the battle include Rystad, "Slaget vid Landskrona", pp.163–8; Isacson, *Skånska kriget*, pp.76–97. Both fundamentally follow the classical interpretation of the battle. A more recent and thorough study is Götesson, *Skånska krigets verkningar*, pp.139–235.

4 Nielsen, "Dansk strategi", p.79.

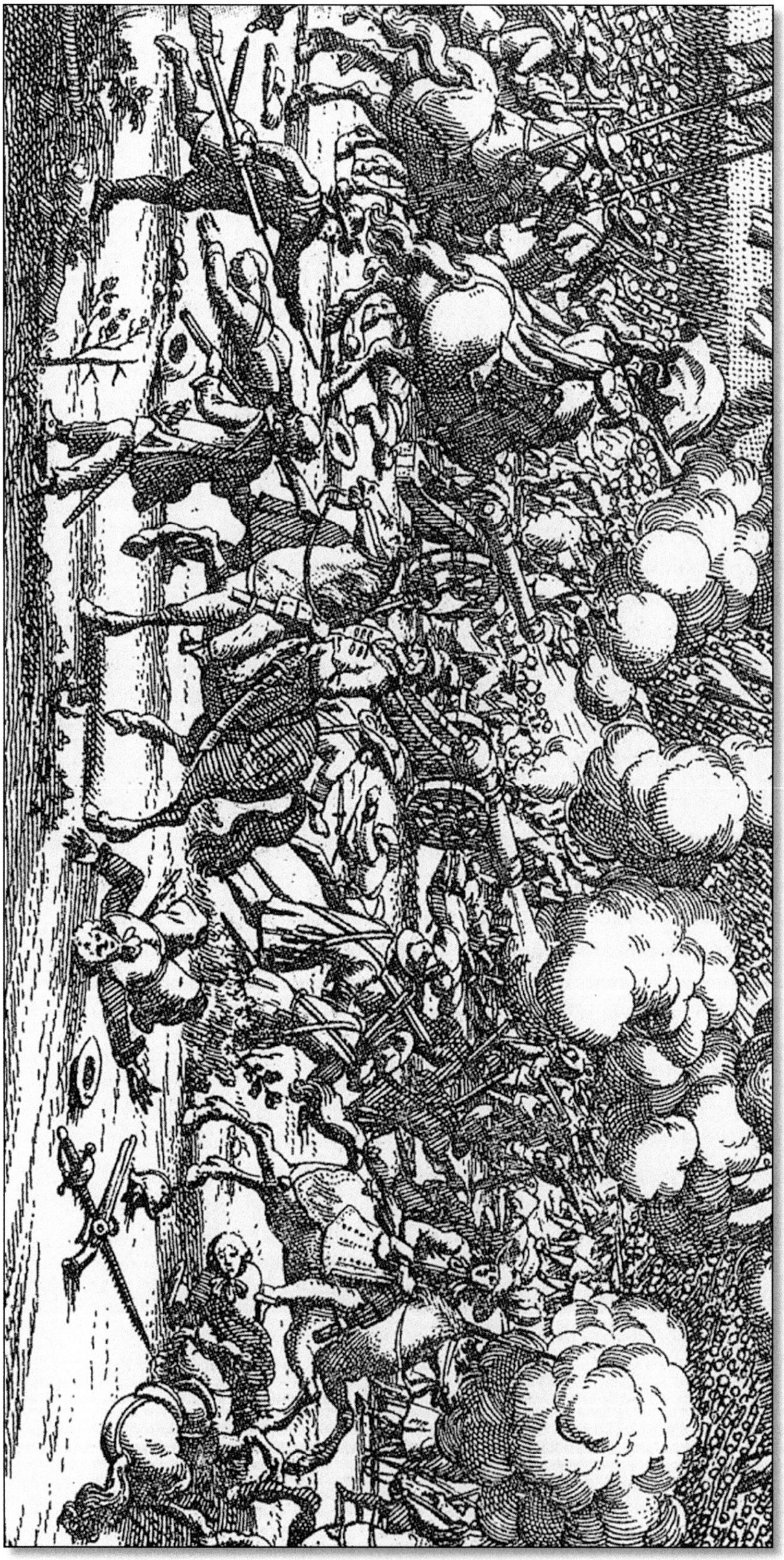

Battle of Landskrona, 1677. Near centre: Musketeers equipped with the old-style bandolier with wooden bottles for gunpowder instead of the new cartridge box.

Scandinavian wings normally (but not invariably) consisting only of cavalry (Appendix IX). This eventually turned out to be a bad decision, since the infantry could not maintain the speed of the cavalry, and thus fell behind both during the advance and the subsequent retreat.

Ascheberg suggested that the Swedish army would move southwest, to reach a position from which they could threaten the Danish flank. King Charles agreed, and the army set out again. The peasant levies were deployed at Tirup church, protected by a *wagenburg* of supply carts.

By 8:00 a.m., the Swedish line had been formed. There was a light breeze, which the Swedes found favourable, since it would blow the smoke of battle against the Danish line, thus providing some cover for the Swedish troops.

King Charles concentrated his artillery, under Colonel Christer Carlsson Lillieberg, in front of the right wing. Lillieberg, who had begun service as a common artilleryman during the Thirty Years' War, had since risen in rank and also been chief of artillery at the campaigns in Germany in 1675 and 1676. King Charles ordered the firing of a double Swedish salute to challenge King Christian.

Christian, who had concentrated his artillery in front of his left wing, that is, opposite the Swedish artillery, did not respond. A third Swedish double salute was fired. Only the Danish artillery at Landskrona replied. Christian wanted the Swedes to attack his new position, since although not comparable to the previous one, it, too, provided good defensive cover. However, it was obvious to the Danes that the Swedish army was both inferior in numbers and weaker in supply. They were not likely to attack a strong defensive position. Moreover, Goltz, too, advised the King to move out his troops, but for another reason. The cover was good but did not allow the Danes to deploy their entire army. He suspected that the Swedes were planning a flank attack and to counter this, he needed more space. In the end, the Danish army deployed in the two usual lines, but with a substantial cavalry reserve in the form of a third line. The reserve, commanded by the redoubtable Major General Meerheim, consisted of units with a large share of veterans.

Between the two armies was a narrow river valley, following the River Råå. The valley floor was about 20 metres below the plain, and the river banks were both steep and muddy. Already before the battle got underway, the Swedish army crossed the river, with some difficulty, and deployed on the western side.

The surviving sources do not give a full picture of the battle, but the main events are known. Still, many events remain obscure, despite both written sources and the results of some battlefield archaeology.[5]

The Swedish Right Wing Versus the Danish Left wing

Real combat began at 10:30 a.m. King Christian led his right wing against the Swedish left wing. However, the infantry battalions deployed in support of

5 Knarrström, *Slagfältet*, pp.109–29.

the Danish cavalry could not maintain the speed of King Christian and the cavalry, so were left behind. This caused some disorder in the Danish line, even though the Swedes lacked flank cover and thus were vulnerable.

Soon after, the Danish left wing, too, charged. Since King Charles had concentrated his artillery in front of the right wing, the Danes suffered casualties and were halted. However, the Danes brought up their own artillery and returned fire. And the Danish artillery was stronger.

Soon after 11 a.m., King Charles, realising that he had nothing to gain by allowing the Danish artillery to overcome his own, led his Drabant Guard, a single squadron of 132 men under the one-armed Colonel Johan Henrik von Naschert, across the valley and up the hill. However, there their progress was hindered by a road flanked on both sides by dry-stone walls, behind which four Danish squadrons waited. The dry-stone walls delayed the King and his men, since any horse that jumped over the first wall then would get stuck between the two walls and often stumble. More cavalry followed him, but then dismounted to remove boulders so as to open up a passage. The heavy Danish fire caused serious losses among the King's cavalry, yet they got across the walled road and charged the four Danish squadrons. The Danes quickly surrounded the little Swedish cavalry force, while King Charles and his men fought for their lives. Fortunately for Charles, his first line was commanded by Ascheberg, who did not hesitate to lead the remaining squadrons in a charge. Two squadrons of the Life Regiment, under Lieutenant Colonel Georg Zelow, managed to get through the walls and charged in support. The Life Regiment was divided between the first and second lines, so Zelow's men were soon followed by two additional squadrons from the Life Regiment, this time under Major General Bielke. Behind him followed the single squadron from the Scania-Bohuslän Dragoon Regiment, under Colonel Mauritz Wilhelm von Post.

In addition, for once the Swedes, too, had deployed some infantry in support of the cavalry wings. Soldiers from the Life Guard, a battalion under Hastfehr, who had been promoted to lieutenant colonel after the Battle of Lund, had by then negotiated the dry-stone walls and, after firing a volley, charged the Danish cavalry.

Then the rest of the Swedish second line followed up the charge. The Västgöta Cavalry Regiment under Colonel Per Hierta, with Major General Schönleben again probably the oldest man on the battlefield, joined the fighting, as did the infantry battalion from the Hälsinge Regiment.

On the Danish side, the infantry from Prince George's Regiment finally reached the battle; however, almost immediately the Danish cavalry was pushed back, which disrupted the infantry, many of whom were ridden down by their own.

A similar fate struck the other Danish infantry, as they arrived in support. The King's Life Regiment and the Queen's Life Regiment were pushed back, too, suffering significant losses. The Danish artillery was captured by the Swedes, who spiked the cannons. Soon many Danes fled, hotly pursued by the Swedish cavalry. Unfortunately for the Danes, this time it was they who were delayed by a dry-stone wall, leading to yet more casualties as the troops desperately attempted to cross.

Cavalry. (Johan Philip Lemke)

Meanwhile, the kind of small skirmishes that mostly go unrecorded in battle histories took place. A few Danes who had taken cover in a thicket opened fire at King Charles. They failed to hit, so Charles, brave to the point of foolhardiness, rode up against them, challenging the Danish soldiers to come out and fight one by one. The Danish soldiers stayed in cover, and as cooler judgement prevailed, the King continued onwards.

Soon the summer heat took its toll, with temperatures rising above 30 degrees. The soldiers were dressed in the same woollen uniforms that they had used in winter, which hardly improved matters. Men and horses collapsed, from exhaustion or heat. One of General Schultz' sons, the 23-year-old Captain Gustav Schultz of the Kronoberg Regiment, collapsed and died without having suffered any wound.[6] King Charles, excited and overheated, is reported to have collapsed twice. On one occasion, he was revived when an anonymous soldier gave him a draught of strong liquor that he had carried into battle.

The combat did not last for more than half an hour but was remarkably hard-fought. No prisoners were taken by either side. King Charles was unwounded, but not all his senior officers fared that well. Colonel von Post suffered two cuts and was shot twice, yet still followed along in the pursuit until he lost consciousness and fell from his horse. He was carried from the field but died on the following day. Ascheberg's horse, Frisk Opp, was shot below him. He soon found another, whose rider had fallen.

Among the Danes, losses were yet higher. Major General Walter, riding with two of his sons, first saw one son mortally wounded, then fell himself.

6 Jacobsen, *Den Nordiske Kriigs Krøniche*, p.130.

Major General Detlef von Rumohr was captured by Captain Bernhard von Liewen of the Life Guard. Liewen, it will be remembered, had distinguished himself already in the Battle of Lund when he had killed a Danish captain in single combat.

The Danish Right Wing Versus the Swedish Left Wing

While the Swedish right wing was victorious, on the other side of the battle the Danes were pushing the Swedes back. Lieutenant General von Baudissin attempted to charge the Swedish left wing in the flank with the Münster dragoons and the Imperial infantry, the originally 1,422-strong Count Strassaldo's Regiment. The charge brought disorder to the Swedish squadrons, which were thrown back into their own second line. Swedish infantry from the Västerbotten Regiment moved forward to support the cavalry, but they suffered numerous casualties from the Danish cavalry, led by King Christian who together with his brother, Prince George, personally killed several Swedes. Perhaps at an early point the reserve under Meerheim was deployed in support, too, which would help explain the rapid success of the Danish right wing. On the other hand, the Danish right wing was probably stronger than the Swedish left wing even without including the reserve. Soon the Swedish lines wavered. To stop the Danish advance, the 60-year-old Field Marshal Helmfelt personally gathered and led a few squadrons from the second line against the Danes. Before the battle, Helmfelt apparently had a dream in which he saw himself fall in the battle, and King Charles had reportedly advised him to heed the dream and not to take any unnecessary risks. Soon Helmfelt's horse was shot under him, collapsing. Helmfelt was thrown, with one of his legs pinned under the dead or dying horse. Helmfelt tried to get up, but a German lieutenant from Gewecke's Cavalry Regiment rushed to him. Despite Helmfelt offering a ransom for his life, the lieutenant ran his rapier through Helmfelt's throat, killing him. The lieutenant then stole Helmfelt's ring. His other clothes and possessions were taken, too, by one or the other of the troops.

After the battle, the ring was identified, proving that Helmfelt was dead. However, his naked body could no longer be identified, so a corpse was selected at random, provided with a proper wig and suitable clothes, and then sent to the Field Marshal's family for burial.[7] Helmfelt was an educated man, and following his last will, Helmfelt's widow bequeathed a substantial part of his fortune to a fund, which still exists, for underprivileged students at Uppsala University.

The Swedes suffered other losses, too. Old Major General Schönleben was badly wounded, like Helmfelt trapped under his dead horse, and was eventually captured as the Danish troops advanced further, pushing the Swedes before them. Colonel Drake, the commander of the Retinue of Nobles, was mortally wounded. On the other wing, the same fate, as noted,

7 Ibid., p.128.

The Swedish peasant levies at Tirup, Battle of Landskrona. (Tapestry based on painting by Johan Philip Lemke; Photo: Medströms)

struck Colonel von Post, the commander of the Scania-Bohuslän Dragoon Regiment, and Lieutenant Colonel Caspar Goës of the same regiment.

The Swedish artillery was lost, too. However, the artillerymen spiked the cannons before the Danes could get to them.

With the Swedish left wing seriously weakened due to the loss of men and, not least significant, both Helmfelt and Schönleben and several regimental officers, the advancing Danes pushed the Swedes back down the valley and into the River Råå. As Swedish survivors scrambled up the slope on the east side of the river, several Danish cavalry units crossed the river, following the Swedes. It seemed likely that the Danish success would result in the entire Swedish left wing fleeing the field.

However, this did not happen. A few Swedish units on the east side of the river, either because they never had crossed in the first place or because they had been able to regroup after being pushed back, now formed up to oppose the Danish advance. This time the Danes were at a disadvantage, since they first had to descend into the river valley, then negotiate the muddy river banks, and finally climb the steep slope under enemy fire. Perhaps foremost of the defending Swedish units was a squadron of the Queen-Dowager's Life Regiment of Horse, commanded by Captain Carl Gustaf Rehnskiöld. This was not Rehnskiöld's first command of a whole squadron; in the Battle of Lund he had assumed command of the squadron when his superior Major Lindhielm had been wounded. His squadron now attacked the Danes who had crossed the river, was surrounded by several Danish squadrons, and a third of the men fell. Yet, Rehnskiöld and the other survivors performed excellently, pushing the Danes back into the river. Most likely, the advancing Danish cavalry that Rehnskiöld defeated had become badly disordered while crossing the river, probably to the extent that the Danish cavalry units could not move at all due to the muddy riverbank and the slope. There is some archaeological evidence that suggests that a large number of cavalry was engaged and lost in this particular place.[8] The King later wrote about Rehnskiöld's "unequalled bravery" during the battle. Within months, he would be promoted to lieutenant colonel, without the need first to serve as major. Soon he would also become head of the regiment, and, in a later war, field marshal.[9]

Major General Jöran Sperlingh assumed command of the Swedish left wing after Helmfelt's death. The left wing withdrew in reasonable order towards Tirup church. There the levied peasants began to make their presence felt, playing their drums, waving their numerous county, district, and hundred flags, and firing muskets. The levies were fundamentally untrained, but they were led by regular officers and had been instructed to stand firm in the face of the enemy, having been taught that flight was tantamount to suicide, as it indeed was if faced by enemy cavalry.

The Danes, failing to realise the nature of the levies, thought that the formation might constitute a large reserve of regular troops. The Danes halted their advance, indeed retreated some distance to reform their lines. This no

8 Knarrström, *Slagfältet*, p.81.

9 Isacson, *Skånska kriget*, p.123 n.14.

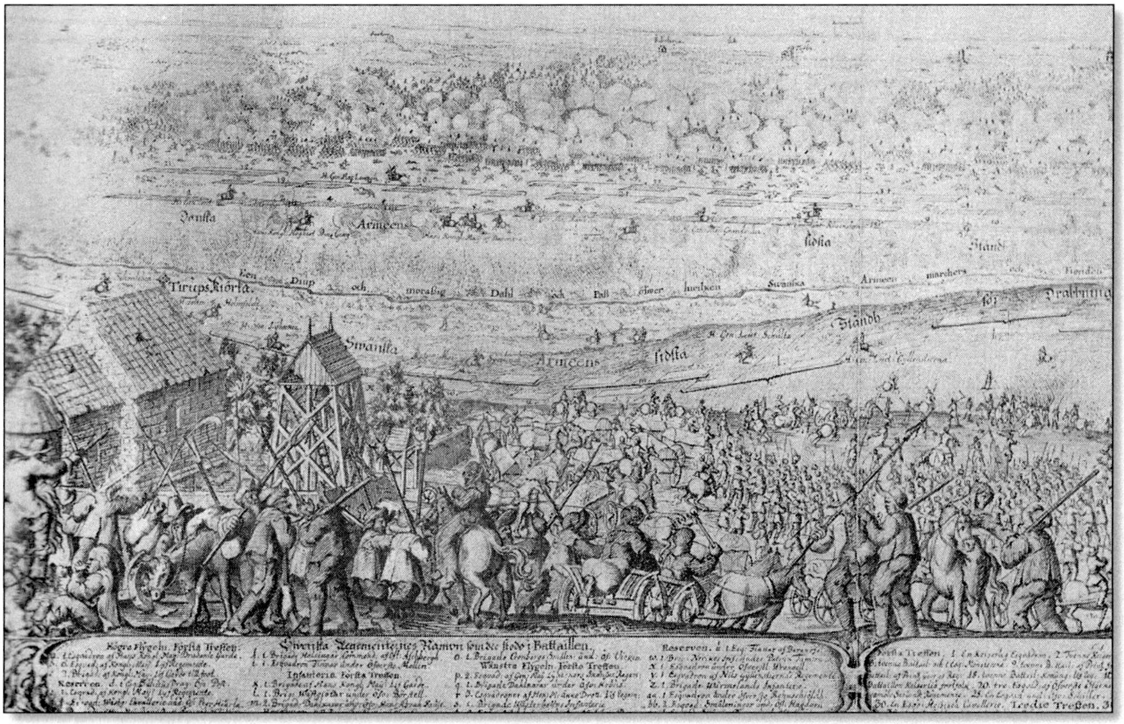

Swedish peasant levies at Tirup Church, during the Battle of Landskrona, 1677.

doubt saved the Swedish left wing. Without joining the fight, the peasant levies may have won the battle. Because the Swedes reformed their line, too, after which they counter-charged the Danish line.

The Struggle Between the Two Centres

In the centre, the two armies had exchanged artillery fire for some time. The Danes used chain shot, a type of cannon projectile formed of two sub-calibre balls chained together. When used against line infantry, chain shot caused terrible slaughter. One such chain shot has been preserved from the Battle of Landskrona, with a length of 45 cm and a weight of 3 kg.[10]

Despite this, the artillery fire was insufficient to decide the battle. The Danish infantry advanced towards their Swedish counterparts. At this point, the three main formations (the wings and the centre) of the Danish army had lost contact with one another. The Danish commander, Lieutenant General Rysensteen, ordered the first line forward. However, the Swedish first line, under Lieutenant General Schultz, pushed back the Danes. The Swedish centre then advanced. The Danish troops grew uneasy; they had seen their left wing flee and lost contact with their right wing.

It has been suggested, based on an archaeological sampling, that the Swedish infantry of the right wing after the defeat of the Danish left wing

10 Knarrström, *Slagfältet*, p.71.

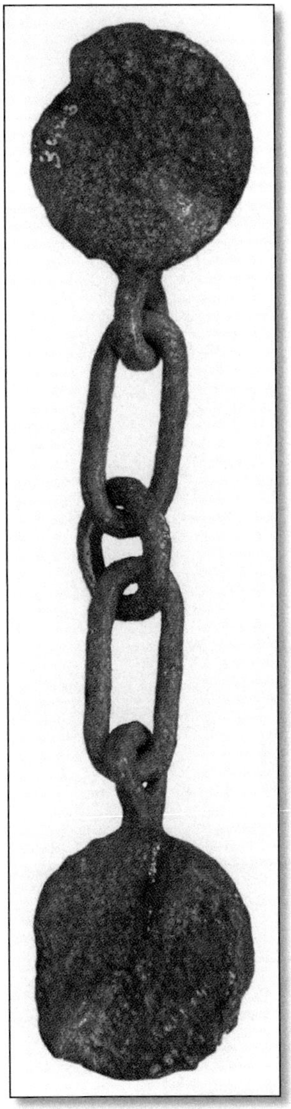

Artillery chain shot, found at Landskrona and likely used by the Danish artillery during the battle. (Photo: Bo Knarrström and Efron & Dotter, 2006)

wheeled to the south so as to attack and turn the Danish centre's flank.[11] If so, this may have been decisive. The Swedish infantry fired a volley, then charged. Rysensteen ordered the second line forward to reinforce the failing, first line; however, his men began to flee. They had lost their will to fight. Even as Rysensteen tried to rally them, some soldiers tried to take cover behind his horse. In time, Rysensteen managed to rally a few soldiers, but most of the centre fled and could not be rallied.

As for the Danish artillerymen, the Swedes were enraged by their use of chain shot. None were spared.

The End of the Battle

At Tirup, King Christian realised that the battle was lost. The presence of the peasant levies played a role, but there were other reasons, as well. From the victorious Swedish centre, Lieutenant Generals Schultz and Gyllenstierna had dispatched seven infantry battalions, around 2,000 men, to move in support of their left wing, facing King Christian. Moreover, from the victorious Swedish right wing, cavalry from the Life Regiment under Bielke and the Västgöta Cavalry Regiment were returning as well, threatening the Danish rear.

By 4:00 p.m., King Christian found it prudent to withdraw with his men. He joined up with the remnants rallied by Rysensteen, then retreated further, leaving two infantry battalions to cover the retreat.

The two rearguard battalions took up a position behind a dry-stone wall. However, Bielke's Life Regiment charged them in the flank. As for Bielke, he was hit by two shots. One of them penetrated behind his cuirass, breaking his collarbone. Nonetheless, he continued the attack. Bielke's men cut down most of the infantry, taking six flags. However, then Bielke collapsed from his wounds and fell from the saddle. Fortunately for him, his men carried him from the field of battle. After a few weeks, he was back on duty. Bielke was later richly rewarded for his deeds at Lund and Landskrona. In June 1678, he was promoted to lieutenant general.

King Christian led the remaining survivors into Landskrona. The Swedish army was too exhausted to pursue.

Danish losses in the battle were almost 2,000 cavalry, 500 infantry, and the entire artillery (the Swedes captured 32 cannons and a mortar).[12] However, they saved their supply train, which was brought into Landskrona before the battle for safekeeping. They had lost 17 cavalry standards and 21 infantry colours, which were taken by the Swedes.

The Danes had suffered losses among officers, too. Among the dead was Major General Walter, Colonel Ramstedt, and several other regimental officers including an otherwise unidentified member of the Montecuccoli family who served as captain, and the head of the Guard Cavalry, Oettingen

11 Ibid., pp.69–70.

12 Rystad, "Slaget vid Landskrona", p.167. See also Ericson et al., *Svenska slagfält*, pp.247–53.

(he died from his wounds in Landskrona, where he had been born, on 24 July).[13] Major General Detlef von Rumohr had been taken prisoner.

The Swedes had lost 20 officers (including Helmfelt, Post, Drake, and Schönleben, who lived but was wounded and in Danish captivity), 17 non-commissioned officers, and 922 men. In addition, 824 men were wounded (about half cavalry, half infantry; or 417 versus 407). On the day after the battle, 86 others were reported as being ill, some no doubt from heat exhaustion. Many of the wounded died from their wounds. Some regiments had suffered significant losses, up to a third of their strength. The Swedes also lost eight cavalry standards, six infantry colours, and two cannons, which were captured by the Danes.[14]

13 Vaupell, *Den danske hærs historie*, pp.183–4.

14 Isacson, *Skånska kriget*, pp.95–6.

24

The Struggle for Swedish Pomerania

The Invasion of Rügen

Following the reverses at Malmö and Landskrona in the summer of 1677, King Christian suddenly attempted to take the island of Rügen, off Swedish Pomerania. Brandenburg and Denmark had previously agreed that Rügen would be given to Denmark after Sweden had sued for peace.

King Christian may have begun to realise that he would not be able to regain Scania, despite his efforts. It seemed he could not make up his mind on whether to focus on reconquering Scania or taking some territory in Pomerania. If the Danish King saw strategic advantages in continuing the removal of the Swedes from northern Germany (and this would have benefited Denmark), it still made little sense to spend his resources there and then, where the Swedes were almost beaten, instead of in Scania, which supposedly was his main objective and where the Danish army had lost every engagement. Perhaps Frederick William of Brandenburg simply was more persuasive than King Christian's own advisors. Meanwhile, Frederick William, as we have seen, again laid siege to Stettin from July 1677 onwards.

King Christian first negotiated the support of 1,500 Brandenburg cavalry and dragoons. Then he had an infantry regiment of 1,600 men enlisted in Brandenburg by Colonel Lehnsdorff on behalf of the Danish Crown.

On 3 September 1677, the Danish main fleet under Niels Juel and King Christian left Copenhagen en route to Rügen, escorted by Tromp and his fleet.[1] Four days later, on 7 September, King Christian and his men landed on Rügen without encountering any resistance.[2] The Danish army, which consisted of 400 horse, some 4,000 infantry, and a strong artillery park, had to a large extent been taken from Landskrona and the field army in Scania.[3] With the reinforcements from Brandenburg, King Christian arrived as

1 Askgaard, "Kampen till sjöss", p.179.

2 Gyllenstierna, "Kriget i Tyskland", p.196.

3 Vaupell, *Den danske hærs historie*, pp.193–4; Tessin, *Die deutschen Regimenter der Krone Schweden 2*, p.38.

the head of an army of some 7,300 men.[4] His immediate objective was to prevent Field Marshal Otto Wilhelm von Königsmarck, then in Stralsund, from repossessing the island. King Christian's ultimate purpose was probably to achieve some kind of success on land before the year ended, and such success seemed increasingly unlikely in Scania.

The ferry connection with Stralsund was on the south side of the island. It was defended by two bastions, known respectively as the old and the new ferry bastion, Altefähr and Neuefähr. Neither was manned by more than a skeleton garrison. In addition, there were only 200 Swedish troops on Rügen. Königsmarck had his main army, some 5,800 men, in Stralsund.[5]

Caught by surprise by the Danish invasion and with a shortage of troops, Königsmarck decided to concentrate his few men in Neuefähr, since it was most easily defended. King Christian, unaware of this weakness and receiving rumours that there was a major Swedish cavalry force on the island, did not attack either bastion but contented himself with establishing a bridgehead for the disembarked troops. Only when the Brandenburg reinforcement had arrived did he move out of the bridgehead, occupying the island.

In October 1677, King Christian returned to Copenhagen. This became a harrowing journey; caught by a storm near Bornholm, the ship drifted perilously close to the shore and almost went aground, where it would surely have shattered. However, thanks to the good seamanship consistently displayed by the Danes, the crew saved the day and their King, who eventually was returned home safe.

The Danish troops on Rügen remained under the overall command of Major General Detlef von Rumohr, who had been exchanged since his capture at Landskrona. As always, they soon began to suffer from attrition, in particular from disease. Moreover, they soon lost Lehnsdorff's newly enlisted regiment. Frederick William of Brandenburg wanted the regiment for the ongoing siege of Stettin and persuaded King Christian to accept a weak cavalry unit in its stead. Again, King Christian seems to have been swayed by the more astute Frederick William.[6]

The Battle of Warksow

Without Rügen, it was difficult to retain Stralsund, which relied on supplies by sea. Moreover, King Charles had ordered Königsmarck to retake Rügen, without which there was no way to communicate with what little remained of Swedish Pomerania. Moreover, the island was an important source of fodder for Königsmarck's cavalry. Königsmarck knew that he had to act fast. If, or rather when, Stettin fell, it was obvious that his adversaries would secure Rügen permanently.

---

4 Tessin, *Die deutschen Regimenter der Krone Schweden 2*, p.39.

5 Gyllenstierna, "Kriget i Tyskland", pp.196–7.

6 Ibid., p.196.

As a result, Königsmarck already by the end of 1677 decided to attempt to regain control over Rügen. He only awaited the opportunity when the straits between Rügen and the mainland would become free of ice. This happened on 5 January 1678, but because of a shortage of vessels and poor weather, the short crossing took two days before it could be completed. On the evening of 7 January, his expeditionary force had landed on the promontory of Prosnitz on the southern coast of Rügen, where Swedish troops still retained Neuefähr. At dawn on 8 January 1678, Königsmarck advanced further into the island. His entire force then consisted of only 3,800 troops, primarily horse.

The coalition that faced him consisted of Danish, Imperial, Münster, Hessian, and Brandenburg units, in total some 2,000 horse and 3,000 foot. The coalition army had deployed in a strong, defensive position northeast of the village Gustow, about 5 km north of Neuefähr. Its centre and left wing was protected by rough terrain. However, Königsmarck was superior in artillery. The Swedish artillery was commanded by Major Johan Siöblad, who a generation later, during the Great Northern War, commanded all Swedish artillery. However, Königsmarck did not deploy his artillery along the entire line of battle, in the Continental manner. Instead he concentrated his firepower where it would overwhelm the enemy. A similar artillery deployment had been used at the Battle of Landskrona, but as we will see, Königsmarck concentrated his firepower to an even higher degree.

The resulting engagement, which took place on 8 January 1678, became known as the Battle of Warksow.

Königsmarck moved his force against the enemy with all speed, since he expected additional Brandenburg reinforcements to move to Rügen from the mainland. He deployed for battle about 1 km from Gustow in two lines (Appendix X).

When the Swedish troops around 9:00 a.m. moved down into the valley south-east of Gustow, they took losses from the enemy artillery fire. Königsmarck accordingly concentrated his force on the right and left only a small unit of dragoons southeast of Gustow, as well as half of his artillery which he deployed in a battery on a hill 700 m south-east of Gustow. Through this concentration of firepower, he forced the enemy right wing, which was deployed in an advanced position before the line of battle, to withdraw to a position close to the other units.

The other half of his artillery, Königsmarck deployed on a hill 500 m north-west of the village Benz. By this means, he could concentrate firepower against the enemy's left-wing cavalry. This was Königsmarck's primary target. When the artillery had softened up the enemy left wing, Königsmarck sent Grothusen's infantry battalions to charge the enemy left wing at the same time as the Swedish cavalry charged.

The Danish commander, Detlef von Rumohr, who had moved forward to observe the enemy's deployment, was hit by a round shot from a cannon, which shattered his left arm, leaving him mortally wounded. This unsettled his men. Rumohr's death was a greater problem than it should have been, since nobody had been appointed to assume control of the coalition army in case of his demise. With Danish, Brandenburg, Hessian, Münster, and Imperial troops all present, there was no obvious candidate to overall command. The

Brandenburg cavalry under Colonel Hülsen on the left wing attempted to counter-charge, but failed. Most of the coalition cavalry on the right wing was sent to support the left wing, but this exposed them, too, to Swedish artillery fire. Moreover, the panicked Brandenburgers disrupted and brought the fresh units along in their flight. Soon the entire coalition cavalry fled.

Königsmarck now sent his second line forward. He also ordered the small cavalry force deployed southeast of Gustow to charge the remaining horse of the coalition right wing, an Imperial dragoon regiment. The dragoons then fled, too.

As a result, the coalition infantry, which so far had hardly taken part in the battle, was left without any cavalry to protect its flanks. Colonel Netzow, who commanded a unit from Münster, conferred with Colonel Georg Wallis auf Karigmain, the senior Imperial officer (of Irish ancestry, the family had been in Imperial service since the Thirty Years' War), who finally had assumed command after the death of Rumohr, about retreating to a better position. The other colonels agreed, and the coalition infantry retreated to a position south-west of Warksow. However, there their exposed flanks were charged by the Swedish cavalry, while Grothusen's infantry charged from the front. Surrounded, the coalition infantry surrendered. It was then around 1:30 p.m.

Meanwhile, Königsmarck had ordered some of his cavalry squadrons instead to pursue the enemy cavalry. As a result, the coalition cavalry surrendered, too.

After the battle and in the days that followed, almost the entire coalition army fell into Swedish captivity. The captured soldiers were enlisted into the Swedish army but stayed on Rügen. As many as 53 standards, two kettledrums, 21 cannons (including those captured on the field of battle), plenty of ammunition, and considerable amounts of supplies fell into Swedish hands.[7] The coalition had lost some 400 killed. Swedish losses were reportedly no more than some 50 dead and 120 wounded.[8]

7 Joose Olavi Hannula, *Hakkapeliter och karoliner: Svenska och finska soldater i strid under 300 år* (np: SMB, 2016; first published in 1939), pp.79–84; Generalstaben, *Karl XII på slagfältet 1*, pp.175–77; Vaupell, *Den danske hærshistorie*, pp.195–8.

8 Tessin, *Die deutschen Regimenter der Krone Schweden 2*, p.40.

25

Stagnation in Scania

Baudissin's Cavalcade

King Charles had, against the odds, won several battles. Yet, it is hard to escape the conclusion that from a Swedish perspective, the entire war had been a series of improvisations. King Charles and his close advisors had been desperate. They had planned no more than one step at the time, knowing that if they failed, there was no need, and no resources, to plan for contingencies.

Despite the Swedish 1677 victory at Landskrona, the strategic situation in Scania remained undecided. The Swedish army dominated most of Halland, Blekinge, and the Scanian plain between Landskrona and Kristianstad. It was domination, not control, since Danish guerrillas and many brigands still operated in northern Scania and Blekinge. However, the Danish army could not carry out regular operations there, nor gather supplies. In August 1677, the Danish field army had been shipped across the Straits to the Danish heartland, leaving a garrison of only 1,400 soldiers in Landskrona.

On the other hand, the Danes still held Landskrona on the coast and Kristianstad, in the inland much further to the east. Landskrona was easily supplied by sea, and could be supplied indefinitely. Kristianstad was in a more precarious position. The Danes managed to get some supplies and funds through, but not enough. The Kristianstad command had to take loans from local merchants and even mint emergency coins to pay for necessary costs. Moreover, the town burghers had to provide food and lodgings on credit to Danish officers, which was unpopular.[1] Despite these arrangements, the supply situation was untenable. This became obvious when on 5 August 1677, Baudissin led eight cavalry regiments and one dragoon regiment out of Landskrona and straight across Scania towards Kristianstad in what became known as Baudissin's cavalcade. The regiments constituted a formidable force: Jutland Retinue of Nobles, under Colonel Rabe von Schilden; 1st Zealand Cavalry Regiment, under Colonel Holger Trolle; 1st Fyn Cavalry Regiment, under Rathlou; 2nd Fyn Cavalry Regiment, under Colonel Balthasar von Arensdorff; 3rd Jutland Cavalry Regiment, under Loren; 4th Jutland Cavalry

1 Gautier, "Krigskostnaderna", p.244.

Cavalry. (Johan Philip Lemke)

Regiment, under Lieutenant Colonel Hans Detlef Steensen; Baudissin's Cavalry Regiment, under K. Örtzen; Grandvilliers's Cavalry Regiment; and Nimpfen's Dragoon Regiment, under Thilo Henrik Nimpfen.[2] King Charles reacted immediately, leading the field army on forced marches to Kristianstad, where he united his men with the containment force already in place. Several skirmishes took place, including one in which Lieutenant Colonel Georg Friedrich von Ascheberg, one of General von Ascheberg's sons who had survived both the battles of Lund and Landskrona, was mortally wounded, eventually dying of gangrene. Baudissin could not get through, and his position being untenable, he returned to Landskrona. Swedish cavalry followed him back, but no engagement took place. Ten days after he had set out, Baudissin and his men returned into Landskrona. The expedition had not been a total failure, since it had given the cavalry the opportunity to bring in some supplies. However, it had no strategic impact.

2 Vaupell, *Den danske hærs historie*, pp.189–90.

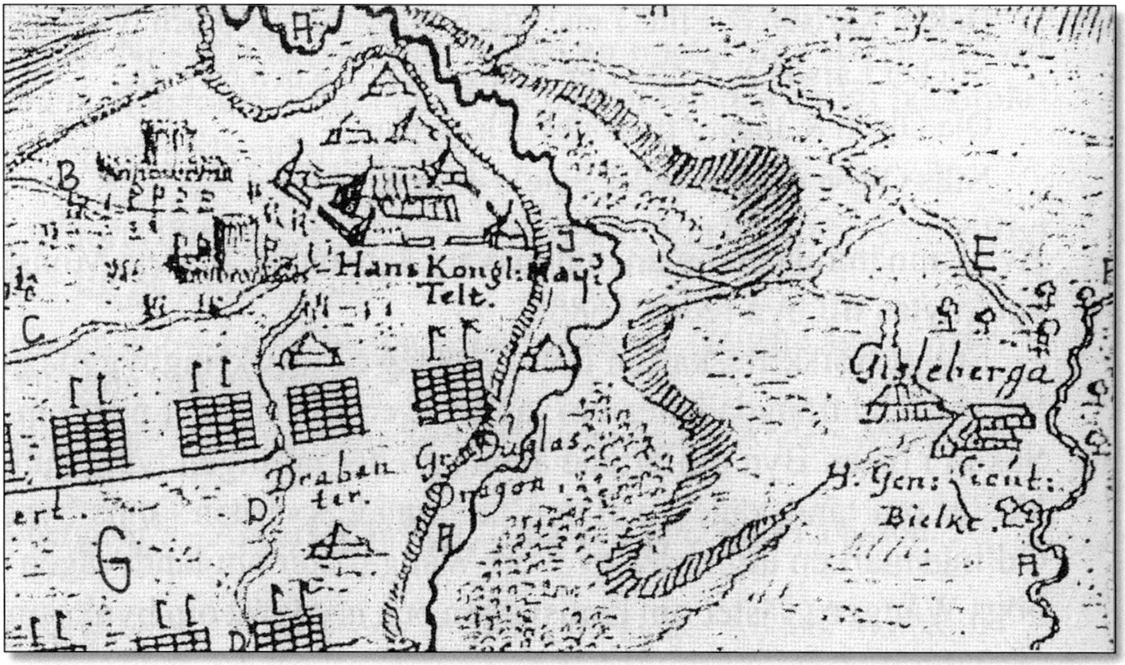

Detail of the Swedish army camp at Norrvidinge, 1678, with the large tent of King Charles in the centre, near the tents of the Drabant Guard, and the tent of Bielke on the right. (Erik Dahlbergh)

Later in the year, the Danes managed to move reinforcements to Kristianstad (a battalion of the 1st Jutland Regiment consisting of 574 men under Putkammer) by landing them at Åhus and marching them to the town east of River Helgeå. They reached the town on 26 September. This temporarily increased the garrison to 2,660 men. Unfortunately, disease and famine due to the lack of supplies remained serious problems. By the end of the year, the garrison consisted of 188 cavalry, 585 dragoons, 1,675 infantry, and 74 artillerymen, in total 2,522 men. However, the garrison only had 107 fit horses, and 500 of the men were laid low from disease. Moreover, the Danish commandant there still lacked funds to pay his troops.[3]

Baudissin's cavalcade had also displayed another turn in the war. In the previous year, Danish troops had been ordered not to harm the peasants and their fields, since it had been assumed that these would be returned to Danish control and therefore were important assets for taxation. However, in a protocol from 8 August 1677, the Danish commissariat ordered that if the peasants were not forthcoming with hay and cattle as required, the troops should seize the needed supplies under threat of 'sword and fire' and through the military means customarily employed on foreign territories.[4]

On the other hand, it was also obvious that the Swedish field army was insufficient to contain both Landskrona and lay siege to Kristianstad at the same time. King Charles deployed his army at Norrvidinge near Landskrona to block further Danish movements. However, the Swedes were not

3 Ibid., pp.199–200.

4 Nielsen, "Dansk strategi", p.84.

sufficiently strong to attempt a siege of either of the two Danish strongholds. The situation in Scania grew increasingly static.

On 18 September 1677, King Christian and all cavalry except a skeleton crew of 10 men per company returned to Copenhagen.[5] Meanwhile, the Danish senior command was ripped apart by personal differences. A Danish officer in Landskrona, Jens Harboe (the brother of the artillery chief, Andreas Harboe), in 1677 described the disputes between the senior commanders, ending with the conclusion (in the mixture of German and French which was common at the time): *Enfin. Es ist all hier rechtes Caos* ("Finally. All here is total chaos").[6] Although there were other quarrels as well, a major cause was that Baudissin in conjunction with the Battle of Landskrona had entered into a dispute with Field Marshal von der Goltz. Baudissin accused his superior of having deployed the army incorrectly, thus causing the defeat. Before the battle, King Christian had replaced Baudissin with Goltz as overall commander, which no doubt also fuelled the animosity. The dispute grew while both men remained in service. Having in August 1677 failed to relieve Kristianstad with the cavalcade, Baudissin was soon dismissed from service, after which he left Denmark. In October 1677, Goltz requested to be relieved from his position as overall commander. He, too, then left Denmark. The dispute between the two men is believed to have ended with a duel in Hamburg in late 1677, which explains why both left Denmark at the time.

Following the resignation of Goltz in October 1677, King Christian replaced him as Danish overall commander with an Imperial officer, Field Marshal Leslie, the commander of the Krain Cavalry Regiment. However, Leslie did not feel sufficiently appreciated, so he resigned already in January 1678. Against his wishes, Friederich von Arensdorff was again appointed overall commander of the Danish army.[7]

There were other disputes, too. King Christian then also had to mediate between Arensdorff, and the recently appointed governor of Landskrona, Rysensteen. The King solved the conflict by removing Rysensteen from his post. Instead he made the indefatigable Meerheim governor of Landskrona.[8]

Meanwhile, Münster again agreed to provide military unit to the Danish Crown. For a subsidy of 73,000 Rigsdalers, Christoph Bernhard von Galen, Prince-Bishop of Münster, for the 1678 campaign season promised to deliver four infantry regiments consisting of a total of 3,812 men, three cavalry regiments consisting of a total of 2,220 men, and 50 artillerymen instead of those who had been lost on Rügen. Hesse-Kassel delivered an infantry regiment of 1,450 men. Lehnsdorff's Regiment, now commanded by Colonel Pflanz, returned from Brandenburg into Danish service. Gewecke's and Goltz's Cavalry Regiments were dissolved. Gewecke instead enlisted two infantry companies for garrison use. An Irishman known as Wulf Henrik Kalneyn

5 Göthesson, *Ställningen vid Norrvidinge*, p.28.
6 Nielsen, "Dansk strategi", p.79.
7 Ibid., p.79.
8 Vaupell, *Den danske hærs historie*, pp.194, 200.

delivered two enlisted companies, and Lieutenant Dubsky re-enlisted his 100 Croat light cavalry.[9]

The Siege of Marstrand

There had also been developments on the Norwegian front. In late June 1677, the Norwegian galley flotilla moved a detachment under Hannibal von Degenfeldt, who had replaced Rysensteen as Norwegian infantry commander, consisting of two infantry regiments (some 2,000 men from the Oppland Regiment, under Colonel Johan Vibe, and Coucheron's Regiment, under Colonel Willem Coucheron, the Dutch fortification officer) to the Bohuslän coast. Count Gyldenløve wanted to carry out a decisive strike against Gothenburg, but King Christian ordered him instead to take the little port of Marstrand north of Gothenburg, which housed a Swedish naval station.[10]

On 30 June 1677, Gyldenløve landed his flotilla on Koön at Marstrand in Bohuslän. On 6 July, the Norwegians began to besiege the citadel, Karlsten. As a first step, Coucheron began to reduce the various outlying forts and bastions around Marstrand. First among them was Hedvigsholm, a small island fort defended by Lieutenant Colonel Andreas Björnsköld and 60 men. Following a few days of hard fighting, Björnsköld was gravely wounded, lost much blood, and after a few days had to leave in search of a surgeon, the only one of which was in Karlsten, Marstrand's citadel. On 20 July, the other survivors of the small garrison withdrew into Karlsten, too. Before leaving, they set the Hedvigsholm fort on fire and arranged to have the gunpowder magazine blown. Gyldenløve then sent seven Norwegian soldiers previously sentenced to death into the abandoned but burning building in order to put out the flames and thereby, if they survived, save the fort. If they came out alive, they would receive an amnesty. The soldiers succeeded.

Gyldenløve could then focus on Karlsten itself, which was held by Colonel Anders Sinclair. Its supplies had run out and losses in men grew, too. Sinclair agreed to surrender, in exchange for being allowed to leave with full honours of war, which was honoured. Sinclair and the survivors were sent to Eda in the Swedish province of Värmland, except about 100 of the wounded, who were allowed to move into Gothenburg for treatment.Of those who marched to Eda, 179 men made it all the way. On 23 July, Karlsten was in Norwegian hands.[11] Gyldenløve appointed Coucheron commandant and he remained there until the end of the war.

Gyldenløve must have celebrated the conquest of Karlsten with mixed feelings. His two best commanders, Colonels Vibe and Iddekinge, had just wounded each other severely in a duel, due to an argument at Gyldenløve's dinner table over which of the two regiments, the Oppland or the 2nd Trondheim, was the first in rank.[12]

9 Ibid., pp.202–3.

10 Vaupell, *Den danske hærs historie*, p.184.

11 Ibid., 185–6; Göthesson, *Ställningen vid Norrvidinge*, p.27.

12 Vaupell, *Den danske hærs historie*, p.184.

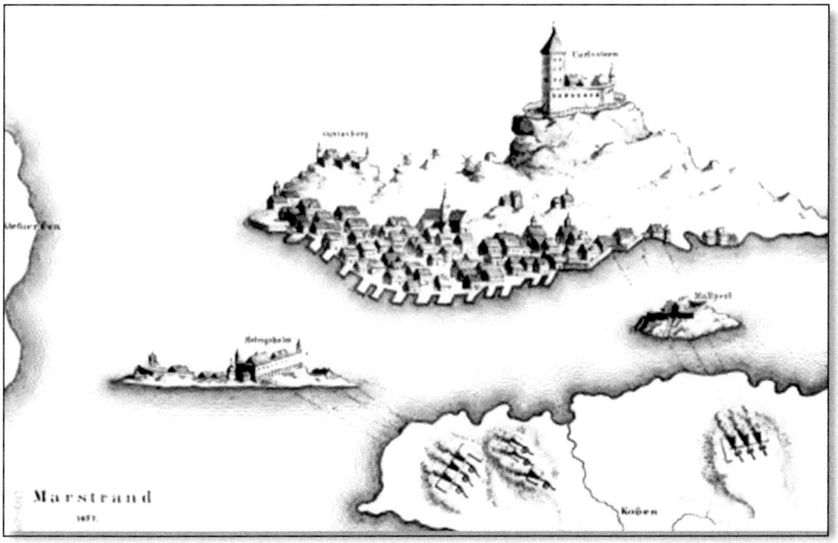

Siege of Marstrand, 1677. (Otto Vaupell, 1872)

Nonetheless, at the same time as Gyldenløve attacked Marstrand, Major General Hans Løwenhielm led 2,000 men across the Swedish border, marching to Uddevalla. Løwenhielm's expeditionary force consisted of two squadrons of Brockenhus's Dragoon Regiment under Bülow and the Søndenfjeld Dragoons under Arnold; and one infantry battalion each from five national regiments that is, 2nd Trondheim, Smaalenene, Bergenhus, Vesterlen, and Akershus Regiments, under respectively Iddekinge, Visborg, Hatten, Christian Vind, and Arnholtz.

In response, Magnus Gabriel De la Gardie, the formerly so powerful Lord High Chancellor and now the overall Swedish commander in western Sweden, led his possibly 1,300 regulars under Colonel Breitholtz and 1,500 levies from Dalecarlia, armed with pikes, morning stars, and *bardiche* poleaxes similar to those that also were used in Poland and Russia, towards Uddevalla. The Dalecarlian peasants, under Governor Gustaf Duwalt, had a reputation for being warlike, but they were untrained and unaccustomed to military discipline. For whatever reason, Løwenhielm retreated towards the Norwegian border.

After capturing Marstrand, Gyldenløve had gone on (requested but unauthorised) leave to Larvik in Norway to get married. However, as soon as he heard that Løwenhielm had retreated, Gyldenløve cut his honeymoon short and on 23 August returned to the Uddevalla region with some 5,600 men, including those of Løwenhielm. Outnumbered, De la Gardie abandoned Kvistrum and withdrew. His retreat did not go well. On 28 August, the Swedish troops attempted to hold off Gyldenløve's men at Kuröd, east of Uddevalla. Arriving at around 5:00 p.m., in the season when daylight lasted long, Gyldenløve ordered the battalions under Iddekinge and Visborg to move to the east, bypassing the Swedish line. De la Gardie, learning of this, ordered his men to retreat to a more easily defended position. However, at this point Gyldenløve ordered Løwenhielm to attack with Brockenhus's Dragoons. Most of the Swedes panicked and fled. A complete disaster was only avoided because a battalion of the Östgöta Regiment under Lieutenant Colonel Zacharias

Below, left; Morning star, Dalecarlia, 1743. An improvised weapon, the appearance of which remained fundamentally unchanged over time. (Army Museum, Stockholm, loan from the Dalarna Museum, Falun; photo: author)

Aminoff, another Swedish noble of Russian origin, managed, briefly, to prevent the Norwegians from crossing the important bridge, while four of the Dalecarlians destroyed a major part of it. The bravery of the four Dalecarlians notwithstanding, it was not a victory. Known as the Battle of Uddevalla, the Swedes lost some 500 men captured and another 800 dead and wounded, at least nine cannons, and most of the supply train. Norwegian losses were small.[13] De la Gardie withdrew across the River Göta Älv. He was subsequently dismissed from his post for failing to keep the Norwegians at bay.

When King Charles on 14 September received the (possibly highly exaggerated) news about the defeat at Uddevalla, he on 17 September set out towards Bohuslän with an expeditionary force of 1,500 cavalry: the Drabant Guard, Life Regiment, Västgöta Cavalry Regiment, and Scania-Bohuslän Dragoon Regiment under Colonel Gustav Douglas. It was imperative to keep Gyldenløve out of Gothenburg. After some skirmishing on the road with Eskild Nielsen's freeshooter company, King Charles arrived in Laholm on 18 September. There he received intelligence that although some Norwegians had established bases around Uddevalla, Gyldenløve and the Norwegian main army had returned to Norway and no longer threatened either Gothenburg or the province of Västergötland. Since the present situation could not easily be amended, the King returned to the Kristianstad area, where the defenders had taken advantage of the decreased pressure by repairing the defences.[14] On 27 September, King Charles and Schultz, who temporarily and on his own initiative had marched to join the King on his journey north towards Bohuslän, resumed the containment of Kristianstad.[15]

Meanwhile, the Norwegian army also attacked further to the north. On 10 August, Major General Reinhold von Hoven and Colonel Georg Christian Schultz led 2,000 men, infantry and dragoons, into the Swedish province of Jämtland. The only Swedish forces in the region were a few companies of the Jämtland Dragoon Regiment, which, however, was permanently dismounted since it lacked horses, and recently conscripted troops from Österbotten in the Swedish-speaking part of Finland. When confronted by the Norwegian dragoons, commanded by Hoven, most of the dragoons mutinied, defecting to the Norwegian side. After all, Jämtland had formerly belonged to Norway. They also persuaded the troops from Finland to surrender. The Swedish commander, Governor Carl Sparre, had to escape in haste, together with his wife, both mounted on the same horse. Sparre then sought out another unit from Finland which was deployed in southern Jämtland. However, on 15 August Hoven and his dragoons defeated them as well.[16] When Field Marshal

13 Nils Axel Kullberg, *Slaget vid Uddevalla år 1677* (dissertation, Uppsala University, 1851); Vaupell, *Den danske hærs historie*, pp.186–7; Petri, *Kungl. Första livgrenadjärregementets historia 2*, pp.422–5.

14 Almgren, "Svensk strategi", p.57.

15 Göthesson, *Ställningen vid Norrvidinge*, pp.27–8.

16 Vaupell, *Den danske hærs historie*, pp.187–8.

Henrik Horn in response led whatever troops that he could raise from the Swedish heartland against the Norwegians, they returned into Norway. The raid, for this is essentially what it was, was over. Although a number of pro-Norwegian locals had been raised, the incursion had no strategic significance and did not impact upon the outcome of the war.

Except Gyldenløve's repeated attempts to take control of Bohuslän, most of which – except Bohus Fortress – he dominated during the war to a higher degree than what King Christian achieved in Scania, the other activities on the Norwegian-Swedish border predominantly consisted of raiding. Although some Norwegian commanders possibly hoped to regain a lost province or two, and some peasants in formerly Norwegian provinces were not averse to the idea, the military activities were nothing but short cross-border raids, mostly with looting as the prime objective. Geographical conditions played a role, too, with the northern reaches of the border becoming increasingly barren and mountainous the further to the north one advanced.

Nonetheless, the border was disputed, and further fighting would follow. In December 1677, King Charles ordered Dahlbergh on a mission to gather intelligence for a future invasion of Norway, to be carried out from Bohuslän by the former Admiral of the Realm, Field Marshal Gustav Otto Stenbock. King Charles had allowed Stenbock to retain his titles and in November 1677 authorised him to lead the western defences, replacing De la Gardie as overall commander in western Sweden. The King had not forgotten the strategic imperative of taking the war to the enemy.[17] In the end, the envisaged invasion never took place, primarily because the Norwegian raiders returned home.

The Surrender of Helsingborg

By late 1677, some of King Christian's advisors, including the aforementioned former ambassador to Sweden, Jens Juel, continued to argue for naval raids on the Swedish coast all the way to Stockholm so that King Charles would have to withdraw army units from Scania. At the same time, they advised attacking Gothenburg from both land and sea. Jens Juel was the brother of Admiral Niels Juel, who on his side advocated an attack on northern Sweden from Trondheim in Norway.

But all these plans necessitated the retention of supremacy at sea. In April 1678, bad news reached King Christian. The Netherlands, now aiming for peace with France, denied the request for a Dutch war fleet. As a result, Tromp left his command by the end of the month, handing it over to Niels Juel. Without a Dutch fleet, the Danish Admiralty abandoned the ambitious plans to attack the Swedes in new theatres of operations. Admiral Juel, with a Danish fleet of 26 warships and three frigates with 1,560 cannons at his disposal, received his orders on 13 May. His primary task was to support the field army in Scania and in particular Kristianstad. He was ordered to raid the ports in the province of Blekinge. In addition, he would pay attention to

17 Lundström, *Erik Dahlberghs dagbok*, p.204.

the Swedish fleet in Kalmar and Stockholm. If it left port, he should defeat it. If not, he should raid the coastal areas and prevent shipping to Stockholm.[18]

In 1678, King Christian appeared to have given up hope of recovering Scania. Instead of increasing efforts to retake the territory, he offered the inhabitants of Scania sanctuaries in the Danish heartland. Some 15,000 people eventually took up the offer, primarily young men who did not wish to serve in Swedish armies. However, despite the King's promises, most ended up in poverty.

Yet, in the summer of 1678 King Christian attempted several offensives. A new contingent of troops from Münster had arrived (from Wedel's, Bassum's, Wendt's, and Rabe's Cavalry Regiments; Hötensleben's Dragoon Regiment; and Wedel's, Gaugreben's, Esch's, Schwarz's, and Frankenstein's Infantry Regiments), to replace the contingent of the previous year which had disbanded. A Hessian infantry formation, Johann auf dem Keller's Regiment, had arrived, too. A Danish army under Major General de Croÿ, who by then had recovered from the wounds sustained at Malmö the previous summer, in May 1678 advanced to recover Helsingborg, the siege of which had been attempted but then abandoned in March 1677. On 9 June 1678, Danish troops, again, gained control of the town. However, the Swedish commandant, Colonel Carl Hård af Segerstad, again withdrew his troops into the citadel, where he held out. In a fantastic ruse, King Christian had two forged letters written and delivered to Hård. The plan was reportedly devised by Croÿ. During the war, Danish guerrillas had repeatedly raided the Swedish communication lines. In the process, they had captured a large number of Swedish letters and documents, including some signed and sealed by King Charles. One of the forged letters delivered to Hård was accordingly made to look like a genuine order from King Charles, signed by the King and also sealed with his personal seal. The letter ordered Hård to surrender Helsingborg in order to spare his men. Amazed, but loyal to King Charles, Hård fell for the ruse and on 27 June surrendered the citadel. He then departed for King Charles's headquarters, where an unpleasant meeting between the two took place. Charles was on his way to relieve Hård. Now Hård had already surrendered the town, and claimed that he had received orders to this effect from Charles! King Charles was furious, Hård was court-martialled, but since he could prove that he had been duped by a nefarious Danish plot and acted in good faith, he was not sentenced to death for cowardice like other commandants who had surrendered. However, he was dismissed from the army.[19]

As for Croÿ, he was in October 1678 promoted to Lieutenant General and appointed commandant in Helsingborg.

18 Askgaard, "Kampen till sjöss", pp.179–80.

19 Vaupell, *Den danske hærs historie*, pp.207–8.

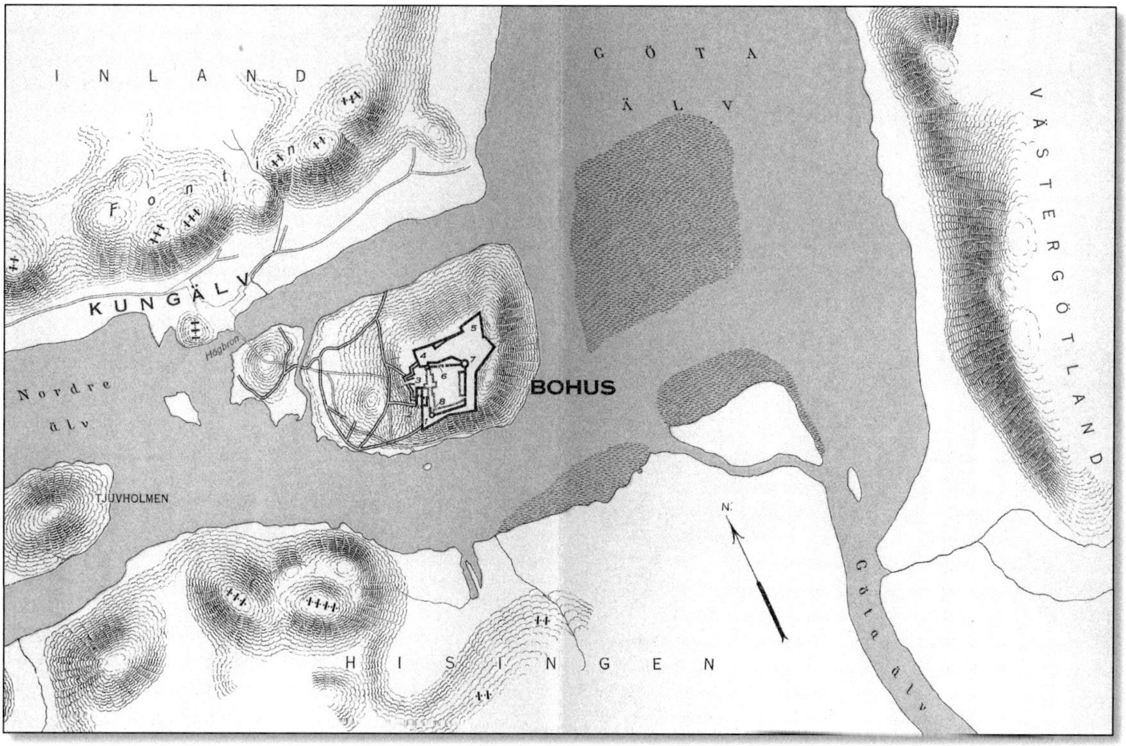

The Siege of Bohus Fortress, 1678

The Second Siege of Bohus Fortress

In April 1678, the Danes planned that a combined Danish-Norwegian army would move against Gothenburg. In preparation of this, a Danish expeditionary force was shipped from Aarhus in Denmark to Uddevalla in Bohuslän, where Gyldenløve also had assembled the Norwegian army, with the cavalry under Duncan, who earlier in the year had replaced Løwenhielm, and the infantry under Degenfeldt. The Danish force, which consisted of the four Jutland Cavalry Regiments, eight battalions from the King's Life Regiment, the Queens' Life Regiment, Prince Frederick's Regiment, Prince Christian's Regiment, and 685 artillerymen with 20 cannons, arrived only by the end of May 1678. It was commanded by Geise, a Brandenburger in Danish service. The combined Danish-Norwegian army, then consisting of 3,589 cavalry and 3,113 infantry, soon found that the Swedes had reinforced the defences of Gothenburg. Gyldenløve accordingly prepared to lay siege to Bohus Fortress instead. Defended by Colonel Friedrich von Börstell, who spent his life at war and had lost an eye at the Battle of Lund, and Lieutenant Colonel Carl Gustav Frölich, who in time was promoted to Major General and ennobled, the fortress had a comparatively small garrison, no more than, at most, 400 men based around a company of the Skaraborg Regiment. From 4 to 21 July 1678, the Danes bombarded Bohus almost without interruption, firing over 2,000, by some accounts 3,600 bombs into the fortress, which almost fell into ruins. Some bombs contained chemical

Siege of Bohus Fortress, 1678. (Johan Philip Lemke)

substances that caused nausea and vomiting.[20] The garrison refused to surrender, however, and the Danes abandoned the siege on 21 July, when a relief force of 6,000 men under Field Marshal Stenbock arrived from Gothenburg with reinforcements. A number of skirmishes took place, in one of which Duncan was wounded. Gyldenløve's men again retreated to Uddevalla, from which the Danish units in August were shipped to Helsingborg. Börstell, who had survived the siege, was promoted to Major General.[21]

For the rest of 1678, the Swedish-Norwegian border was fairly quiet.

20 Petri, *Kungl. Första livgrenadjärregementets historia 2*, p.451. On early modern Scandinavian chemical warfare, see also Michael Fredholm von Essen, "Early Eighteenth Century Naval Chemical Warfare in Scandinavia: A Study in the Introduction of New Weapon Technologies in Early Modern Navies", *Baltic Security and Defence Review* 13: 1 (2011), pp.122–51.

21 Vaupell, *Den danske hærs historie*, 203–4; Gulowsen, *Gyldenløvefeiden*, pp.157–83; Petri, *Kungl. Första livgrenadjärregementets historia 2*, pp.445–51.

The Swedes Retake Kristianstad

The Danes had won supremacy at sea, but could they retain it without the Dutch? For the first time during the war, King Charles in 1678 put an experienced naval officer in command of the navy. Admiral Hans Wachtmeister was not only a proven naval commander, he had also, it will be remembered, commanded a squadron at the Battle of Lund and worked with irregulars in Bohuslän. Admiral Wachtmeister's orders, dated 18 April 1678, was to move the main fleet into Kalmar. There the fleet, 18 ships of the line, five frigates, and five other ships with a total of 1,387 cannons, could take advantage of a protected port within reach of the theatre of operations and, in particular, Stralsund in Pomerania. Wachtmeister would be on the spot to take the initiative, if an opportunity arose. Wachtmeister left Dalarö on 6 June with 31 ships. On 12 June, he had reached southern Öland.[22]

Niels Juel had left port on 1 June with 22 warships. Soon the Danish and Swedish fleets made visual contact. However, on 14 June Wachtmeister, following orders, sailed into Kalmar. No battle took place, and Juel found it inopportune to attack Kalmar. During the summer of 1678, both fleets operated more cautiously than in the past. Neither side wanted to risk a major battle under unfavourable circumstances. Danish warships carried out several raids on Swedish territory. On 4 July, for instance, the Danish main fleet under Juel again took Ystad which they then looted. The Swedes used Ystad for the transit of supplies to besieged Malmö. King Christian had ordered Juel to 'bring the inhabitants to ruin, capture the young men, kill the horses, remove the cattle, and by such means prevent the enemy from receiving supplies'.[23]

Meanwhile, Dahlbergh, with some 9,500 men, laid siege to Kristianstad. A number of skirmishes took place, as Danes carried out sallies and Swedish troops assaulted the Danish fortifications. The Danes also made attempts to relieve Kristianstad. On 15 July 1678, King Christian led 11,000 men, half of them mounted, from Landskrona towards Kristianstad.[24] It was essentially a repeat of Baudissin's cavalcade the previous year, but with more troops. Moreover, King Christian's attack formed part of a combined land-sea operation. On 20 July, Admiral Juel landed some 600 troops and three cannons under Colonel Jacob Wilhelm Stuart at Landön on the shore east of Åhus with orders to break into Kristianstad, or, if this failed, to create a diversion to enable King Christian to attack from another direction. Juel brought a substantial squadron, consisting of two large warships, four small warships, and four other ships including a fireship. The Danish troops fortified their position. On 21 July, the Swedes responded. Colonel Axel Wachtmeister led 200 cavalry and 500 foot including grenadiers against the Danish position. According to the report to the King, they drove the Danes back into the sea, killing 115 of them at the cost of only 3 Swedish troops. Among the dead was Captain Krumsee, the former Danish commandant of Karlshamn.

22 Askgaard, "Kampen till sjöss", pp.180–1.
23 Ibid., pp.180–1.
24 Almgren, "Svensk strategi", p.59.

On 27 July, Juel landed yet more troops, some 1,000 men under Colonel Stuart, near Karlshamn further to the east. Aided by a pro-Danish renegade known to history only under the nickname Pickedala-Ola, they managed to penetrate into the town, before they were pushed back by Swedish troops under the efficient Johan Gyllenstierna. Meanwhile, the Swedes had managed to bring artillery to bear on Juel's ships, so they had to raise anchor and leave. A few remaining Danes were captured on the same day, including one irregular, whom the Swedes promptly executed. In total, the Juel's fleet had lost some 400 dead and 30 captured. Juel was highly dissatisfied, and following the defeat, he made a formal complaint about Stuart, who was dismissed from the army.[25]

Meanwhile, the Danish main army shrank rapidly. A list of troops dated 21 July shows that the field army then consisted of 10,912 men (with 28 cannons, three mortars, and 154 carts), of whom 5,222 were cavalry and dragoons (including 874 Münster troops). It follows that the infantry and artillerymen then constituted 5,690 men. Whether officers and non-commissioned officers were included remains unclear. Most of the horse were Danes, while the majority of the infantry were enlisted Germans. But already when King Christian on 23 July reached Önnestad, 13 km north-west of Kristianstad, some units had been ordered elsewhere, and illness and desertions had taken their toll. A list from this date shows that out the 4,364 specifically Danish cavalrymen and dragoons, only 3,224 remained (there are no comparable data for the non-Danish horse, or for the infantry and artillery). A quarter of the mounted troops had disappeared. Within a week, yet more troops had been lost. It can accordingly be estimated that the Danish field army then consisted of no more than some 8,000 men.[26] Moreover, several regiments lacked gunpowder, while the infantry of Prince George's Regiment lacked ammunition and grenades. Nonetheless, the colonels were willing to take the chance of offering battle. A few skirmishes followed, but the Swedish army had a strong position, so there was little King Christian felt that he could do. In fact, it remains unclear if King Christian even went to Kristianstad with the resolve to offer battle. After several meetings with his council of war, and much hesitation. King Christian on 25 July ordered the commandant in Kristianstad, Carl Henrik von der Osten, to abandon the town, if he could negotiate honourable terms.[27] In the final analysis, the purpose of the expedition seems not to have been to defeat the Swedes in open battle, but to outmanoeuvre them, hoping that they would abandon the siege.

It seems clear that King Christian by then, if not before, had given up his last hope of regaining Scania. On 29 July, he issued an order that the towns and estates of Scania such as Lund, Laholm, Knutstorp, Eriksholm, Rosendal, Ystad, Trelleborg, Simrishamn, and Skanör, as well as all windmills, all supplies and fodder, and all ships and boats should be burned. Except for the easily supplied Landskrona, the Danes were leaving. King Christian

25 Vaupell, *Den danske hærs historie*, p.210.

26 Knud Fabricius, "'Terror Panicus' og Christianstads undsætning 1678", *Historisk Tidsskrift* 11:2 (Copenhagen 1949), pp.467–92, on pp.484–5.

27 Ibid., pp.487, 489.

returned to Copenhagen on 30 July.[28] Further instructions followed on 9 August, when Arensdorff issued an order to the freeshooter captains to burn all supplies they could find, including all crops, whether already harvested or not, together with the existing infrastructure. The intention was to ruin the country. The freeshooters, who had been promised a new life in Denmark, did not hesitate to carry out the order, nor they did they neglect to extort payments from any Scanians who had money or valuables.[29] These actions, probably more than any others, swayed the population from Danish to Swedish sympathies.

King Charles took advantage of the situation by informing the Danish commandant in Kristianstad, von der Osten, that King Christian had left the army. The latter faced a hopeless task. Of the original garrison of 4,300 men, by March 1678 only 2,045 had remained, and of these, only 1,206 had been fit for duty (data from 6 March).[30] At this point, only 1,028 soldiers remained.[31] Disillusioned and well aware of his lack of supplies, von der Osten on 1 August agreed to surrender. The final negotiation to surrender Kristianstad was concluded on 4 August, when von der Osten and Ascheberg signed the agreement. After the formalities, Ascheberg treated the Danish officers to a good dinner. On 5 August, the surviving Danes left Kristianstad, marching away with full honours of war. They were then sent, under guard, to Helsingborg from which they would be shipped to Denmark. King Christian was not angry; he soon appointed von der Osten the new commandant in Landskrona.

On the night between 6 and 7 August, the Danish relief army left Önnestad. The siege was over. The Danish army returned to Landskrona, burning everything in its path. As before, King Christian felt a need to find a scapegoat for the failure, and the natural one was his overall commander, Friedrich von Arensdorff, whom he in August 1678 dismissed from his post, and then court-martialled, accused of dereliction of duty. As new overall commander, King Christian appointed Lieutenant General Gustav Wilhelm von Wedel, the Prussian officer who then led the Münster reinforcements. He retained the position until the end of the war, perhaps because no major actions then took place.[32]

For King Charles, the surrender of Kristianstad was a major victory, since he no longer needed to divide his forces but could concentrate them around Landskrona and Helsingborg. King Charles marched his army to Gudmundstorp, where it rested for a week. With new reinforcements from the Swedish heartland as well as from Bohus and Gothenburg, the Swedish troops by then numbered some 11,000 men. However, by then it was clear that the war fundamentally was over.

As August shifted into September 1678, King Christian finally decided to offer battle. Having just received reinforcements from Norway, his army

28 Ibid., p.490.

29 Knarrström and Larsson. *Hans Majestäts friskyttar*, p.104.

30 Fabricius, "Terror Panicus", pp.344–5.

31 Jensen, *Den skaanske krig*, pp.344–5, 385.

32 Nielsen, "Dansk strategi", p.79.

then consisted of 58 squadrons and 20 battalions, or almost 15,000 men. The Swedish field army had received reinforcements, too, and then consisted of 47 squadrons and 14 battalions, or some 12,000 men. However, King Charles was no longer the desperate firebrand that he once had been, seeking battle at all costs. Realising that he had more to gain from diplomatic activities in Europe, where peace negotiations were already underway, King Charles refused to humour King Christian.[33]

33 Almgren, "Svensk strategi", p.59.

26

The Fall of Stralsund

Despite Königsmarck's efforts, Stralsund could not be saved. In the summer of 1678, the Danes raided Rügen several times. In addition, Frederick William of Brandenburg in early September assembled 15,000 Brandenburg troops on Usedom, which he intended to move to Rügen, protected by 11 warships. He had agreed with King Christian that they would invade Rügen together and then share the island. (The warlike Prince-Bishop Christoph Bernhard von Galen of Münster wanted in, too, but King Christian said that the island was too small to divide further; besides, the Prince-Bishop died of natural causes in September and his successor wished to discontinue Münster's participation in the coalition.)[1] Meanwhile, King Christian shipped 2,000 troops to Rügen: three battalions of 2nd Zealand, 1st and 2nd Jutland Regiments, and the survivors from Kristianstad under Colonels Knoblauch, Fuchs, and Trop. As commander of the Danish expedition, he selected Hans Løwenhielm, who had been ordered from Norway for this purpose.[2]

Königsmarck had received intelligence on the Danish-Brandenburgian plans, but there was little he could do to thwart them.

The first Danish and Brandenburg troops again landed on Rügen on 12 September 1678.[3] They recaptured the island quickly, since the soldiers pressed into Swedish service after the Battle of Warksow handed over the fort of Neuefähr without a fight to the Brandenburgers.

With Rügen in the coalition's hands, the turn had come to Stralsund. On 24 September, Frederick William of Brandenburg began to ship his troops on Rügen to the mainland. A few days later, the siege of Stralsund began. On 10 October 1678, Frederick William began to fire incendiary bombs into the town. With most of its southern half destroyed already on 11 October, Königsmarck entered into negotiations for surrender, which were concluded on 15 October.[4]

1 Gyllenstierna, "Kriget i Tyskland", p.197.
2 Vaupell, *Den danske hærs historie*, p.212.
3 Askgaard, "Kampen till sjöss", p.181.
4 Gyllenstierna, "Kriget i Tyskland", p.198; Anne Grabinsky, *Die Stralsunder Doppelkatastrophe von 1678/80: Wiederaufbau nach zwei vernichtenden Stadtbränden* (Berlin: Lit, 2006), p.12.

Siege, probably 1670s. The infantry wear sleeveless coats with tails fastened at the back. (Johan Philip Lemke)

Immediately after the conquest of Stralsund, Frederick William turned to Greifswald, the last remaining Swedish-held territory on the German coast. Greifswald was defended by a garrison of 460 men. On 15 November, after a few days of artillery bombardment, the town could no longer be defended. Greifswald surrendered on 17 November.[5] Only a minor part of the Swedish army was recovered and brought to the Swedish mainland. King Christian did not want the survivors from Stralsund and Greifswald to be immediately redeployed in Scania, so he sent them to Kalmar instead. He needed not worry; the ships that carried the prisoners of war were less fortunate than King Christian had been on his similar journey in the previous year. The transports went aground at Bornholm, where some prisoners drowned, others were butchered by the islanders as they came ashore, and most of the survivors were interned on the island in violation of the terms of their agreement to surrender.

5 Gyllenstierna, "Kriget i Tyskland", p.198.

27

The End of the War

The Swedish Invasion of Prussia

By the winter of 1678/1679, the strategic situation on the Continent had changed. France, Sweden's ally and ostensible protector, had during the autumn of 1678 made peace with the Netherlands and Spain, which were Denmark's allies. France accordingly promised to send a fleet to the Baltic in support of Sweden. The fleet was supposed to arrive in May 1679, bringing 10,000 French troops that would support a projected Swedish invasion of Zealand (the Danes had worried about a French fleet ever since 8 December 1676, and on 13 October 1677 they received intelligence, which turned out to be faulty, that a French fleet was on its way to Gothenburg[1]). Again, King Charles hoped to take the war to his enemies, moving the theatre of operations from Scania to Denmark. At the same time, he had again ordered an expeditionary force to move from Livonia through Prussia towards Brandenburg and the occupied Pomerania. Admiral Wachtmeister was ordered to wait in Kalmar for the promised French fleet to arrive. Then, and only then, would he go on the offensive.[2] However, in the end no French fleet materialised. There was thus no chance to invade Denmark, regardless of how well-intentioned such a plan was from a strategic perspective.

Then there was the planned attack on Brandenburg-Prussia from Livonia. As noted, the appointed expedition commander, Field Marshal Bengt Horn, had delayed so long that he only arrived in Riga in January 1678. King Charles therefore removed him from his command. By February 1678, the expedition had finally been organised, consisting of somewhat more than 6,000 men and an artillery contingent. Moreover, in spring 1678 King Charles appointed a new commander, Field Marshal Henrik Horn. Horn probably accepted the task with mixed feelings, since he by then had already failed to reach Pomerania once, as commander of the fleet. Besides, he arrived in Riga only in September 1678. But then events moved fast. Horn immediately mustered his forces, which had grown into a total of

1 Askgaard, "Kampen till sjöss", p.185 n.33, p.186 n.34.
2 Ibid., p.182.

11,200 men (14 cavalry, six dragoon, and 12 infantry regiments). As head of fortifications and intelligence, Horn appointed Lieutenant Colonel Paul von Essen, a Livonian noble. The expeditionary force left Livonia in October 1678. However, the political understanding with Poland was already gone, and no Polish support was forthcoming. Besides, the already from the outset poor roads had deteriorated further because of heavy rains. The march to the Prussian border took a month. As usual under such campaign conditions, the army suffered losses from disease and famine.

Horn's advance into Prussia was the first full-scale Swedish invasion of enemy territory during the war. On 6 December, he captured the town of Tilsit. He stayed for some time there to gather new supplies. This was prudent; King Charles had ordered him to conserve his forces, find a defensive location, and await reinforcements in spring 1679. However, when Horn on 6 January 1679 arrived at Wehlau, he received intelligence that Frederick William of Brandenburg led an army of 7,000 men against him, and indeed already had deployed 4,000 men near Königsberg.

With his customary vigour, Frederick William attempted to outflank the Swedish expedition. Taking a page out of the Swedish book, he boldly marched his army across the ice of the frozen Vistula and Curonian Lagoons (Frisches Haff and Kurisches Haff). The two Brandenburgian armies reunited in Königsberg. Detaching 5,000 men to Tilsit, Frederick William led the rest in an attempt to prevent Horn's retreat. On 29 January 1679, the Swedish army beat off Frederick William's men at Tilsit. Yet, since supplies of all kinds were lacking, including horses, and Horn had suffered considerable attrition among his men from disease and famine, he already on 9 January had decided to return to Livonia. Horn outmanoeuvred Frederick William by unexpectedly choosing the (even worse) inland roads instead of those along the shore that he had used on his way to Prussia. Horn returned to Riga on 4 February with the survivors of his expedition, some 5,000 men.[3] The strategy to bring the war to Brandenburg did not produce any lasting gains, yet it had succeeded in forcing Frederick William to move his available forces far to the east, away from his Danish ally.

As for King Christian, he fully expected a French incursion into Holstein. He accordingly concentrated the Danish army in the south, under Field Marshal Lieutenant Wedel, in anticipation of the French threat.[4] With both main adversaries now having to defend their external borders, there was no longer any immediate strategic threat to the Swedish heartland. In Scania, only the indefatigable Meerheim, governor of Landskrona, continued active combat operations. Like before, he led raids into the Swedish hinterland, killing and capturing men and supplies. Not averse to harsh methods, he was known to employ torture against those captives he believed to be Swedish spies.[5]

3 Hans Ulfhielm and Eric Granefelt (eds.), *Kungl. Artilleriet: Svenska Artilleriet i Östersjöprovinserna 1561–1721* (np: Militärhistoriska Förlaget, 2005), pp.180–81; Holm, *Översikt över Sveriges krig*, pp.154–7; Gyllenstierna, "Kriget i Tyskland", p.199; Almgren, "Svensk strategi", p.58.

4 Nielsen, "Dansk strategi", p.89.

5 Vaupell, *Den danske hærs historie*, pp.200–201.

The Fighting in Bohuslän

Although King Christian had given up on Scania, his half-brother, Count Gyldenløve, and his Norwegian troops were, like Meerheim, not yet out of the picture. Serious fighting still took place in Bohuslän. In February 1679, Gyldenløve again advanced into Sweden. The winter was very cold, but this was an advantage, since it enabled the Norwegians to move fast, while the Swedish garrisons did not expect any hostilities, and thus were taken by surprise.

On 15 February, Gyldenløve led 2,000 foot, 800 horse, and 10 cannons into the province of Dal. He divided his troops into three flying columns. Gyldenløve led the first, ravaging the provinces of Värmland and Dal and burning many villages. Cicignon (who in autumn 1678 had replaced Degenfeldt as infantry commander), with the second, did likewise, but following another route. Duncan, with the third column, led some cavalry against Åmål at Lake Vänern.

At the same time, and further to the north, the able Colonel Vibe led 1,200 men and 6 cannons against Eda.[6] Yet, while the raids were devastating, these expeditions were eventually abandoned, as Swedish troops assembled and slowly prepared their defences.

More fighting followed between Count Gyldenløve's and Field Marshal Stenbock's troops in Bohuslän, in particular around Uddevalla. In March 1679, Stenbock and Lieutenant General Mörner led almost 7,000 men from Vänersborg towards Uddevalla. However, the Swedes did not manage to break through the well-prepared Norwegian defences, and eventually, the Swedes had to retreat to Gothenburg.[7]

The Norwegians were not the only ones who went on the offensive. Much further to the north, a Swedish expeditionary force from Jämtland under Colonel Anders Planting-Bergloo, the head of the Jämtland Dragoon Regiment, in July advanced to Røros in Norway, where there were important copper mines. The expeditionary force, which consisted of 1,400 horse and 800 foot, burned the town but then, as Gyldenløve dispatched reinforcements to Trondheim, on 1 August withdrew into Jämtland.[8]As with the Norwegian cross-border offensives, the Swedish one, despite having the specific objective to destroy the copper works, was essentially a raid.

The Peace Treaties

Admiral Juel received his orders for the 1679 sailing season only on 31 May 1679. In essence, his orders were to prepare for another invasion, but this time in the vicinity of Kalmar.[9] However, the plan was as ambitious as it was unrealistic. Moreover, the Danish commanders could not agree on where to land. Instead, fighting was limited to a few skirmishes with the Swedish

6 Ibid., pp.216–17.

7 Ibid., pp.217–18; Almgren, "Svensk strategi", p.61.

8 Vaupell, *Den danske hærs historie*, pp.204, 218; Almgren, "Svensk strategi", p.61.

9 Askgaard, "Kampen till sjöss", p.181.

fleet in Kalmar, before the Danish fleet withdrew to Gotland.[10] During the summer, a Swedish fleet attempted to retake Gotland. However, the attempt failed.[11] Denmark retained Gotland until some time after peace was declared.

In Scania, King Charles remained cautious. By the end of July, he assembled an army of some 11,000 men, which he used to contain, but not lay siege to, Helsingborg.[12] Swedish forces under Stenbock also continued to make attempts on Uddevalla, but with no more success than previously. However, by September the Swedish troops abandoned the attempt.[13] King Charles informed Stenbock that he was free to withdraw and to go into winter quarters. By then peace negotiations were already ongoing, and peace was approaching.

There were internal quarrels among Sweden's enemies. King Christian and the Dukes of Lüneburg argued over possession of Bremen-Verden. Frederick William of Brandenburg wanted Swedish Pomerania, but Emperor Leopold foresaw future problems and did not wish to see the rising Brandenburg-Prussia grow even stronger. So the common front collapsed. Peace was negotiated in Nijmegen over an extended period of time between the second half of 1678 and late 1679 with the Holy Roman Empire, a number of German states, and, finally, the Netherlands. At the same time (26 January 1679 (O.S.) / 5 February 1679 (N.S.)), the Treaty of Celle was signed between Sweden and the Dukes of Lüneburg. In exchange for ceding control of the towns of Thedinghausen and Dörverden, Sweden's sovereignty over Bremen-Verden was confirmed. However, following the Treaty of Nijmegen, Wildeshausen and its surrounding district, which had been ceded to Sweden in the 1648 Peace of Westphalia and remained geographically separated from the rest of Bremen-Verden, had to be pawned to the Prince-Bishop of Münster, with which a peace was signed on 19 March 1679, until Sweden could afford to pay the Prince-Bishop the amount of 100,000 Riksdalers, which was stipulated in the treaty.

Having in May sent an army across the Rhine and into Brandenburgian territory, France forced Brandenburg to settle at Saint-Germain-en-Laye on 19 June (O.S.) / 29 June (N.S.) 1679. In the peace treaty, Sweden recovered all its Pomeranian possessions except the former Swedish eastern bank of the River Oder which was ceded to Brandenburg (excepting the towns of Gollnow and Damm). Even so, Gollnow (modern-day Goleniów) had to be pawned to Brandenburg, until Sweden could repay the amount of 50,000 Thalers (which only became possible in 1693). Damm (modern-day Dąbie) remained in Swedish hands.

The lost towns were not crucial to Sweden. Nonetheless, King Charles was enraged that King Louis XIV of France had concluded peace agreements on his behalf, without consulting him. For the rest of his life, King Charles could not forgive the French. Yet, without French diplomatic support, it is unlikely that Sweden would have been able to regain, and retain, its lost German territories.

10 Vaupell, *Den danske hærs historie*, p.219.

11 Almgren, "Svensk strategi", p.61.

12 Ibid., p.61.

13 Vaupell, *Den danske hærs historie*, p.220.

France also exerted pressure on Denmark, to the extent of sending troops into the Danish possession of Oldenburg. Denmark suddenly stood alone against both Sweden and France. Moreover, by then, as noted, Denmark was close to financial bankruptcy. In the August 1679 peace of Fontainebleau, Denmark lost all its conquests, including Wismar. In a separate agreement, France also saw to that Denmark had to relinquish control over Holstein-Gottorp, which was returned to its Duke. Naturally, Denmark also failed to recover the provinces *previously* lost to Sweden. At the September 1679 peace of Lund, Sweden retained both the formerly Danish provinces and its exemption from the Sound Tolls. Following negotiations in Lund between Swedish and Danish delegations, which included the Swedish Royal Councillor Johan Gyllenstierna and the Danish Minister Jens Juel, the peace agreement between Denmark and Sweden was signed on 18 September 1679 (O.S.). The Danes also agreed to leave Gotland. However, after the peace treaty was signed, they destroyed Visby's defences and also blew up the remains of Visborg Castle.

The Scanian War was over. On 15 October, King Charles mustered the field army at Ylleshed, where he earlier had defeated King Christian. He thanked the regiments for their service, and then released them.[14] Paradoxically, the army then assembled was probably both the largest and the best supplied of all Swedish armies since the outbreak of war.

With peace followed the long-postponed royal wedding. On 6 May 1680, the Danish Princess Ulrika Eleonora and King Charles finally married. Out of loyalty to her betrothed's country, the Princess had spent much of the war engaged in charitable work among Swedish prisoners-of-war, something that was sorely needed. For the rest of her life, she continued to devote considerable efforts to charity, at times pawning her jewellery to defray expenses. She was beloved by all, except her mother-in-law, who never accepted her.

14 Göthesson, *Ställningen vid Norrvidinge*, p.73.

28

The Aftermath and Legacy of the Scanian War

One could argue that the real winner of the Scanian War was Louis XIV of France. Not only because it was he who pushed through the peace agreements that ended the war, but because the Scanian War had given him the time and means to carry through his own strategic objectives. During the almost five years that the war had lasted, Sweden's improvised defences had kept busy the entire military might of Denmark and Brandenburg, and a major part of the Dutch navy, preventing them from taking part in the broader conflict with France.

Another winner was Frederick William of Brandenburg, henceforth known as the Great Elector. Although his territorial gains were modest, the army that he and Derfflinger had built and used with great success ultimately grew into the army of Prussia. Moreover, the anniversary of the victory at Fehrbellin became a holiday that was celebrated in Germany until 1914, when on the same day (28 June N.S.), the Archduke Franz Ferdinand of Austria was assassinated, which led to the First World War and the downfall of the army and dynasty the ancestors of which once had defeated Wrangel and Königsmarck.

Sweden's experiences in the Scanian War laid the foundation for the first substantial reform of the Swedish army since the Thirty Years' War. Having inherited a state ruined by an inept regency government, an army and navy that lacked everything from funding to trained men, and a multitude of hostile neighbours, King Charles made sure that this would not happen again. Based on what he had learnt, King Charles restructured the Swedish army and established a comprehensive military system that enabled Sweden repeatedly to mobilise trained armies during the even more devastating Great Northern War which followed a generation later.

There was also a financial component of the reform. In December 1680, King Charles requested the parliament to carry out a major *reduktion*. Three-quarters of the previously alienated lands were returned to the Crown, leaving only a third of the total in noble hands. King Charles did not even spare his few close friends, such as Bielke, who suffered massive financial loss through the *reduktion*. Sweden became an absolute monarchy, not as in Denmark by a revolution from above but by the parliament's reinterpretation of existing law. The *reduktion* returned revenues of four million Riksdalers to the Crown. The national debt, the servicing of which had been a significant problem since 1648, fell from 40 to 50 million Riksdalers in 1681 to a mere 10 million by 1697.[1] Henceforth, Sweden did not need to depend on foreign subsidies.

The military system introduced by King Charles was an improved version of the *indelningsverk*, the allotment authority. This took the rest of Charles's reign to implement and was his key achievement in building a military state. Its purpose was to ensure the production of a continuous stream of recruits to refill the ranks when men were lost in war. This had been a key problem during the Scanian War, when recruitment primarily derived from conscription. The Crown abandoned the practice of periodic conscriptions in which it sought to raise whatever number of troops was needed. Instead, individual provinces contracted to raise and maintain regiments of a set size in both peace and war. To spread the load of recruiting and maintaining a soldier, farms were grouped together to share the burden. Farmers were not required to serve themselves, so they could recruit a soldier who would serve in exchange for the provision of a house and pay. As a further boon, the system was established by the parliament, so was not the result only of the assertion of an absolute monarchy but rested on consent and a sense of legitimacy within the population. By the time of Charles's death in 1697, his introduction of the *indelningsverk* had resulted in the creation of a well-trained, native, and professional standing army with a constant size of no less than 10 cavalry and 22 infantry allotted regiments, a total of 11,000 horse and 25,000 foot. Soldiers were well equipped, and the institution of provincial regiments resulted in high morale and esprit de corps. Moreover, government funding was sufficient also to maintain a force of 8 enlisted cavalry and 15 enlisted infantry regiments to garrison the overseas provinces, a major reconstruction of the navy, and the establishment of a new naval base in the south.[2]As a consequence of the defeats at sea and in response to the threat from Denmark, the Admiralty had realised that there was an urgent need for a naval base closer to the theatre of operations than the existing one at Stockholm. In 1679, King Charles ordered the foundation of Karlskrona, in Blekinge, which in 1680 became the key naval base in Sweden.

The Scanian War, like the Thirty Years' War before it and the subsequent Great Northern War, displayed a continuation of the distinctive Swedish offensive strategy that since the time of Gustavus Adolphus had come to characterise the Swedish art of war. On the Continent, strategies were often defensive, even when the available resources would have allowed for an offensive strategy. Not so in Sweden. There, as we have seen, King Charles and his senior commanders itched for going on the strategic offensive, by bringing the war to their enemies, even when resources were inadequate or lacking altogether. It was taken for granted that the offensive, not a stubborn defence, would win the war.

1 Alf Åberg, *Karl XI* (Stockholm: Wahlström & Widstrand, 1958), p.119.

2 Lars Ericson Wolke, *The Swedish Army in the Great Northern War 1700–21: Organisation, Equipment, Campaigns and Uniforms* (Warwick: Helion, 2018).

The same can be said, in even stronger terms, for the Swedish choice of tactics. King Charles and his senior commanders sought battle and would attack under most circumstances. Some would explain this as the result of a perception of invincibility of Swedish arms that derived from stories of Gustavus Adolphus with which King Charles and his generation had grown up. However, this would not be the full explanation. For most of the war, King Charles sought battle and had his men charge the enemy not because he believed his army was invincible but because he was acutely aware of everything that the army lacked, in resources, manpower, supplies, money, and so on. Simply speaking, King Charles had to engage the enemy and win quickly, because he knew that he could not afford a prolonged war. One could argue that this choice was no choice at all, since the lack of resources precluded other options. The result was a set of aggressive tactics that suited Sweden, with its relatively small population and less than impressive economy. The Scanian War thus laid the foundation for the distinctive Swedish tactics employed during the subsequent Great Northern War and used to great effect by King Charles XI's son and successor, King Charles XII.

While Swedish tactics already at the time of the Thirty Years' War had focused on the offensive, the tactics employed during the Scanian War were singularly aggressive and became known as the *gå på* ('go at them') approach, after the command *Gå på!* which was the order to charge. As a result, the shock derived from firepower became fully integrated with the forward movement, which culminated in the hand-to-hand combat phase which aimed to destroy the cohesion of the enemy unit. The combination of firepower and movement was decisive for gaining and holding the initiative, which enabled a smaller force to attack a larger one with some hope of success. Moreover, Sweden retained the pike, even as the rest of Europe began to regard this weapon as obsolete. Swedish cavalry tactics, too, grew increasingly aggressive, in fact even more so after the war. The artillery, however, had to adopt a subordinate role. Not even regimental artillery had the mobility to follow the rapid charges henceforth aimed for, so while still employed during sieges, artillery from this time comparatively seldom played a prominent role on the battlefield, at least not until the second half of the subsequent Great Northern War. When used, however, the aim was to concentrate artillery fire for particular tactical tasks such as had been done at Landskrona and to an even higher degree at Warksow, not to disperse the artillery along the entire front line which remained the Continental model.

The Swedish model also had an impact on tactical doctrines used elsewhere. Already on 3 August 1677, after the defeats at Lund and Landskrona, the Danish army modified its own tactics following the Swedish model. On this date, the Danish cavalry was ordered to abolish the caracole and adopt the same aggressive tactics as the Swedes, that is, charging home with the rapier.[3] The Danish instruction was fundamentally a copy of Ascheberg's orders before the Battle of Lund. And the Swedish command *Gå på!* made such an impact in northern Germany that it survived, in its Low German form, as

3 Jensen, *Den skaanske krig*, p.292.

Gah to! which for many years continued to be used, with the same meaning, among Pomeranian and Prussian troops. On the other hand, the Danes abandoned, for a generation, the experiment with national units consisting of conscripts and instead reverted to enlistment as the means to raise troops.

King Charles never forgot the Battle of Lund. For the rest of his life, he would respect the anniversary of the battle, not with celebration but with prayer and solitude. The Battle of Lund had taught him the human cost of war, and he was determined not to be dragged into such a calamity again.[4] Charles was still a man of his times; he knew that Sweden had a warlike reputation to uphold, needed to safeguard, through military means, its position in the world, and that a Swedish king, even one with absolute power, first and foremost was a military commander. He congratulated those of his commanders, such as Königsmarck and Bielke, who won renown in foreign wars; he continued, when needed, to dispatch Swedish troops abroad to assist his allies; but he was very aware of the human cost in doing so and tolerated no waste in human lives. On several occasions, he expressed his unwillingness to send troops to those wars which Sweden was treaty-bound to support but for which Charles saw little utility. And when some of the Swedish subsidy regiments sent in support of the Dutch as part of the League of Augsburg were all but destroyed in the French victory at Fleurus in 1690, King Charles angrily noted to his friend Bielke that his men were too dear to him to be 'brought to the slaughter bench'.[5] Charles had good reason to use such language. At Fleurus, Erskine's Regiment lost 95 percent of its 876 officers and men including both the colonel and all captains, while Bielke's Regiment lost more than 80 percent of its 993 officers and men. Both regiments had been raised in Bremen-Verden, for which Sweden had fought hard in the Scanian War.[6]

As for the other survivors of the war, they continued their lives. King Christian spent time hunting and with his mistress, and between these pursuits, he presided over major legal reforms in both Denmark and Norway, as well as the support of colonies and trading stations in the Caribbean, West Africa, and India. His brother, Prince George, in 1683 married the daughter of King James II of England and remained there as the Duke of Cumberland.

Gustav Adolph von Baudissin left Denmark after his 1677 dismissal from the army. His rival Joachim Rüdiger von der Goltz left Denmark, too. Their dispute is believed to have ended with a duel between the two in Hamburg in late 1677. Both survived, and later on, Goltz fought at the 1683 siege of Vienna.

So did Charles Eugène de Croÿ, who went into Imperial service in 1681. Wounded in the siege of Vienna, he later served as Field Marshal in the war against the Ottoman Turks in 1687–1693. In 1699, he entered first Polish, then Russian service, until he was captured at Narva in 1700 by Swedish King Charles XII.

4 Rystad, *Karl XI*, pp.97, 359.
5 Ibid., p.276.
6 Robert Hall; Iain Stanford; and Yves Roumegoux, *Flags and Uniforms of the Dutch Army 1685–1715* Vol. 1: *Cavalry, Dragoons, Artillery & Subsidy Regiments*(Romford: Pike and Shot Society, 2014), pp.166, 171.

Nils Bielke lost most of his property through the *reduktion*, and his friendship with King Charles did not sway the King to offer any relief. Disillusioned, Bielke received the King's approval to go into foreign service. In 1683, he participated in the Swedish relief force to Vienna, following the Emperor's call for support against the Ottoman Turks.[7] In 1684, he went into Bavarian service and soon fought the Ottoman Turks in Hungary, participating in the conquest of Pest and Ofen in 1686 and in the Second Battle of Mohács in 1687.

Otto Wilhelm von Königsmarck, too, participated in the Swedish relief force to Vienna. In 1685, Königsmarck took service with the Republic of Venice. Alongside the Doge of Venice, Francesco Morosini, he led the Venetian conquest of the Morea in the early years of the Morean War 1684–1699 between Venice and the Ottoman Empire as commander of the Venetian land forces. He served in this role when Venetian artillery fire in 1687 accidentally destroyed major parts of the Parthenon, which the Ottoman Turks used for ammunition storage.

Immediately after the war, Rutger von Ascheberg was appointed Governor-General of first Gothenburg, then Scania and all the former Danish provinces in the south. He worked to improve conditions for their inhabitants so that they would adjust to life as Swedes. He also made sure that the University of Lund again became a centre of learning. King Charles said that whatever he had learnt about military matters he had learnt from Ascheberg, and that he regarded him as a father.[8]

Erik Dahlbergh stayed in service, in 1693 rising in rank to Field Marshal and Governor-General of Bremen-Verden. In 1696, Dahlbergh was appointed Governor General of Livonia, in which role he served in the early years of the Great Northern War.

7 Rosander, *Sveriges fältmarskalkar*, p.198.

8 Åberg, *När Skåne blev svenskt*, p.202; citing a letter from King Charles to Nils Bielke.

Appendices

Appendix I. Danish Army Regiments, 1675[1]

Cavalry

The Guard Cavalry (*Garden til Hest*)
Zealand Retinue of Nobles (*Sjællandske Rostjeneste*)
Jutland Retinue of Nobles (*Jydske Rostjeneste*)
Life Regiment Cavalry (*Livregiment til Hest*)
1st Zealand Cavalry Regiment (*1. Sjællandske Rytterregiment*)
2nd Zealand Cavalry Regiment (*2. Sjællandske Rytterregiment*)
1st Fyn Cavalry Regiment (*1. Fyenske Rytterregiment*)
2nd Fyn Cavalry Regiment (*2. Fyenske Rytterregiment*)
1st Jutland Cavalry Regiment (*1. Jydske Rytterregiment*)
2nd Jutland Cavalry Regiment (*2. Jydske Rytterregiment*)
3rd Jutland Cavalry Regiment (*3. Jydske Rytterregiment*)
4th Jutland Cavalry Regiment (*4. Jydske Rytterregiment*)
Schleswig Cavalry Regiment (*Slesvigske Rytterregiment*, also known as *Sønderjydske Rytterregiment*)
Baudissin's Cavalry Regiment (*Baudissins Rytterregiment*)
Rauch's Cavalry Regiment (*Rauchs Rytterregiment*)
Gewecke's Cavalry Regiment (*Geweckes Rytterregiment*)

Dragoons

Walter's Dragoon Regiment (*Walters Dragonregiment*)
Örtzen's Dragoon Regiment (*Örtzens Dragonregiment*)
Rantzau's Dragoon Regiment (*Rantzaus Dragonregiment*)

Infantry

The King's Life Regiment (*Kongens Livregiment*)
The Queen's Life Regiment (*Dronningens Livregiment*)
The Commanding General's Regiment (*Feltherrens Regiment*)
The Field Marshal Lieutenant's Regiment (*Feltmarskalløjtnantens Regiment*)
1st Zealand Regiment (*1. Sjællandske Regiment*)
2nd Zealand Regiment (*2. Sjællandske Regiment*)

1 Primarily based on Vaupell, *Den danske hærs historie*; Jensen, *Den skaanske krig*.

1st Fyn Regiment (*1. Fynske Regiment*)
2nd Fyn Regiment (*2. Fynske Regiment*)
1st Jutland Regiment (*1. Jydske Regiment*)
2nd Jutland Regiment (*2. Jydske Regiment*)
3rd Jutland Regiment (*3. Jydske Regiment*)
4th Jutland Regiment (*4. Jydske Regiment*)
Schleswig Regiment (*Slesvigske Regiment*)
Holstein Regiment (*Holstenske Regiment*)
Plön Regiment (*Plønske Regiment*)
Maximilan Rosencrantz's Regiment (*Rosencrantz' Regiment*)
Lübbe's Regiment (*Lübbes Regiment*)
Baudissin's Regiment (*Baudissins Regiment*)
Lütken's Regiment (*Lütkens Regiment*)
Bremer's Regiment (*Bremers Regiment*)
Degenfeldt's Regiment (*Degenfeldts Regiment*)
Harlov's Regiment (*Harlovs Regiment*)
Schönfeldt's Regiment (*Schönfeldts Regiment*)

Field Artillery

One unit, consisting of 4 companies

Note. The national regiments were, despite their names, most commonly known by the names of their colonels, even when members of the same family commanded several regiments. All regiments were based in Denmark.

Appendix II. Norwegian Army Regiments, 1675[2]

Cavalry

Recke's Regiment (*Reckes Regiment*), consisting of 496 men in 2 squadrons, under Colonel Mathias Didrik von der Recke

Dragoons

Søndenfjeld Dragoons (*Søndenfjelds Dragoner*), consisting of 150 men in 1 squadron, under Johan Arnold
Nordenfjeld Dragoons (*Nordenfjelds Dragoner*), consisting of 150 men in 1 squadron, under Mathias Eriksen Orning

Infantry

Akershus Regiment (*Akershusiske Regiment*), consisting of 1,500 men, under Major General Hans Løwenhielm
Oppland Regiment (*Oplandske Regiment*), consisting of 1,500 men, under Colonel Christoffer Fredrik Gersdorff

2 Primarily based on Vaupell, *Den danske hærs historie*, 102-3; Jensen, *Den skaanske krig*, 45; Gulowsen, *Gyldenløvefeiden*

Smaalenene Regiment (*Smaalenske Regiment*), consisting of 1,500 men, under Colonel Eiler Visborg
Vesterlen Regiment (*Vesterlenske Regiment*), consisting of 1,500 men, under Colonel Mogens Krag
Bergenhus Regiment (*Bergenhusiske Regiment*), consisting of 1,700 men, under Colonel Bendix von Hatten
Trondheim Regiment (*Trondhjemske Regiment*), consisting of 2,000 men, under Lieutenant General Henrik Rüse von Rysensteen
Marine Regiment (*Marineregiment*), consisting of 1,000 men, under James Hamilton
Enlisted companies (garrison units), in total 486 men, under Reinhold von Hoven, Marthin Jørgen Rochlinge, Speckhahn, and Hirsfeld

Artillery

One unit, consisting of 106 men with 18 three-pounders and 8 six-pounders

Appendix III. Swedish Army Regiments, 1675[3]

Cavalry

His Majesty's Drabant Guard (*Kunglig Majestäts drabantgarde*), formally the mounted unit of His Majesty's Life Guard of Horse and Foot (*Kunglig Majestäts Livgarde till häst och fot*), based in Sweden (E)
The Retinue of Nobles in Sweden and Finland (*Adelsfanan i Sverige och Finland*), based in Sweden and Finland
The Retinue of Nobles in Livonia (*Adelsfanan i Livland*), based in Livonia
The Retinue of Nobles in Estonia (*Adelsfanan i Estland*), based in Estonia
The Retinue of Nobles in Ingria (*Adelsfanan i Ingermanland*), based in Ingria
The Retinue of Nobles in Pomerania (*Adelsfanan i Pommern*), based in Pomerania
The Retinue of Nobles in Bremen-Verden (*Adelsfanan i Bremen-Verden*), based in Bremen-Verden
Life Regiment of Horse (*Livregementet till häst*), based in Sweden
Västgöta Cavalry Regiment (*Västgöta kavalleriregemente*), based in Sweden
Åbo and Björneborg County Cavalry Regiment (Åbo och Björneborgs läns kavalleriregemente), based in Finland
Småland Cavalry Regiment (*Smålands kavalleriregemente*), based in Sweden
Nyland and Tavastehus County Cavalry Regiment (*Nylands och Tavastehus läns kavalleriregemente*), based in Finland
Östgöta Cavalry Regiment (Östgöta kavalleriregemente), based in Sweden
Viborg and Nyslott (Karelian) Cavalry Regiment (*Viborgs och Nyslotts (Karelska) kavalleriregemente*), based in Finland
Scanian Cavalry Regiment (*Skånska kavalleriregementet*), based in Sweden

3 Primarily based on Tessin, *Die deutschen Regimenter der Krone Schweden* 2; Höglund, *Skånska kriget*, in particular 72-8 on seniority system

The Queen-Dowager's Life Regiment of Horse (*Riksänkedrottningens livregemente till häst*), based in Sweden
Bünow's Cavalry Regiment (*Bünows kavalleriregemente*), based in Pomerania
Giese's Cavalry Regiment (*Gieses/Geijsos kavalleriregemente*), based in Pomerania (E)
Holstein-Eutin's Cavalry Regiment (*Holstein-Eutins kavalleriregemente*), based in Pomerania (E)
Knausdorff's Cavalry Regiment (*Knausdorffs kavalleriregemente*), based in Pomerania (E)
Meyer's Cavalry Regiment (*Meyers kavalleriregemente*), based in Pomerania
Wittenberg's Cavalry Regiment (*Wittenbergs kavalleriregemente*), based in Pomerania
Wrangel's Cavalry Regiment (*Wrangels kavalleriregemente*), based in Pomerania (E)
Planting's Cavalry Regiment (*Plantings kavalleriregemente*), based in Pomerania (mostly E)
Mengden's Cavalry Regiment (*Mengdens kavalleriregemente*), based in Livonia (E)

Dragoons

Scania-Bohuslän Dragoon Regiment (*Skåne-Bohusläns dragonregemente*), based in Sweden
Viborg Dragoon Regiment (*Viborgs dragonregemente*), based in Finland
Savolax Dragoon Regiment (*Savolax dragonregemente*), based in Finland
Holstein-Eutin's Dragoon Regiment (*Holstein-Eutins dragonregemente*), based in Pomerania
Wangelin's Dragoon Regiment (*Wangelins dragonregemente*), based in Pomerania (in part E)

Infantry

His Majesty's Life Guard on Foot (*Kunglig Majestäts Livgarde till fot*), based in Sweden (E)
German Life Guard of Foot (*Tyska livgardet till fot; Deutsches Leibregiment zu Fuß*), based in Pomerania (E)
Uppland Regiment (*Upplands regemente*), based in Sweden
Skaraborg Regiment (*Skaraborgs regemente*), based in Sweden
Åbo County Regiment (Åbo läns regemente), based in Finland
Södermanland Regiment (*Södermanlands regemente*), based in Sweden
Kronoberg Regiment (*Kronobergs regemente*), based in Sweden
Jönköping Regiment (*Jönköpings regemente*), based in Sweden
Björneborg Regiment (*Björneborgs regemente*), based in Finland
Dalecarlia Regiment (*Dalregementet*), based in Sweden
Östgöta Regiment (Östgöta regemente), based in Sweden
Tavastehus Regiment (*Tavastehus regemente*), based in Finland
Hälsinge Regiment (*Hälsinge regemente*), based in Sweden
Västgöta-Dal Regiment (*Västgöta-Dals regemente*), based in Sweden
Elfsborg Regiment (*Elfsborgs regemente*), based in Sweden
Viborg County Regiment (*Viborgs läns regemente*), based in Finland

Savolax County Regiment (*Savolax läns regemente*), based in Finland
Västmanland Regiment (*Västmanlands regemente*), based in Sweden
Västerbotten Regiment (*Västerbottens regemente*), based in Sweden
Kalmar Regiment (*Kalmar regemente*), based in Sweden
West Nyland Regiment (*Västra Nylands regemente*), based in Finland
East Nyland Regiment (Östra Nylands regemente), based in Finland
Närke-Värmland Regiment (*Närke-Värmlands regemente*), based in Sweden
Scania-Halland Regiment (*Skåne-Hallands regemente*), based in Sweden
Scania-Blekinge Regiment (*Skåne-Blekinge regemente*), based in Sweden
Österbotten Regiment (Österbottens regemente), based in Finland
Colony Regiment (*Koloniregementet*), based in Livonia, Estonia, and Ingria (E)
Jämtland Regiment (*Jämtlands regemente*), based in Sweden
Mountain County Regiment (*Bergsregementet*), based in Sweden (E)
The National Commanding General's Life Regiment of Foot (*Riksfältherrens livregemente till fot*), based in Pomerania (E)
Horn's Regiment (*Horns regemente*), based in Bremen-Verden (E)
Delwig's Regiment (*Delwigs regemente*), based in Pomerania (E)
Haren's Regiment (*Harens regemente*), based in Pomerania (E)
Helmfelt's Regiment (*Helmfelts regemente*), based in Pomerania (E)
Duke of Holstein-Eutin's Regiment (*Hertigen av Holstein-Eutins regemente*), based in Pomerania (E)
Duke of Saxony-Gotha's Regiment (*Hertigen av Sachsen-Gothas regemente*), based in Pomerania (E)
Oxenstierna's Regiment (*Oxenstiernas regemente*), based in Pomerania (E)
Tungel's Regiment (*Tungels regemente*), based in Wismar (E)

Artillery

The Artillery Regiment (*Artilleriregementet*), which included both the field artillery and all garrison artillery units (E)

Note. Units are listed in rough order of seniority. However, the seniority system primarily concerned the regiments in Sweden and Finland and does not seem to have encompassed most regiments in Germany and Livonia. E = enlisted.

Appendix IV. Annual revenues available to the Swedish Crown, 1674[4]

Territory	Riksdalers
Swedish heartland	2,367,289
Finland	353,126
Scania, Halland, Blekinge (formerly Danish)	353,279
Bohuslän (formerly Norwegian)	6,163
Livonia	219,262
Estonia, Ingria	44,160
Pomerania, Wismar	216,888
Bremen-Verden	268,499
Totals	**3,945,688**

Appendix V. Tentative Order of Battle at Fehrbellin, 18 June 1675[5]

The Swedish Army
Commander: Lieutenant General Wolmar Wrangel af Lindeberg.

Right wing: Cavalry
Wittenberg's Cavalry Regiment, under Colonel Leonard Johan Wittenberg.
Bünow's Cavalry Regiment, under Colonel Günther von Bünow.
Holstein-Eutin's Cavalry Regiment, under Colonel Jacob von Bülow.
Östgöta Cavalry Regiment, under Colonel Adam Wachtmeister.

In total, 14 squadrons.

Centre: Infantry
Commander: Major General Henrik von Delwig.
German Life Guard on Foot, under Major General Otto Johan von Grothusen.
National Commanding General's Life Regiment on Foot, under Lieutenant Colonel Claus Ulrik von Schwerin.
Jönköping Regiment, under Colonel Gustav Horn.
Helmfelt's Regiment.
Delwig's Regiment (1 battalion), under Lieutenant Colonel von Maltzahn.
Duke of Saxony-Gotha's Regiment.
Hälsinge Regiment, under Major General Jacob Johann von Wulffen.
Field artillery, consisting of 7 cannons

4 Source: Magalotti, *Sverige*, 33
5 Various, often contradictory sources

In total, 8 battalions

Left wing: Cavalry
Åbo and Björneborg County Cavalry Regiment, under Colonel Bernhard Otto von Liewen.
Småland Cavalry Regiment, under Colonel Friedrich von Buchwald.
Giese's Cavalry Regiment, under Major General Johann von Giese.
Planting's Cavalry Regiment.

In total, 10 squadrons.

The Brandenburg Army

Commander: Frederick William of Brandenburg.

Right wing: Cavalry
Commander: Frederick, Prince of Hesse-Homburg.
Life Regiment Cavalry (*Leibregiment*), under Colonel Ulrich Hipparchos von Promnitz.
Hesse-Homburg's Cavalry Regiment.
Mörner's Cavalry Regiment, under Colonel Berndt Joachim von Mörner.
Görtzke's Cavalry Regiment, under Lieutenant General Joachim Ernst von Görtzke.
Prinz's Cavalry Regiment, under Colonel Johann Friedrich von Printz.
Bruckdorff's Cavalry Regiment (1 squadron), under Alexander Magnus von Bruckdorff.
Kurprinz Cavalry Regiment, Lieutenant Colonel Johann Christoph von Strauss.
Lüdeke's Cavalry Regiment, under Major General Lüdeke.

Left wing: Cavalry
Commander: Field Marshal Georg von Derfflinger.
Trabant Guard (*Trabantengarde*) Cavalry (1 squadron), under Lieutenant Colonel Hans Albrecht von Wolffersdorff.
Prince of Anhalt's Cavalry Regiment (3 squadrons), under John George, Prince of Anhalt-Dessau.
Derfflinger's Cavalry Regiment, under Captain Jacob Ernst von Kottwitz.
Bornsdorff's Dragoon Regiment (1 squadron), under Colonel von Bornsdorff.
Derfflinger's Dragoon Regiment (1 squadron).
Grumbkow's Dragoon Regiment (1 squadron).
Croÿ's Cavalry Regiment (1 squadron).
Frankenberg's Cavalry Regiment.

Artillery.

Appendix VI. The Danish Invasion Force, 1676[6]

Cavalry
1st Zealand Cavalry Regiment, under Friedrich von Arensdorff
2nd Zealand Cavalry Regiment, under Detlef Rantzau
1st Fyn Cavalry Regiment, under Jacob Duncan
2nd Fyn Cavalry Regiment, under Conrad Reventlow
1st Jutland Cavalry Regiment, under Hans Friedrich von Lewetzow
2nd Jutland Cavalry Regiment, under Jacob von Bülow
3rd Jutland Cavalry Regiment, under Anders Sandberg
4th Jutland Cavalry Regiment, under Carl von Arensdorff

Dragoons
Walter's Dragoon Regiment, under Georg Trop
Ramstedt's Dragoon Regiment, under Nicolaus Helmich Ramstedt

Infantry
The King's Life Regiment, under Niels Rosencrantz
The Queen's Life Regiment, under Joachim von Schack
Prince George's Regiment (formerly the Commanding General's Regiment), under Dietrich Busch
Weyher's Regiment, under Thomas Meldrum
1st Zealand Regiment, under Jean de la Haye
2nd Fyn Regiment, under Siegwert von Bibow
4th Jutland Regiment, under Ægedius Kristof Lützow
Plön Regiment, under Conrad Brinck
Rosencrantz's Regiment, under Maximilian Rosencrantz
Degenfeldt's Regiment, under Hannibal von Degenfeldt
Stuart's Regiment, under Jacob Wilhelm Stuart

Note. Except the named provincial regiments, all were enlisted, in some cases just before the invasion.

Appendix VII. Order of Battle at Halmstad (Fyllebro), 17 August 1676[7]

The Swedish Army
Commander: Field Marshal Simon Grundel Helmfelt, with King Charles nominally in command.

Right wing: Cavalry
Commanders: King Charles, with Lieutenant General Rutger von Ascheberg in command of the first line, and Major General Leonard Johan Wittenberg

6 Primarily based on Colonel Maximilian Rosencrantz's disposition of the invasion fleet, manuscript, 1676.

7 Primarily based on Stade, "Slaget vid Halmstad," 96–8; with additional data on the Danish army from Vaupell, *Den danske hærs historie*, 125

in command of the second line.
His Majesty's Drabant Guard, consisting of 2 squadrons, under Lieutenant Colonel Hans Henrik von Siegroth.
The King's Life Regiment of Horse, consisting of at least 6 squadrons, under Colonel Nils Bielke.
Småland Cavalry Regiment, consisting of 2 squadrons, under Colonel Elias von Hagendorn.

Centre: Infantry
Commanders: Lieutenant General Martin Schultz in command of the first line, and Major General Barthold de Mortaigne in command of the second line.
His Majesty's Life Guard on Foot, consisting of 3 battalions, under Colonel Christoffer Gyllenstierna.
Skaraborg Regiment, consisting of 1 battalion, under Colonel Frederik von Börstell.
Kalmar Regiment, consisting of 1 battalion, under Lieutenant Colonel Erik Soop.
Dalecarlia Regiment, consisting of 1 battalion, under Colonel Hans Abraham Kruuse af Verchou.
Artillery, consisting of approximately 16 cannons.

Left wing: Cavalry
Commanders: Lieutenant General Wilhelm von Fersen in command of the first line, and Major General Johan Benedikt von Schönleben in command of the second line.
Västgöta Cavalry Regiment, consisting of 4 squadrons, under Colonel Per Hierta.
The Queen-Dowager's Life Regiment of Horse, consisting of 2 or 3 squadrons, under Lieutenant Colonel Fritz Wachtmeister.
Scania-Bohuslän Dragoon Regiment, consisting of 2 squadrons, under Major Peter Weinholtz (formally under Colonel Mauritz Wilhelm von Post who did not participate).

In addition, the Scanian Cavalry Regiment, consisting of 1 squadron (in reality 1 company), under Lieutenant Colonel Georg Johan Maydell, took part in the battle, in an unknown position which enabled them to reinforce the centre.

In total, 18–20 cavalry squadrons, 6 infantry battalions, and some hundred artillerymen, or some 6,000 men.

The Danish Army
Commander: Major General Jacob Duncan

Cavalry
A composite regiment (of eight national cavalry regiments), consisting of 500 men, under Colonel Burchard Heinrich Münchhausen.
Trop's Dragoon Regiment (formerly Walter's Dragoon Regiment), consisting of 500 men, under Colonel Georg Trop.

Infantry
Rosencrantz's Regiment, consisting of at least 640 men in 2 battalions, under Colonel Maximilian Rosencrantz and Lieutenant Colonel Frederik Wilhelm von Warnstedt.
2nd Fyn Regiment, consisting of at least 276 and 412 men, respectively, in 2 battalions, under Hans Detlef Steensen and Paul Rantzau (regiment formally under Colonel Christoph Hans Schack who did not participate).
Holstein Regiment, consisting of 292 men in 1 battalion, under Behrends (formally under Colonel Johan Vogt who did not participate).
Bremer's Regiment, consisting of 304 men in 1 battalion, under Kardorff.

Artillery
3 twelve-pounders.
About 10 regimental cannons.
2 mortars.

In total, 2,924 men in addition to officers and artillerymen, as presented. However, there is reason to believe that at least Rosencrantz's Regiment and the 2nd Fyn Regiment consisted of more men than given above. Since at least a few hundred officers and artillerymen need to be added to the total strength, the real total is estimated to have been closer to 4,000 men, and at least no less than 3,500.

Appendix VIII. Order of Battle at Lund, 4 December 1676[8]

The Swedish Army
Commander: Field Marshal Simon Grundel Helmfelt, with King Charles nominally in command.

Right wing: Cavalry
First line, commanded by Lieutenant General Otto Wilhelm von Fersen:
Viborg Dragoon Regiment, consisting of 260 men in 2 squadrons, under Colonel Gotthard Johan von Budberg.

8 Primarily based on Jensen, *Den skaanske krig*, 178–81; Stade, "Slaget vid Lund," 112–17; Wahlöö and Larsson, *Slaget vid Lund*, 92–5.

His Majesty's Drabant Guard, consisting of 150 men in 1 squadron, under Lieutenant Colonel Hans Henrik von Siegroth.
Life Regiment of Horse, consisting of 530 men in 5 squadrons, under Colonel Nils Bielke.
Åbo-Viborg Cavalry Regiment (Åbo-Viborgs kavalleriregemente), consisting of 303 men in 4 squadrons, under Colonel Klas Johan Baranoff.

In total, 1,243 men in 12 squadrons.

Second line, commanded by Major General Leonard Johan Wittenberg:
Scania-Bohuslän Dragoon Regiment, consisting of 60 men in 1 squadron, under Lieutenant Colonel Caspar Goës (formally under Colonel Mauritz Wilhelm von Post who did not participate).
The Retinue of Nobles, consisting of 200 men in 2 squadrons, under Colonel Johan Christersson Drake af Torp och Hamra.
The Reinforcement of Nobles in Götaland (*Adelns fördubbling i* Götaland), consisting of 170 men in 2 squadrons, under Colonel Christoffer von Güntersberg.
Old Smålanders (*Gamla Smålänningar*; formally the Blekinge Cavalry Regiment, *Blekingska regementet till häst*), consisting of 120 men in 1 squadron, under Colonel Hans Andersson Ramsvärd.
The Civil Service's Temporary Regiment (*Civilstatens bevillning*), consisting of 100 men in 1 squadron, under Lieutenant Colonel Axel Rehnskiöld.

In total, 650 men in 7 squadrons.

Right wing totals: 1,913 men in 19 squadrons.

Centre: Infantry
First line, commanded by Lieutenant General Martin Schultz:
His Majesty's Life Guard on Foot, consisting of 600 men in 3 battalions, under Colonel Christoffer Gyllenstierna.
Skaraborg Regiment, consisting of 243 men in 1 battalion, under Colonel Frederik von Börstell.
Dalecarlia Regiment, consisting of 125 men in 1 battalion, under Colonel Hans Abraham Kruuse af Verchou.
Västgöta-Dal Regiment, consisting of 96 men in 1 battalion, reportedly under Colonel Lars Axel Mörner af Tuna.
Hälsinge Regiment, consisting of 101 men in 1 battalion, under Lieutenant Colonel Georg Friedrich von Ascheberg.
Närke-Värmland Regiment, consisting of 117 men in 1 battalion, under Lieutenant Colonel Alexander Tomson.
Västernorrland Temporary Regiment (*Västernorrlands tremänningsregemente*), consisting of 176 men in 1 battalion, under Lieutenant Colonel Zacharias Ribbing.

Artillery: a total of 8 six-pounders and possibly 4 three-pounders, deployed in the centre between the infantry battalions.

In total, 1,458 men in 9 battalions.

Second line, commanded by Major General Barthold de Mortaigne:
Viborg Dragoon Regiment, consisting of 126 men in 2 squadrons.
Old Östgötians (*Gamla Östgötar*), consisting of 66 men in 1 squadron, under Colonel Otto Vellingk.
Gästrike-Hälsinge Reserve Regiment (*Gästrike-Hälsinge tremänningsregemente*), consisting of 193 men in 1 battalion, under Colonel Peter Örneklou.
Old Östgötians, consisting of 66 men in 1 squadron, under Colonel Vellingk's second-in-command, Lieutenant Colonel Johan Anders von der Pahlen.
Savolax Dragoon Regiment, consisting of 90 men in 1 squadron.
Småland Dragoon Regiment (*Småländska dragonregementet*; recently raised as a temporary regiment), consisting of 100 men in 1 squadron, under Colonel Abraham Cronhiort.

In total, 641 men in 1 battalion and 6 squadrons.

Centre totals: 2,099 men in 10 battalions and 6 squadrons.

Left wing: Cavalry
First line, commanded by Lieutenant General Johan Galle:
Småland Cavalry Regiment, consisting of 90 men in 1 squadron, under Colonel Elias von Hagendorn.
Viborg and Nyslott (Karelian) Cavalry Regiment, consisting of 600 men in 5 squadrons, under Colonel Bernhard Mellin.
Västgöta Cavalry Regiment, 400 men in 4 squadrons, under Colonel Per Hierta.
Savolax Dragoon Regiment, consisting of 295 men in 2 squadrons, under Colonel Herman von Burghausen.

In total, 1,385 men in 12 squadrons.

Second line, commanded by Major General Johan Benedikt von Schönleben:
The New Retinue of Nobles (*Adelns fördubbling i Svealand; Nya Adelsfanan*), consisting of 590 men in 4 squadrons, under Colonel Robert Lichton.
The Queen-Dowager's Life Regiment of Horse, consisting of 140 men in 2 squadrons, under Lieutenant Colonel Fritz Wachtmeister.
Savolax Dragoon Regiment, consisting of 98 men in 1 squadron.

In total, 828 men in 7 squadrons.

Left wing totals: 2,213 men in 19 squadrons.

Army totals: The Swedish army consisted of 44 squadrons of cavalry and dragoons, 10 battalions of infantry, and some artillery, the latter served by some hundred artillerymen. Total numbers, including officers (not counted above), were likely about 7,500 men. In addition, there was personnel in the supply train, including those too ill to fight, but their number is unknown.

The Danish Army
Commander: King Christian, with General Carl von Arensdorff.

Right wing: Cavalry
Commander: Lieutenant General Friedrich von Arensdorff.
First line, commanded by Major General Hans Wilhelm Meerheim:
Örtzen's Dragoon Regiment, consisting of 3 squadrons, under Colonel Detlef von Örtzen.
The Guard Cavalry, consisting of 3 squadrons, under Colonel Samuel Christoffer Plessen.
Life Regiment Cavalry, consisting of 3 squadrons, formally under Major General Hans Wilhelm Meerheim.
1st Jutland Cavalry Regiment, consisting of 3 squadrons, under Colonel Hans Friedrich von Lewetzow.
Zealand Retinue of Nobles, consisting of 2 squadrons, under Colonel Christian Christoffer Holck.

In total, 14 squadrons.

Second line, commanded by Major General Detlef Rantzau:
Baudissin's Cavalry Regiment, consisting of 3 squadrons, under Lieutenant General Gustav Adolph von Baudissin.
2nd Zealand Cavalry Regiment, consisting of 2 squadrons, under Major General Detlef Rantzau.
1st Fyn Cavalry Regiment, consisting of 3 squadrons, under Lieutenant Colonel Bernhard Christopher Kaas (formally under Major General Jacob Duncan who did not participate).
1st Zealand Cavalry Regiment, consisting of 3 squadrons, formally under Lieutenant General Friedrich von Arensdorff.

In total, 11 squadrons.

Right wing totals: 25 squadrons.

Centre: Infantry
Commander: Major General Joachim von Schack.
First line, commanded by Major General Joachim von Schack:
The King's Life Regiment, consisting of 2 battalions, under Colonel Siegwert von Bibow.
Prince George's Regiment (*Prinds Jørgens Regiment*; formerly the Commanding General's Regiment), consisting of 2 battalions, under Colonel Anton Günther Pottendorff.
Stuart's Regiment (*Stuarts Regiment*), consisting of 1 battalion, under Colonel Jacob Wilhelm Stuart.
Croÿ's Regiment (formerly Degenfeldt's Regiment; Degenfeldt had been promoted to major general and sent to Norway), consisting of 1 battalion,

under Colonel Charles Eugène de Croÿ.
Prince Frederick's Regiment (*Prinds Frederiks Regiment*; formerly the Field Marshal Lieutenant's Regiment), consisting of 2 battalions, under Colonel Thomas Meldrum.
The Queen's Life Regiment, consisting of 2 battalions, under Colonel Wilhelm Erhorn.

In total, 10 battalions.

Second line, commanded by Colonel Johan Caspar von Cicignon:
Lütken's Regiment, consisting of 1 battalion, under Colonel Detlef Lütken.
4th Jutland Regiment, consisting of 1 battalion, under Colonel Ægedius Kristof Lützow.
1st Fyn Regiment, consisting of 1 battalion, formally under Colonel Johan Caspar von Cicignon.
Commandeered sailors, consisting of 3 battalions known respectively as the King's Squadron (*Kongens Eskadre*), the Queen's Squadron (*Dronningens Eskadre*), and Prince George's Squadron (*Prinds Georgs Eskadre*).
3rd Jutland Regiment, consisting of 1 battalion, under Colonel Barthold Bülow.
Plön Regiment, consisting of 1 battalion, under Colonel Conrad Brinck.

Artillery: Approximately 56 cannons of various calibres, deployed between the infantry battalions, possibly under Major Andreas Harboe.

In total, 8 battalions.

Centre totals: 18 battalions.

Left wing: Cavalry
Commander: Major General Anders Sandberg.
First line, commanded by Major General Anders Sandberg:
3rd Jutland Cavalry Regiment, consisting of 3 squadrons, formally under Major General Anders Sandberg.
Jutland Retinue of Nobles, consisting of 2 (3?) squadrons, under Colonel Mogens Kruse.
2nd Fyn Cavalry Regiment, consisting of 3 squadrons, under Colonel Conrad Reventlow.
2nd Jutland Cavalry Regiment, consisting of 3 squadrons, under Colonel Jacob von Bülow.
Rauch's Cavalry Regiment, consisting of 2 squadrons, under Colonel Gottfried Rauch.
Schleswig Cavalry Regiment, consisting of 3 squadrons, under Colonel Henrik Sehested.

In total, 16 squadrons.

Second line.
4th Jutland Cavalry Regiment, consisting of 3 squadrons, formally under Carl von Arensdorff.
Brockenhus's Dragoon Regiment (*Brockenhus' Dragonregiment*; formerly Rantzau's Dragoon Regiment), consisting of 3 squadrons, under Colonel Jørgen Brockenhus.

In total, 6 squadrons.

Left wing totals: 22 squadrons.

Army totals: 41 cavalry squadrons, 6 dragoon squadrons, 18 infantry battalions, and some 56 cannons. Cavalry and dragoons consisted of at least some 4,700 to 5,000 men, while infantry strength was some 5,800 men. With officers included, the total Danish strength was at least some 11,000 to 11,500 regulars. In addition, there were some 1,300 sailors, and an unknown number of supply train personnel.

Appendix IX. Order of Battle at Landskrona, 14 July 1677[9]

The Swedish Army

Commander: Field Marshal Simon Grundel Helmfelt, with King Charles nominally in command.

Right wing
First line, commanded by General Rutger von Ascheberg (cavalry) and Major General Barthold de Mortaigne (infantry):
His Majesty's Drabant Guard, consisting of 142 men in 1 squadron, under Lieutenant Colonel Johan Henrik von Naschert.
Life Regiment of Horse, consisting of 6 squadrons, under Lieutenant Colonel Georg Zelow.
His Majesty's Life Guard on Foot, consisting 2 battalions, under Lieutenant Colonel Jacob Johan Hastfehr.

In total, 7 cavalry squadrons and 2 infantry battalions.

Second line, commanded by Major General Nils Bielke:
Scania-Bohuslän Dragoon Regiment, consisting of 1 squadron, under Colonel Mauritz Wilhelm von Post.
Life Regiment of Horse, consisting of 1 squadron, under Major General Nils Bielke.
Västgöta Cavalry Regiment, consisting of 4 squadrons, under Colonel Per Hierta.

9 Primarily based on Götesson, *Skånska krigets verkningar*, 159–77.

Jämtland Regiment, consisting of 1 battalion, under Captain Bengt Ribbing.
Hälsinge Regiment, consisting of 1 battalion, under Lieutenant Colonel Georg Friedrich von Ascheberg.
Viborg and Nyslott (Karelian) Cavalry Regiment, consisting of 1 squadron, under Colonel Bernhard Mellin.

In total, 7 cavalry squadrons and 2 infantry battalions.

Artillery, under Lieutenant Colonel Christer Carlsson Lillieberg.

Right wing totals: 14 cavalry squadrons, 4 infantry battalions, and artillery.

Centre: Infantry
First line, commanded by Lieutenant General Martin Schultz (assisted by infantry commanders Major General Barthold de Mortaigne and Major General Jöran Sperlingh):
His Majesty's Life Guard on Foot, consisting of 1 battalion, under Lieutenant Colonel Jacob Johan Hastfehr.
Skaraborg Regiment, consisting of 1 battalion, under Colonel Frederik von Börstell.
Dalecarlia Regiment, consisting of 3 battalions, under Colonel Hans Abraham Kruuse af Verchou.

In total, 5 infantry battalions.

Second line, commanded by Lieutenant General Christoffer Gyllenstierna:
Kalmar Regiment, consisting of 1 battalion, under Lieutenant Colonel Erik Soop.
Kronoberg Regiment, consisting of 2 battalions, under Colonel Henrik von Wicken and Lieutenant Colonel Carl-Gustav Skytte.

In total, 3 infantry battalions.

Centre totals: 8 infantry battalions.

Left wing
Commander: Field Marshal Simon Grundel Helmfelt.
First line, commanded by Major General Jöran Sperlingh (infantry) and Major General Johan Benedikt von Schönleben (cavalry).
Scanian Cavalry Regiment, consisting of 2 squadrons, under Major Henrik von Crefeld.
Dalecarlia Regiment, consisting of 1 battalion, under Major Peter Trotzig.
The Queen-Dowager's Life Regiment of Horse, consisting of 3 squadrons, under Lieutenant Colonel Mårten Grelsson Lindhielm.
Västerbotten Regiment, consisting of 1 battalion, under Colonel Evert Horn.
The Retinue of Nobles, consisting of 2 squadrons, under Colonel Johan Christersson Drake af Torp och Hamra.

In total, 7 cavalry squadrons and 2 infantry battalions.

Second line, commanded by Colonel Georg Henrik Lübecker.
Åbo-Viborg Cavalry Regiment, consisting of 1 squadron, under Colonel Klas Johan Baranoff.
Närke-Värmland Regiment, consisting of 1 battalion, under Lieutenant Colonel Alexander Tomson.
Wrangel's cavalry (*Wrangels ryttare*), consisting of 1 squadron, under Lieutenant Colonel Mauritz Fredrik Wrangel.
Gyllenstierna's Cavalry Regiment (*Gyllenstiernas kavalleriregemente*), consisting of 1 squadron, under Colonel Nils Gyllenstierna (formerly the Civil Service's Temporary Regiment, now reorganised as an enlisted regiment).
Värmland Regiment, consisting of 1 battalion, under Colonel Göran Stierna.
Småland Cavalry Regiment, consisting of 2 squadrons, under Colonel Per Jönsson Stålhammar.
Scania-Bohuslän Dragoon Regiment, consisting of 1 squadron, under Lieutenant Colonel Caspar Goës.
Old Östgötians, consisting of 1 squadron, under Colonel Otto Vellingk.

In total, 7 cavalry or dragoon squadrons and 2 infantry battalions.

Left wing totals: 14 cavalry or dragoon squadrons and 4 infantry battalions.

Peasant levies
4,000 levied Småland peasants led by their county governors, Augustin Leijonsköld and Gustav Lilliecrona.

Army totals: 28 cavalry or dragoon squadrons and 16 infantry battalions. Total strength was 8,522 men excluding officers, non-commissioned officers, and artillerymen, accordingly somewhat higher than 9,000 men. One near-contemporary document records 8,836 excluding officers and non-commissioned officers. To this total can be added the 4,000 levied peasants, who did not actively participate in the battle.

Note. There is documentary evidence that a squadron of Colonel Hans Andersson Ramsvärd's Old Smålanders, too, participated in the battle, since a payment to the men of this regiment for expenses incurred in the battle was recorded. However, this regiment is not mentioned in any existing order of battle and its location in the battle line remains unknown. It is possible that the regiment for unknown reason arrived late, so was not recorded in the order of battle.

The Danish Army
Commander: King Christian, with Field Marshal Joachim Rüdiger von der Goltz.

Right wing
First line, commanded by King Christian, Prince George, Field Marshal

Joachim Rüdiger von der Goltz, and Lieutenant General Gustav Adolph von Baudissin:
Grandvilliers's Regiment, consisting of 2 battalions, under Major General Grandvilliers (from the Münster contingent).
Netzow's Regiment, consisting of 2 battalions, under Colonel Netzow (from the Münster contingent).
Count Tecklenburg's Regiment, consisting of 2 battalions, under Colonel Tecklenburg (from the Münster contingent).
Grandvilliers's Cavalry Regiment, consisting of 1 squadron, under Colonel Bassum (from the Münster contingent).
Count Strassaldo's Regiment, consisting of 1 battalion, under Colonel Georg Wallis auf Karigmain (from the Imperial contingent).
Krain (Carniola) Cavalry Regiment, consisting of 1 squadron, under Field Marshal Lieutenant Jacob Leslie (from the Imperial contingent).
Baudissin's Cavalry Regiment, consisting of 1 squadron, formally under Lieutenant General Gustav Adolph von Baudissin.
2nd Fyn Cavalry Regiment, consisting of 2 squadrons, under Balthasar von Arensdorff.
2nd Zealand Cavalry Regiment, consisting of 2 squadrons, under Major General Detlef Rantzau.
Life Regiment Cavalry, consisting of 1 squadron, under Adam Hans Bars.

In total, 8 squadrons and 7 infantry battalions.

Second line, commanded by Major General Grandvilliers and Major General Detlef Rantzau:
Life Regiment Cavalry, consisting of 1 squadron.
Count Strassaldo's Regiment, consisting of 1 battalion (from the Imperial contingent).
Grandvilliers's Cavalry Regiment, consisting of 1 squadron (from the Münster contingent).
Jutland Retinue of Nobles, consisting of 2 squadrons, under Colonel Mogens Kruse.
3rd Jutland Cavalry Regiment, consisting of 3 squadrons, under Colonel Lorenz Styrke.
Schumacher's Dragoon Regiment, consisting of 1 squadron, under Colonel Schumacher (from the Münster contingent).
Ramstedt's Dragoon Regiment, consisting of 2 squadrons, under Colonel Nicolaus Helmich Ramstedt.

In total, 10 squadrons and 1 infantry battalion.

Third line, commanded by Major General Hans Wilhelm Meerheim:
The Guard Cavalry, consisting of 3 squadrons, under Joachim von Oettingen.
Goltz' Cavalry Regiment (formerly Rauch's Cavalry Regiment), consisting of 2 squadrons, formally under Field Marshal von der Goltz.
Gewecke's Cavalry Regiment, consisting of 2 squadrons, under Colonel Jacob Gewecke.

Schleswig Cavalry Regiment, consisting of 3 squadrons, under Colonel Conrad Friderich Rewentlow.
In total, 10 squadrons.

Right wing totals: 28 squadrons and 8 infantry battalions.

Centre
Commander: Lieutenant General Henrik Rüse von Rysensteen.
First line, commanded by Lieutenant General Henrik Rüse von Rysensteen:
Prince Frederick's Regiment, consisting of 3 battalions, under Colonel Thomas Meldrum.
Artillery, consisting of at least 25 cannons and 8 mortars, under Lieutenant Colonel Braune (Münster contingent) and Major Andreas Harboe (Danish contingent).

In total, 3 infantry battalions and artillery.

Second line, commanded by Major General Joachim von Schack:
Prince Christian's Regiment (*Prinds Christians Regiment*; formerly Maximilian Rosencrantz's regiment), consisting of 1 battalion, under Johan Anton Elnberger.
2nd Zealand Regiment, consisting of 1 battalion, under Colonel Christian Lange.

In total, 2 infantry battalions.

Centre totals: 5 infantry battalions and artillery.

Left wing
Commanded by Lieutenant General Friedrich von Arensdorff.
First line, commanded by Major General Hans Walter and Major General Detlef von Rumohr:
Nimpfen's Dragoon Regiment (*Nimpfens Dragonregiment*; formerly Örtzen's Dragoon Regiment), consisting of 1 squadron, under Thilo Henrik Nimpfen (also known as Nymphius).
Reinhard Keller's Cavalry Regiment, consisting of 1 squadron, under Lieutenant Colonel Wilhelm von Hornum (from the Hessian contingent).
1st Zealand Cavalry Regiment, consisting of 2 squadrons, formally under Lieutenant General Friedrich von Arensdorff.
The King's Life Regiment, consisting of 2 battalions, under Reinhard Keller.
4th Jutland Cavalry Regiment, consisting of 3 squadrons, under Major General Hans Walter.
Prince George's Regiment, consisting of 2 battalions, under Colonel Anton Günther Pottendorff.
Schleswig Regiment, consisting of 1 battalion, under Bartolomeus Veit Henrik Schönberg.
1st Fyn Cavalry Regiment, consisting of 2 squadrons, under Colonel Christopher Otto Schack.

3rd Jutland Regiment, consisting of 1 battalion, under Colonel Barthold Bülow.

In total, 9 squadrons and 6 infantry battalions.

Second line, commanded by Major General Hans Friedrich von Lewetzow.
1st Zealand Cavalry Regiment, consisting of 2 squadrons, formally under Lieutenant General Friedrich von Arensdorff.
The Queen's Life Regiment, consisting of 1 battalion, under Colonel Hans Georg von Schulenburg (or Colonel Wilhelm Erhorn).
1st Jutland Cavalry Regiment, consisting of 3 squadrons, under Colonel Herman Franz von Schwanewede.
Christian Juel's Cavalry Regiment, consisting of 2 squadrons, under Colonel Christian Juel-Rysensteen.
Zealand Retinue of Nobles, consisting of 1 squadron, under Colonel Rabe von Schilden.
Reinhard Keller's Cavalry Regiment, consisting of 1 squadron, under Lieutenant Colonel Kristof Lorenz Reitzenstein (from the Hessian contingent).
Brockenhus's Dragoon Regiment, consisting of 3 squadrons.

In total, 12 squadrons and 1 infantry battalion.
Left wing totals: 21 squadrons and 7 infantry battalions.
Army totals: 49 squadrons and 20 infantry battalions, in total some 11,000 to 12,000 men including officers.

Appendix X. Order of Battle at Warksow, 8 January 1678[10]

The Swedish Army
Commander: Field Marshal Otto Wilhelm von Königsmarck.

Right wing: Cavalry
Commander: Major General Friedrich von Buchwald.
First line:
Königsmarck's Life Regiment of Horse (*Königsmarcks Leibregiment zu Pferd*; formerly Holstein-Eutin's Cavalry Regiment), consisting of 4 squadrons, under Magnus Johann von Tiesenhausen.
Composite unit of different cavalry regiments, consisting of 3 squadrons, under Colonel Arvid Gyldenär.
Second line:
Östgöta Cavalry Regiment, consisting of 3 squadrons, under Blechert Wachtmeister.

10 Primarily based on a preserved order of battle, referred to as *Bataille, der Königl: Schwedischen Trouppen, wieder die Dähnen auf der Insel Rügen, den 8 Januari 1678 erhalten*; later studies are generally irreconcilable.

Centre: Infantry
Commander: Major General Otto Johan von Grothusen.

First line:
German Life Guard on Foot, consisting of 1 battalion, under Major General Otto Johan von Grothusen.
The National Commanding General's Life Regiment on Foot, consisting of 1 battalion, under Colonel Claes Ulrik von Schwerin.
Västmanland Regiment, consisting of 1 battalion, under Colonel Sabel.
Uppland Regiment, consisting of 1 battalion, under Count Gustav Carlson.
Artillery, consisting of 21 cannons, under Major Johan Siöblad.

Left wing: Cavalry
Commander: Colonel Bernhard Otto von Liewen.

First line:
Åbo and Björneborg County Cavalry Regiment, consisting of 3 squadrons, under Colonel Bernhard Otto von Liewen.
Composite unit of different cavalry regiments, consisting of 3 squadrons, under Colonel Jürgen Mellin.
Second line:
Wangelin's Dragoon Regiment, consisting of 2 squadrons, under Berndt Wangelin.
Småland Cavalry Regiment, consisting of 2 squadrons, formally under Major General Friedrich von Buchwald.

The Coalition Army
Commander: Major General Detlef von Rumohr.

Right wing: Cavalry
Commander: Lieutenant Colonel Iversen (from Denmark).

First line:
Composite unit of different cavalry regiments, consisting of 3 squadrons (from Denmark).
Grandvilliers's Cavalry Regiment, consisting of 2 squadron, under Colonel Bassum (from the Münster contingent).
Schultz's Dragoon Regiment, consisting of 1 squadron (from the Imperial contingent).
Second line:
Composite unit of different cavalry regiments, consisting of 3 squadrons (from Denmark).
Schultz's Dragoon Regiment, consisting of 2 squadrons (from the Imperial contingent).

Centre: Infantry
Commander: Colonel Georg Wallis auf Karigmain (from the Imperial contingent).

First line:
Count Strassaldo's Regiment, consisting of 800 men in 2 battalions, under Colonel Georg Wallis auf Karigmain (from the Imperial contingent).
Netzow's Regiment, consisting of 400 men in 1 battalion, under Colonel Netzow (from the Münster contingent).
Keller's Regiment, consisting of 200 men in 1 battalion, under Colonel Johann auf dem Keller (from the Hessian contingent).
Second line:
Keller's Regiment, consisting of 400 men in 2 battalions, under Colonel Johann auf dem Keller (from the Hessian contingent).
The King's Life Regiment, consisting of 300 men in 1 squadron, under Reinhard Keller (from Denmark).
Artillery, consisting of 12 to 16 light cannons.

Left wing: Cavalry
Commander: Colonel Wilhelm Friedrich von Hülsen (from Brandenburg).

First line:
Hülsen's Cavalry Regiment, consisting of 3 squadrons, under Colonel Wilhelm Friedrich von Hülsen (from Brandenburg).
Reinhard Keller's Cavalry Regiment, consisting of 2 squadrons, under Lieutenant Colonel Wilhelm von Hornum (from the Hessian contingent).
Görtzke's Dragoon Regiment, consisting of 1 squadron, under Görtzke (from Brandenburg).
Second line:
The Retinue of Nobles (composite unit), consisting of 2 squadrons (from Denmark).

Composite unit of different dragoon regiments, consisting of 3 squadrons (from Brandenburg).

Colour Plate Commentaries

A. The Swedish Army, Battle of Lund, 1676

1. Mounted Drabant, His Majesty's Life Guard of Horse

His Majesty's Drabant Guard served as the personal bodyguard of the King of Sweden and was the most prominent unit in the Swedish army. Its men followed King Charles wherever he went, and despite a high casualty rate in battle, the Drabant Guard never let Charles down. Since 1657, the unit had formed part of His Majesty's Life Guard of Horse and Foot. From 1675, the Drabant Guard formed the only mounted unit of the Life Guard. It consisted of enlisted soldiers, many of whom in time became officers in King Charles's army, since service in the Life Guard in many ways functioned as an officer training school.

Although records detailing the Drabant Guard uniforms have been preserved, questions still remain on how the Drabants dressed when on campaign. It cannot even be determined with any degree of certainty whether the Drabants wore breastplates or not at the Battle of Lund. They probably received them only the following year, but if so, why did regular cavalry units receive theirs before the Drabant Guard? Or did the Drabants arm themselves individually? Probably not, but we simply do not know. Contemporary paintings are of little help, because the only certain depiction of a Drabant guardsman at Lund shows him from the back, so only the grey regulation-issue cloak is visible.

In 1675–1676, Drabant guardsmen on ceremonial duty at court wore buff coats with chest buttons. Swedish buff coats usually did not have chest buttons, since they interfered with the breastplate. A set of buff coats with chest buttons was captured by Danish troops at Stade in Bremen-Verden in 1676 (and have been preserved in museums in Copenhagen and Stade). Although these buff coats were not used by the Drabant Guard, and may not even have been made in the Swedish heartland, it is conceivable that Drabant guardsmen then wore buff coats of this pattern. However, there is no evidence that they wore such dress on the battlefield. It is also possible that Drabants wore regular buff coats in battle, like the Life Regiment of Horse did, but if so, they presumably also wore breastplates over their buff coats. Another possibility, and the one chosen for this plate, is that the Drabant cavalrymen dressed according to regulations, that is, in French-style blue coats with yellow lining. This was also the uniform which King Charles later on recommended for all Swedish troops, and the one which in time became the archetypal Carolean uniform. It would not be strange if the Drabant Guard was the first cavalry unit which received the new uniform. This might also explain why breastplates were only issued later, when it had been found that battle conditions still demanded it.

As compared to Denmark and the German principalities, Sweden faced a disadvantage when raising cavalry. Danish horses were considerably bigger than Swedish ones. They were also better fed. Swedish horses were no larger than ponies, with a height of 140 cm as measured behind the saddle. The Danes would joke that a Swedish horse could walk below the belly of a Danish horse. However, they were hardy and strong and could survive periods of lack of fodder far better than the Danish ones.

2. Trooper, Life Regiment of Horse

The Life Regiment of Horse was unusual among conscripted regiments since its intake of recruits derived from different regions of the Swedish heartland. In part for this reason, the Life Regiment was regarded as a select elite unit. Under the command of Nils Bielke, the Life Regiment lived up to its reputation. Its men were dressed and armed in the traditional manner, each with a breastplate over his buff coat and with black, high riding boots. The lower end of the buff coat was often turned back in the manner shown so as to enable easier movement. This is what the bulk of the Swedish cavalry looked like during the Scanian War. Many of the cavalrymen depicted as following King Charles in contemporary paintings no doubt belonged to the Life Regiment. At this time, breastplates were commonly painted black, but later on, both newly-issued ones and many of those that remained were instead polished so as to give a shining appearance.

At the Battle of Lund, and on a number of other occasions, Swedish soldiers wrapped a wreath of straw around their left arms and put a whisk of straw in the band around their hats, in the manner shown in this plate.

3. Trooper, Baranoff's Åbo-Viborg Cavalry Regiment

The Åbo-Viborg Cavalry Regiment was an enlisted unit raised in Finland in 1676. From the outset, each man was uniformed in a red French-style coat with blue lining and, as headgear, a *karpus* in same colours. As a newly raised unit, it did not receive breastplates until in 1679. Like all cavalry, they wore black, high riding boots. This soldier, like most others, wore his hair tied up with a ribbon

The carbine arrangement is usually reconstructed as in this plate, but as noted, at this time the carbine possibly hung with the butt down. One reason for this might be that it facilitated movement with the carbine loaded.

B. The Swedish Army, Battle of Lund, 1676

1. Pikeman, Västgöta-Dal Regiment

The issuing of new uniforms was seldom completed rapidly, since soldiers were expected first to wear out their old uniforms. This meant that several styles of uniforms might appear simultaneously within the same unit. The soldiers of the Västgöta-Dal Regiment suffered from inconsistencies more than most, since in 1675 coats in no less than three different colours were ordered on separate occasions: first blue, then brown with red lining and border, and finally grey with yellow lining and border. In 1676, five hundred sets of grey coats with yellow lining and yellow borders were finally distributed. This pikeman is dressed in a grey coat with yellow lining, but the yellow border which should have been visible is not. On his head, he wears a fur-lined, grey *karpus* which might or not have been regulation issue but certainly was helpful in winter.

His rapier hangs from a waistbelt. More common still was to carry the rapier in the old style, hung from a baldric.

2. Musketeer, Dalecarlia Regiment

At the time of the Battle of Lund, the Dalecarlia Regiment had been issued with blue French-style coats with red lining, blue breeches, and black hats. However, this musketeer has, like many other soldiers, for one reason or another retained the old style of baggy breeches, which he wears together with stockings.

The musketeer is depicted with a new flintlock musket and cartridge box. However, in the early years of the war the matchlock musket still remained in near-universal use, together with the old-style bandolier with wooden bottles for gunpowder. Moreover, Swedish orders and post-war regulations still included explicit references to musket fork rests. This does not reconcile with the paintings purporting to be from the war, since most do not show either style of equipment. Danish illustrations, for instance the Rosenborg Castle tapestries, frequently show bandoliers, but they are not as clear with regard to what the bandoliers were used for. The tapestries were based on a series of paintings by artists such as Claus Møinichen, Christian Morholt, and Peder Andersen which were produced in the period 1686–1688. Likewise, most of the Swedish battle paintings were produced in the years after the war by Johan Philip Lemke. However, Lemke based the details of his paintings on sketches that he had made of continental, probably French soldiers, before he even arrived in Sweden. Although most of the battle paintings were inspected and approved by the respective king who had ordered them, this only proves that the general outline of the battles was correct. Since in particular King Charles was in the process of modernising both uniforms and equipment according to the Continental style, he is unlikely to have complained if his chosen artist depicted the men under his command with slightly more up-to-date equipment than had actually been used in that particular battle.

3. Artilleryman, Artillery Regiment

All Swedish artillery technically belonged to the Artillery Regiment. Most artillerymen were dressed in practical, grey French-style coats with blue lining and grey hats. This artilleryman wears the old-style baggy breeches under his coat, together with grey woollen stockings. The shade of grey of his uniform derived from natural wool, so might vary slightly between different individuals.

While all units suffered from significant wear and tear of uniforms when on campaign, the artillery and the navy may have suffered most. Already in

1677, a report noted that the Artillery Regiment, both in garrisons and in the field artillery, had worn out their uniforms to the extent that the men were essentially "naked" and could no longer go on campaign.

C. The Danish Army, Battle of Lund, 1676

1. Trooper, Life Regiment Cavalry

While many Danish cavalrymen still wore buff coats or jerkins, although reportedly of less sturdy leather than the Swedish elk-skin buff coats, many had already been issued light grey French-style coats. This trooper also wears the traditional, grey wide-brimmed felt hat. Like all cavalry, he has been issued black, high riding boots. He also carries a rapier and a carbine. No doubt, he had been trained to use the carbine in the caracole, which during the war, and in the face of more aggressive Swedish tactics, finally was abolished within the Danish cavalry.

Like the situation in the infantry, most cavalrymen still wore their rapiers hung from a baldric. However, the waistbelt was becoming increasingly common. The cavalryman would also bring two wheellock pistols, carried in holsters fixed to the front of his saddle. Only one Danish cavalry regiment had been issued breastplates, so this Life Regiment cavalryman would not have one.

2. Musketeer, the Queen's Life Regiment

Like several other regiments, the uniform colours of the Queen's Life Regiment depended on when a particular uniform item had been issued. However, in this regiment, the base coat colour was from 1669 always red. At the beginning of the Scanian War, red coats with yellow lining and yellow stockings were apparently most common, and this combination remained prevalent after the war as well. However, some uniforms issued during the war may have come with green or blue lining instead of yellow.

The black hat is of a modern, stiffer type than the traditional wide-brimmed variety. Like the cartridge box, it carries the royal cypher of King Christian V and replaced the previous model during the war. Again, most soldiers would still have carried the rapier hung from a baldric.

3. Officer, Prince George's Regiment

Although officers acquired their own uniforms, they would in most cases, and certainly so in Denmark, follow the base colour of the regiment in their choice of uniform. Since 1670, Prince George's Regiment had a blue base colour, so this officer wears a blue, French-style coat, for obvious reasons considerably more embellished than the coat of a common soldier. Along its seams and edges, the coat is decorated with lace trim, in this case silver ribbon. An infantry officer customarily wore a gilded gorget with King Christian's royal cypher and a crown. Officers in some regiments wore sashes. In 1668, the officers of this particular regiment (which then had been known as the Commanding General's Regiment) had worn blue sashes with mixed gold and silver fringes, and clearly this officer still retains his sash. He also wears a plumed hat, perhaps with the plume made of ostrich feathers, and black, high riding boots, since a senior officer would be mounted on horseback. In battle, he might still dismount and lead on foot.

D. The Danish army, Battle of Lund, 1676

1. Pikeman, 1st Fyn National Regiment

Since 1675, the 1st Fyn National Regiment wore green coats with yellow lining. This soldier's hat is decorated with the royal cypher, and he carries his rapier in a baldric in the common manner. The pike was still in widespread use and was not regarded as obsolete, even though the number of pikes in the Danish army grew smaller and King Christian in October 1678 ordered that pikes should be abandoned and replaced with muskets and swinefeathers. The pike shafts may have been painted black, since this seems to have been a common practice in Germany.

2. Musketeer, Sailors' Battalion

Before the Battle of Lund, the Danes formed 12 companies of commandeered sailors into three sailors battalions, named in the manner of the navy respectively as the King's Squadron, the Queen's Squadron, and Prince George's Squadron. The sailors were ordered to serve as infantrymen, something for which they were untrained. They were armed and organised in the manner of the regular infantry, with pikes (up to 30 percent of the total) and snaphance muskets as primary weapons. Most of the sailors received red coats to look like soldiers, which they wore with possibly white stockings. However, this sailor still wears his daily shipboard dress, which consists of a hat, jacket, baggy breeches, and woollen stockings. Probably a Dutchman, he is armed with one of the snaphance muskets used by the Dutch navy as shipboard weapons. Others were armed with half-pikes, crude morning stars, pistols, and cutlasses.

3. Danish Irregular

The irregulars who served in the Danish freeshooter companies were not always former peasants but most dressed as rural countrymen, since they often tried to pass as locals to avoid discovery. This irregular is armed with a musket and along fighting knife, which is barely visible under his jacket. A probably typical, preserved such knife has a 37 cm long blade reminiscent of the later Bowie knife. Others used rifled hunting weapons and probably operated as snipers.

E. Swedes, Danes, and Norwegians

1. Officer, Swedish Naval Regiment, 1676

The Naval Regiment (*Marinregementet*) was an infantry regiment raised in 1676 in Bohuslän and Halland. Officers wore French-style blue coats with red cuffs, red breeches, and white stockings. The seams of the officer's coat is decorated with lace trim. Officer also wore gilded gorgets, decorated with the royal cypher. The men of the Naval Regiment wore blue coats, too, but without red cuffs and other decorations, and grey woollen breeches.

The sketch shows an infantryman who carries his rapier in the old style, hung from a baldric instead of from a waistbelt.

2. Swedish Sailor

Common sailors did not wear uniforms and looked much the same whether in the Danish or the Swedish navy. Marine archaeology, in particular from the site where the Swedish flagship *Kronan* sank off Öland, has yielded much evidence on how Swedish sailors dressed at the time. A sailor would receive a jacket and a pair of blue or grey baggy woollen breeches. In addition, he would receive a linen shirt, long woollen stockings, and a pair of greased-leather shoes. At this time, most would bring their own headgear. There is some evidence that sailors later also received blue coats and hats.

Officers, as always, dressed in greater variety and in better clothes. Again archaeological finds from the Kronan gives a good picture of their dress, ranging from scarlet jackets to wolf-skin coats for cold weather.

3. Musketeer, Norwegian Akershus Regiment

The Norwegian regiments were dressed and equipped in similar style to the Danish regiments. This musketeer wears a light grey French-style coat with green lining and, as headgear, a *karpus* in same colours that were characteristic of the uniform of the Akershus Regiment. Like many Swedish units, he still wears the old-style baggy breeches.

Most still wore the rapier hung from a baldric, but as in Denmark and Sweden, the waistbelt was coming into fashion.

F. Swedish Standards

1. Cavalry Regimental Standard, Baranoff's Åbo-Viborg Cavalry Regiment, 1676

When raised, the regimental standard of the Åbo-Viborg Cavalry Regiment was blue with a border of yellow and blue silk. It displayed the royal cypher, the crown, and palm branches, a symbol of victory, in yellow. A new system for standards and colours had been introduced in 1672, based on the concept that all provincial regiments should have the coat of arms of the province in which they were raised on their colour. However, it took time before the new system was fully applied, and Baranoff's standard, too, did not correspond to the new system.

2. Cavalry Standard, Vadsbo Company, Life Regiment of Horse, 1679

The regimental standard of the Life Regiment of Horse was white, carrying the coat of arms of the Kingdom of Sweden. In addition, each company had its own standard. These were white, too, but with a motto in Latin, in gold letters on a blue base, and the coat of arms of the province from which the company derived, in a canton in the upper corner. This company standard derives from the Vadsbo Company. It carries the motto *Constanter* ("Standing fast") and the black eagle on yellow shows that the company derived from the province of Värmland. This was then not quite true, since Vadsbo in 1658 had been transferred to Västergötland. However, many standards were old and they were not changed unnecessarily.

3. Infantry Company Flag, Dalecarlia Regiment, 1676

The Dalecarlia Regiment in 1676 received eight company flags, one white for the Life Company and seven blue, for the other companies. Each had the arrows and crown that constituted the coat of arms of Dalecarlia, a green laurel, and four black grenades with red flames. The flags followed the new system introduced four years earlier.

4. Infantry Company Flag, Västgöta-Dal Regiment

The company flags of the Västgöta-Dal Regiment followed the new system, with the red bull of the provincial coat of arms prominently displayed in the centre, surrounded by a green laurel and four black grenades with red flames in the same manner as the flags of the Dalecarlia Regiment.

G. Danish Standards, Battle of Lund, 1676

1. Infantry Regimental Colour

One of several Danish regimental colours taken at the Battle of Lund and currently preserved in the Swedish Trophy Collection (reference: Army Museum, Stockholm,AM.080172). It is not always possible to identify to which regiment they belonged. Made of yellow cloth, this colour is fairly representative of the Danish infantry regiments, but of unknown identification. As was common with Danish colours, it also included a canton with a Danish cross (*Dannebrog*) in the upper corner. The breadth of the colour is 150 cm and its length 170 cm. The stave (from ferrule to finial) is 253 cm long.

2. Infantry Company Flag, 3rd Jutland Regiment

Another of several Danish regimental colours taken at the Battle of Lund and currently preserved in the Swedish Trophy Collection (reference: Army Museum, Stockholm,AM.080054), this can be identified as belonging to the 2nd company of the 3rd Jutland Regiment, under Colonel Barthold Bülow. Again, the colour also included a canton with a Danish cross (*Dannebrog*) in the upper corner. The breadth of the colour is 205 cm and its length 230 cm. The stave (from ferrule to finial) is 307 cm long.

No less than three company flags of this regiment were taken at Lund and remain preserved in the Swedish trophy collection (references: Army Museum, Stockholm,AM.080054, AM.080055, and AM.080056).

3. Infantry Flag, Sailors' Company

One of several Danish sailors battalion flags taken at the Battle of Lund and currently preserved in the Swedish Trophy Collection (reference: Army

Museum, Stockholm, AM.080178). Made of yellow woollen cloth, the hearts were painted in red directly on the cloth. The breadth of the colour is 177.2 cm and its length 237.8 cm. The stave (from ferrule to finial) is 216 cm long. As usual with Danish colours, it also included a canton with a Danish cross (*Dannebrog*) in the upper corner. Because of its pattern, this was presumably a sailors' company flag.

H. Swedish, Danish, and Norwegian Standards

1. Swedish Infantry Colour, Naval Regiment, 1676

The Naval Regiment followed the general style of the provincial regiments, except that it had a white ship with Swedish flags instead of a provincial coat of arms displayed in the centre, surrounded by four black grenades with red flames. There may have been a plan to add a laurel for the company flags, but no flag with this motif is preserved.

2. Danish Cavalry Standard, 1676

One of several Danish cavalry standards taken at the Battle of Lund and currently preserved in the Swedish Trophy Collection (reference: Army Museum, Stockholm,AM.080263). The motto, in Danish, is *Lycken bær manden ofver bæcken* ("Fortune carries the man across the stream"). It has been identified as belonging to the 2nd company of the 1st Zealand Cavalry Regiment, under Friedrich von Arensdorff. The breadth of the colour is 62.5 cm and its length 59 cm. The stave (from ferrule to finial) is 307 cm long.

3. Danish Infantry Colour, Sailors' Battalion

Another of several Danish sailors battalion colours taken at the Battle of Lund and currently preserved in the Swedish Trophy Collection (reference: Army Museum, Stockholm,AM.080116). Made of woollen cloth, the breadth of the colour is 175 cm and its length 200 cm. The stave is 237 cm long. Designed as a Danish cross (*Dannebrog*), this can likely be identified as the battalion colour of the King's Squadron of the commandeered sailors. Since a similar flag exists in the Trophy Collection that likely can be identified as the battalion colour of the Queen's Squadron (AM.080115), we can assume that Prince George's Squadron fielded a similar colour, too, with the appropriate name cypher.

4. Infantry Flag, Norwegian Sailors' Company

Yet another of several Danish sailors battalion flags taken at the Battle of Lund and currently preserved in the Swedish Trophy Collection (reference: Army Museum, Stockholm, AM.080079). Because of the Norwegian lion in the centre of the Danish cross (*Dannebrog*), it has been attributed to a Norwegian sailors' company that fought within one of the Danish sailors battalions. The colour probably derived from the Norwegian warship *Norske løve* ("Norwegian lion"). The breadth of the colour is 177 cm and its length 244 cm. The stave is 290 cm long.

Further Reading

With the exception of a few engagements fought on the Continent, most battles during the Scanian War took place in southern Sweden. It is accordingly unsurprising that almost all studies of the war were carried out in the Scandinavian countries, and in particular in Sweden and Denmark. For this reason, most remaining sources as well as later studies are in Danish, Norwegian, or Swedish. Previous research and publications on the Scanian War can be said to have gone through four phases, which in its broad outlines mirror those of military history elsewhere in Western Europe. First, already at the time of the war a significant number of news pamphlets were produced, purporting to detail and explain the various actions undertaken. Most were propagandistic in nature. Second, renewed interest in the war occurred in the late nineteenth century, especially in relation with the bicentennial anniversary of the Battle of Lund. This stimulated research in the purely military aspects of the war and was frequently carried out as part of the growth in military history as a field of study within the general staffs that then were being formed, following the Prussian example, in many European armies. Several participants in the war had left diaries, including King Charles, Rutger von Ascheberg, Erik Dahlbergh, Nils Bielke, and two young lieutenants, Nils Skytte and Johan Adolph Clodt von Jürgensburg. As a result, what can almost be termed official Danish, Norwegian, and Swedish military histories of the organisation, tactics, and events during the war were published. Based on the diaries and national archive sources, these histories tend to report facts as they were recorded. However, most information on opposing forces that was found in the national archives derived from intelligence or assessments that frequently exaggerated their number and strength. It follows that the histories are generally reliable when it comes to descriptions of their own units and activities but far less so with regard to those of their opponents. Thus, histories such as those by Vaupell, Jensen, Björlin, and Gulowsen are best read together, not separately.

In the first half of the twentieth century, research on the Scanian War entered a third phase, this time taking place also among civilians, with Swedish historians from the University of Lund at the forefront. For the first time, the economic and cultural effects of the war were being studied as well. Then, following a post-second world war hiatus when all military aspects of history were regarded as anathema among Scandinavian academics, interest in the war was rekindled by amateur military historians from the 1970s and in particular the 1980s onwards. In this fourth phase of research, a renewed interest was devoted to the archival sources, which unearthed plenty of previously ignored data on the military units that participated in the war, with a particular focus on uniforms, flags, and organisation. This also led to several new popular histories of the war, of varying standards of research and attention to details, which in turn inspired the first, and under-resourced, attempts at battlefield archaeology. Several recent archaeological excavations have increased our knowledge of the Scanian War, as well as the conditions of late seventeenth-century battles in general.

However, hardly any of this research was published in English. For this reason, the following bibliography is limited to the works most frequently referenced in notes and most useful for continued research. Other works are only mentioned in the notes.

Åberg, Alf (ed.), *Fältmarskalken Rutger von Aschebergs journal och korrespondens till år 1680*. Stockholm, Historiska Handlingar 34:1, 1951: 1–267.

Alm, Josef. *Blanka vapen och skyddsvapenfrån och med 1500-talet till våra dagar*. Stockholm: Rediviva, 1975. First published in 1932.

Alm, Josef. *Eldhandvapen 1: Från deras tidigaste förekomst till slaglåsets allmänna införande*. Stockholm: Rediviva, 1976. First published in 1934.

Almgren, Carl Eric. "Svensk strategi och krigsledning". Göran Rystad (ed.). *Kampen om Skåne*. Lund: Historiska Media, 2005: 33–74.

Askgaard, Finn. "Kampen till sjöss". Göran Rystad (ed.). *Kampen om Skåne*. Lund: Historiska Media, 2005: 171–86.

Bauer, Frank. *Fehrbellin 1675: Brandenburg-Preußens Aufbruch zur Großmacht*. Potsdam: Kurt Vowinckel-Verlag, 1998.

Bellander, Erik. *Dräkt och uniform: Den svenska arméns beklädnad från 1500-talets början fram till våra dagar*. Stockholm: P.A. Norstedt & Söner, 1973.

Bergström, O. (ed.). *Öfverste Nils Skyttes dagbok 1675–1720*. Stockholm: P.A. Norstedt & Söner, 1901.

Björlin, Gustaf. *Kriget mot Danmark 1675–1679*. Stockholm: P.A. Norstedt & Söner, 1885.

Cohrt, Poul T. "Landstigningen vid Råå". Göran Rystad (ed.). *Kampen om Skåne*. Lund: Historiska Media, 2005: 22–9.

Ericson, Lars; Martin Hårdstedt; Per Iko; Ingvar Sjöblom; and Gunnar Åselius. *Svenska slagfält*. np: Wahlström & Widstrand, 2003.

Fabricius, Knud. "'Terror Panicus' og Christianstads undsætning 1678", *Historisk Tidsskrift* 11:2 (Copenhagen 1949): 467–92.

Gautier, Henrik Didier. "Krigskostnaderna och den danska statens finanser". Göran Rystad (ed.). *Kampen om Skåne*. Lund: Historiska Media, 2005: 232–51.

Glete, Jan. *Navies and Nations: Warships, Navies and State Building in Europe and America, 1500–1860*. 2 vols. Stockholm: Almqvist & Wiksell

International, Acta Universitatis stockholmiensis (Stockholm Studies in History) 48: 1, 1993.

Göthesson, Lars-Åke. *Ställningen vid Norrvidinge hösten 1678: Erik Dahlberghs bataljplan över Karl XI:s fältläger vid Norrvidinge och Dagstorp*. Kristianstad: Monitor Förlaget, 2005.

Götesson, Lars-Åke, *Skånska krigets verkningar i Landskronatrakten 1676–1679*. Visby: Nomen, 2014.

Gulowsen, I. *Gyldenløvefeiden 1675–1679*. Christiania: Videnskabs-Selskabet, 1906.

Gyllenstierna, Ebbe. "Kriget i Tyskland". Göran Rystad (ed.). *Kampen om Skåne*. Lund: Historiska Media, 2005: 187–203.

Hasselager, Olaf; and Torstein Snorrason. *Danish Uniforms, Colours and Standards 1675–1679*. Online publication, 2000.

Hildebrand, Sune (ed.). *Hakvin Spegels dagbok*. Stockholm: P.A. Norstedt & Söner, 1923.

Hildebrand, Sune (ed.), *Karl XI:s almanacksanteckningar*. Stockholm: Norstedt & Söner, 1918.

Hinze, Uwe-Rolf. *Die Schlacht von Fehrbellin: Der Sieg Brandenburgs über Schweden 1675*. Karwe: Edition Rieger, 2010.

Höglund, Lars-Eric. *Skånska kriget 1675–79: Fanor och uniformer*. Karlstad: Acedia Press, 1999. Published in English as *The Scanian War 1675–1679: Colours and Uniforms*. Karlstad: Acedia Press, 1999.

Holm, Torsten. *Översikt över Sveriges krig under 1600-talets senare hälft*. Stockholm: Militärlitteraturföreningen 148, 1927.

Isacson, Claes-Göran. *Skånska kriget 1675–1679*. Lund: Historiska Media, 2000.

Jacobsen, Sthen. *Den Nordiske Kriigs Krøniche*. Ed. Martin Weibull. Lund: Gleerups, 1897.

Jensen, Niels Peder. *Den skaanske krig 1675–1679*. Copenhagen: Det nordiske forlag, 1900.

Johansen, Katia; and Peter Kristiansen. *Rosenborgtapeterne: Christian Vs sejre i Skånske krig 1675–79*. Copenhagen: De Danske Kongers Kronologiske Samling på Rosenborg, 1999.

Johansson, Björn Axel (ed.). *Regalskeppet Kronan*. Höganäs: Bra Böcker, 1985.

Klinkenborg, Melle. *Fehrbellin: Nach Berichten und Briefen der führenden Männer*. Leipzig: R. Voigtländer, 1913.

Knarrström, Bo. *Slagfältet: Om bataljen vid Landskrona 1677 och fynden från den första arkeologiska undersökningen av ett svenskt slagfält*. Saltsjö-Duvnäs: Efron & Dotter, 2006.

Knarrström, Bo; and Stefan Larsson. *Hans Majestäts friskyttar av Danmark*. Stockholm: Riksantikvarieämbetet, 2008.

Lundgren, Kurt. *Regalskeppet Stora Cronan: Byggandet, slaget och undergången 1676*. np: SMB, 2014.

Lundström, Herman (ed.), *Erik Dahlberghs dagbok (1625–1699)*. Uppsala: Almqvist & Wiksell, 1912.

Magalotti, Lorenzo. *Sverige under år 1674*. Stockholm: Rediviva, 1986. First published in 1912.

Nielsen, K.V. "Dansk strategi och krigsföring". Göran Rystad (ed.). *Kampen om Skåne*. Lund: Historiska Media, 2005: 75–91.

Petri, Gustaf. *Kungl. Första livgrenadjärregementets historia 2: Östgöta regemente till fot 1619–1679*. Stockholm: P.A. Norstedt & Söner, 1928.

Rosander, Lars. *Sveriges fältmarskalkar: Svenska fältherrar från Vasa till Bernadotte*. Lund: Historiska Media, 2003.

Rystad, Göran. *Karl XI: En biografi*. Lund: Historiska Media, 2003.

Rystad, Göran (ed.). *Kampen om Skåne*. Lund: Historiska Media, 2005.

Rystad, Göran. "Slaget vid Landskrona". Göran Rystad (ed.). *Kampen om Skåne*. Lund: Historiska Media, 2005: 163–8.

Rystad, Göran. "Snapphanarna och 'det lilla kriget'". Göran Rystad (ed.), *Kampen om Skåne*. Lund: Historiska Media, 2005: 283–98.

Sello, Georg. "Fehrbellin". *Deutsche Zeitschrift für Geschichtswissenschaft* 7 (1892): 282–318.

Seitz, Heribert. *Svärdet och värjan som armévapen*. Stockholm: Kungl. Armémuseum, 1955.

Stade, Arne. "Christian V i slaget vid Lund: En huvudvärk för den danskakrigspropagandan". *Historisk Tidsskrift*. New Series 15. Copenhagen, 1983–1985: 23–54.

Stade, Arne. "Stade, Arne. "Slaget vid Halmstad (Fyllebro)". Goran Rystad (ed.). *Kampen om Skåne*. Lund: Historiska Media, 2005: 95–106.

Stade, Arne. "Slaget vid Lund", Göran Rystad (ed.), *Kampen om Skåne*. Lund: Historiska Media, 2005: 107–162.

Tessin, Georg. *Die deutschen Regimenter der Krone Schweden 2: Unter Karl XI. und Karl XII. (1660–1718)*. Cologne: Böhlau, 1967.

Ulfhielm, Hans; and Eric Granefelt (eds.). *Kungl. Artilleriet: Svenska Artilleriet i Östersjöprovinserna 1561–1721*. np: Militärhistoriska Förlaget, 2005.

Vaupell, Otto. *Den danske hærs historie til nutiden og den norske hærs historie indtil 1814*, Vol. 1. Copenhagen: Gyldendal, 1872.

Wahlöö, Claes; and Göran Larsson. *Slaget vid Lund: Ett mord och icke ett fältslag*. Lund: Historiska Media, 1998.

Weibull, Martin (ed.). "Johan Adolph Clodts anteckningar", *Historisk Tidskrift* 3 (1883): 203–24, 279–322.

Wernstedt, Folke. *Kungl. Svea livgardes historia -4: 1660–1718*. Stockholm: Stiftelsen för Svea livgardes historia, 1954.